Cherokee History
and the Spirit Family

James Neil Barnes

UNG
UNIVERSITY of
NORTH GEORGIA™
UNIVERSITY PRESS

Copyright © 2023 by James Neil Barnes

All rights reserved. No part of this book may be reproduced in whole or in part without written permission from the publisher, except by reviewers who may quote brief excerpts in connections with a review in newspaper, magazine, or electronic publications; nor may any part of this book be reproduced, stored in a retrieval system, used in any way with AI, or transmitted in any form or by any means electronic, mechanical, photocopying, recording, or other, without the written permission from the publisher.

Published by:
University of North Georgia Press
Dahlonega, Georgia

Printing Support by:
Lightning Source Inc.
La Vergne, Tennessee

Color image of Annie Spirit Mayes Snell by her great-great-grandaughter Mary Ann Casem, designer, educator, and visual storyteller.

Cover and book design by Corey Parson.

ISBN: 978-1-959203-17-9

For more information, please visit: http://ung.edu/university-press
Or e-mail: ungpress@ung.edu

This book is dedicated to my daughters Deborah Elaine Barnes and Sociana Duigan Clark, my grandchildren Brendan Barnes Casey, Erin Barnes Casey, Lucia Susan Spencer Clark and William John Simon Clark, and Anne Louise Fuhrman, my wife and accomplice in life.

> I have been and still am a seeker. I have ceased to question stars and books;
> I have begun to listen to the teaching my blood whispers to me.
> Hermann Hesse (Demian)

This quote from Theda Perdue has stayed with me while writing this book:

> Loyalty to each other, concern for the spiritual power in their way of life, and their insistence upon the fundamental importance of tribal unity and harmony . . . . No one can study the Cherokee without coming away with deep respect for their dignity, their familial commitment, their intelligence, and their profound generosity of spirit.[1]

The words of Bartholomé de las Casas in 1555 also resonate. A conference in Valladolid, Spain was called to decide what to do with the native peoples in the New World that Spain claimed. Juan de Sepulveda debated Bartholomé claiming the alleged superiority of Spaniards to Indians:

> In wisdom, skill, virtue and humanity these people are as inferior to Spaniards as children are to adults and women to men . . . almost—I am inclined to say—as between monkeys and men.

De las Casas replied:

> The Indians are not ignorant, inhuman or bestial, rather, long before they heard the word Spaniard they had properly organized states, wisely ordered by excellent laws, religions and customs. They cultivated friendship and bound together in common fellowship, lived in populous cities in which they wisely administered the affairs of both

peace and war justly and equitably, truly governed by laws that at very many points surpass ours, and could have won the admiration of the sages of Athens.

Thank you Bartholomé!

The beginning of my library for this book included Emmet Starr's *History of the Cherokee Indians*, family roll cards from various censuses, valuations of improvements in 1819, 1828, 1835 and the Dawes Roll enrollment cards at the end of the 19th century. This drawing in Starr's History reminds me of Mayan temples I've visited over the years, linking the Cherokees to the larger Amerindian reality.[2]

Table of Contents

Foreword ix
Preface: Annie Spirit's Family and Early Life. xv
Chapter 1: Ludovic Grant and the Spirit Family 1
Chapter 2: Some Important Back History 8
Chapter 3: Heroines and Heroes 35
Chapter 4: Battle of Horse Shoe Bend. 43
Chapter 5: Buffalofish Spirit. 48
Chapter 6: Lithia Springs 55
Chapter 7: John Huss Spirit. 58
Chapter 8: Samuel Houston Mayes 62
Chapter 9: Cherokee Lives Before the Trail of Tears 66
Chapter 10: Sequoyah. 80
Chapter 11: The Ridges 90
Chapter 12: Jackson's Removal Act 98
Chapter 13: The Treaty Party 118
Chapter 14: Chief Ross's Final Efforts. 129
Chapter 15: The Roundup and Exodus 150
Chapter 16: Cherokee Genocide 159
Chapter 17: Rebuilding 174
Chapter 18: John Huss Spirit and The International Indian Council . 195

Chapter 19: Female and Male Seminaries 201
Chapter 20: Annie Spirit and Samuel Mayes 212
Chapter 21: The 1850s in the Cherokee Nation. 217
Chapter 22: Slavery 221
Chapter 23: Keetoowah, Masons, and the Golden Circle 228
Chapter 24: The Civil War in Indian Territory 234
Chapter 25: Aftermath of War. 264
Chapter 26: New Start 272
Chapter 27: Life Goes On. 289
Chapter 28: Outlaws and Heroes – Ned Christie Revealed 304
Chapter 29: The 1890s – Decline of Sovereignty 313
Chapter 30: A Note on the Hotel Hazel. 332
Chapter 31: A New Century 336
Chapter 32: End of the Dream 343
Chapter 33: Epilogue 359
Acknowledgements 364
Appendices (available online) 367
Notes 368
Bibliography. 434
Index 447

Foreword

This book tells the history of Cherokees from the mid-1700s to the early 1900s, illustrated with maps, paintings, photographs and supported by original documents. My great-great grandmother Annie Spirit's life from 1826 to 1910, and the lives of her grandparents, parents, aunts and uncles, siblings, cousins, children and grandchildren illuminate and parallel the rise and fall of the Cherokee Nation. How they responded shows the resilience of the Cherokee people in never giving up on their destiny. I have drawn on contemporary sources for details about what they faced during each generation, as the boundaries of their territory shrank until they lost their homeland in the east, and finally their sovereignty in the west. The appendices contain original documents that are brought together for the first time. My goal has been to write a compact history that brings to light information and features people often left out of other histories.

A photo of Annie taken around 1900 has peered down at me for the past thirty years since I found it in the Cherokee Nation's archive in Tahlequah. Her piercing eyes are partly responsible for my writing this book. Researching her family's story deepened my understanding of the suffering of Cherokees and other Native Americans in the 18th and 19th centuries as they were forced to give up their ancestral lands and move west to "Indian Territory." After being rounded up there was heavy loss of life in the stockades, on their arduous trips west and after they arrived. No one knows how many Cherokees died. After removal, their struggle didn't end, as greed and racism underpinned how the US dealt with native Americans, leading to the forced dissolution of their sovereignty in the early 20th century. The unpaid arrears owed to the Cherokee people and to all first peoples are enormous. I see my Cherokee ancestors and their progeny with Scottish, Irish, and English spouses spreading out in a complicated multi-layered pattern. They are my teachers, heroes, and heroines. I salute their dignity as men and women, fathers and mothers, stoic in the face of trauma suffered simply because they were Cherokee at the wrong times and places. Annie's mother, aunts, grandmothers and great-grandmother helped save their culture as they steadily lost their homeland. They survived moving west, enduring arduous years rebuilding the Cherokee Nation.

As federal and state politicians conspired to remove Cherokees from their land, their culture was gravely threatened. What the US government did was so extreme that it remains difficult to accept even today. How an independent sovereign nation's lands, acknowledged in treaty after treaty, could have been taken away so cavalierly continues to astonish me. The 1835 census shows that Cherokees still owned about 1,700,000 tillable acres in Georgia alone, with many more acres of forests, rivers, lakes, marshes and mountains. Significant Cherokee tracts also remained in Alabama, Tennessee and North Carolina. Consider this map of the Cherokee, Choctaw, Creek, Chickasaw and Seminole tribes' ancestral lands in the southeast and imagine what it meant to lose them.[3]

Cherokees were forced to play an elaborate three-dimensional game of chess they did not design and whose rules they didn't fully understand. Yet Cherokee culture was flowering even in the face of the growing threats from officials in Georgia, Tennessee, Alabama, North Carolina and the federal government. Towns, farms, ferry crossings and businesses were growing rapidly. Cherokees were proud of their culture and expected to be treated fairly by Congress and the Supreme Court, but they were forced off their land at gunpoint.

The Civil War brought to the forefront every lingering grievance in the Cherokee Nation, triggering violence that almost tore it apart, yet in a few years they found the healing path and that dark past quickly receded. The 1870s and 1880s were a time of great progress. The Nation was once again in control of its territory, with a democratically elected government and free public schools that educated their children to a high standard. There was much to be proud of. But the US intervened once again in the 1890s, demanding that Cherokees give up their sovereignty. Desire for their land and resources, coupled with endemic racism, led the US to force Cherokees and other Indians to accept what they termed "allocations." This suggested that the Indians were somehow homesteaders, while all remaining communal lands were taken and sold to people who poured into Indian territory. Stripping the Cherokees of their schools, their beloved newspaper, their land and their very way of life took away everything that made them who they were. This seemed to be what the US government desired—a type of cultural genocide of an entire nation of people.

In spite of every negative thing she experienced during her life, Annie was resilient and focused on the future. This book tells what her generation experienced as they dreamed of overseeing their own nation, taking many concrete steps to that end. But their dream ended in the early 1900s when their government, courts, schools, and press were abolished, and the State of Oklahoma was established in 1907. Imagining what family members experienced, heard, read and thought has been a long exercise in humility. I hope that my evolving empathy has led to a path that rings true. Annie's summary of her life in the Preface is italicized to indicate that it is my attempt to provide her a voice. Family members played prominent roles in the Cherokee Nation during the final thirty years of Annie's life, including the tenures of Joel and Samuel Mayes, Jr. (her first husband Samuel Mayes' sons with Nannie Adair), her fourth cousin Dennis Wolfe Bushyhead, and her third cousin Thomas Buffington as Principal Chief. Her son William Penn Mayes (Billy), my great-grandfather, served as Interpreter for the Senate for ten years, working on tribal business with his half-brothers Joel and Samuel when they were Chiefs. Known as Billy, he was a successful farmer near Grove in Northeast Indian Territory, with the largest orchard in the area. In the mid-1890s he and his wife Annie Harper Gladney opened the Hazel Hotel in Grove, named after one of their daughters, my great-aunt Hazel. In its day it was the most important hotel in the region, known for its lodging and food. They lived there together until she died in 1929. The hotel burned down in October 1933. William died of a stroke in Tahlequah at the age of eighty-seven on November 16, 1944, five months after I was born.[4] Of course I never knew him nor did he meet me, but his presence has hovered over me all my life.

During the past thirty years I've traveled to Tahlequah, Grove, and other places in northeast Oklahoma, visiting libraries, newspapers, museums, graveyards and the Cherokee National Headquarters. I found the Talbot Museum in Colcord to be a small treasure trove of Cherokee documents, books and maps, including several involving my extended family In Grove it was pleasing to find the location of the Hazel Hotel. Using maps from before the Grand River dam was built, I drove down dusty roads to locate family farms. My great-grandfather extolled the hunting and fishing while growing up on Honey Creek in the 1860s and 1870s, and Annie's farm was her refuge until the end of her life. Although part of Honey Creek was submerged by Grand Lake, it remains a beautiful stream with superb trout fishing.

Wanting to learn more about the Spirit family's lives prior to removal from Georgia, Alabama, and Tennessee in the 1830s, I traveled there in October 2015 with Charley Cope, an old friend from Michigan Law School. Our quest was to locate the area on the south side of the Etowah River where Annie and her family lived prior to being deported in 1838 and visit Amerindian sites. The Echota Mounds Museum of the Mississippian culture was particularly moving, with its dioramas of a typical community in the 1500s when de Soto arrived. The reconstructed New Echota Capitol in northern Georgia is a national treasure, reflected in the simple beauty of the Supreme Court, Council House, and homes and projecting a rich, peaceful ambience. There are numerous Cherokee sites open to the public in northern Georgia and southern Tennessee, including Joe Vann's home, John Ross's house, The Ridge's mansion and Sequoyah's memorial museum in Vonore, Tennessee. I found numerous documents about my family. That trip provided a powerful impetus to write this book.

My hope is that it will be both an inspiration and a resource for people of all ages, whether they are well-versed in Native American history or are coming to the topic for the first time. In my lifetime, first nations throughout the Americas have made amazing strides forward in recapturing their own narratives and in obtaining legal protection of their rights. Perhaps this personal history will help build momentum towards those goals.

Preface: Annie Spirit's Family and Early Life

My history and that of the Spirit family and of the Cherokees intertwine. My life and memories connect with those of the Cherokees. They may seem random in their order, but they're all connected because of who I am, who my family is, and who the Cherokees are. I'm a Trail of Tears survivor, born in the spring of 1826 in the Cherokee Nation, now northern Georgia. I was named Ah-ni-wa-ke but everyone calls me Annie.[5] My mother was born into the Deer Clan (Ani'-Awi'), one of our seven clans. The others are Blue, Long Hair, Bird, Paint, Wild Potato and Wolf. The number seven is important to us spiritually as there are seven levels in the Cherokee universe. A baby typically receives his or her name seven days after birth, during a naming ceremony that requires immersion in a stream seven times. Seven councilors preside over the seven regular festivals, and in olden times there was a sacrifice every seventh day.[6]

I'm not quite the full blood many people assume.[7] From long ago I inherited white genes from Ludovic Grant, whose half-Cherokee daughter Mary married my great-great grandfather Old Sconti Spirit.[8] My father, known simply as The Spirit, was born about 1797, and my mother, Chowyoucah, was born into the Swimmer family around 1790.[9] I was the eldest of their three children: Charles and Watt arrived in 1832 and 1834 respectively. My mother's first marriage to George (Oo-you-tah) Vann brought an alliance with the Terrapin and Vann families. One of the most astute people I ever knew, George was a cousin of Chief James Vann.[10] Educated at the Spring Place Moravian Mission School, his analysis of any problem was superb. He was like a second father to me, and I was close to his children with my mother, my half-siblings Annie, Elsie and Weely Vann, and my stepsister Lydia, his daughter with E-Li-Si Ratt. Weely was ten when I was born, and Annie was three, while Elsie and Lydia were six or seven years older than me. My mother also had my half-sister Susan with David Sconti after removal.[11] All my siblings except for Lydia were raised together.[12]

My maternal grandmother Chi-Wa-Yu-Ga was born about 1765 and married into the Swimmer clan. She saw so much in her long life, could analyze situations clearly and quickly, and was my teacher about everything having to do with nature. She died in 1860 when I was thirty-five. Her sons Jess and Jim Swimmer helped raise me, as maternal uncles often do in Cherokee society.

I was especially close to my paternal grandfather Buffalofish (Da-gah-sah-tah) and his wife Wo-de-yo-he.[13] In 1826, they and most of the extended family lived not far from Buzzard Roost Island on the Chattahoochee River in what today is Georgia. That's about sixteen miles from Lithia Springs, an important spiritual site for Cherokees. My father and mother moved from there to Dykes Bend along the Etowah River two years after I was born.[14] Buffalofish and his other sons and daughters joined us there in 1829 and 1830 following the loss of their farms and ferry because of the infamous "Coffee Line" seizure by Andrew Jackson's agents, General John Coffee and US Commissioner Joseph McMinn.[15] Each had secret financial interests in that land. Their erroneous map forced many

Cherokees with significant farms, mills, and ferries to move,[16] including my grandfather Buffalofish and his family. They lost everything, including their proximity to Lithia Springs.

My great-grandfather Old Spirit, sometimes called Old Sconti, was married first to Mary Blaylock. They had one child:[17]

- John Spirit (We-Cha-Lah-Nae-He) was born in 1787. As a young man he lived near Battle Creek, Tennessee, and eventually moved close to his father and Susannah in northeastern Alabama. After becoming a disciple of the Moravian church and a preacher, he changed his name to Huss in honor of the Czech Moravian martyr John Hus. He was married to Nancy Gourd with whom he had a son, William, around 1814. She was married to two other men - Alexander McCoy, with whom she had John Lowrey McCoy, and John Blaylock, with whom she had Jefferson Blaylock. John also married Nancy Mush, who had three girls with two other men—Jane Jennie, Mary Sally, and Rachel. The girls were adopted by John, taking the Huss name. Reverend John was a fountain of support after removal west. As a Supreme Court judge, he was skilled at explaining things logically. Everyone loved his preaching, always in Cherokee since he spoke little English.

Old Spirit later married Susannah (Tsah'wah'u'gah). They lived for many years near Creekpath, Alabama not far from their friend George Guess (Sequoyah). They and several thousand other Cherokees moved west because of treaties signed from 1815 to 1819, trading their Alabama lands for what were supposed to be equivalent parcels in Arkansas. In 1823, Sequoyah moved permanently near where Spirit and Susannah were living. Old Spirit died in Arkansas in 1828 when I was just two, but he remains alive in my mind through Susannah's stories. Each of their children was important in my life:[18]

- Betsy Spirit, born in 1777, had a liaison with Sequoyah. In 1797, they had a son named Big Dollar George, who married Tianna Knightkiller and fathered four children.[19]
- Buffalofish was born about 1780 and married Wo-de-yo-he, born the same year. They established a large farm on the Chattahoochee River and began raising a family. They became successful, with three slaves[20] to help manage their farms and orchards, a large stable of horses and a herd of cattle. Their sons Alexander Buffalofish (Oo-ta-lah-nah), Eagle-on-the-roost (Wa-Lu-Kil-Lah), Crying Snake (Enoh'li-kah), and Charlie Buffalofish were always there for the family. Their daughter Nakey married Nitts, one of Big Nitts' sons, and they had seven children: Levi, Ice, Ah-claw-se-nee, Oo-nah-stul-lah, Te-tah-te-yas-kee, Caty and Lydia. Their daughter So-Wa-Chee married Sawney Vann, a partner with Buffalofish in many ventures, including a ferry near Buzzard Roost Island. They had three children: Arch, Jennie, and Lewis. Crying Snake, an orator of some note, transfixed people with passionate, articulate speeches. As a young girl, I tried to learn how to mimic his cadences, which were rolling and sonorous. He married Alcie Vann. Charlie Buffalofish, their youngest child, married Sallie Wool Frisley, and their son Hunter (Canahelage), born in 1849, grew up with my children.
- David Sconti Spirit was born in 1781. He used the Sconti name in honor of his grandfather, Old Sconti. He married Mary Buffington, and they had David, Susie, and Peggy. He and my mother also had a child together, Susannah (Susan) Sconti.[21]
- Caty Spirit was born in 1790. She married Knightkiller, and they had two sons: David, born in 1816 and Henry a few years later. After removal west, they lived along Honey Creek. It broke my heart when she died rather suddenly in 1869, almost eighty.

In 1848, I married Samuel Houston Mayes, a white man with whom I had three daughters and a son. During the Civil War, I married Simon Snell, a full-blood Cherokee, with whom I had one son. In my later years, I've used the name Snell or Snail (I-la-qui), as there isn't agreement on which English translation is best. I have thirty-one grandchildren and thirty-two great-grandkids, who have brought me great happiness and optimism about the future of the Cherokee Nation.[22]

When my family lost their land in 1838, they were living in the old Chattoogee District near the confluence of the Etowah and Oostannallah Rivers—the 'Head of Coosa' in our parlance. Today that is Rome, Georgia. Our farms were located a few miles east of Coosa on the south side of the Etowah River across from where Dykes Creek flows into the river. It's a beautiful area, tucked into the large undulating, snake-like loops of the river, with rich land, fecund marshes, creeks thick with fish and crustaceans, and forests full of wildlife. We had a stone fish weir on the Etowah, whose free-flowing water was pure.

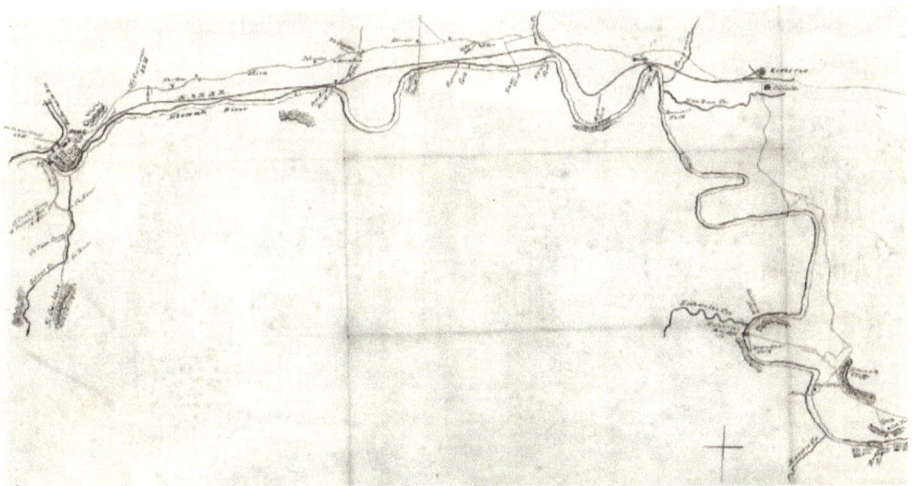

Map of the Etowah River

This map shows that district with Georgia's lottery numbers: our farms were on the south side of the Etowah to the left of the large bend and extending west and south in Sections 305, 306, 334 and 335.[23]

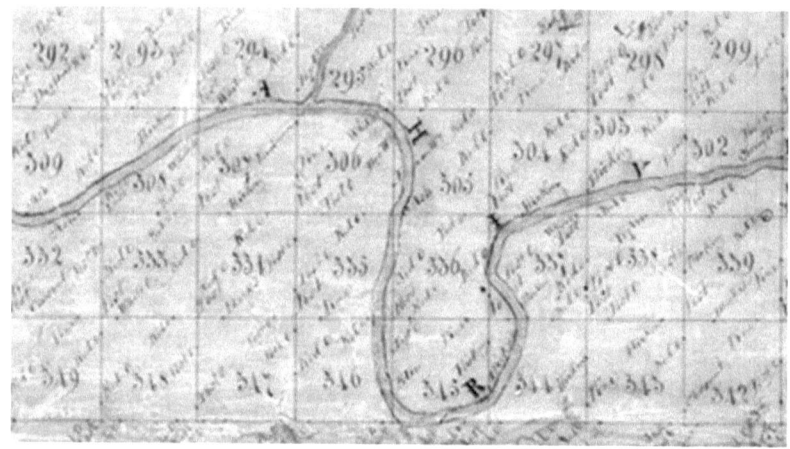

Chestnut, white oak, and hickory were the main hardwoods in our forests. Our homes and barns were made of all three woods and were comfortable and warm, especially in the cold winters and hard rains times in the spring. Our house was similar to this one. I felt safe there.

Every clan has its own 'sacred' wood. It's oak for the Deer Clan. Our forests were filled with many other species—chestnut, hickory, elm, maple, poplar, loblolly pine, cedar, magnolia, persimmon, dogwood, mulberry, redbud, and mimosa. Poplars were especially suited for making large dugout canoes. This one pictured below is over thirty feet long, carved from a single large poplar around 1790.

Traditional drums were made from cedar. Many Cherokees carry a small piece of cedar wood in their medicine bags, and cedar is placed above the entrances to homes to protect against entry of evil spirits. The wood of the cedar tree plays a powerful protective role for us as part of our creation story:

> The Creator accepted the gratitude of the people and was glad to see them smiling again. However, during the time of the long days of night, many of the people had died, and the Creator was sorry that they had perished because of the night. The Creator placed their spirits in a newly created tree. This tree was named Ah-see-na loo-guh. . . . When you smell the aroma of the cedar tree or gaze upon it standing in the forest, remember that if you are Tsalagi . . . , you are looking upon your ancestor.[24]

We spent many winter evenings shelling chestnuts around the fire together. My mother and grandmothers made large flat loaves of chestnut bread, wrapping individual servings in corn shucks. Absolutely delicious! We pounded hickory nuts into mush and added boiling water to make a rich and nourishing drink. Corn mixed with ground hickory nuts yielded another staple food. We made our furniture from white oak, and hickory had many uses, including the pestles for grinding corn and mashing chestnuts.

In the spring, dogwood and redbud flowers lit up the forest's edge. In summer, mimosa blossoms attracted butterflies and bees, and the intense fragrance of magnolia blossoms lingered for weeks. Under the forest canopy, we found spicebush, witch hazel, pawpaw, wild hydrangea, pepperbush, bloodroot, larkspur, trillium, hepatica, violets, ginger, mint, and wild potato. "Moccasin flower" (Lady's Slipper) was used by healers for heart trouble. Bloodroot provided the red dye for baskets.

Mushrooms were prolific in spring and autumn; I enjoy every variety. A richness buried in deep memory is unlocked every time I eat one. Nuts, berries, and edible plants were abundant. Mosses and lichens were used to prepare a form of salt. Nearly every family had fruit trees. Peach was the most popular, but we also grew apple, cherry, pear, quince, and plum trees. Valuation agents in 1835 and 1836 counted more than sixty-three thousand peach trees on Cherokee land in Georgia alone! My father, grandfather, and uncles all had large orchards.

Most families owned horses, cows, pigs, goats, sheep, and dogs. My grandmother Wo-de-yo-he was the horsewoman of our family. When they lived at Buzzard's Roost, she owned more than twenty and loved to ride along the Etowah River. In Georgia, Cherokees owned more than 80,000 head of livestock in 1835. Our dogs were named Ruby (for her coloring) and Lightning (one of the fastest dogs I ever knew). They were short-haired, about two feet tall and very intelligent, my devoted companions. They were very important to us, serving as companions and guardians as well as carrying loads in pouch bags that fit over their backs.

My siblings, cousins, and I roamed the forests, swamps, rivers, and streams, learning paths and crossings by memory. It would be hard to overstate the extent of the beautiful lands bequeathed to us by the Creator. The wild Tennessee, Oostannallah, Coosa, and Etowah Rivers and their many winding tributaries were the liquid sinews binding everything together. Look at the map and imagine our lives amid those interwoven creeks, swamps, and rivers. We were blessed with endless bottomland on which to grow crops; hardwood and pine forests covered much of the land; and game was abundant, even though our ancestors had been hunting there for centuries. A Cherokee would never kill a wolf, which were messengers to the spirit world.

Many Cherokees operated ferry crossings. One not far upriver from our farm on the Etowah was owned by Samuel Mayes, a white man married to Nannie Adair from an illustrious Cherokee family. Sam took a shine to me when I was about eighteen. Although a lot older, he was persuasive, and Cherokees didn't have a strict view of marriage or monogamy anyway. In 1833, he stood up for Cherokees by refusing to sign the Georgia loyalty oath required of all white men with Indian wives, going to prison over that. Acting in solidarity with his Cherokee family, he gave up everything when they departed for the west in 1837. Decades later, two of his children with Nannie—Samuel and Joel—became chiefs. They were family, and I was close to them and Sam's other children.

My grandmothers seemed to know everything about how to catch fish (atsat'i). First, dig up roots of the Venus Fly Trap and trout lilies, chew a small piece and put it onto the bait. Saliva was a key aspect of this technique. I learned the cues nature gives us about the most auspicious fishing times, gleaning them from the seasons, lunar cycles, weather, insect hatchings, and time of day. We usually fished in the early morning or late afternoon gliding into the twilight. The simple companionship of fishing with my family and friends has stayed with me all my life. It was strictly forbidden to eat gar. Our grandmas showed us how a gar's lower jaw could be dried and used to make scratches on skin as part of a treatment for certain diseases or, sometimes, when they wanted to make a disciplinary point—I hated being scratched because of doing something wrong! Catfish were considered unclean and were not commonly eaten.

Sports and games played a crucial role in our social lives. The most important was stickball (anitsodi). Stickball is called "the little brother of war" and in the past was used to decide conflicts instead of engaging in warfare. Stickball was bloody and dangerous. The men often fasted, abstained from sex, were ritually scratched by a medicine man—each team had one—went to water and prayed before playing. I noticed when I was about five that just before a ball game the men and boys slathered an oily looking substance on their bodies. Mother told me that ballplayers rub themselves with fresh eel skins to become slippery. Women often tied up their hair with eel skins to make it sleek, a practice I adopted as a teenager. I was worried it would smell, but curing the skins removes the odor. Although both men and women played stickball, it was more important for men. A medicine man tosses a small ball made of deer hair and hide into the air to begin, and the players use hickory sticks to hit and cup it. There is no set number of players required, but the teams must be equal. Seven points are scored when the ball strikes a wooden fish on the top of a pole approximately 25 feet tall, and two points are awarded when the ball strikes the pole.

Cherokee Stickball set[25]

Hearing the women sing their special ball stick song is really something. This is how the players look when dressed for a match.

Stickball Players[26]

Another important game I liked to watch as a child is Cherokee marbles. We called it Five Hole (Di-ga-da-yo-s-di). It requires considerable skill to shape marbles from sandstone, smoothed round to the size of a small billiard ball. Play takes place on a course approximately one hundred feet long, with five two-inch holes about 25 feet apart in an L-shaped space. Each player has one marble and must keep track of its location as well as the opposing players' marbles. The players toss the marbles at the holes in sequence, trying to knock other marbles out of the way and be first inside a tiny ring around each hole. Elders say the game goes back more than a thousand years.[27]

Many activities for girls were carried out in small groups, which nourished our social fabric. I was particularly interested in basket weaving, bead work and making useful object from clay. My grandmothers taught us the art of weaving baskets and mats. First, they showed us where to gather the right canes for each type of basket and harvest tree-barks for dyes. Second, the process of cutting canes into strips and weaving them together took patience and time. It was normal then for all young girls to learn designs that were beautiful and functional, like this classic red pattern.

This traditional basket design made of river cane is strong and well-balanced, one of my favorites.

Grandmother Chi-Wa-Yu-Ga showed us where to find the right clay to make bowls, jugs and plates. I loved the earthy feeling of blending different clays with water to prepare to construct a bowl.

Learning when the clay was ready was a skill that took some time. She built hot fires in which to harden them. I became a competent potter, striving to make traditional bowls like this one.[28]

Cherokees like beautiful beads. My aunts and grandmothers had superbly decorated necklaces and bags. We were lucky to have artisans who made things that are both functional and beautiful, like this bandolier bag.

Great-grandmother Susannah gave me a pair of beaded moccasin slippers like this when I was about six.[29]

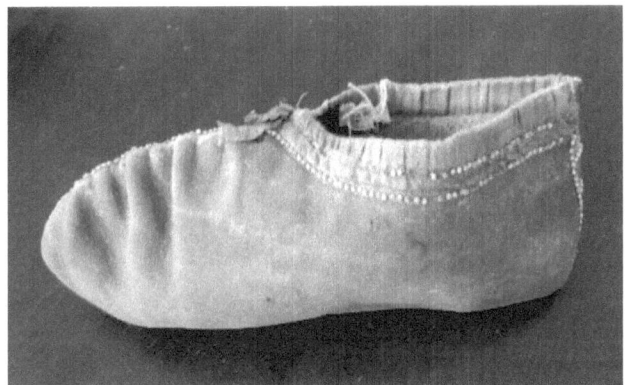

Flickering memories beckon me, a long thread unspooling from my brain laden with images and sounds from my early years when life was simpler, and normal. My grandparents taught us about the origin of the universe and our place in it. Some might call this a myth, but to me it was real and compelling.

When the Earth began there was just water. All the animals lived above it and the sky was beginning to become crowded. They were all curious about what was beneath the water and one day Dayuni'si, the water beetle, volunteered to explore it. He went everywhere across the surface, but he couldn't find any solid ground. He then dived below the surface to the bottom and all he found was mud. This began to enlarge in size and spread outwards until it became the Earth as we know it. After all this had happened, one of the animals attached this new land to the sky with four strings. Just after the Earth was formed, it was flat and soft, so the animals decided to send a bird down to see if it had dried. They eventually returned to the animals with a result. The land was still too wet, so they sent the great buzzard from Galun'lati to prepare it for them. The buzzard flew down and by the time he reached the Cherokee land he was so tired that his wings began to hit the ground. Wherever they hit the ground a mountain or valley formed. The animals then decided that it was too dark, so they made the sun and put it on the path in which it still runs today.[30]

Buffalofish told us the proper ways to honor the spirits, the correct medicine for many ailments, and the origins of our major festivals. One of his most useful pieces of advice was simply to be patient, but also to stand up for ourselves and fight for what is right. The centerpiece of our daily walks along the river was history that he taught us through stories about people and important events. The name 'Pathkiller' had come up at dinner one day, and I asked Buffalotfish about him the next morning.

"Pathkiller was one of our greatest chiefs. Born in 1745 and renowned for his erudition, he was called the Last of the Cherokee Kings. He led us through many difficult moments. Pathkiller had an elegant way of analyzing things, and it was a great experience just to speak with him. In 1827, he died at home, where he operated an important ferry on the Coosa River. Major Ridge bought his entire property."

"Who is Major Ridge?" I asked. "I'd love to see that ferry crossing! Will you take me there?"

"That's a long story. I'll tell you more about Major Ridge another day; he's an amazing man." We continued down to the weir to get fish for supper. I remember often walking with his hand in mine, especially when it was cold or the terrain was uneven, listening to him speak in his soft voice. He was compelling about the place of water in our lives. "Going to water" was his favorite ritual, and it quickly became mine, too. Almost every Cherokee village was located near a river, stream, or lake and children learned how to swim at an early age.

"Immersion and bathing in running water is an ancient belief," he told us one morning. "The murmurs of moving water are voices communicating with us, but one must be patient and listen carefully to understand their meanings."

"Are you sure, Grandpa?" my brother Charles asked. "I don't hear them."

Holding our hands, he led us down to the edge of the creek, near where a bed of rocks created an area of resistance, and we knelt on our haunches to hear better. "Close your eyes and listen," he suggested. He was right—I could hear chattering, like a different language being warbled, and other larger sounds that had never caught my attention before. It was incredibly peaceful, and I remember how safe I felt there with him by the rippling water.

When I was about ten, my grandmothers Wo-de-yo-he and Chi-Wa-Yu-Ga described the taboo against menstruating women swimming near fish weirs and traps—it was thought the fish might be contaminated. I didn't understand this restriction, asking many questions about it, but they were clear about its importance; mama backed them up, so I accepted the proscription. I tried to teach my daughters this rule, but they thought it old-fashioned and didn't go along with it. I can see their point.

Going to water was so important for Cherokees that most mornings, no matter how cold, we would bathe together in the river, face east, and pray. Giving thanks for a new day, we washed away feelings that might separate us from our neighbors. The family went to water together at sunrise of every new moon as part of a special ceremony. Going to water was essential for postpartum and post-menstrual cleansing, and preparations for sporting events—especially our great ball game. This has stayed with me all my life.

One of my fondest memories is the Green Corn dance under a full moon in August when the corn is first ripe enough to eat. Kernels from the corn gathered from each of the seven clans were placed onto the sacred fire, along with a deer tongue. The festival features the frenzied music of the water drum—an earthen pot or kettle with a skin stretched over the top with an inch or so of water inside, a river-cane flute, which is about twelve inches long with six holes that produce intricate melodies, and percussive shrieks. We have several forms of trumpets made from buffalo horns, long neck gourds, or the thigh bone of a crane. Turtle shells are used for rattles, a single rattle held by men and turtle shell shackles placed on women's legs. As a young girl, I learned the woman's part of many dances. The festival cleansed the community by encouraging everyone to get rid of useless things, including grievances and feuds. The fasting and dancing went on for two or three days, and then the feast began: roast corn, corn soup, and corn bread.

The clan council usually gathered at some point during the week to hear the most distinguished member review the history of the clan for the past year, commending those for some deed that brought honor to the clan and chastising those who had done something dishonorable. I recall the suspense as we listened for the names! When I was growing up, clan relationships were still important, despite the Council having abolished the "blood law" in 1820. Cherokee belief is that the world and life must stay in balance (tohi) to keep spiritual peace. Reciprocal hospitality remained a paramount clan responsibility. One could travel to any village and easily find clan members to stay with. Maternal uncles (e-du-tsi) were very important. Blood brothers (anadanvtli) were seen as standing so closely together as to form one person from a clan perspective. The paternal grandfather's and maternal grandfather's clans were important for the extended family.

Priests produced a new "pure" fire at the conclusion of the festival, which every household carried to their hearths. After painting ourselves white, we would all head to the river in a procession with the Archi Magus, who would jump in first, then we all followed. It was an inspiring ceremony! A rule of the festival was that young men had to wait each year until then to look for brides. As an annual event bringing together people from around the Nation, it allowed us to visit relatives, tell stories, trade goods, participate in sports and dances, and look for mates!

Every girl was taught how to cook and bake. The most important ingredient was corn (Selu). We learned how to shuck it, crush it into powder, leach it with lye to prepare hominy (ganohena), boil it for mush, and bake bread with it. We also made bean bread (Gadu tuya), which was delicious and filling, an lobloly, a bread for special occasions made with persimmons, pumpkin, and peaches. Whenever I think of cornbread, it reminds me that Selu—the corn mother—and Kanat'i—the hunter father—were the parents of all Cherokees. Besides corn, we grew wheat, rye, and oats, and there was a mill nearby to grind them into flour. Everyone had chores on the farm. I was first drawn to tending berries and tomatoes. Mother gave me a little blackberry patch when I was about five, and I graduated to tomatoes soon thereafter. How much do I like tomatoes? Have you ever tasted a Cherokee Purple?

One thing I'd like to mention is how important it was to take care of our teeth were. Very rarely did anyone have a decayed tooth. I think there are two reasons for this. First, our diet was perfectly balanced, and we grew up chewing nuts in profusion, which strengthens teeth. Second, correct breathing was taught from birth, always through the nose, never through the mouth, which maintains the mouth's shape and protects teeth. A child was never allowed to sleep with his or her mouth open, and as we walked or ran it was important to breath only through our noses.[31]

The most important thing I recall about my early years was Sequoyah's wonderful invention of a Syllabary of all the basic sounds in our language. When I was born many Cherokees had already learned how to read and write using his simple approach. By the time I was five I yearned to learn too. Given our association with Sequoyah through great-aunt Betsy, great-grandfather Spirit and Uncle John Huss Spirit, our family fully endorsed this. They agreed I could begin class at a nearby mission school. Like most, I found it easy to learn how to read and write. One day in early 1832, I ran in exclaiming, "I can read, I can read!" The larger world opened up quickly as the new weekly newspaper *The Cherokee Phoenix* was discussed regularly, providing the main way we heard about the larger world as well as about our ambitious plans and successes. I devoured it, learning new words and expressions every day.

I was enveloped by my family then in a huge, protective web, enclosed by love and affection. There has always been a flame burning inside me for the deep contact with relatives that I experienced then, and I've reached out widely. Like all my people, I've experienced sorrows and heartbreak, as well as my share of happiness and joy. Life is such a strange mixture of the most prosaic things that provide solace and joy amid the harsh realities we sometimes face on the curves of history. I carried the history of the rich Cherokee culture with me on the Trail of Tears and afterwards in the west. My sense of injustice about what happened to every Cherokee family has remained with me. But being a daughter, mother, grandmother and great-grandmother, with intricate webs of family around me, has compensated for our travails. I am proud to be Cherokee.

1

Ludovic Grant and the Spirit Family

Ludovic Grant was born in Aberdeenshire, Scotland on August 19, 1688. When he was born, no one could have guessed that he would become a key figure in Cherokee history and the Spirit family. Ludovic lived with his father William and his mother, Katherine Gordon, with three siblings in the village of Fyvie. The family had no idea their lives would be swept up in the venom between Catholics and Protestants. The history of struggle between Protestants and Catholics in the United Kingdom was long and sometimes bloody.

King James II, a Catholic and a Stuart, ruled Scotland, Ireland and England from 1685 to 1688. James' elder daughter, Mary, was a Protestant and it was felt that time would solve the religious problem many had with James as she would inherit the throne. But on June 10, 1688 he had a son, James Francis Edward, displacing Mary and raising the prospect of a longer-term Catholic dynasty ruling the three countries. At the same time, James' government was prosecuting seven bishops from the Protestant Church of England for seditious conspiracy. Although they were acquitted on June 30[th,] many anti-Catholic riots broke out in England. English nobles wrote to King William III of Orange in the Netherlands urging that he come to the assistance of protestants by overthrowing James. King Louis XIV of France launched what became the Nine Years War in September 1688 in alliance with the Dutch. On November 5th William landed in Devon with 20,000 men, advancing quickly on London. The Royal English Army disintegrated; James and his family were exiled to France and William assumed the throne of England, Ireland and Scotland.

Those who supported the Stuarts were called "Jacobites" as the Latin for James is Jacobus. Although the Treaty of Limerick in 1691 was meant to put to rest the Jacobite rebellion in Ireland and Scotland, its terms were harsh: Irish and Scottish Catholics were excluded from voting, sitting in Parliament, purchasing land, possessing firearms, owning horses or educating their children. All clergy who refused to swear an oath of allegiance to King William were expelled. In exile, the Stuarts held court at the palace of Saint-Germain-en-Laye near Paris. King James was the last Catholic King of England, dying in a French monastery in 1701. But his death didn't still the long-simmering anger of many Scots, or the ambition of James III to restore the Stuarts to power.

The Earl of Mar raised the exiled Stuart standard at Braemar on September 6, 1715, beginning the Jacobite uprising and triggering war with England. It didn't go well for the Jacobites. Ludovic, part of a Highland Jacobite group led by Thomas Forster, was on the losing side. Captured at the battle of Preston, England on November 14, 1715, he was imprisoned for six months in Chester Castle. Luckier than many others who were executed by King William, Ludovic was banished to Charles Town in the new world. Sailing as an indentured servant on the *Susannah* on May 7, 1716, he arrived in late July, probably as part of the group purchased by Deputy Governor Craven. After his servitude ended in 1723, Ludovic decided to become a trader with Indians. He became fluent in Cherokee, registering as an official trader with the Cherokee nation in 1725 and obtaining a license from England.

He moved to Great Tellico, a village located between the Valley and Overhill towns in Tennessee on a stream running from the Little Tennessee River to the Hiwassee River. There he met his wife from the longhair—Ani'Gilâ'hi—clan. Many people have posited that her name was "Eughioote." They were no doubt married in a typical Cherokee wedding at a Green Corn Festival. As the groom, he presented meat, symbolizing his ability to care for his wife. She would have given Ludovic an ear of corn representing Selu, the corn mother, representing her ability to take care of him. The Green Corn Dance involved everyone, giving thanks for the harvest. A medicine man sacrificed seven ears of corn, one for each clan, in the sacred town fire. [32]

Their daughter Susannah Catherine was born about 1727, and Mary arrived in 1729. They were raised in Great Tellico.[33] Also in 1729, Sir Alexander Cumming visited the Cherokees, hoping to secure their allegiance to the British crown. He met Ludovic in Keowee, who agreed to be one of his guides. They went up the Keowee path to Niquassi (near present-day Franklin, North Carolina) where they were met by a delegation from the Middle and Overhill towns. Ludovic had learned Cherokee well enough to be the official interpreter. A few months later, claiming to have been given the authority to name Moytoy of Tellico as Emperor, Cumming invited several Cherokee leaders to travel to England to meet the King. They boarded the English Man-of-War *Fox* in Charles Town on April 13, 1730, landing on June 5th in Dover, England. On June 22nd, they were presented to the King, who signed Articles of Friendship and Commerce: "The King gives to the Cherokee Indians the privilege of living where they please." A warrior named Ketagustah laid a bundle of feathers on a table before the King, saying "This is our way of talking, which is the same to us, as your letters in the book are to you; and to you, beloved men, we deliver these feathers, in confirmation of all we have said, and of our agreement to your articles."[34] Attacullaculla made a short speech, noting that Cherokees looked on King George "as the Sun and . . . father...For though we are red, and you are white, yet our hands and hearts are joined together . . . . In war, we shall always be with you."[35]

Engraving of the 1730 Cherokee Delegation[36]

When the Cherokees returned home laden with presents from the King, Moytoy charged them with illegally selling their homeland for signing the Treaty of Dover. Although the Treaty didn't contain any land cessions, it stipulated that only England could build forts or trade with Cherokees.[37] After appearing before the Cherokee Council, they were found not guilty. Years later, Ludovic set the record straight: "It is about thirty years since I went into the Cherokee Country where I have resided ever since . . . I speak their language. I have often been consulted by them about their affairs, and . . . I may therefore say with great certainty that if ever there had been any such surrender I must have heard of it, but I have never heard of such thing . . . ."[38]

Around 1746, Ludovic and his wife established a general store in Tomatly, located on the Valley River in the Snowbird Mountains of North Carolina. He was a famous trader and negotiator by 1751. The August 1751 Act that reorganized the Indian trade listed Cornelius Daugherty and Ludovic Grant as traders of record for the Valley Towns, with Cotocanahut, Nayowee, Tomatly and Cheewohee listed next to Grant's name. Ludovic witnessed the Fort Prince George land-cession treaty by the Cherokee Nation to the King of England on November 24, 1753.[39] The signers and witnesses at Keowee show the extent of his connections: Wauhatchee from Keowee; Outacite; Corane the Raven; Canacaugh the Great Conjuror of Keowee; Sinnawa the Hawk's Head; Nelle Wagalche of Toxowa; Yohoma of Keowee; Canasaita of Keowee; Yorhalche of Toxowa; Owasta of Toxowa; South Carolina Governor James Glen; and James Beamer, a leading trader with the Lower Towns. Ludovic had an extensive correspondence with Governor Glen from 1751 through 1756, which details his relationships with Cherokee chiefs and warriors. He died in Charles Town (called Charleston today) on October 5, 1757.

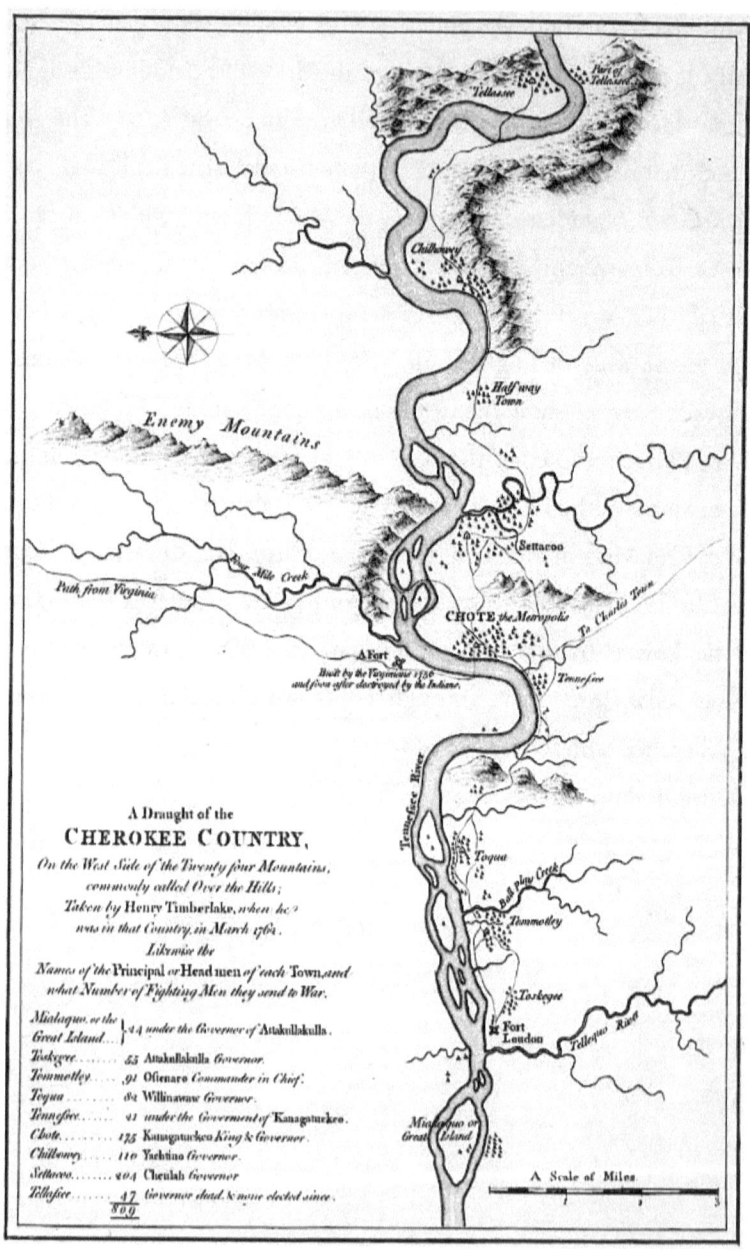

Topographical Map of the Central Cherokee Nation 1762[40]

Ludovic's daughter Mary married Old Sconti Spirit about 1750.[41] That union produced Annie's great-great aunts Lydia in 1756 and Peggy (Chi-goo-ie) in 1758, and Annie's great-grandfather Spirit in 1760. Peggy married William Shorey, with whom she had Elsie in 1798, Lydia in 1803, and Elizabeth around 1804. Mary Grant also married Colonel William Emory, a Scot born in 1728 who moved to South Carolina with his family in 1737. Mary and William had a son, William, Jr., in 1744 and two daughters, Mary in 1746 and Elizabeth in 1748, who were The Spirit's half-siblings. Elizabeth and Mary each married several times and had numerous children, who were Annie's great aunts and uncles in the Martin, Fields and Buffington families.[42]

Ludovic's daughter Susannah married Robert Emory in 1743, with whom she had one child in 1744, also named Susannah. She also was married to John Martin, Richard Fields and John Stuart, bearing ten children with those three men. With Stuart she had a son named Oo-no-du-tu (Bushyhead) in 1767, the father of Reverend Jesse Bushyhead, one of The Spirit's cousins. Mary and Susannah's children were in Annie's life because those who moved west were from families that played important roles in the Nation, including Reverend Jesse Bushyhead. Educated at Candy Creek Mission, Bushyhead taught at several schools in that area as a young man. He was elected Chief Justice of the Supreme Court on October 17, 1840, replacing John Martin and serving until his untimely death in 1844. His son Dennis Wolfe Bushyhead was an important figure in the Nation, elected Chief in 1879. (We'll learn more about Dennis later.[43]) Grant's legacy includes his descendants from the Buffington, Emory, Fields, Martin, Beck, Daniel, Rogers, Fawling and Spirit families. I wish there had been more white people like him—generous, wise and willing to give credit to the Cherokees for their knowledge and culture.

2

Some Important Back History

To understand Cherokee history when Annie was alive, it is essential to study what happened in the eighteenth century. This map of the political geography of eastern North America when George Washington was born in 1732 shows the overlay of Indian lands against the claims of England, France, and Spain at the time.[44]

When Annie's great grandfather Spirit was born in 1760, the Cherokee Nation comprised well over 100,000 square miles, encompassing parts of eight US states today. It was the largest Indian tribe in North America, with the Appalachians at its heart. Simple roads crossed the land, while rivers and streams were the sinews connecting the Nation.

Cherokees had plenty of troubles with the English, who bribed them to give up land and sometimes attacked their villages without provocation. At the same time, the English often expressed sympathy with the situation of the Cherokees' if that helped them fend off the French, and they cultivated Cherokee leaders. Likewise, colonial leaders, including the young George Washington and Thomas Jefferson, developed alliances with some Cherokees. In 1756 General Dinwiddie and George Washington wanted their help against the French, who were establishing a fort at the mouth

EASTERN NORTH AMERICA AT THE TIME OF WASHINGTON'S BIRTH

of the Tennessee River and expanding Fort Duquesne. Henry Timberlake, a British officer who served with Washington, appreciated the Cherokees' diplomatic and battle skills, and induced Dinwiddie to invite Ostenaco and Attacullaculla to Williamsburg to discuss mutual interests. On his way there, Ostenaco stayed with Thomas Jefferson, driving down Duke of Gloucester Street in the governor's coach between an honor guard of militia. Dinwiddie promised Ostenaco and Attacullaculla that he would build a fort in the Overhill Cherokee country for protection against the French and provide them with guns and ammunition if they sent warriors to help defend Virginia. It was to be called Fort Loudon. The Cherokees did send some warriors and were generally helpful to Dinwiddie and Washington, but it never seemed good enough. Both men denigrated the Cherokees in their written reports and diaries, never understanding the real situation from the Cherokee perspective.[45] Attacullaculla wished to return to England to meet the King again, hoping that would restore the commitments made in 1730, but colonial officials rejected the visit as too expensive.[46]

One of the worst assaults by English troops against the Cherokees took place in 1759 under Governor William Lyttelton of South Carolina, whose forces attacked undefended Cherokee towns in South Carolina, Tennessee, and Georgia in reprisal for the English defeat at Fort Loudon. The commander of English forces reported on his success: "All their towns . . . besides many little villages and scattered homes, have been burnt; upward of 1400 acres of corn . . . entirely destroyed; and near 5000 Cherokees, including men, women and children, driven to the mountains to starve."[47]

The Cherokee population was geographically concentrated differently than in the 1830s when their lands were seized. This 1760 map by Thomas Kitchin shows their main settlements:[48]

Several Cherokee chiefs were invited to London in May 1762, accompanied by Henry Timberlake. Ostenaco, Cunne Shote, and Woyi were keen to discuss enhancing trade and security. The Indians had an audience with King George III and their portraits were painted. The delegation's visit helped secure the Proclamation Line of 1763, which forbade white settlers

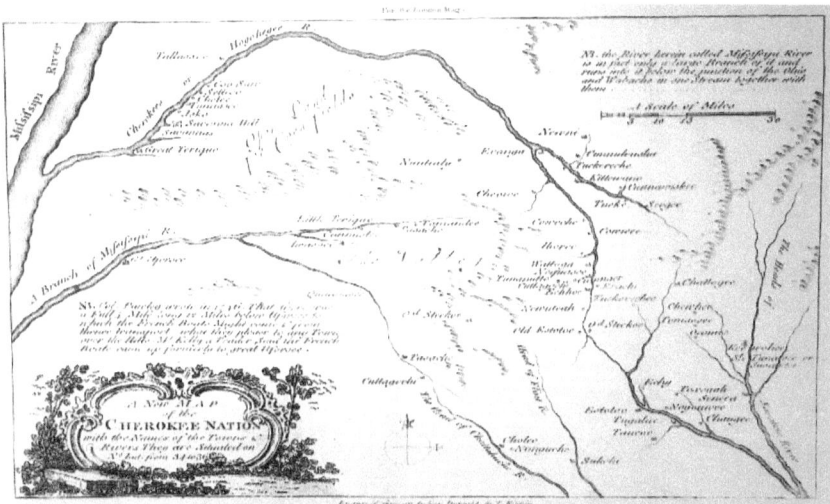

from claiming land west of the Appalachian Mountains, the first English attempt to maintain order along the frontier lands they had won from France. This painting of the Cherokee delegation shows their formal dress for the audience with the King:

Atawayi (Wood Pigeon), Kunagadoga (Standing Turkey) and Utsidihi (Ostenaco)[49]

Sir Joshua Reynolds painted Ostenaco, and Francis Parsons painted Cunne Shote (Oconastota) while they were in London in 1762.[50]

Ostenaco and Cunne Shote (Ocanastota)

That Royal Proclamation decreed that all Indian relations would be directed by London rather than individual colonies, dividing its North American territory into four large administrative areas: Quebec, East and West Florida, and Grenada. It set the Appalachian Mountains as the boundary between the colonies and Indian territory, leaving all land to the west in Indian control, thereby undercutting land-grabs by George Washington and other principals in the Ohio and Mississippi Companies. It prohibited any "private Person . . . from [buying] any Lands reserved to the said Indians within those parts of our Colonies where We have thought proper to allow Settlement" and all purchase or settlement west of the Appalachian Mountains.[51]

Ostenaco and Timberlake returned to London in 1764 to plead with the King to respect the 1763 official Borders Map and stop the hordes of white invaders pouring in. The King pretended he had no time in his busy schedule to see them, and their requests were met with silence. Still, the alliance with England continued. The English Parliament enacted the Quebec Act in 1774, transferring all the territory between the Ohio and Mississippi Rivers to Canadian jurisdiction, further undermining Washington's and other speculators' efforts to carve out vast estates there. In the spring of 1775, Dunmore went further, ruling that Washington's personal surveyor, George Crawford, wasn't qualified, thereby threatening all of Washington's land patents totaling about twenty-three thousand acres. Likewise, Washington's purchase of veterans' claims to thousands of acres of 'bounty' lands was ruled illegal by Lord Dartmouth. Washington had hoped that his Mississippi Company would obtain about two and one-half million acres of Indian land, but he was was forced to give up that dream.[52]

Cherokees were excellent diplomats. Their problem was power: they didn't have enough of it to stand up against the tidal wave of immigration pouring over their territory. In 1775, the great Cherokee War Chief Dragging Canoe (Tsi'yu-gunsini), a son of Attacullaculla, spoke these prescient words: "Whole nations have melted away like snowballs in the sun before the white man's advance. They leave scarcely a name of our people except those wrongly recorded by their destroyers…Finally the whole country, which the Tsalagi and their fathers have so long occupied, will be demanded, and the remnant of the Ani Yvwiya, The Real People, once so great and formidable, will be compelled to seek refuge in some distant wilderness . . . We will hold our land."[53]

That year the Transylvania Company, represented by Richard Henderson and Daniel Boone, decided to acquire most of what is now Kentucky. Their proposed Treaty of Sycamore Shoals required the Cherokees to give up around twenty million acres in Kentucky and Tennessee in exchange for two-thousand pounds sterling and around eight-thousand pounds worth of guns, ammunition, beads, and blankets. Dragging Canoe and some of the

14 | Some Important Back History

other chiefs involved refused and left the negotiation, but Oconostota and Raven Warrior, plied with alcohol, signed the Treaty giving away the traditional hunting grounds in Kentucky. Dragging Canoe remained totally opposed, warning the colonialists that they were purchasing a "dark and bloody ground."[54] Charles C. Royce drew a detailed map of the original Cherokee Nation's boundaries showing the major cessions made through the years, which puts into focus what the Cherokees lost from the mid-1700s to 1838:[55]

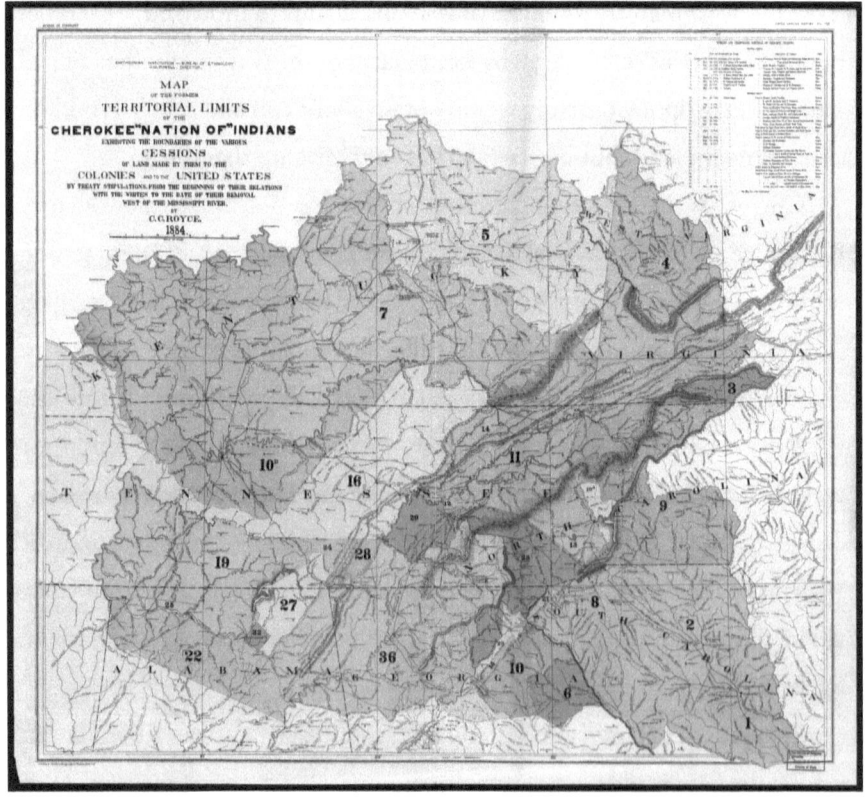

Royce Cherokee Cessions Map 1884

Partly at Washington's urging, Virginia declared independence in 1776 in order not to be blocked by England any longer. Adopting a constitution that annulled the Quebec Act, Virginia created the County of Kentucky that covered most of what they wanted. Washington and other speculators drooled at the prospect.[56] But the Revolutionary War with England took precedence over everything else. When Washington was chosen to serve as General of American forces, he badly needed the support of Indians, and in January 1777, he asked Nathaniel Gist, a prominent trader who had married into the Cherokee Nation, to raise five hundred Cherokee troops, promising that the Indians would be paid the same as colonial soldiers and would receive ammunition and supplies. Gist began his negotiations quickly, since all treaties with England were nullified by the Revolutionary United States Government and Cherokees hoped for a peaceful relationship. But what Washington most wanted was to replace the English treaties with new agreements that would remove Cherokee authority. By May, he helped conclude an agreement with them to give up virtually all their remaining land in South Carolina. A peace treaty was signed with Virginia and North Carolina in July on the Long Island of the Holston River, forcing Cherokees to sign away more than five million acres in western North Carolina and eastern Tennessee. Corn Tassel, the first 'beloved man,' was invited to address the US Congress in July 1777 in connection with the Holston treaty:[57] "It is a little surprising that when we enter into treaties with our brothers, the whites, their whole cry is more land! . . . You marched into our territories with a superior force. Your numbers far exceeded us, and we fled to the stronghold of our extensive woods, there to secure our women and children. Thus, you marched into our towns; they were left to your mercy. You killed a few scattered and defenseless individuals, spread fire and desolation wherever you pleased, and returned again to your own settlements. Were we to inquire by what law or authority you set up a claim . . . I answer, none! Your laws do not apply in our country, nor ever did."[58]

Most Cherokees strongly opposed the Treaty. Dragging Canoe led a band of Overhill Cherokees to an area seven miles upstream from where the South Chickamauga Creek joins the Tennessee River, near present-day Chattanooga, establishing Old Chickamauga Town and ten others in 1777.[59] John McDonald owned a trading post nearby that supplied the Chickamauga Cherokee with guns, ammunition, and supplies. The Chickamaugas included some white men who supported the British, black slave refugees, and Indians from several different tribes. Secretary of War Henry Knox termed them "the germ of the evil" and committed himself to their destruction.[60] Evan Shelby's troops attacked them in 1779, burning the eleven towns and around twenty-thousand bushels of corn. He sent word of their success to Patrick Henry and Thomas Jefferson. Dragging Canoe didn't give up.[61] In the end, Washington didn't include Cherokee troops in his army during the Revolutionary War, continuing to have a fraught relationship with Indians generally and exploiting them whenever it suited his purposes. He often denigrated them as not being worth the cost. Even when Cherokee chiefs begged him to help their starving people, he turned a blind eye. He was forever interested in their lands but not much in being allies. As historian Colin Calloway puts it, "Instead of being remembered for employing Indians in his armies during the Revolution, Washington would be remembered for sending his armies against them."[62]

Washington planned and executed a major attack against the Iroquois in the summer of 1779 because of their continued support for the English, stating he wanted to "distract and terrify the Indians."[63] His meticulous plan envisioned burning down their main villages and destroying their crops. His first target was the Onondaga capital village, with Colonel Goose Van Schaick leading five hundred men. They destroyed the village, burned crops, killed at least twelve people, and took many prisoners. Contemporaneous accounts accused the American troops of raping women and killing children.[64] To continue the war against the Iroquois, he tapped Major General John Sullivan, laying out these objectives: "the total destruction and devastation of their settlements and the capture of as many prisoners of every age and sex as possible. It will be essential to ruin their crops now in the ground and prevent them from planting more."[65]

As he prepared for the assault in the summer of 1779, General Sullivan raised a toast to his officers promising "civilization or death to all American savages."[66] He moved forward with a force of more than four-thousand troops, almost one-quarter of Washington's army. In late August at Newtown on the Chemung River, Sullivan's force destroyed everything in that beautiful town, which was better built and supplied than typical American settlements of the day. His troops burned the Indians' extensive cornfields, destroying all crops his troops didn't need. For the next month they methodically destroyed villages and crops as they neared Chenussio, the largest Seneca town. As the army swept in, burning more than one hundred and twenty homes, all the gardens and seven hundred acres of cornfields, an unknown number of Iroquois were killed. Washington carefully monitored the progress of the campaign, writing Sullivan that he "should have completed the entire destruction of the whole settlements of the Six Nations, excepting those of the Oneidas and such other friendly towns as have merited a different treatment."[67]

Although Washingon hoped this campaign would convince Indians not to support England, many tribes opposed America until the end of the war. His troops committed many travesties in Indian country, including the notorious massacre of Moravian Christian Indians at Gnadenhütten and endless raids against Shawnees by General George Rogers Clark. Those troops spared neither women nor children. By war's end, most Indians in the various theaters of war opposed the colonists.[68] Washington tried to distance himself from the worst atrocities, writing Congress that they were not "committed under my Direction, or by any parties of Continental Troops; nor have they been sanctified by any Orders from me . . . ."[69]

Even those who did support Washington, such as the Oneidas, fared poorly at his hands, with many forced to live in squalid camps. Still, they celebrated the war's end with the surrender of General Cornwallis at Yorktown in October 1781.[70] But Colonel John Sevier attacked the Cherokees in 1782, driving Dragging Canoe and his brothers Little Owl, Badger, and Turtle-at-Home further south, where they established five lower towns below the Tennessee River Gorge: Running Water Town, Nickajack, Long Island, Crow Town, and Lookout Mountain Town.[71] Using Running Water as his base, Dragging Canoe and his warriors mounted attacks on white settlements around the region for the next several years. When the Peace of Paris was signed in 1783, ending the Revolutionary War, England ceded all the land east of the Mississippi, south of the Great Lakes, and north of Florida. Indians weren't mentioned, abandoning them to their fate.

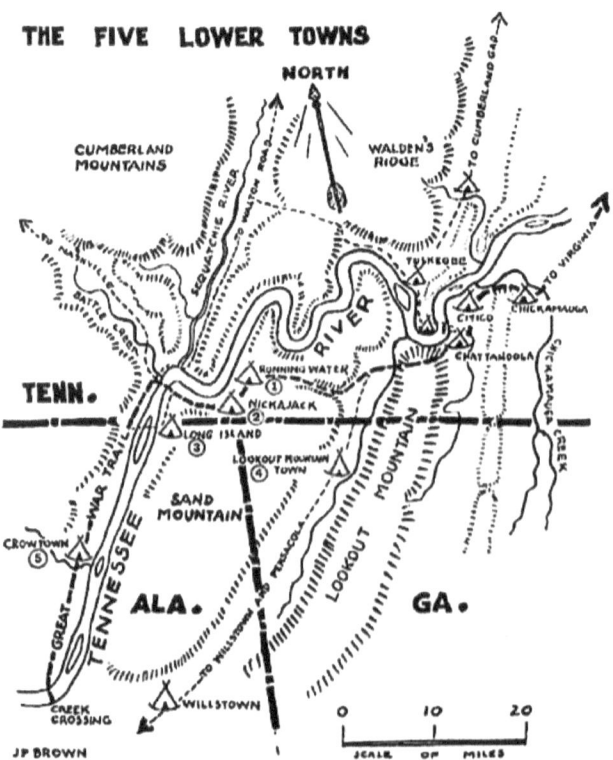

Area Around the Five Lower Towns[72]

The first agreement signed by Cherokees, Choctaws, and Chickasaws with the new US government was the Treaty of Hopewell on November 28, 1785. The US acknowledged full Indian ownership of their lands, laying out the official boundaries of the three Nations and guaranteeing perpetual protection by the Federal Government. That was a decent beginning, if only it had proved to be the true model of their relationships with the United States. But the Hopewell Treaty and its boundaries were never enforced by the US or the states, regardless of who was President. During the next few decades, additional treaties required Cherokees to give up more and more land. They expected those "gifts" would bring peace, but the appetites for Cherokee land by colonialists were insatiable. George Featherstonhaugh, one of the Cherokees' staunchest friends, described their dilemma: All the agreements signed with the US "were treaties of cession that Government always guaranteed to the Indians, in the most solemn form, that portion of their territory which was not ceded" but there was no "security for the performance of these treaties."[73]

An early example of US perfidy was the assassination of Chief Corn Tassel in 1788. When Major James Hubbard from the illegally declared 'state of Franklin' in North Carolina, under the command of John Sevier, went to Corn Tassel's home in Toquo, the US flag given to him at the signing of the Hopewell Treaty flew on his front porch. Hubbard invited Corn Tassel and other warriors to attend a "peace" meeting, where they were axed to death, a horrible, almost unimaginable crime. Following that travesty, Dragging Canoe continued to protect their Cherokee towns by conducting periodic raids against white settlements along the Hiwassee River, but superior American forces defeated him in 1789 at the Battle of Flint Creek in Alabama. In May that year, twenty-four Cherokee chiefs at Chota sent George Washington a letter carried by the elderly chief Rising Fawn, asking the US to abide by the Treaty of Hopewell and to stop invading their remaining lands. It included this moving statement: "We are neither Birds nor Fish, we can neither fly in the air nor live under the water, therefore we hope pity will be extended towards us: We are made by the same hand and in the same shape with yourselves . . . ."[74]

In reply, Washington promised to respect the Hopewell Treaty, but his choice of William Blount as Indian Commissioner, a major speculator in Indian lands, belied a serious commitment. When Washington named Blount as Governor of the new territory of North Carolina, he promptly appointed the notorious Sevier as Brigadier-General of the militia. Both Blount and Sevier were principals in the Tennessee Yazoo Company that advertised farmland in the Muscle Shoals area owned by the Cherokee Nation.[75] At the same time, the official position of the US government, as voiced by War Secretary Henry Knox, was clear about the Indians' legal rights: "The Indians being the prior occupants, possess the right to soil. It cannot be taken from them unless by their free consent . . . . To dispossess them . . . would be a gross violation of the fundamental laws of nature, and of that . . . justice which is the glory of a nation."[76]

The 1791 Treaty of Holston was designed to end hostilities between the US and the Cherokees, affirming their sovereignty while providing the US with the exclusive right to trade with the Cherokee Nation and prohibiting diplomatic relations with other countries. The Cherokees agreed to give up an additional 2.6 million acres of land. Article II laid out the responsibilities of the US and the states for their citizens vis-à-vis Cherokees: "If any citizen or inhabitant of the United States, or of either of the territorial districts of the United States, shall go to any town, settlement, or territory belonging to the Cherokees, and shall there commit any crime upon, or trespass against the person or property of any peaceful and friendly Indian or Indians . . . such offender or offenders shall be subject to the same punishment . . . as if the offence had been committed within the jurisdiction of the State or district to which he or they may belong against a citizen or white inhabitant thereof."[77]

Dragging Canoe, Bloody Fellow, Doublehead, John Watts, and Little Turkey grudgingly signed the Treaty, but they were so upset when it wasn't enforced that Bloody Fellow, a chief of the Five Lower Towns led a delegation to Philadelphia to protest, which included Kingfisher, Nontuaka, Teesteke, Katigoslah, Suaka, Jane Dougherty and their interpreter, James Carey. They met with Washington and Knox on January 4, 1792, asking that all white settlement in the Muscle Shoals area be stopped, for squatters to be removed and for the annuity to be increased from $1000 to $1500. Washington agreed, and the Treaty of Holston was amended accordingly. Washington even gave Bloody Fellow the honorific title of General. The Cherokees left for home pleased with the negotiation. Yet just six months later, after nothing had been done to stop the hordes of squatters flooding in, Bloody Fellow issued this angry statement: "Congress are Liars, General Washington is a Liar & Governor Blount is a Liar."[78]

After a brief pause, Dragging Canoe and his followers continued to fight. He died of natural causes at Running Water Town on February 29th after dancing all night in celebration of a new alliance with the Muskogee and Choctaw. His nephew John Watts assumed command, immediately traveling to Pensacola to seek the Spanish Governor's support, but he declined to help the Cherokees. Isolated and outgunned, Watt and his followers fought on for two more years. After James Ore's militia destroyed Running Water and Nickajack in 1794, Watts moved the resistance to Willstown, which continued until the signing of the Treaty of Tellico Blockhouse in 1798, essentially an addendum to the Treaty of Holston.[79] Article 1 states it was negotiated "for the purpose of doing justice to the Cherokee Nation" but required additional large cessions of land. As usual, the treaty promised that the US "will continue the guarantee of the remainder of their country forever, as made and contained in former treaties."

Painting of Dragging Canoe[80]

Tecumseh, an important Shawnee chief who tried to unify Indians to secure their homelands, was a good friend to the Cherokee Nation. He supported Dragging Canoe's campaigns in the 1780s and 1790s. Born in 1768 in western Ohio to the Shawnee chief Puckshinwa and his wife Methoataske, during a meteor shower, his name means "shooting star" or "the panther passing across." He and his brother Tenskwatawa started a pan-Indian movement in Prophetstown near Lafayette, Indiana Territory in 1808, traveling widely to build a broad alliance. While he was away in 1809, Governor William Henry Harrison marched his troops to Prophetstown intending to destroy it. Tenskwatawa rallied the Indian warriors to resist, but they were overwhelmed by Harrison's forces at the Battle of Tippecanoe and fled. Harrison's troops burned Prophetstown to the ground. Although some Cherokees saw that as prophetic of their likely future, most continued to both resist and co-exist with white culture.

During the War of 1812, Tecumseh fought with British troops at the siege of Detroit, where US forces were defeated. He joined British Major-General Henry Proctor to fight in Ohio, but Harrison defeated them, driving thousands of warriors and their families to Canada. The US attacked the British and Indians at the Battle of the Thames on October 5, 1813, killing Tecumseh. Through the next few years, most of the remaining Indian-controlled land in the eastern US was seized and the Indians driven west of the Mississippi. There were many Trails of Tears as various Indian Nations bravely struggled against being forced to give up their homes. In this context, Tecumseh's advice on life and death is as relevant today as when he wrote it:

> So live your life that the fear of death can never enter your heart. Trouble no one about their religion; respect others in their view, and demand that they respect yours. Love your life, perfect your life, beautify all things in your life. Seek to make your life long and its purpose in the service of your people. Prepare a noble death song for the day when you go over the great divide. Always give a word or a sign of salute when meeting or passing a friend, even a stranger, when in a lonely place. Show respect to all people and grovel to none. When you arise in the morning give thanks for the food and for the joy of living. If you see no reason for giving thanks, the fault lies only in yourself. Abuse no one and no thing, for abuse turns the wise ones to fools and robs the spirit of its vision. When it comes your time to die, be not like those whose hearts are filled with the fear of death, so that when their time comes they weep and pray for a little more time to live their lives over again in a different way. Sing your death song and die like a hero going home.[81]

24 | Some Important Back History

Painting of Tecumseh Based on a Contemporary Drawing[82]

Perhaps Cherokees should have learned the big lesson earlier as they tried various strategies to counter pressures to take their land. While the historical context during the years leading up to the Trail of Tears was fluid and occasionally hopeful, the overarching reality from the mid-1700s on featured a series of solemn treaties signed by the British and US, which both governments violated with impunity. George Washington, the first US President, never understood or respected Indians, although they loomed large in his world. He spent a good portion of his adult life making speculative investments in Indian lands.[83] As one writer summarizes Washington's operative reality, "Indian land dominated his thinking and his vision for the future. Indian nations challenged the growth of his nation. A thick Indian strand runs through the life of George Washington as surely as it runs through the history of early America."[84] By the end of his life, Washington had accumulated more than 45,000 acres in Kentucky, Ohio, Pennsylvania, and West Virginia. A large percentage of the federal budget during his presidency was dedicated to wars against Indians as he supported policies to divest them of millions of acres.[85] "Washington, more than most, had a hand on the scales and was instrumental in the dispossession, defeat, exploitation, and marginalization of Indian peoples. He rarely used the term 'Indian country'—he called it 'wilderness', 'the frontier', 'the Ohio country', 'the west'—but he lived his whole life with one eye on it and one foot in it."[86]

Washington's last letter to the state governments before giving up his role as Commander-in-Chief of the Continental Army describes Americans as the "sole Lords and Proprietors of a vast Tract of Continent."[87] Although Indian sovereignty was proclaimed in the first treaty signed by the US in 1778 with the Delaware Nation, the US systematically asserted authority over Indians everywhere.[88] Still, Washington regularly spoke of having amicable relations with them, welcoming a delegation of thirteen Cherokee chiefs to his Market Street home in Philadelphia on Saturday afternoon, June 14, 1794. Several members of his cabinet—Jefferson, Hamilton, Knox, and Colonel Timothy Pickering—were present. Everyone smoked and passed around the long-stemmed pipe "in ritual preparation for good talks and in a sacred commitment to speak truth and honor pledges made."[89]

Thomas Jefferson also invested in Indian land while ostensibly supporting Indian rights. He wrote General Knox on August 10, 1791, "I am of opinion that Government should firmly maintain this ground; that the Indians have a right to the occupation of their lands independent of the States within whose chartered lines they happen to be . . . [U]ntil they cede them by treaty . . . no act of a State can give a right to such lands . . . ."[90] But he did little to support those fine thoughts, hoping that Indians learning farming and trades such as weaving would be induced to give up their territories and survive as citizens on smaller parcels. Obviously, that was a foolish notion to say the least. Beginning in 1803, Jefferson stopped referring to Indians as "Friends and Brothers," instead addressing them as "My children" and signing his letters as "Your Great Father."[91] He described his big-picture plan to General William Henry Harrison, Governor of the

Indiana Territory: "To promote this disposition to exchange lands which they have to spare and we want, for necessities which we have to spare and they want, we shall push our trading houses, and be glad to see the good and influential individuals among them in debt; because we observe that when these debts get beyond what individuals can pay, they become willing to lop them off by a cession of lands."[92]

Reading the words of Washington, Knox, and Jefferson as they dismantled Indian lands while justifying their policies as "protecting" them reveals their hypocrisy and deceit. George Calloway, who wrote a seminal history of George Washington's relations with Indians, notes that the "formula they developed—land for civilization—became a strategy for American expansion and a hallmark of US Indian policy for one hundred years. So did the readiness to wage war on Indians who refused the deal."[93]

Long before the Trail of Tears, a few Cherokee leaders thought it would be wise to explore other options. Some left as early as 1782 when they received permission from Don Estevon Miro, Governor of Louisiana, to move to Spanish territory west of the Mississippi River.[94] The Bowl, an important Cherokee chief, moved in 1794 with a large entourage, eventually settling in what became Texas. Chief Tahlonteskee announced in 1806 that he was moving west, stating at a Council meeting: "Whites will never be satisfied with treaties that leave Indians some land." He was married to Jennie Lowrey, sister of Assistant Principal Chief George Lowrey and a close friend of Annie's great-grandfather Spirit. In July 1809, he and around one-thousand followers moved to the Saint Francis River area of Arkansas with their livestock, slaves, plows, looms—everything needed to make a new life there. Ceding their part of the tribe's ancestral lands in Alabama in return for the new territory, they moved to the Arkansas River Valley between Point Remove Creek and the mouth of the Poteau River in 1812, the same area where Spirit and Susannah settled in 1819. At first, Tahlonteskee was happy to have moved: "I am here settled, fond of my situation, loving my present house and field." But he became increasingly disturbed that what he'd imagined was a peaceful place, where Cherokees could once again be masters of their fate, was increasingly disturbed by hordes of white hunters pouring in to kill buffalo: "They do not destroy less than five thousand buffaloes every summer for no other profit but the tallow . . . a thousand weight of meat is thrown away for no other profit than perhaps 20 pounds of tallow. This is a thing which will render game shortly scarce and we must then see our children suffer."[95]

Painting of a buffalo hunt in Thomas McKenney's History of the Indian Tribes of North America[96]

Tahlonteskee also was distressed about continuing conflicts with the Osages, the traditional owners in the area, and other tribes forced to flee their homelands in Ohio, Indiana, Illinois, and other states—Delawares, Weas, Kickapoos, Piankeshaws, Peorias and many more, all putting additional pressure on the Osages. But no matter what happened, he was determined to stay, saying "I will not move again!" The Treaty of the Chickasaw Council

House was signed in September 1816, with the Cherokees giving up about 3,500 square miles in Alabama for allegedly equivalent land in Arkansas. That was followed by the Treaty of the Cherokee Agency on July 8, 1817, which ratified and extended the earlier agreement, signed by Major General Andrew Jackson for the US, Cherokees who still resided east of the Mississippi, and those who had moved to the Arkansas River area. Article Eight guaranteed title in fee simple to Cherokee heads of households who chose to remain in the East, while Article Twelve assured that all Indian lands would be protected from white intruders. Jackson obtained about two million acres of land in North Carolina and Tennessee for the US from the deal.

Jackson was instrumental in negotiating various cession treaties as Commissioner and General, usually coupled to "investments" in Cherokee land. The Cumberland Valley was being overrun with white families desperate for their piece of Indian land, and Jackson was only too happy to help. In a letter to his friend John Coffee, Jackson predicted that this approach to obtaining cessions "will give us the whole country [the entire Southeast] in less than two years."[97] Jackson and Secretary of War John C. Calhoun pressed the Cherokees for another large cession, culminating in a Treaty dated February 27, 1819 that covered four million acres. The stipulations in the 1817 Treaty were supposed to be maintained, including fee-simple reservations of six-hundred and forty acres to each household that chose not to emigrate west. But this was a ruse. As Christopher Vandeventer, chief clerk of the War Department, wrote to Lewis Cass, "The great object is to remove, altogether, these tribes beyond the Mississippi. If that be accomplished, every difficulty is removed; there then ceases to be any question about the tenure by which the Indians shall hold lands."[98]

The 1817 and 1819 agreements provided for "equivalent" land in the west, free transport and food on Government boats, and compensation for the homes and farms left behind. Although paltry, those sums were paid, but no assistance was provided for farming implements and supplies following removal. Samuel Houston played a major role in convincing Cherokees to leave their ancestral lands and move to Arkansas. As a boy, he ran away from home to live on the banks of the Hiwassee River in Tennessee, where he learned to speak Cherokee and participated in their ball games and dances while living with Chief John Jolly's family. He loved the Green Corn dance and is said to have been a decent dancer. In 1817, General Jackson recommended to War Secretary Calhoun that Houston be named sub-agent for the Government. He was confirmed on October 21st and in that capacity worked with Chief Jolly to convince many Cherokees to move west.

Jolly departed in 1818 with sixteen boats and 330 people, settling near Spadra Bluffs. Each of his 108 warriors received a new rifle. Their early impressions were favorable: rich riverbanks and flood plains, hardwood forests like those in Alabama and Georgia, plentiful water, and lots of game including buffalo, elk, wild turkeys, migrating geese, and ducks. But they quickly began to see the flaws in the new land, which wasn't theirs but someone else's. Far from the empty virgin territory they were promised, it was partly occupied by Osages, who were extremely unhappy about the growing Cherokee settlements. Sometimes they blocked access to crucial salt sources and hunting grounds, raiding Cherokee settlements to steal animals and weapons. In response, Tahlonteskee's warriors struck back. Although the situation became increasingly tense, small numbers of Cherokees continued to move to Arkansas. Collectively they became known as the "Old Settlers."

Tahlonteskee hoped that missionaries would bring education to the west, and in late 1818 requested the American Board of Commissioners for Foreign Missions to establish a new mission in Arkansas. Although he didn't live to see it, Dwight Mission was established in the spring of 1820, near present-day Russellville. When Tahlonteskee died in 1819, John Jolly was elected to succeed him. He hoped to reunite all Cherokees. Later that year, representatives from 54 towns and villages gathered in Echota to adopt articles of governance to protect Cherokee lands both east and west. A standing committee of thirteen people was formed to administer the affairs of the whole Nation, confident that they could protect the Cherokee Nation by standing together.

Painting of Chief Jolly by George Catlin[99]

By 1819, several thousand Cherokees lived in Arkansas, including Annie's great-grandparents Spirit and Susannah; Spirit lived there until his death in 1828. The Cherokees built homes, created farms and established a traditional government. Jackson was happy with this result, using it to press for all southeastern Indians to give up their lands, but his long-term goal was set back in 1821 when the Supreme Court ruled in *Johnson v. McIntosh*[100] that the Indians, as "original inhabitants . . . were admitted to be the rightful occupants of the soil, with a legal as well as just claim to retain possession of it." In establishing the principle of Aboriginal Title, Chief Justice Marshall stated that Congress could no more steal Indian land than it could take land from white people. Daniel Webster was the Cherokees' lawyer in that case. John Ross wrote about it in 1822, "I can't believe that the United States Government will still continue . . . removing nation after nation of them from the lands of their fathers into the remote wilderness."

Daniel Webster in 1835[101]

The Bureau of Indian Affairs was created in 1824 as part of the War Department. Rather than trying to assist Indians, much less implement the Supreme Court's 1821 decision that they had the right to control their own lands, its official mission was to expedite removal. Chief Ross presented President Monroe a detailed history of Cherokee relations with the United States in early January 1824, insisting that his statements denying Cherokee sovereignty lacked any merit. The President responded dismissively on January 19th. Ross wrote War Secretary Calhoun a pointed response on February 11th: "The Cherokee nation have never promised to surrender at any future period, to the United States, or Georgia, their title to lands; but, on the contrary the United States have, by treaties, solemnly guaranteed to secure to the Cherokees forever their title to lands which have been reserved by them: therefore, the State of Georgia can have no reasonable plea against the Cherokees for refusing to yield . . . territory twice as large, west of the Mississippi, as the one now occupied by the Cherokees east of that river . . . .all the money now in the coffers of your treasury would be no inducement for the nation to exchange or to sell their country."[102]

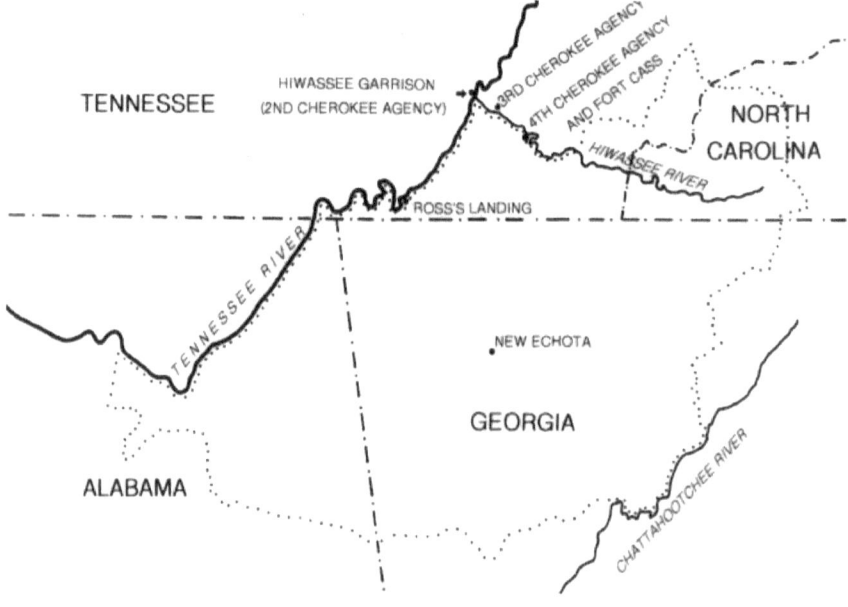

Map of Cherokee Nation 1819-1835[103]

Representatives of Shawnees, Ottawas, Wyandots, Tuscaroras, and Miamis gathered in Kaskaskia, Illinois in October, invited by the Western Cherokee Chief Takatoka, recently named "Beloved Man" (Ani-Kituwagi). John Jolly was there, along with Spring Frog, Young Glass, John Drew, Corn Tassel, Tahlone and Witch. Following days of discussions, they agreed to invite the tribes east of the Mississippi to join them in Arkansas, but they needed clarity from Washington on the legal extent of their new lands and sent a delegation to Washington to obtain those details. On the way, Takatoka became sick with a fever, dying near the Mississippi River. The rest of the delegation made it to Washington, where they learned that the US had no interest in the proposal but instead wanted them to give up their Arkansas land and move further west to what was called Lovely's Purchase. That was rejected, and they returned home deeply distressed.[104] The Cherokee Council formally resolved "unanimously, with one voice and determination, to hold no treaties with any Commissioners of the United States to make any cession of lands, being resolved not to dispose of even one foot of ground." The was popular with all Cherokees wherever they lived and whatever their political views, including the Spirit family.

But President Monroe, pressed strongly by General Jackson, continued pursuing his aggressive goal of removing all the Indians in the east, initiating new treaties—often well-lubricated by bribes and alcohol—with the Osages, Chippewas, Dakotas, Sacs, Foxes, Winnebagoes, Miamis, and Ottawas. All were forced to trade their lands for a pittance and move west. Cherokees held out longer than most in the face of intransigent US pressure. Duncan G. Campbell, the Commissioner nominated by Monroe to negotiate with the Cherokees in 1823, put it starkly: If Cherokees "cherish the idea of independence and self-government, the sooner they are corrected the better. The United States will not permit the existence of a separate, distinct, and independent Government within her limits."[105] His words fell on deaf ears in the Cherokee Nation, which was building its new capitol and focused on educating its people.

President Monroe was pressed by Georgian officials to honor the terms of its 1802 Compact with the US, which implied removing all Indians in the state at some future time. The Compact wasn't worded precisely. In his reply, Monroe acknowledged that the Compact didn't envision or authorize force, writing that "any attempt to remove them by force would, in my opinion, be unjust."[106] In his eighth and final annual message to Congress in December 1824, Monroe stated that forcible removal would be "revolting to humanity and utterly unjustifiable." He called for Cherokees to voluntarily move to what were described as vast uninhabited lands west of the Mississippi River. But just five weeks before leaving office he formally declared that removal of the Indians was of "paramount importance" to the US: "Experience has clearly demonstrated that in their present state it is impossible to incorporate them in such masses, in any form whatsoever, into our system."[107]

But the Cherokees proceeded during the next few years to prove they were fully capable of managing their own affairs, while continuing to fend off assaults on their sovereignty. Based on the traditional Cherokee spiritual path called "Kituhwa" named after their "mother town" that was the capital prior to Chota. It was the place where the Creator gave the laws and first fire to the people. Kituwah Mound is located near present-day Bryson City, North Carolina. Kituhwa and Keetoowah (A-ni-kee-too-wah-gee) have essentially the same meaning, although in the 1890s the mostly full-bloods who were most fiercely against loss of sovereignty were called Keetoowah. They saw land cessions as treason. Legends say the name was given after seven of the wisest men climbed the highest peak and fasted for seven days and nights, asking the Creator for guidance. On the seventh night of their fast, the Creator said: "You shall be Kituwah."[108]

In the 1820s they built a beautiful new capitol in New Echota, wrote a constitution, established a court system and legislature, and started a public school system that should have been the envy of the colonialists. The Cherokee Nation was blessed with many wise heroes and heroines as they negotiated their path forward in the face of implacable opposition from the US and individual states.

3

Heroines and Heroes

In the late 1700s and early 1800s, two people stand out as models of how Cherokees dealt with conflict between their society and white settlers. Although neither was a member of the Spirit family, they illustrate the qualities that Cherokees brought to the table in negotiating a path forward. Nanye-hi and Tah-Chee inspired the entire Cherokee Nation.[109]

There are many stories about Nanye-hi, no doubt some of them exaggerated. She is thought to have been born around 1738 into a powerful family in the Wolf clan, living near Chota in the hills of what today is Eastern Tennessee.[110] Her mother most likely was Na-Ni, born around 1716, while her father was a displaced Delaware named Five Killer (Skayagustuegwo), born in 1710.[111] Her grandmother was probably Nancy Moytoy, born around 1683, and her grandfather was likely White Owl Raven, born about 1680. Assuming that is true, her maternal grandfather was Amatoy Moytoy, born in 1640, and her grandmother Quatsy was born around 1650. She experienced violence in her early life given the ongoing struggle with European settlers as well as other tribes. Nanye-hi's first husband, Tsu-la Red Fox Kingfisher, was killed in a 1755 raid on the Creeks, sometimes called the Battle of Taliwa. She was fighting beside him. After he fell, she rallied the warriors and led the charge that brought victory. In her honor, she was named Ghighau (Beloved Woman), which meant that she sat on the Council of Chiefs, headed the Women's Council and had power over the fates of prisoners. Sometimes known as Agi-ga-u-e (War Woman), she prepared the "white drink" made from Yaupon Holly for the warriors who planned to attack the Carter's Valley, Holston, and Watauga settlements in July 1776, and regularly helped prepare that drink for the younger men going to war, a sacred ritual.[112]

As a member of the Wolf Clan, Nanye-hi came from a group noted for its healers. A legend tells of an old man with sores all over his body who showed up among the Cherokee seeking help. A woman of the Wolf Clan helped him, and in return he taught the women of the Clan the cures of the plant world, telling them they would be the healers in their communities.[113] Nanye-hi always saw herself as a healer and peacemaker. She married Bryant Ward, an Irish trader born in Antrim around 1730, on September 18, 1756. Their daughter Elizabeth was born on September 18, 1757. Bryant brought his son John Jack with him into Cherokee country, who married Catherine McDaniel, a daughter of William David McDaniel and Sookie Hopper. It is unclear how long Bryant and Nanye-hi stayed together. She raised Elizabeth and her children with Kingfisher—Catherine, born in 1752, and Five Killer (Hi-s-gi-di-hi), born in 1755. As Nanye-hi learned more about American and English customs, she concluded that co-existence was both necessary and possible. She spent her life supporting peace. The conclusion of the French and Indian War in 1763 provided a brief and hopeful moment, but large-scale incursions by white settlers continued incessantly, and peace was illusory. In the 1770s, as threats of war emerged between England and the colonies, most Cherokees supported the British. Nanye-hi disagreed, personally warning white settlers of possible Cherokee attacks. She used her power to free captives, most famously Lydia Bean, who was tied to a stake prior to her imminent execution. Striding to the prisoner, Nanye-hi cut her loose, taking her to her own home for safety while tempers cooled. Lydia taught Nanye-hi how to make butter and cheese, which led her to introduce cows and dairy products into the Cherokee economy, a profound development.

US Colonel William Christian led eighteen-hundred soldiers against Cherokee towns in October 1776, demolishing several but sparing Nanye-hi's out of respect for her. Following US independence, she continued pressing for peaceful coexistence. After warning settlers of an impending Cherokee attack in 1781, her entire village was captured. The US delivered an ultimatum: immediate negotiations. The Cherokee accepted, naming Nanye-hi as their chief negotiator. At the successful conclusion of the talks held on the Long Island of the Holston River, she made this statement: "You know that women are always looked upon as nothing; but we are your mothers; you are our sons. Our cry is all for peace; let it continue. This peace must last forever. Let your women's sons be ours. Let our sons be yours. Let your women hear our words."

Nanye-hi and Corn Tassel played a key role in negotiating the Hopewell Treaty in November 1785. Hundreds of Cherokees arrived on November 18th at the South Carolina plantation owned by General Andrew Pickens, who had been given 573 fertile acres on the Keowee River by George Washington for his service during the Revolutionary War and then greatly expanded the plantation. It had been Cherokee land, but because they had supported England they would have to pay. The US appointed three commissioners to negotiate, Colonel Benjamin Hawkins from North Carolina, Joseph Martin from Virginia and General Lachlan McIntosh, an important Georgia rice farmer, all slave owners.[114] Nanye-hi argued that the land surrounding the plantation remained Cherokee territory and asked for help in removing the hundreds of white squatters who had invaded the area.

The commissioners replied that there was nothing they could do, prompting this riposte from Corn Tassell: "Are Congress, who conquered the King of Great Britain, unable to remove these people?"[115]

Inviting the commissioners to smoke her pipe of peace and friendship, Nanye-hi expressed hope that the "chain of friendship will never more be broken." The Cherokees were in a weak negotiating position and agreed after ten days to accept the US conditions: return all the slaves they had liberated during the war, agree on a new boundary that ceded considerable additional territory, and accept the protection of the US. For its part, the US agreed that territory beyond the new boundary remained Cherokee and undertook to stop white encroachment. The first Treaty of Hopewell was signed on November 28, 1785.[116] Nanye-hi was satisfied with the result, thinking that peace and respect would follow.

But as the hordes of white settlers kept coming, she changed her opinion on how much compromise could be tolerated. For the next 25 years, she was a sought-after advisor, working closely with the Women's Council and increasingly worried about the loss of Cherokee land. She and the Women's Council sent this message to the all-male Cherokee National Council on May 2, 1817: "The Cherokee ladies now being present at the meeting of the chiefs and warriors in council have thought it their duty as mothers to address their beloved chiefs and warriors . . . Your mothers and sisters ask and beg of you not to part with any more of our land . . . .But keep it for our growing children, for it was the good will of our creator to place us here . . . .Therefore, children, don't part with any more of our lands but continue on it & enlarge your farms. Cultivate and raise corn & cotton and. . . . have a great many grandchildren who I wish to do well on our land."[117]

When organizing another petition to the National Council on June 30, 1818, she again urged the Cherokee not to give away their land: "As the Cherokee nation have been the first settlers of this land; we therefore claim the right of the soil . . . .Now the thought of being compelled to remove to the other side of the Mississippi is dreadful to us, because it appears to us that we, by this removal, shall be brought to a savage state again . . . ."[118]

When the land on which Nanye-hi's home stood was sold in 1819, she moved back to Chota and spent her remaining years running an inn at Woman Killer Ford, along the Ocowee River on the Federal Road in what is now Polk, Tennessee. She died on March 20, 1824. I'm glad she didn't have to experience the Trail of Tears, but her moral courage and leadership would have been welcome. She was a great Cherokee heroine.

***

Tah-Chee means "Dutch" in Cherokee. He was sometimes called Captain William Dutch for reasons lost to history. His name written in Cherokee is Tatsi. Born about 1790 at Turkey Town near the Coosa River in Alabama, not far from where Annie's great-grandfather Spirit lived, he was the third son of Skyugo, a famous chief. To escape continuing struggles with whites, the family moved to Arkansas when he was a young boy, initially living in the St. Francis River area. An uncle prepared his first gun by cutting off part of the barrel to make it easily managed by the young boy. When he was about thirteen years old, he was allowed to participate in a long hunting expedition and was absent a year. That set the pattern of his life.

A renowned hunter and warrior, a legend on the plains as a lone hunter with three large dogs running alongside his horse, Tah-Chee was curious about other cultures, learning to speak Osage—with whom the Cherokees were often at war—and other dialects. He both fought against and hunted with the Osages. Once, he set out alone with his three dogs on a long hunt, going up the Arkansas River by canoe to the mouth of the Neosho River, where he hid the canoe in thick underbrush and traveled on foot to the

Missouri river. After hunting and trapping for several weeks, he returned to his canoe with 90 beaver skins. When he got home, he learned that one of his mother's relatives had been killed by an Osage during his absence and wanted to immediately avenge her death. Joining the war party headed by his uncle Cahtateeskee Dirt Seller, he was surprised when at their first encampment, Dirt Seller raised him to the station of warrior and presented him with a war club: "I present this to you; if you are a Brave, and can use it in battle, keep it; if you fail in making it, as a warrior should, effective upon the living, then, as a boy, strike with it the bodies of the dead!"[119] Tah-Chee killed two Osages, returning with their scalps to participate in his first scalp dance to honor the victory. It made a big impression on him.

When Cherokee Agent Edward DuVal tried in 1824 to convince Cherokees residing south of the Arkansas River to move north to where some Cherokee had been emigrating since 1817, Tah-Chee refused to go. He told DuVal that "they never again meant to join the main body of the Nation" but "intended to go in the other direction and settle . . . beyond the Red River, within the Spanish provinces."[120] His village was three miles west of Danville, Arkansas on Dutch Creek, where his main hunting area was the Fource Valley. Dutch Creek Mountain was named after him.

When the US signed a treaty in 1828 with Cherokees living in his family's northeast Alabama homelands to exchange their land for a large tract of several million acres in Arkansas, it made him so angry that he moved to the Red River area in Texas, where Chief Bowles had established a large Cherokee community. Tah-Chee honed his warrior status in battles against the Tawakanaks and Commanches there. He left Texas in 1831, moving to the mouth of the Canadian River in the Cherokee Nation West, where he built a large home and continued breeding and raising horses. He was chosen by Colonel Arbuckle to guide US Army troops on expeditions and ended up feeding the troops through his uncanny understanding of buffalo.

In that capacity, he helped lead the Dragoon expedition into Comanche territory, where he met the painter George Catlin in 1834, who described him as "one of the most extraordinary men that lives on the frontier at the present time." Colonel August Chouteau wrote in 1833 that "Dutch (Tahchee) is looked upon as the most sagacious and daring war Captain in the Cherokee Nation west of the Mississippi . . . [he] may be known . . . by his remarkable black, keen, restless eyes."[121] James Hall described him: "He is five feet eleven inches high, of admirable proportions, flexible and graceful in his movements, and possesses great muscular power and activity; while his countenance expresses a coolness, courage, and decision, which accord well with his distinguished reputation as a warrior."[122]

Although Tah-Chee was an excellent warrior, he was also a diplomat, using his knowledge and skills to help find peace. He became a key liaison between the Old Settlers and Chief John Ross following removal and was a representative at the 1835 Camp Homes Treaty negotiation, which established peace between the US and the Cherokee, Comanche, Wichita, Creek, Choctaw, and Osage tribes. Tired of war and happy with his diplomacy, he built a house on the Canadian River, married, and became a farmer. His herd of cattle was the largest in the region and his love for ponies was legendary. Elected as a Senator on the National Council in 1841, 1843 and 1847, he continued to play an important role in the Cherokee Nation, and signed the Washington treaty on August 6, 1846 as „Wm. DUTCH" along with John Huss Spirit. Diplomacy ran in the family. His father signed the Treaty of the Holston on July 2, 1791, the Treaty of Philadelphia on June 26, 1794 (as Skyuka), and the first Treaty of Washington on January 7, 1806 as Skeuha.

Tah-Chee represents well the struggles that Cherokees faced. An astute warrior and hunter who became a linguist and diplomat, he died too young on November 12, 1848. This 1837 lithograph by Albert Newsam based on a painting by Charles Bird King shows him in his fine clothing, typical of how many Cherokees dressed in those days.[123] Cherokee men loved their colorful turbans!

Cherokee warriors demonstrated their intelligence and prowess in many battles in the 18th and early 19th centuries, perhaps most famously at Horseshoe Bend in 1814.

4

Battle of Horse Shoe Bend

A few words about the Battle of Horse Shoe Bend (Tohopeka) are in order, given that Cherokees prevented Andrew Jackson and his second in command, General John Coffee, from being defeated there. Some say the Cherokees saved Jackson's life. Several relatives in the extended Spirit family fought on Jackson's side at this Battle and others during the Creek Wars.[124] Once Major Ridge agreed to help Jackson fight the Creeks, he sent runners around the Nation asking for volunteers. More than 800 experienced warriors formed a Company, including John Ross serving as an adjutant. Along with Colonel Pathkiller and Lieutenant Colonel John Lowrey, he marched the men to Jackson's headquarters at Ten Islands, Alabama to discuss strategy. Jackson assigned Colonel Gideon Morgan to lead the Cherokee Company. They moved quietly the next morning towards the Creeks' fortified camp, located on a tight bend of the Tallapoosa River that was protected by water. The only entrance was blocked by a high log barrier. The middle of town was dominated by a tall red pole with dozens of white scalps dangling down.

The forces engaged on March 27th at the Horse Shoe Bend, not far from present-day Dadeville. Jackson led his main force toward the breastworks, while General Coffee and a detachment of militia joined the Cherokees in fording the Tapaloosa to come around from behind. At first, the Creeks, under the leadership of Chief Menawa and William Weatherford—a formidable warrior—held out against Jackson's forces, with defenses that seemed impregnable:[125]

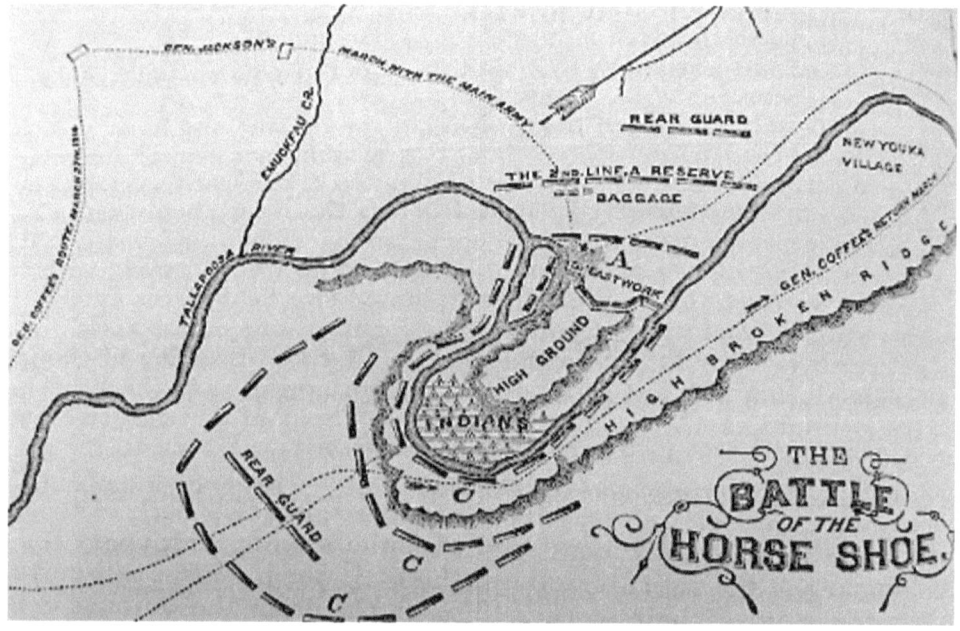

Jackson described the difficult setting his troops faced as the battle began:

> It is impossible to conceive a situation more eligible for defence than the one they had chosen and the skill which they manifested in their breastwork was really astonishing. It extended across the point in such a direction as that a force approaching would be exposed to a double fire, while they lay entirely safe behind it. It would have been impossible to have raked it with cannon to any advantage even if we had had possession of one extremity.[126]

After the fighting had raged for several hours, the Creeks' defenses held firm against Jackson's two artillery cannons pounding their positions, with only a few wounded. Ridge proposed that Private Tocqua, nicknamed The Whale, would swim across the river with his son-in-law Corporal Charles Reese and one other man to a spot facing the rear of the fort and retrieve two canoes left on the beach. They successfully ferried Major Ridge and his company across the river, back and forth, as only a few could fit in a canoe on each trip, and they came under fire. Tocqua was wounded.[127] The majority of the Creeks were surprised and quickly overwhelmed. Ridge fought several hand-to-hand, killing one warrior in the water with his knife and leaving him floating face down with blood swirling everywhere.[128] Soon, Jackson's forces were able to clear the barrier at the fort's entry and poured in, pressing the Creeks man to man, chasing everyone who ran into the forest or the river. Trapped between the two forces, the Creeks decided to fight to the last man. After several hours, eight-hundred Creek warriors were dead, with Weatherford being one of the few to escape. Ross compiled a list of Cherokees lost: eighteen killed and thirty-six wounded. One of the dead was the son of Walkingstick, an important Cherokee leader and diplomat born in 1755 who lived near Annie's grandparents in the 1820s, ten miles from Buzzard's Roost, and supported their claims against the US in 1842. No one in the Spirit family was killed, but several were wounded. Tocqua later described what they had done: "By this exploit our warriors were enabled to cross the river and obtain other canoes by which they succeeded in carrying over a force strong enough to attack the enemy in the rear. And by keeping up a hot fire soon dislodged them from their breast works. They were then pursued . . . until the victory was gained."[129]

Indian Agent Return J. Meigs described the decisive role played by Cherokee warriors: " . . . the daring intrepid & preserving bravery of the Cherokee warriors probably saved the loss of 1000 white men."[130] But as the weary Cherokee warriors traveled back home after the battle, they learned that while they were fighting to save Jackson, his Tennessee Militia had been looting and pillaging Cherokee villages and farms, stealing horses, slaughtering hogs and cattle, and taking food and clothing from people in the villages. Agent Meigs was stunned by the devastation. Ridge demanded compensation for the lost animals, food, and supplies. Jackson rebuffed the claim as a groundless falsehood and, in fact, took the opportunity to extend the boundaries of his "settlement" with the Creeks to include another huge tract of Cherokee land in Northern Alabama, over two million acres.[131] Ridge decided to ride to Washington, D.C. to speak directly with President Madison, departing late in 1815 with John Ross, Colonel Lowrey and a few others. They arrived in late January 1816 to find the Capitol still devastated by the British attack on the city in late 1814. The White House was a ruin. On March 22nd Ross and Ridge presented a summary of the devastation wrought by the Tennessee Militia to President Madison in Octagon House, where his offices were relocated while the White House was being rebuilt. With the support of Secretary of War Crawford, $25,000 was provided as compensation, and a beautiful rifle was given to Tocqua for his leadership and bravery in swimming back and forth across the river.[132]

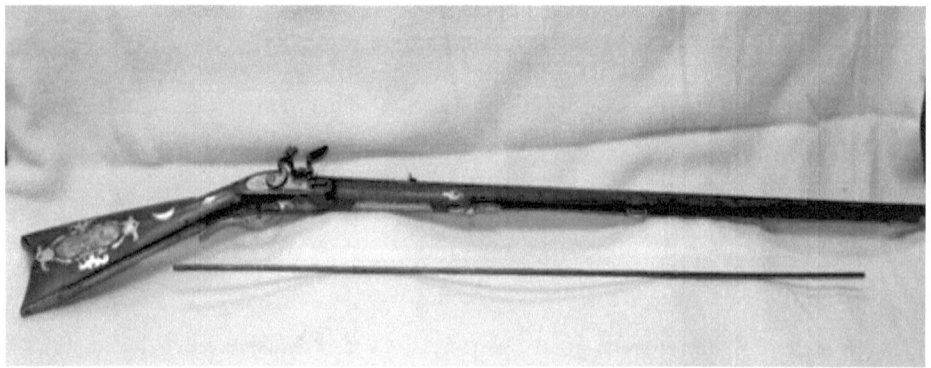

The Battle of the Horse Shoe was effectively the end of the Red Stick War, fought by the US with the Creeks during 1813 and 1814 and what amounted to a civil war inside the Creek Nation. Jackson forced the Creeks to give up more than twenty-one million acres in Alabama and Georgia and move west. The victory put Jackson firmly in the national spotlight. Later, when he ignored the Cherokee petitions to stay in their native land, Chief Junaluska (Gu-Ka-Las-Ki), who personally recruited one-hundred warriors and helped save Jackson's life at Horse Shoe Bend, put it best: "If I had known that Jackson would drive us from our homes, I would have killed him that day at the Horse Shoe."[133]

After returning home to Oostanaula in early April, Major Ridge personally took charge of verifying the true Cherokee boundaries with the Creeks, providing those details to Secretary Crawford. President Madison was said to be on his side, but Jackson was furious and tried to buy another huge section of Cherokee territory. That effort failed when Ridge stated forcefully that none of the land was for sale at any price. But a few months later, Jackson's $5,000 bribe to a few chiefs partly succeeded; one million more acres were lost as Madison went along with the deal. To drive the knife in, Jackson was named Commissioner in charge of Cherokee land claims, using that position to promote his dream of driving all Indians in the Southeast from their ancestral lands while padding his personal holdings.

Many positive things occurred between 1814 and 1835 as Cherokee creativity and resourcefulness successfully built its Nation, including constructing a new Capitol at New Echota. What was life like for Cherokees then? What were their expectations and hopes? It's time to learn more about Annie Spirit's grandfather Buffalofish.

5

Buffalofish Spirit

Annie's Grandfather Buffalofish (Da-Gah-Sah-Tah) was born around 1780 when his father, The Spirit, and his mother Susannah (Tsah'wah'u'gah) were twenty years old. At the time, The Spirit lived along Mouse Creek in Tennessee, where he married his first wife, Mary Blaylock. She was a half-blood daughter of Nancy Gourd, a full blood Cherokee, and John Blaylock, a white captive of the Cherokees. Later, Spirit married Susannah, and they moved to Creekpath, Alabama, where they were neighbors of Major George Lowrey and Sequoyah. It is likely that Buffalofish was born there.

After Buffalofish married War-te-yoh-he, they began farming and raising a family at Buzzard Roost on Sweetwater Creek, a tributary of the Chattahoochee River, in District 18 of the old Cherokee Nation. That's about sixteen miles southwest of Marietta, Georgia in Cobb County, near Austell and Lithia Springs, a site of great spiritual significance for Cherokees. Sweetwater Creek was named after Ama-kan-as-ta (Sweet Water), a local Cherokee chief.[134] There is evidence of Woodland (1,000 B.C. to 900 A.D.) and Mississippian (900 A.D. to 1,600 A.D.) villages as well as Paleo-Indian mounds from 10,000 B.C. along the river. In the early 1800s the Creeks established a village named Buzzard Roost along the southeast bank of the

Chattahoochee River, about one mile below the mouth of Utoy Creek. Today it is Sweetwater Creek State Park, a beautiful area near Lithia Springs.

Chattahoochee River near Buzzard Roost

The first reference to Buffalofish in a US document was on September 5, 1814. He received $25 at the Cherokee Agency, likely a treaty benefit. There are periodic references to him in Moravian journals, particularly regarding his friendship with US Cherokee Agent Colonel Return J. Meigs. For example, he is recorded as returning on June 3, 1819 from a visit with Meigs, who at that time was a neighbor of Chief Chuleoa. Eventually the community where he lived was named Buffalo Fish Town in his honor. War-te-yoh-he and Buffalofish had at least eleven children, including:[135]

- The Spirit, Annie's father (1792-1851) married Chowyouka Swimmer (1790-1861)
- Crying Snake (E-nah-da-gah) married Alcie Vann
- Alexander Buffalofish (Oo-ta-lah-nah) married A-toh-hee Cornsilk and had a son named Ben Buffalofish

- Naky or Nakey married Nitts (O-Ne-Hut-Tee), son of Stitches and had several children: Levi, Ice, Ah-claw-se-nee, Oo-nah-stul-lah, Te-tah-te-yas-kee, Caty, and Lydia
- So-Wa-Chee married Sawney Vann (1792-1860) and had a number of children: Arch, Jennie, Moses, Lewis, Tah-no-lee, Jack, and De-gu-tlu-ga-sky
- Charlie Buffalofish (?-1850) married Sallie Tail Frisley (1822-1902) and had five children: Hunter Poorbear Buffalofish (1849-?), Peggy, Nellie, Charlie, and Yo-nu-la-so-dah
- Eagle-on-the-Tree or Eagle-on-the-Roost (Wa-lu-kil-lah)

This family tree shows Buffalofish's great-grandparents down to An-na-wa-ki Spirit:

SCONTI, Old (ca1726 - 1765)
b. ca 1726
d. 1765
& **GRANT, Mary** (1729 - 1782)
b. 1729
d. 1782

SPIRIT, The (1760 - 1828)
b. 1760
d. 1828
& **TSAH-WAH-U-GAH, Susannah** (1760 - 1860)
b. 1760
d. 1860

SPIRIT, Buffalofish (1780 - 1842)
b. 1780
d. 1842
& **WO-DE-YO-HE** (1780 - 1859)
b. 1780
d. 1859

Spirit (1797 - 1851)
b. 1797
d. 1851
& **SWIMMER, Chowyouka** (1790 - 1861)
b. 1790
d. 1861

SPIRIT, Ah-na-wa-ki (1826 - 1910)
b. 1826
d. 20 Feb 1910
& **MAYES, Samuel Houston** (1803 - 1858)
b. 11 Apr 1803
d. 30 Dec 1858

The Treaty of Indian Springs on January 8, 1821 records Buzzard's Roost as being on Creek land, "beginning on the east bank of the Flint River . . . to the head of the principle western branch; from thence the nearest and direct line to the Chattahoochee River, up the eastern bank . . . to the Shallow ford . . . provided . . . that if the said line should strike the Chattahoochee River below the Creek Village Buzzard's Roost, there shall be a set-off made so as to leave the said village within the Creek Nation."[136] Soon thereafter the Cherokees and Creeks negotiated a treaty that left the area under Cherokee control. When the 1830 census was taken in Cobb County, Major James Montgomery outlined the limits of Cherokee territory there: "Starting at Buzzard Roost Island on the Chattahoochee, he followed 'an old Indian trail' that soon passed the homes of Buffalo Fish and Dick Scott."[137] In spite of robust Cherokee documentation of their agreement with the Creeks in the early 1820s to mark the boundary, the US wanted the area. Jackson engaged one of his business partners, Colonel Coffee, to draw a new map to achieve that.

In 1829 the so-called "Coffee Line" was officially marked from the Lower Shallow Ford on the Chattahoochee through upper Cobb and Paulding County to the Alabama line. Cherokee citizens living south of the line, now claimed by Georgia, were forced to leave their farms and resettle north of the new boundary line. Buffalofish and his extended family were forced to abandon their houses, fields, a valuable ferry, many animals, tools, and household items. Their neighbors Walkingstick, Drowning Bear and several other families also had to leave. None of the Cherokees received any compensation despite filing claims in 1836 and 1837. After removal, they filed new claims in 1842, which are discussed in Chapter 17. In the 1820s, Buffalofish and Crying Snake had a share in a ferry on Sweetwater Creek, located five miles above its mouth, in partnership with Drowning Bear, Stop, Ca-su-an-ga, Sickawie, and Sweetwater, as reflected in this decision on their claim for $1260 dated February 11, 1837.[138]

Buffalofish 1837 Ferry Claim

Boundary disputes involving Cherokees and their white neighbors were covered extensively in the *Cherokee Phoenix*, often attested to by Cherokee leaders, including Buffalofish, such as this letter on December 21, 1929:[139] "The undersigned are all men of old age, and have been Chiefs of rank in the Cherokee Nation for many years, and make the following statements, before Gen. John Coffee . . . .[T]he Chiefs of the two nations, in 1821, entered into a written agreement definitively establishing the boundary between the two Nations; commencing at Buzzard Roost on the Chattahoochee River, thence to the Coosa River, opposite to the mouth of Will's Creek, thence down the southeast bank of the Coosa River to a point opposite to the lower end of the Ten Islands . . . .The Cherokees have been and are exclusively in the occupancy and possession of the Country lying north of said line . . . . Going Snake, Sleeping Rabbit, Choonukee, Taleskee, Cahnohtle, Buffaloe Fish, A. Smith, Choonoolungske, Spring Frog."

This and numerous other letters in the *Cherokee Phoenix* show how conclusive the Cherokee position was and the extent to which Jackson and his cronies went in seizing that land. It also puts into perspective the claims filed in 1836, 1837 and 1842 by Buffalofish and his family, discussed in Chapter 17. A decision on one of Buffalofish's claims on February 10, 1837 valued his twenty-five-acre farm there at $797.50 including spoliation,[140] based on an earlier evaluation by Shaw and McMillan, two of the Georgian appraisers hired by the government.[141]

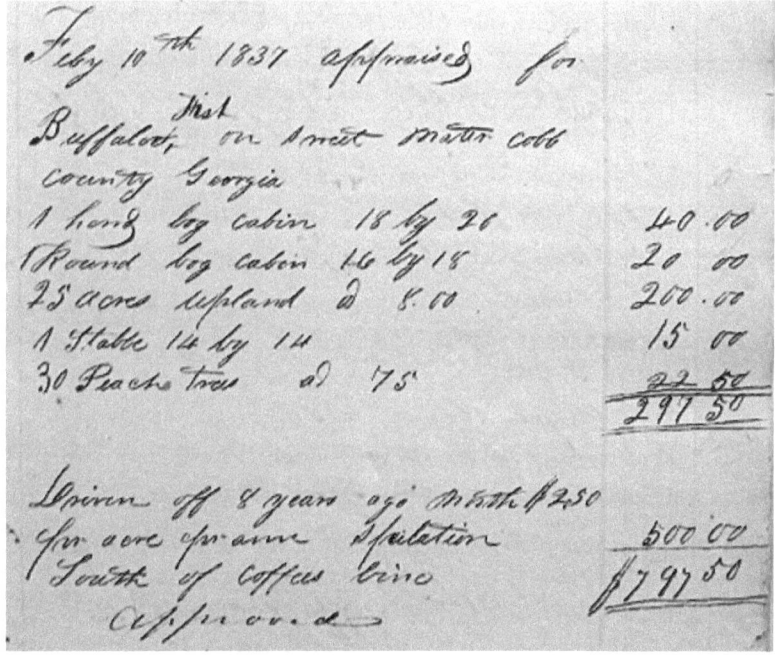

Buffalofish 1837 Farm Claim

Although good records of similar property owned by white families do not exist, most observers consider the appraisals of Cherokee farms and other assets to be well below their intrinsic values. The appraisal process was intensely political, as part of the goal of forcing Cherokees off their land. As a matrilineal society, women owned much of a family's property.

Buffalofish's wife possessed far more wealth, totaling several thousand dollars. Although Buffalofish and the Spirit family were reluctant to leave their farms, which they had held on to in the face of ongoing pressure and threats, they thought it would be possible to enjoy life free from border strife if they relocated to Dykes Bend. Thus, they moved to the south bank of the Etowah in 1829 and 1830, establishing new farms near Annie's parents' farm.[142] By 1835, Buffalofish and his extended family had built new homes, barns, and other buildings, clearing acres of farmland along the Etowah. He supervised construction of a farmhouse for two of his grandchildren, his deceased daughter's orphans named Assetetu Wiper and Teeartoonskie Baker. The 1836 valuation by Waters and Burns, two other government-appointed appraisers, allotted them $140 for their farm "near Dykes. Baker & wife both dead. Valued for his heirs, Buffalo Fish's grandchildren." The property evaluations carried out in 1835 show that Buffalofish and Wo-de-yo-he were well-off, with two homes, extensive fields, out-buildings, more than twenty horses, a large herd of cattle, and three slaves.

For the few years between 1830 and 1835, Buffalofish's and Wo-de-yo-he's lives were relatively peaceful. All their grandchildren were nearby, and several of their old friends had moved with them. One thing they all missed was Lithia Springs, a sacred area that had been central to their lives.

6

Lithia Springs

When the Cherokee first arrived in Georgia hundreds of years ago, they believed that Yowa, the creator, had guided them to an area with seven springs, where healing waters flowed from a stone temple built by the ancients. Those who lived around the springs rarely got sick. Its waters were mineral laden. Seen as powerful by the people, they became a symbol of long life and health.

Creeks also lived in that area and the boundaries were disputed. Believing the springs were on their land, the Cherokees challenged the Creeks to play a ball game, with the winner taking control. The Cherokees won. Cherokee Chief Ama-Kanasta (Sweetwater) was the Chieftain of Lithia Springs and the surrounding area in the late 1700s. He took his name from the "sweet water" that flowed from the ancient springs. It was an important site for all Cherokees, but especially for those who lived in the vicinity. They called them "Powder Springs" because the sediments from the sulfur-laden water was dry as powder. Among the minerals found in the springs are Lithium, Silica, Sulfur, Sodium Dioxide, Potassium Oxide, Lime, Magnesium, Phosphorus Pent Oxide, Arsenic, Hydrogen Sulphide, Alumina and Ferric Oxide.[143]

Archaeological excavations have turned up Neolithic artifacts, proving the Amerindians came to Lithia Springs for healing and spiritual reasons since prehistoric times. Buffalofish, Wo-de-yo-he and their children lived not far away. When I visited in 2015, there seemed to be music in the land, with light-toned raspings of insects, a lovely range of bird trills and warbles, the whispers of leaves and boughs moving in the wind and burbling from small streams. The unfolding beauty swept me away as I thought about the ceremonies that Cherokees carried out there. Standing at the sacred well and looking at the giant smiling turtle carved from blue quartz granite centuries ago, did I just imagine absorbing its ancient auras and spirituality?

Giant Stone Turtle at Lithia Springs[144]

Prior to removal, Georgia began selling gold rights in the area. In the 1832 lottery 40-acre parcel including the springs was auctioned off to Phillip J. Crask for $18.50; because Cherokees still occupied the area, he sold it to John Boyle in 1837 for $12.50. After the Cherokees were moved west in 1838, Boyle sold the land to Colonel Rogers and former ex-Governor Charles MacDonald for $500. They had no interest in the spring but wanted to use the creek that flowed into the Chattahoochee to build a mill, which was successful, eventually leading to founding the town of New Manchester.[145]

In 1887, the Sweetwater Park Hotel opened for visitors wanting treatments and bathing at the now world-famous spot. Sweetwater Creek, on which Buffalofish Spirit and his family lived, is the source of the springs. Like most Cherokees who lived in the area, members of the Spirit family visited it periodically until they left their homeland in 1837 and 1838, including Buffalofish's half-brother John Spirit. This advertisement shows the hotel and springs in 1888.[146] Today, Lithia Springs State Park is a major tourist destination.

World Famous Lithia Spring Water Vapor Baths

7

John Huss Spirit

John Spirit was born in 1787 to The Spirit and Mary Blaylock.[147] As a young man, he moved to Battle Creek, and in the 1820s relocated to Will's Valley with the Lowreys to be close to his father, The Sprit., and his step-mother Susannah.[148] He was often called Captain Spirit because of his service as Company Leader of the Cherokee Light Horse guards in 1825.[149] After being baptized in 1824 along with his mother Mary, wife Nancy Gourd, and sister Christianna, John decided to become a minister.[150]

John and Nancy had a son, William, around 1814. Being a pious man who took literally the Bible's commandments to help orphans, the sick, and the poor, he adopted her son with John Blaylock (Jefferson Blaylock) and Alexander McCoy (John Lowrey McCoy). Likewise, he adopted the three daughters of his second wife, Nancy Dorcas Mush (Rachel Crawfish, Jane Jennie Huss, and Mary Sally Huss). He paid for each one's education and tried to steer them on a good path, not always with success.[151]

Elected in 1828 to the Supreme Court along with Andrew Ross and Walter Scott "Red Watt" Adair, he served with distinction until being replaced in 1834 by Archibald Fields, Annie's third cousin. He outlined in the *Phoenix* his philosophy about who is qualified to be elected to the National Council, countering English-speaking mixed bloods who proposed to restrict the candidates to people like themselves. His arguments in favor of a democratic approach won the day: "This would be a great evil, for it would appear like creating a division among the people. It is well-known that the poor and uneducated feel that those who talk English are overbearing . . . Both the upper and lower houses should be mixed with English-speakers and non-English-speakers so that they would have to learn to work together . . . Wherever a people preserve a regular system of Government, that community is firmly established. So let it be with us Cherokees . . . "[152]

John regularly inveighed against drunkenness, which he viewed as the greatest evil bedeviling his people,[153] and kept a journal of his meetings with a wide range of people as he rode far and wide proselytizing. This is illustrated in his diary entry for March 1829 after leaving Willstown: "I then . . . spent the night at the house of Mr. John Ridge…The next night I spent at Archy Downing's . . . .I had appointed a meeting on the Sabbath at Rising Fawn's . . . .The people were very attentive to my discourse, and their number was considerable . . . ."[154]

Captain Spirit was ordained as a Cherokee evangelist on July 20, 1834 at the Brainard Mission in Tennessee, home to a group of Presbyterian missionaries associated with the American Board. He took the last name Huss in honor of a famous Bohemian Catholic priest Jan Hus, who lived from about 1369 to 1415. He led an early reform movement against the Catholic hierarchy, denouncing the moral failings of bishops and the pope from his pulpit, and was the founder of the Huttite movement. Although popular among the population, Hus was arrested and charged with religious crimes by papal authorities at the Council of Constance. On June 15, 1415 he was tried by three bishops. John Hus was condemned to death by the Bishop of Lodi, Giacomo Balardi Arrigoni, on July 6th and burnt at the stake. The people of Bohemia responded with large protests. After Pope

Martin V authorized execution for all Hus supporters a revolt broke out. The fighting ended only in 1436 after the Basil Compacts were signed, allowing Bohemia to practice its own form of religion.[155]

John Spirit was inspired by this history while studying to become minister and decided to take that name. The service in English was interpreted by Elias Boudinot, while Huss's sermon in Cherokee was interpreted by Stephen Foreman. Huss spoke little English, while Stephen, the only other ordained Cherokee preacher at that time, was fluent in both languages, having studied at the Union Theological Seminary in Virginia and Princeton Theological Seminary in New Jersey. A renowned speaker with few equals, Huss told parables grounded in his deep knowledge of the Bible. His sermon that day was reported nationally in *The Missionary Herald*, an important periodical published by the American Board of Commissioners for Foreign Missions, citing Matthew 13 and 14: "Enter ye in at the strait gate, for wide is the gate, and broad is the way, which leadeth to destruction . . . .Because strait is the gate, and narrow is the way which leadeth unto life, and few there be that find it.' . . . and it is now left to your choice into which you will enter. Now then, my friends, I ask you, what will you do?"[156]

John Huss played a large role in Cherokee society and in the lives of the Spirit family. As we will learn in Chapter 14, he decided to leave the Cherokee Nation prior to the Trail of Tears, moving his large family in 1837. Although he had obtained a reservation of 640 acres in Hall County under the 1819 Treaty, little good that did him—or most anyone who believed they would be able to keep their land. Before removal, he had several farms: Mercier, Howard, Nicholson, Qua'quaw and Day, comprising more than two hundred acres of cultivated land with numerous houses, stables, barns, kitchens, a smokehouse, and slave quarters. He was awarded $7,637 for his improvements and $1,288 for dispossession, but it's unclear if he ever received the money.

After removal, he resumed his life as a preacher in 1837 on Honey Creek, maintaining connections with many important missionaries. One can see the esteem in which he was held in this 1843 report by the Society for Propagating the Gospel Among the Indians: "Huss is a man of strong mind, good sense and great native eloquence. He is . . . greatly respected by his own people . . . He has for more than twenty years been an exemplary Christian. Having a clear and active mind, and a thirst for Christian knowledge, he availed himself of every accessible means of obtaining it."[157] He was both a claimant and witness on several family claims in 1842, including for his son William Huss and his wife's son Jefferson Blaylock.[158] Ironically, William and his cousin David Knightkiller, a first cousin of Annie Spirit, ended up being anti-religion, accused of breaking windows in the Mount Zion meeting house and other similar incidents.[159] William died young in 1844 from natural causes.

Huss was one of the signers of the Washington treaty on August 6, 1846 as a member of the Treaty Party. That treaty stabilized the Cherokee Nation after years of arguments with the US about the status of the Cherokee Nation and the duties of the US under the New Echota Treaty. Huss regularly met and corresponded with Reverend Samuel Worcester. An example is the letter Worcester wrote Reverend Treat on June 6, 1849 about Huss's difficult family situation. Reporting that, when Huss married Nancy Mush, he welcomed her daughter Jane and her six children—born of different fathers, including George Lowrey, Rider Fields, Nelson Ore, Jefferson Pack and James Landrum—and all the children were baptized. It was a complex and complicated family.[160] Huss never publicly complained about any of this, his focus being the church, which was full every Sunday. His preaching was widely admired around the Cherokee Nation. He died at home in Honey Springs in 1858, the same year as my great-great grandfather, Samuel Houston Mayes.

8

Samuel Houston Mayes

Samuel Mayes was a white man whose ancestors came to the US from Ireland and Scotland in the late 1600s and early 1700s.[161] Born along the Tennessee-Georgia border on November 11, 1803, he was the youngest of four. His mother, Charlotte Samuels, died during childbirth. She had moved to the Cherokee nation as a young woman to work as a missionary. Samuel's sister Lucy Ann arrived in 1789, and Sarah Charlotte was born in 1793. Their father, John Mayes, was born in Paxtang, Pennsylvania in 1768 and moved his family to Habersham County, Georgia while a young man. He recorded a deed of gift with the Habersham County clerk on May 11, 1820, giving his "beloved son Samuel Mayes" his land, tools, and several slaves.[162] He died in 1822. Samuel's paternal grandparents were Lt. Andrew Jackson Mayes and Mary Rutherford, both of Irish descent, whose parents emigrated to the United States. Andrew fought in the American Revolution in South Carolina.[163]

In 1824, Samuel married Nancy Adair, daughter of two prominent Cherokees, Black Watt Adair and Rachel Thompson. Black Watt was born in Adairsville, Georgia in 1783 and died there in 1835 just after learning his extensive farms were being taken by white settlers. Rachel was born in the

Cherokee Nation in 1786. Black Watt's grandmother was Nancy Lightfoot, whose mother was Ga-ho-ga. Samuel and Nancy had eleven children, two of whom became Chiefs: my great uncles Joel Bryan Mayes and Samuel Houston Mayes, Jr. In a broad sense, it wasn't an untypical Cherokee family of the day; there had been a lot of intertwining of Cherokees and whites during the preceding 75 years. When Samuel married Annie Spirit in 1848, it interlinked these two interesting families. His sister Lucy Ann Mayes also married a Cherokee, George M. Ward, whose mother, Catherine McDaniel, was a descendant of Old Hop Moytoy.[164]

Samuel and Nancy had five slaves who helped them work their extensive farms along the north side of the Etowah River[165] including 269 acres of improved land and 200 acres of fenced woodland. They owned four nearby farms named Ka'nan'sausky, Lily Consene, Squel'look, and Miller. They also operated an important public ferry across the Etowah near the mouth of Bolton's Creek, which is where he and Annie Spirit likely met when she was a girl. Samuel was always loyal to his Cherokee family. He was arrested by the Georgia Guard in 1831 for refusing to sign the oath of allegiance to Georgia required of all whites who had married Cherokees. While awaiting trial, he was confined at Camp Gilmer before being sentenced by Judge Clayton in Lawrenceville on September 15th to four years of hard labor at the Milledgeville Penitentiary.[166] Camp Gilmer was a rough place, akin to a dungeon. He was locked up with Samuel Worcester and several other missionaries who also had refused to sign the oath. While incarcerated together, they wrote a letter to the warden, Colonel Nelson, on July 16, 1832 asking for permission to hold a prayer meeting. Their request was summarily denied.[167]

The missionaries' case resulted in the famous Supreme Court decision *Worcester v. Georgia*. Mayes was released in late 1832 on the condition that he sign the oath and promise not to come back to the area. In the end, he never signed the oath and moved his family west in 1837, losing much of what he had built up over the years. We'll learn more about the *Worcester v. Georgia* case in Chapter 12 and about Samuel's life in Chapter 20. The lives of the overwhelming number of Cherokees who remained on their ancestral lands in the 1830s before the Trail of Tears were difficult and yet uplifting, as they continued struggling together to keep their sovereignty and stand up to the United States. But the odds were against them.

9

Cherokee Lives Before the Trail of Tears

When Annie was born in 1826, it was a time of grand experimentation and rapidly developing self-confidence for the Cherokees. Cherokee towns were democratic, and everyone participated, including women, who owned most of the homes, farms, and mills, which were inherited matrilineally. Women were the mainstay of the farms and small businesses, were involved in trade and negotiations, and were often artists. They were open about marriage, and there was absolute equality: either a man or woman could dissolve a marriage and choose a new partner, while family links were always maintained and nourished. In the 18th and 19th centuries, Europeans found the role of women in Cherokee society difficult to accept. Imagining a "petticoat" government based on their own limited perspectives, they were unable to envision a society in which women and men were equal. Cherokees had a lot to teach their American and English friends, if only they'd been willing to listen.

Sexual freedom was a key aspect of personal freedom. Being ashamed of physical desire was contrary to that. There was no shame in sex. Marriage decisions were made by women, who accepted an offer or not, and men moved into the home and village of the bride's mother. Likewise, divorce was simple: a woman could put her husband's personal items outside the door, and the marriage was over. It was a classic matrilineal culture, which gave women immense influence and power.

In the 1820s and 1830s, Cherokee villages and farms featured comfortable wooden houses, barns, corncribs, smokehouses, and other outbuildings. Most people had modest farms. Collectively, they built schools, courthouses, stores, mills, warehouses, roads, ferries, and boat landings. There were no disputes over who had which parcel of land or how large a home was, and no one was homeless. Except for the wealthier, most people wove their own clothes. Some made beautiful baskets and pottery. Everyone produced enough food for their own needs with often a modest surplus. They had large apple and peach orchards, well-maintained gardens, and thousands of cows and horses. In ancient times, Cherokees were growing crops as well as hunting and, by the year 1000 A.D., had a varied diet of meat, fish, corn, and other vegetables, along with every berry and nut that nature produces. The Cherokees' great Chief John Ross—nicknamed "White Bird"—described their land and state of development to Albert Gallatin in a letter on February 27, 1826:

> Our country is well adapted for the growth of Indian corn, wheat, rye, oats, Irish and Sweet Potatoes, which are cultivated by our people. Cotton is universally raised for domestic consumption & a few have grown it for market, and have realized very good profits. I take pleasure to state that there is not to my knowledge a solitary Cherokee to be found who depends upon the Chase for subsistence. Every head of family has his own farm and house... A great portion of Cherokee clothing is furnished from our own people and fancy goods such as silks, calicoes, cambrics, handkerchiefs and shawls, etc. are introduced by native Merchants from the adjoining states.[168]

Only 1/8th Cherokee by blood, Ross was 100 percent Cherokee in his heart. One of nine children of Daniel Ross and Mollie McDonald, he grew up in an Indian community called Tahnoovayah on the Coosa River and was educated at a local school started by his father under the tutelage of John Barber Davis. When they were older, he and his brother Lewis were sent to Kingston Academy where their English skills were polished.[169] No one served the Cherokee Nation longer or better.

Drawing of John Ross as a young man[170]

In the 1820s, Cherokees created a written language so simple and ingenious that it was easily learned by most of the people within a few years. They built an educational system second to none, providing free education to everyone—Cherokee, white, mixed, and black. Some children were educated at religious schools, and a few teenagers went to boarding schools up north on scholarships provided by the missionaries. Supported by the increasing literacy affected by Sequoyah's syllabary and extensive intersections with people from various countries, Cherokees in the 1820s and 1830s constructed a prosperous, modern life. In 1822, their Supreme Court was established along with two lower courts, and a written Constitution modelled after that of the US was adopted on July 26, 1827. They created an elected legislature and upper house to enact statutes and ordinances. The press was free, and a wide range of religious belief was supported. The economy was booming as they adopted technology and tools to carry on trades and farming while maintaining the core of traditional Cherokee society. From their perspective, there was no reason why Indian and white cultures could not coexist. They built their first Council House in New Echota in 1819, in honor of the original town of Chota.[171]

Sketch of first council house at New Town (New Echota, Georgia)

Cherokee surveyors laid out the new town with care. Their carpenters constructed beautiful buildings for the Supreme Court and Council House with special touches appropriate for each structure. The windows were perfectly symmetrical and superbly glazed. The Cherokee Nation came together there in a profound way as the new capital was being built, a showcase to the world, however brief in time it was allowed to survive. These images are of the recreated buildings constructed with such pride in New Echota during the 1820s.[172]

Supreme Court

Supreme Court Interior

Council House

Vann's Tavern

Tavern Interior

Typical Cabin

In October 1827, a prospectus announced a free weekly bilingual newspaper called the *Cherokee Phoenix*. Its first number was published by Elias Budinot and Elijah Hicks on February 21, 1828; its crest, a phoenix rising from a blanket of flames with the word "protection" written between its wings and on either side the characters spelling "The Phoenix Will Rise." That first issue became a treasured family item. It included "The Lord's Prayer" in Cherokee and English. This is the Cherokee version:

ᎣᎩᏙᏓ ᏍᎦᎳᏗ ᎮᎲ, ᎦᎸᏉᏗᏳ ᎨᏎᏍᏗ ᏕᏣᏙᎥᎢ.
ᏣᎬᏫᏳᎯ ᎨᏒ ᏩᏍᎩᎦᎵ. ᎠᏂ ᎡᎶᎯ ᎠᏂᎦᏎᏍᏛ ᏄᏍᏛᏉᎡᏛ,
ᎾᏍᎩᏯ ᏍᎦᎳᏗ ᏂᎦᏎᏍᏗᏍᎪ.
ᏂᏓᏙᏓᏈᎢᏓᏝ ᎤᎩᏓᏴᎥᎯ ᎣᎩᎥ ᎠᎾ ᎢᎦ.
ᎠᎴᏍᎩᏈᎥᏃ ᏍᎦᎩᏎᏑᎯ, ᎾᏍᎩᏯ ᏥᏓᎦᏍᏓᏂᏗᎮ ᎢᎦᏐᏅᎢ.
ᎠᎴ ᎳᏍᏗ ᏣᎳᏫᏍᏛᏍᎨ ᎨᏒ ᎤᏓᏍᎩᏂᏲᏍᎬᎥᎩ,
ᏍᎩᏅᏓᏛᏍᏛᏅᎥᏎᏃ ᎤᏂ ᎨᏒᎢ. ᏣᏪᎵᏎᏃ ᏣᎬᏫᎯ ᎨᏒᎢ, ᎠᎴ
ᏣᏂᎦᏗᎢ ᎨᏒᎢ,
ᎠᎴ ᎠᎵᎦᎸᏗᎧᎥ ᎨᏒ ᏂᎦᏛᎢ. ᎠᎺᏅᎢ. ᎡᏍ

In 1829, the masthead was expanded to the "*Cherokee Phoenix and Indians' Advocate*," as the paper covered politics, education, farming, and religion. Readers expressed their points of view in letters to the editor. Annie loved visiting the printing house, smelling the ink, watching the type being set, and hearing the noise made by the press. The most satisfying aspect for her was seeing the result, the paper in all its glory, printed in this small building.[173]

All the important Cherokee Chiefs strongly supported teaching everyone the written language and fully endorsed the newspaper, which was the main vehicle for bringing the whole nation together. Unity was crucial. Among them was Chief Pathkiller, who passed away on January 8, 1827. Born in 1745, he fought on the British side in the Revolutionary War, experiencing the huge changes in his people's lives over the decades. Although a traditionalist, he supported opening the Nation to missionaries, education, and modern farming, and endorsed having written laws. He'd been ailing for a few years, leaving much of the work to his deputy Charles Hicks, a mentor to John Ross along with The Ridge, one of the most important Cherokees of that time. (We'll learn more about the Ridge later.) Ross and The Ridge were pleased that Hicks was immediately named Principal Chief, but just two weeks later he died on January 20th. Hicks had been working with Ross and the new Indian Commissioner, Hugh Montgomery, on the first canal project through Cherokee territory. The Ridge delivered the eulogy for his old friend at Spring Place. Politically, the deaths of Pathkiller and Hicks couldn't have come at a worse moment, with the Cherokees being pressed by the governors of Georgia, Tennessee and North Carolina to give up more land, while Jackson was campaigning for the Presidency.

As President of the National Committee, Ross was thrust into a leadership role along with The Ridge, Speaker of the Council. In the spring, Ross moved his family from his grandfather's cabin near Lookout Mountain close to New Echota, building a beautiful two-story house 70 feet long and 20 feet deep on 175 acres near The Ridge's large property. It became a small plantation farmed with the labor of the twenty slaves he'd inherited from his grandfather, and Ross started a ferry service at the confluence of the Coosa, Etowah, and Oostanaula Rivers. This map was drawn by Charles Royce in 1884 based on old maps showing the central Cherokee Nation around 1828 and the confluence of those rivers:[174]

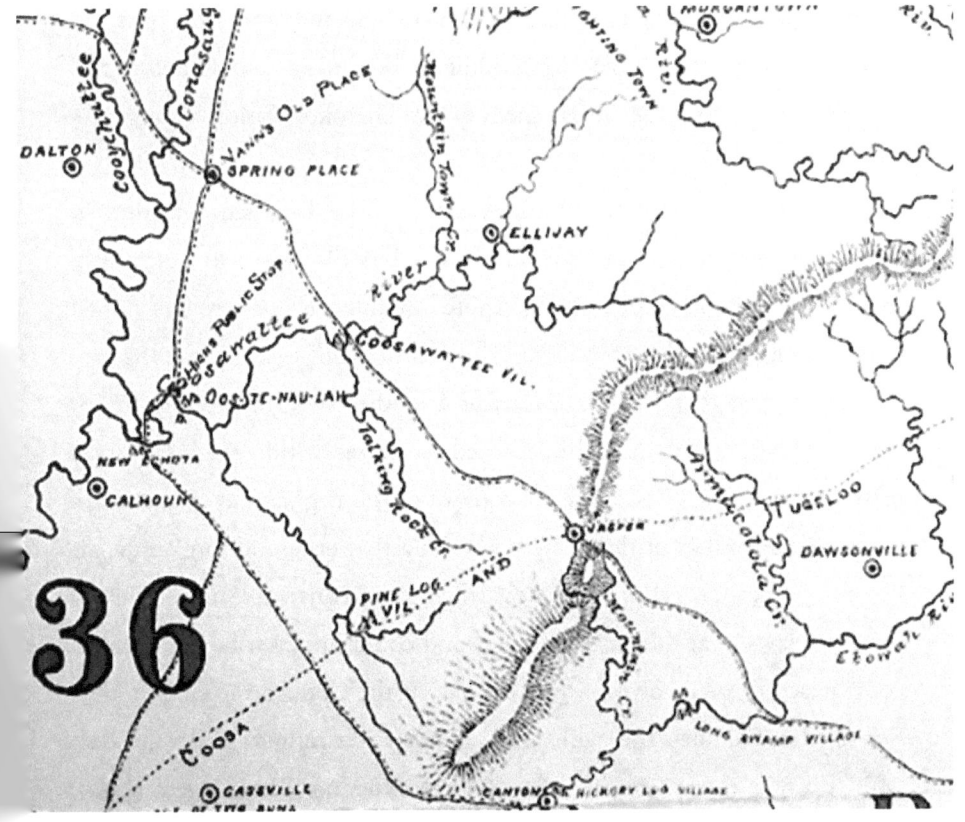

One key task was preparing a written constitution for the first time. For the next several months Ross and Ridge met almost every day to craft it. The document, which drew heavily for its structure, philosophy, and wording on the US Constitution, was presented on July 3, 1828. Article 1 protects all Cherokee land from encroachment by the Federal Government, states, or individuals. The preamble states:

> We, the Representatives of the people of the Cherokee Nation, in Convention assembled, in order to establish justice, ensure tranquility, promote our common welfare, and secure to ourselves and our posterity the blessings of liberty; acknowledging with humility and gratitude the goodness of the sovereign Ruler of the Universe, in offering us an opportunity so favorable to the design, and imploring His aid and directions in its accomplishment, do ordain and establish this Constitution for the Government of the Cherokee Nation.[175]

During the constitutional convention, White Path led a faction in opposition, urging a return to older ways, but his view was not widely shared. The Constitution was agreed to on July 26th. Cherokees hoped that it would solve their problems with Georgia and other states. Instead, Georgia argued that it violated Article 4 of the US Constitution, which says that "No new State shall be formed or erected within the jurisdiction of any other State . . . without the consent of the Legislatures of the States concerned as well as of the Congress." Using that excuse, Georgia officials began to annex Cherokee lands, declaring that Indians were subject only to Georgia's laws, that they had no rights and could not even be witnesses in court proceedings involving white people. At the Council meeting in New Echota that October, the main business was selecting new leaders to deal with this new threat from Georgia. Neither Ross nor The Ridge ran and, without any drama, William Hicks was chosen Principal Chief to complete his brother's term. Ross was elected Assistant Principal Chief, which suited him perfectly. The Ridge began subtly promoting Ross as the next Chief, often through articles in the *Phoenix*, which had quickly become essential to the life of the Nation. In one article, he warned about electing leaders who could be manipulated by whites, referring to the conditions in Arkansas where thousands had moved, concluding: "Let us hold fast to the country, where we remain."

But there were endless political pressures for the US government to take more Indian land. Tennessee and Alabama forced President Quincy Adams in March 1827 to instruct General James Cocke to purchase 504,000 acres in North Carolina for construction of the Hiwassee-Conasaga Canal. Cocke offered Ross $10,000 for the land, presented on a take-it-or-leave-it basis that came out of the blue. It was soundly rebuffed by Ross and the Cherokee National Council on October 11th: The "Cherokee Nation has *no more land to dispose of and* . . . cannot accede to your propositions."[176] The US Senate had discussed the canal on February 19th, approving the requested $10,000 without any consideration of the land to be taken for the project. Tennessee had chartered the Hiwassee Canal Company a year earlier with a mandate to build the canal, and a similar company was chartered in Alabama. They had to drop the idea when the Cherokees refused to sell the land, which was probably just as well as it was estimated to need fifteen locks and a large reservoir costing over one million dollars.[177] The Cherokees stood strong together in stopping the project.

Meanwhile, the Cherokees who had moved west during the prior decades, called the "Western Cherokee," also were being pressured. The US wanted them to trade their Arkansas land between the White and Arkansas Rivers and move further west. Some of the leaders agreed with this since the territory was under constant threat from other tribes; on the other hand, they'd been promised the land in perpetuity. A delegation including Black Fox (Enolee), John Rogers, Tom Graves, Thomas Maw, George Marvis, John Looney and Sequoyah traveled to Washington at the end of 1827 with the goal of securing clear title to their Arkansas lands, plus an outlet to the western buffalo prairies. Instead, after weeks of discussion with the intransigent US negotiators, they agreed to the trade.[178] In May 1828, the Western Cherokee chiefs signed a new treaty with the US without approval from the main part of the Cherokee Nation, obtaining seven million acres running along the Arkansas, Canadian and Grand Rivers. Leaving aside how it was negotiated, it contained important commitments in Article 2, which the entire Cherokee Nation supported:

> The United States agree to possess the Cherokees, and to guarantee it to them forever, and that guarantee is hereby solemnly pledged, of seven millions of acres of land . . . .In addition to the seven millions of acres thus provided for, and bounded, the United States further guarantee to the Cherokee Nation a perpetual outlet, West, and a free and unmolested use of all the Country lying West of the Western boundary of the above described limits, and as far West as the sovereignty of the United States, and their right of soil extend.

Tahlonteeskee was established as the Capitol of the Western Cherokees near Chief Jolly's home, about two miles up the Illinois River from its mouth on the Arkansas River, named in honor of the prior chief, Jolly's brother. Following the Cherokee Constitution, the Western Council elected chiefs for four-year terms, while judges and Lighthouse Guards were elected every two years. Four districts were created: Sallisaw, Lee's Creek, Illinois, and Neosho, each with two representatives. All of these changes were approved by the National Cherokee Council in New Echota.

Meanwhile, life was good in New Echota, which had become a modern town. People were building houses, stores, farms, mills, and ferries in profusion across the Cherokee Nation. With more and more people able to read, the *Phoenix* was increasingly popular. Everyone looked forward to the annual National Council meeting and elections, which were covered extensively in the newspaper. More than a thousand people arrived for the meeting on October 13th, opened by Hicks with the annual Chief's address. That was the first time there was a vote for Principal Chief for a set term of four years, just as in the US Constitution. The two candidates were Hicks and Ross. Hicks had every reason to imagine he would be chosen, but The Ridge's quiet lobbying paid off when Ross was elected by a vote of 34-6 on October 17th. George Lowrey was elected Assistant Principal Chief and The Ridge was named Counselor to Ross. John Martin was elected Treasurer.

Ross and The Ridge held the reins of power in the Cherokee Nation, which was increasingly tied together by Sequoyah's Syllabary that provided everyone the ability to communicate in writing. It was a life-changing development. Sequoyah provided the glue that the Nation needed so badly.

Charles Bird King Portrait of Chief Ross at Forty-Three[179]

10

Sequoyah

John Huss Spirit and Annie's great-grandfather Spirit and Susannah lived for many years near Creekpath, Alabama. One of their neighbors and friends was George Guess, better known as Sequoyah, who lived up the road in Willstown. After the 1817 and 1819 treaties between the US and Cherokees living in Alabama, Spirit and Susannah moved to Arkansas, along with the so-called Old Settlers. Clearing land for crops and livestock, they collectively built barns, houses, grist mills, and towns, and established a new government based on a traditional approach. The naturalist Thomas Nuttall described the area in 1819: "Both banks of the river, as we proceeded, were lined with the houses and farms of the Cherokees, and though their dress was a mixture of European and Indian taste, yet in their houses, which are decently furnished, and on the farms, which were well fenced and stocked with cattle, we perceive a happy approach to civilization. Their numerous families, also well fed and clothed, argue a propitious progress in their population. . . . Some of them are possessed of property to the amount of many thousands of dollars, have houses handsomely and conveniently furnished, and their tables spread with our dainties and luxuries."[180]

Spirit and Susannah decided to move from Alabama to Arkansas in 1819 because they were tired of fighting with whites over land. He was a spiritual man and wanted to live the rest of his life according to the old ways. Though Annie never knew him, his influence was huge because of her grandmother Susannah's stories about him and Sequoyah. Susannah lived to a great age, dying in 1860 near Annie and her children in the Cherokee Nation west.

John Huss Spirit stayed in Alabama and was a close associate of Sequoyah's in refining the alphabet and played a major role in translating the Bible into Cherokee, perceiving quickly how valuable it would be for the people. The two of them went through it together line by line[181] and the American Board of Commissioners for Foreign Missions wrote warmly about their collaboration: "The improving state of this nation is a circumstance that has excited considerable interest by the invention of eighty-six alphabetical characters of letters by which . . . our people write correctly in our own language . . . . I enclose you a list of these letters as a sample of the forms . . . made out by Captain Spirit."[182] The American Board of Commissioners continued detailing the event by stating: "At candle light we attended a Cherokee meeting, conducted by John Huss (or Spirit), who is an uncommonly interesting man. He understands his native language only. His exhortations are heard with pleasure, as they are always fraught with good sense and energy. As a speaker he has, perhaps, few equals. His knowledge of the Bible we thought excellent . . . ."[183]

When Sequoyah was born in Tuskegee near Fort Loudon on the Tennessee River to Wu-te-he, a full-blood Cherokee, and Nathaniel Gist, there was no way to imagine his future importance.[184] As a young man, he left the Overhills area and moved to Willstown, near John Spirit. He served as a private in the war against the Creeks in 1812 despite a bad leg, fighting alongside Andrew Jackson at the Battle of Horse Shoe Bend on

March 27, 1814.[185] A polymath, he taught himself to be both a silversmith and blacksmith, making the tools needed for those trades and inventing several new ones. He was an excellent artist as well as the best salt maker in the Nation. Two of his uncles were chiefs: Taluntuskee (the Overthrower) and Kahn-Yah-Tah-Hee (First to Kill). He had no English yet fathomed an elegant way to record Cherokee sounds and syllables in a simple written form, combining sounds to make words and phrases. He spent years by himself developing it, claiming he got a key insight from listening to birds, trying several approaches before coming up with 86 characters to represent the syllables from which all Cherokee words are formed.

In February 1818, Sequoyah joined his good friend John Jolly's group of Cherokees who were moving to Arkansas pursuant to the 1817 Treaty, refining his syllabary during their time traveling west. They arrived on the north side of the Arkansas River, not far from the Illinois River, and began establishing a new life there.[186] By 1821, Sequoyah felt his work was almost finished and traveled back home to show it to friends there. He started with his neighbor George Lowrey, who lived three miles away and was skeptical about what Sequoyah had been doing, not believing it was possible to write in Cherokee. "Show me how it works," Lowrey is said to have requested.

Sequoyah asked his daughter Ayoka to repeat the first few sounds of the syllabary, which she did without hesitating. Then Sequoyah left the room. Lowrey asked Ayoka to write down some words in another room so that her father couldn't hear or see them. In a few minutes they returned. Ayoka proudly showed it to Sequoyah, who read the words Lowrey had specified without a mistake. Lowrey immediately became a believer, urging him to complete the syllabary and begin teaching people to use it. The syllabary was adopted formally by the Council later that year and, in 1822, Sequoyah returned to Arkansas, carrying written messages from home to Chief Jolly and the others who had emigrated. Quickly people began writing back and forth.[187]

Modern Painting of Sequoyah and Ayoka[188]

He was excited about showing Old Spirit and other emigrants their language in written form. No other Indian had ever done that. Ta-ka-to-ka was a conjurer as well as the war chief, and he invited Sequoyah to his village to teach his first class in Arkansas. At the beginning, he asked each person to say a word, which he wrote down and then asked Ayoka to come in and read them. She got every word right. He began teaching classes that were open to everyone. People caught on quickly, able to learn to read and write within a month.[189] His invention was put to good use by recording important documents that previously were only oral. Sequoyah's first composition was about the boundary lines between Cherokee country . . . Georgia and Tennessee. He had been called on to speak on the subject at a court held at Chatonga, and read his statement while people drew near to stare as he made what seemed to be just strange marks on pieces of paper.[190]

Sequoyah had several wives and an estimated twenty children.[191] Around 1796, he had a relationship with Annie's great-aunt Betsy Spirit, born in 1777, and they had one child, Big Dollar George, in 1797.[192] His best-known wife was Sally Waters, whom he married in 1815. They had Tessey, perhaps his closest child, and Polly. The Cherokee Council awarded him a silver medal in 1824 in token of his genius and in gratitude for the service rendered to his people. The medal, made in Washington, was inscribed on one side with two pipes and on the other with his profile. Chief John Ross wrote this letter to Sequoyah about the medal: "Mr. George Gist (Sequoyah), My Friend—The Legislative Council of the Cherokee Nation in the year 1824 voted a medal to be presented to you, as a token of respect and admiration for your ingenuity in the invention of the Cherokee Alphabetical Characters . . . . In receiving this small tribute from the representatives of the people of your native land, in honor of your transcendent invention, you will, I trust, place a proper estimate on the grateful feelings of your fellow countrymen . . . ."[193]

On September 29, 1825, Cherokee preacher David Brown wrote from Willstown to Jeremiah Evarts, one of the main American missionaries working in the Nation, about translation of the Bible. He noted that "Brother Huss will be transcribing it on the plan of G. Guess, that it may be open to the inspection of our people." The National Committee and Council agreed on November 2, 1826 to build a printing office twenty-four by twenty feet, one story high with a shingle roof, one fireplace, chinked and lined on the inside with narrow plank, with the necessary benches and type desks. With Samuel Worcester's support, Elias Boudinot raised the funds to buy the printing press and type by making a series of paid speeches in Philadelphia and other cities. They were popular and soon he had raised sufficient funds. In early 1828, the press and type were shipped by water from Boston to Augusta and transported from there to New Echota by wagon. The first issue of the *Cherokee Phoenix* was published on February

21st in parallel columns of Cherokee and English. That was a great day for the Cherokee Nation. The typefaces were miracles of beauty and function, while the printing press was modern and functional.[194]

Sequoyah traveled with a group of Old Settler Arkansas Cherokees to Washington, D.C. in late 1828 to sign a treaty containing an honorarium for him in Article Five and that also allowed him to use another saline since his first one in Arkansas had been confiscated: "It is further agreed that the United States will pay five hundred dollars for the use of George Guess (Sequoyah) . . . for the great benefit he has conferred upon the Cherokee people . . . from the use of the alphabet discovered by him, to whom also in consideration of his relinquishing a valuable saline, the privilege is hereby given to locate and occupy another saline on Lee's Creek." Although the Treaty of May 1828 promised Sequoyah $500 for the benefits of his invention and $1000 for a new printing press, money for the new press was never received. Sequoyah did receive cash and goods worth an estimated $389.75[195] but as late as June 16, 1838, Sequoyah had not received one penny of the compensation he had been promised for his property and buildings in the Cherokee Nation East.

The 19th Report of the American Board of Foreign Missions in 1828 reported the rapid success of the population in learning the alphabet: "It is an unexampled fact, that in some places nearly all the adult population, and in the tribe at large, more than one half, are actually capable of reading in their own language . . . having learned from small manuscripts, and without ever having become acquainted with any other alphabet, or possessed a single page of a printed book in any language."[196] The paper's name was changed to "Cherokee Phoenix and Indians' Advocate" in 1829, produced weekly for the next few years and then irregularly until its demise.

Sequoyah settled on Big Skin Bayou near present-day Sallisaw, Oklahoma where he built this log cabin, a museum today:[197]

While in Washington, D.C. in 1828, Sequoyah was interviewed by the author Samuel Lorenzo Knapp, which resulted in his first lecture the following winter. Extracts were published in the Niles' Weekly Register extolling his painting skill and beginning to provide him with a national audience: "Sequoyah has also a great taste for painting. He mixes his colors with skill; taking all the arts and sciences of the tribe upon the subject, he added to it many chemical experiments of his own, and some of them were very successful, and would be worth being known to our painters. For his drawings he had no model but what nature furnished, and he often copied them with astonishing faithfulness . . . He had never seen a camel hair pencil when he made use of the hair of wild animals for his brushes."[198]

When schools were provided in each district in 1832, Sequoyah was employed to supervise the teaching of his syllabary and paid $400 annually, four times more than the Chief received.[199] Over the years, numerous men came to meet him in his home, which was near the military road from Fort Smith to Fort Gibson. John Stuart of the US Seventh Infantry published "A Sketch of the Cherokee and Choctaw Indians" in 1838 that was advertised in the *Arkansas Gazette*, which included this extract: "George Guess (Sequoyah), the inventor of the Cherokee alphabet, is a man of about sixty years of age. He is of middle stature, and of rather a slender form, and is slightly lame in one leg, from disease when young...His eyes are animated and piercing, showing indications of a brilliancy of intellect far superior to the ordinary portion of his fellow men . . . . He is inquisitive, and appears to be exceedingly desirous of acquiring information on all subjects. . . . . He has been in the habit, ever since he could apply his language in that way, of keeping a journal of all the passing events which he considered worthy of record; and has . . . quite a volume of such matter."[200] A Philadelphia merchant named John Alexander stopped by in 1839, recording these impressions in his diary: "I found the old gentleman's farm to consist of 10 acres cleared land and 3 small cabins clustered together; his stock is 2 mules, 3 yoke oxen, a wagon with a small stock of cattle and hogs. He has had five wives and 20 children . . . . He is of a pleasant countenance & indicates a good deal of genius. He conversed very freely on various topics, becoming very animated when my answers and questions pleased him."[201]

In the years following the Nation's move west, Sequoyah went on missions to Washington, D.C. from time to time. While there in 1841, he met delegations from other tribes and decided to write a book on Indian life. After returning home, he put his provisions and writing materials in an oxcart, planning to visit Indians of the plains and mountains. William A. Phillips, a Scot who served in the Civil War on the Union side, wrote a book about Sequoyah: "One of the most remarkable features of his experience was the uniform kindness with which his brethren of the prairies received him. They furnished him means too, to prosecute his inquiries in each clan or tribe. He made several journeys, always inquiring for Cherokees.[202] He had with him a two-wheeled cart drawn by a single ox, and a boy 17 years of age. The cart was filled with matter printed in the Cherokee language. His destination was the homes of the Zunis, Hopis and other tribes of New Mexico and Arizona. Some of these Indians heard of his coming and sent a delegation many miles to the east to meet and welcome the 'Wise man of the Cherokees,' as he was known to all tribes, east, south and southwest."[203]

In 1843, the Cherokee Nation voted to provide Sequoyah a literary pension, the only such act ever by the tribe. The pension was passed on to his widow.[204] Sequoyah is thought to have died in San Fernando, Mexico in August 1843 while taking documents and newspapers to Cherokees living there, hoping to induce them to rejoin their families in the new territory. A report on his final journey is in Appendix 2.[205] Sequoyah's death wasn't reported in the Cherokee Nation for almost two years, when some of his comrades returned from Mexico and gave this statement to Cherokee agent Pierce Butler: "Warrens trading house, Red River, April 21, 1845. We the undersigned Cherokees direct from the Spanish dominions, do hereby certify that George Guess (Sequoyah), of the Cherokee Nation, Arkansas, departed this life in the town of San Fernando in the month of August 1843, and his son (Chusaleta) is at this time on the Brasas River, Texas. About 30 miles above the falls, and intends returning home this fall. Given under our hands day and date above, Standing Rock, by mark, Standing

Bowles, by mark, Watch Justice, by mark, witness Daniel C. Watson and Jesse Chilsom."[206]

Sequoyah's statue was placed in Statuary Hall in the US Capitol building on June 6, 1917. Sculpted by Vinnie Ream Hoxie and George Julian Zolnay, Sequoyah was the first and only native American honored there. Oklahoma Senator Owen made an address that captures the essence of his genius: "It is a strange thing that no alphabet in all the world reaches the dignity, the simplicity, and the value of the Cherokee alphabet as invented by Sequoyah . . . . With the Sequoyah alphabet a Cherokee could learn to spell in one day . . . .So great an intellectual accomplishment was this that Canon Kingsley named the great red cedars of California, which towered as high as 400 feet into the air and which were 25 feet through at the base, "Sequoias," because they were typical of this great North American Indian."[207] To me, Sequoyah is the greatest Cherokee hero. Charles Bird King painted him in 1836 holding his syllabary.[208]

11

The Ridges

Another great hero in the Cherokee pantheon, who played key roles in the maturing of the Cherokee Nation and was a friend of the Spirit family, was The Ridge—Ka-Nun-Da-Cla-Geh. His name means "the man who walks on the mountaintop." Born in Tennessee in the early 1770s and grandson of chiefs Oconostota and Attacullaculla, he closely followed the prophecies of the medicine men as a young warrior. His mother was half Cherokee—her grandfather a Highland Scot, like Annie Spirit's 4th great grandfather Ludovic Grant. His father taught him to bathe and then recite the hunter's prayer every night: "Give me the wind. Give me the breeze. O Great Earth Hunter, let your stomach, the ground, cover itself; let it be covered with leaves. And you, O Ancient Red Fire, may you hover about my breast while I sleep. Now let good dreams come."

He married a full-blood Cherokee, Sehoyah Wickett, in the early 1790s and they moved to Pine Log, in present-day Bartow County, Georgia. President George Washington's "civilization" policy for Native Americans led government agent Benjamin Hawkins to provide The Ridge with new farm implements and Sehoyah with a spinning wheel and loom so that the young couple could learn white ways. But still, as a young man he was completely opposed to giving up the homeland: "Now mark what our forefathers told us. Your elder brother will settle around you—he will encroach upon your lands, and then ask you to sell them to him. When you give him a part of your country, he will not be satisfied, but ask for more . . . He will teach your women to spin and weave . . . and teach you to cultivate the earth. He will even teach you to read and write . . . But these are but means to destroy you, and to eject you from your habitations."[209]

Near the end of Jefferson's presidency, Chief Black Fox began advocating exchanging all Cherokee land for new territory in the West. His allies included the Glass, Turtle at Home, and Chief Tahlonteskee. Without going through normal procedures, they negotiated with Indian Agent Return J. Meigs and then called a Council meeting at Red Clay for endorsement of their radical plan. Buffalofish Spirit and his father were there. At first, no one spoke against Black Fox's proposal. But increasingly agitated, The Ridge delivered this speech on the spur of the moment: "My friends, you have heard the talk of the principal chief. He points to the region of the setting sun as the future habitation of this people. As a man he has a right to give his opinion; but the opinion he has given as the chief of this nation is not binding . . . to drag this people, without its consent, from their own country, to the dark land of the setting sun. I resist it here, in my place, as a man, as a chief, as a Cherokee . . . . What are your heads placed on your bodies for, but to think, and if to think, why should you not be consulted? . . . I, for one, abandon my respect for the will of a chief, and regard only the will of thousands of my people."[210]

The mood changed dramatically. As though everyone had been waiting to hear such words, the room filled with acclamations. The Council modified the delegation to include The Ridge and a majority opposed to the proposal. That proved to be one of the most illuminating times in his life, as he met President Jefferson and other important people. He returned home determined to help his people in any way possible.

After the Creek War ended in 1814, The Ridge made several trips to Washington to help negotiate boundaries, meeting Presidents Monroe and Madison. In the 1820s, he was one of twelve men selected to administer justice, riding the judicial circuit around the Nation. Before long, he was named head of the group, entrusted with enormous discretion. He became a strong proponent of connecting all parts of the Nation with roads and ferries to support economic and political development. Wanting to provide their children with a modern education, Ridge and Sehoyah enrolled their eldest child John at the Spring Place Moravian Mission, where he learned to read and write while studying mathematics and history. Next, he attended the Brainerd Mission School run by the American Board of Commissioners for Foreign Missions, where he did brilliantly.

One of a few Cherokees selected to attend the Mission School in Cornwall, Connecticut, John studied under Reverend Herman Daggett, where he met his future wife, Sarah Northrup. After a two-year engagement, they married against the advice of family and under harsh pressure from many white people, who couldn't fathom why she would marry a savage. But, as one writer described her, "She loved the young Indian, who, abandoning the bow and the tomahawk, had successfully cultivated the arts of peace, and the literature of the white man. She possessed too, a missionary spirit... with the belief, that it was her duty to embrace the opportunity offered her, of becoming a messenger of peace . . . ."[211] As they began married life in New Echota, they were filled with shared dreams of free public education leading to universal literacy and a peaceful, equitable relationship with the US. They had six children. John traveled to Washington frequently as an advisor and interpreter, equally articulate in English and Cherokee.

Charles Bird King portrait of John Ridge[212]

The Ridge often was asked to help other tribes negotiate with the US. He assisted the Creeks in 1825 to settle their long-running dispute, writing a speech for Chief O-Pothle-Yoholo to deliver to General Gaines. That was so successful he was invited to Washington to meet the President. Arriving in December with John, David Vann, and thirteen Creek chiefs, they took rooms at Brown's Indian Queen Hotel. After several weeks the Government agreed to pay $217,600 for the remaining Creek land in Georgia and expenses for the move west, plus a perpetual annuity of $20,000 per year. He met privately with General Jackson while in Washington, writing him afterwards: "My heart is glad when I look upon you. Our heads have become white. They are blossomed with age . . . When first we met we were taking the red path . . . War is no more heard in our land. The mountains speak peace. Joy is in our valleys . . . The meeting of friends gladdens the heart. Our countenances are bright as we look on each other."[213]

Occasionally The Ridge's old war-like skills were useful. An important pocket of land in northwest Georgia along the Alabama border that Cherokees won from the Creeks in 1821 had been recognized as Cherokee territory by the US in 1826. But Georgia refused to accept that, allowing dozens of white settlers into the area. When the Cherokees appealed to the federal government for help in removing them in 1828, Jackson appointed General Coffee to investigate. Surprisingly, he ruled in favor of the Cherokees but told Ross it was up to him to kick out the settlers. Ridge was delegated to do this, and assembling a sizable group of warriors, he visited each of the eighteen white families who had settled there. At each farm he gave them time to gather their belongings and leave, then set fire to the structures. That was effective for a time.

In the autumn of 1829 Ridge, John, and Elias Boudinot still strongly supported the death penalty for giving away Cherokee land. Ironically, it was under the terms of that law that they would lose their lives ten years later. They gradually changed their minds about removal. Why? I think it was partly because John married Sarah Northrop, a white missionary's daughter, while Elias married Harriet Ruggles Gold, daughter of a Cornwall doctor. Both men were educated in New England. Elias was born Gul-la-gee-nah (Buck Watie) in 1802. In 1817, he was invited by the American Board of Commissioners for Foreign Missions to attend school in Cornwall, Connecticut. On the way, he was introduced to the President of the American Bible Society and decided to adopt his name: Elias Boudinot. After completing his studies in 1822, he began giving public lectures around the country about the Cherokees' condition. Understanding that many white people harbored feelings of revenge for what they imagined Indians had done to them, he spoke directly: "Our fathers, too true, did you the injury, but where are they? Their bones now moulder beneath some lonely shed, and the scanty earth which covers them is now all they can claim . . . Their possessions once were great—a boundless country, supplying them with game—and the multitude of the watery elements were theirs. You now live on their ruins! Can you still harbor revenge?"[214]

Although tending towards optimism about the possibilities for rapprochement with white society, once Boudinot had fallen in love with a white woman and experienced prejudice so directly, he wrote honestly about his feelings, as in this letter to the editor of the Christian Herald: "Prejudice is the ruling passion of the age, and an Indian is almost considered accursed . . . If an Indian is educated in the sciences, the classics, astronomy, moral and natural philosophy . . . yet he is an Indian, and the most stupid and illiterate white man will disdain and triumph over this worthy individual."[215] Boudinot spoke at the First Presbyterian Church in Philadelphia on May 26, 1826. All his speeches that year were drawn from his pamphlet *An Address to the Whites*, which supported his fundraising to buy a printing press for the Cherokee Nation: "What is an Indian? Is he not formed of the same materials with yourself? For 'of one blood God created all the nations that dwell on the face of the earth.' . . . You here behold an <u>Indian</u>, my kindred are Indians, and my fathers sleeping in the wilderness grave - they too were Indians. But I am not as my fathers were, broader means and nobler influences have fallen on me . . . I ask you, shall red men live, or shall they be swept from the earth? With you and this public at large, the decision chiefly rests."[216]

Boudinot's greatest writing took place during the years he served as Editor of the *Phoenix*, the bilingual newspaper that he conceived of and carried forward. In that position he responded to many issues in the U. S., and the paper was distributed widely around the country. In 1828 when the House Committee on Indian Affairs requested an appropriation of $50,000 for removal of Indians from the southeast, he wrote "Where have we an example in the whole history of man, of a Nation or tribe, removing in a body, from a land of civil and religious means, to a perfect wilderness, in order to be civilized?"[217] His 1829 editorial took on Secretary of War John Eaton's claim that Cherokee sovereignty ended during the Revolutionary War because they sided with England: "It appears now . . . that the illustrious Washington, Madison and Monroe were only tantalizing us . . . Why were we not told long ago, that we could not be permitted to establish a government within the limits of any state? [H]ow happens it now . . . that a storm is raised by the extension of tyrannical and unchristian laws, which threatens to blast all our rising hopes and expectations?"[218]

Charles Bird King painting of The Ridge[219]

John Ridge and Elias Boudinot were intellectuals who exerted a powerful influence on The Ridge. He changed his mind, agreeing that the

Cherokee future would be better if they made the best deal possible and moved west. Earlier, without his wise counsel Chief Ross arguably wouldn't have been a success. The fact that The Ridge and Ross came to loggerheads in the mid-1830s over removal doesn't detract from his overall legacy. But the reality that The Ridge was willing to sell the Nation for a pittance at the behest of Andrew Jackson can't be ignored either. He was dealt a certain hand of cards in the real world, playing them honestly and well as President Jackson unleashed his draconican plan to remove all Indians in the southeast from their homelands. Jackson's Removal Act was a radical departure that undermined all the treaties so solemnly signed by the US with the Cherokees and other Indian Nations.

12

Jackson's Removal Act

Like all Cherokee families, the Spirit clan suffered directly from Andrew Jackson's campaign to take Indian land and move the tribes west. In the 1828 Presidential election against John Quincy Adams, he promised that if elected, he would force all Indians in the eastern half of the country to give up their homelands. In contrast, Adams believed that past Indian treaties should be honored, supporting sale of Indian land only when negotiations were fair. He overturned Jackson's "deal" between Georgia and the Creeks, terming it fraudulent. Jackson's team spread vile lies about him, including that he gave a Russian Minister an American girl as a sex-slave. Adams replied in kind, calling Jackson a murderer and accusing him and his wife Rachel of adultery and bigamy since she wasn't divorced from her first husband at the time of their marriage. It was a sleazy campaign in every respect. Jackson's white nationalist rhetoric won him the Presidency, with a decisive victory in the Electoral College. That same year, Annie's grandfather Spirit died in Arkansas and his wife Susannah moved back to the Cherokee Nation to live with Annie and her family along the Etowah River.

Jackson introduced his Indian Removal Act in early 1829. It contained a timeline for complete removal but was silent on the tribes' sovereign rights, nor did it provide for compensation and removal costs. The President's rhetoric was all about the "march of civilization," by which he and his allies meant one thing: white domination with docile tribes "falling into line" and moving west. Almost immediately after the election, Georgia passed legislation to strip Cherokees of their sovereignty and rights. Chief Ross, Edward Gunter, Richard Taylor and William Coodey departed for Washington in early January 1829, settling into Williamson's Hotel a few weeks later, ready to begin meeting with new cabinet officials and members of Congress. But Jackson's election had engendered even stronger anti-Indian thinking among top government officials. Most everyone Ross met with refused to help, and the delegation departed at the end of April without having resolved anything. Their only solace, a thin reed to be sure, was this paragraph in Jackson's Inaugural Address: "It will be my constant and sincere desire to observe toward the Indian tribes . . . a just and liberal policy . . . ."[220]

Buffalofish, his wife Wo-de-yo-he, and their children who lived on Sweet Water Creek near Buzzards Roost were forcibly dispossessed of their large farms in 1829. Having lost most of their horses and cattle, they moved to the Etowah River near Annie's family late in the year and began to rebuild their lives. They did not want to move west. The Jackson Administration's policy is perhaps best shown in Secretary of War Eaton's response to Chief Ross's anguished letters to the President about Georgia's act of December 20, 1828. Eaton informed Ross on April 18th that the Cherokee Nation had never been a sovereign political entity within the boundaries of Georgia: "If, as is the case, you have been permitted to abide on your lands from that period to the present, enjoying the right of soil and the privilege to hunt, it is not thence to be inferred, that this was anything more than a permission growing out of compacts with your nation . . . [R]emove west, where you will find no conflicting interests."[221]

The *Cherokee Phoenix and Indians' Advocate* published many letters and stories about these developments. A typical example is a letter on March 4, 1829 entitled "To the Cherokee People" written by Annie's uncle Crying Snake and eight other elders: "If the country, to which we are directed to go is desirable and well-watered, why is it so long a wilderness and wasteland and uninhabited by respectable white people . . . if the running streams were as transparent as crystal, and silver fish abounded in their element in profusion we should still adhere to the purposes of spending the remnant of our lives on the soil that gave us birth and rendered dear from the nourishment we receive from its bosom."[222]

Missionaries tried to inform the public about the Removal Act's implications for Indians. In August, Jeremiah Evarts, Secretary of the American Board of Commissioners for Foreign Ministers, wrote twenty-four essays in the *National Intelligencer* about the Cherokees' plight, using the pseudonym William Penn. They were influential nationally, leading many people to support the Cherokee cause.[223] Echoing Jefferson's language in the Declaration of Independence, Evarts wrote passionately that "The Cherokee are human beings, endowed by their Creator with the same natural rights as other men," noting that their territory "was in possession of their ancestors . . . and has come down to them with a title absolutely unencumbered in every respect."[224] Evarts went to great lengths to educate the public about the long history of treaties between the US and the Cherokees, and the fact that the Indians were always perceived to be Nations possessing sovereignty. He noted that the 1798 Tellico Treaty committed the United States to "continue the GUARANTY of the remainder of their country FOREVER . . . ." Predictably, Jackson was unimpressed. His first message to Congress on December 8th characterized Cherokee attempts to create a sovereign state within Georgia as "pretentious", informing the Indians inhabiting parts of Georgia and Alabama that their attempt to establish an independent government would not be countenanced by the US. and advising them to emigrate beyond the Mississippi or submit to the laws of those states.[225]

An article about the Removal Act was published in the *Phoenix* the following week, asking if Jackson possessed a moral compass. Clearly, he had little capacity to understand what is fair and what is wrong but, driven by prejudice and fear, he embraced unfairness and darkness. Evarts believed that it would stain the country's moral fabric if Congress went along with Jackson's removal plans, writing "it will be known by all men, that in a plain case, without any plausible plea of necessity . . . the great and boasting Republic of the United States . . . incurred the guilt of violating treaties . . . before the eyes of the American community . . . ."[226]

Jeremiah Evarts circa 1845[227]

In July 1830 the Cherokees prepared an appeal to Congress that succinctly outlined the history of their relations with the United States.

It is a moving document: "We appeal to the judge of all the earth, who will finally award us justice, and to the good sense of the American people, whether we are intruders upon the land of others. Our consciences bear us witness that we are the invaders of no man's rights—we have robbed no man of his territory—we have usurped no man's authority, nor have we deprived any one of his unalienable privileges. How then shall we indirectly confess the right of another people to our land by leaving it forever? On the soil which contains the ashes of our beloved men we wish to live—on this soil we wish to die."[228]

In September 1830, Methodist missionaries James Trott and Dickerson McCloud drafted a Resolution opposing the Removal Act that was circulated widely around the country by Moravian, Baptist, Presbyterian, and Congregationalist ministers. Public opinion against the Removal Act was growing around the country, but Jackson tirelessly promoted it.[229] The country was divided, with people from all walks of life and every region opposing it. Even the Superintendent of the Bureau of Indian Affairs, Thomas McKenney, publicly termed the Removal Act a "mockery" of justice. Shortly after he went to the White House to formally protest, he was fired, ironically while in Philadelphia meeting with the publisher of his new book *History of the North American Indians*.

Stepping up the pressure, Jackson stopped complying with treaty requirements for annual payments to be paid directly to the Cherokee Nation. He ordered Secretary of War P.G. Randolph to inform Chief Ross that the practice of paying annuities to the Treasurer of the Cherokee Nation would be discontinued and instead paid to individuals.[230] The Cherokee National Council fought vigorously against this, but Jackson was intransigent. With the payments in limbo, Ross asked sympathetic members of Congress for help. Representative Bates of Massachusetts introduced legislation to reverse the policy on March 1, 1831: "I deny the right of the Executive to make this order. These annuities are debts due to the Indians—not gratuities . . . "[231] Despite Congressional pressure, Jackson continued pushing for individual payments, and US Agent H. Montgomery agreed, requiring on June 15th that the head of each family come to the Agency to receive their payments.[232]

The Removal Bill was debated in Congress in late 1830. The Cherokee National Council prepared a "Memorial" for the full Senate and House of Representatives laying out why the Removal Act should be defeated. One of the most important documents the Cherokees ever wrote, the Memorial encapsulates their existence as a people:

> The undersigned memorialists humbly make known to your honorable bodies, that they are free citizens of the Cherokee Nation . . . . Will you listen to us? Will you have pity upon us? You are great and renowned—the nation which you represent is like a mighty man who stands in his strength. But we are small—our name is not renowned . . . The land on which we stand we have received as an inheritance from our fathers who possessed it from time immemorial, as a gift from our common father in heaven . . . This right of inheritance we have never ceded, nor ever forfeited...What great crime have we committed, whereby we must forever be divested of our country and rights?[233]

Senator Theodore Frelinghuysen of New Jersey spoke for six hours on the Senate floor, summarizing the history of whites trampling on Indian rights and calling for the Removal Act to be defeated: "I believe, Sir, it is not now seriously denied that the Indians are men, endowed with kindred faculties and powers with ourselves; that they have . . . are justly entitled to a share in the common bounties of a benignant Providence . . . . I ask in what code of the law of nations . . . their rights have been extinguished? The question has ceased to be—What are our duties? An inquiry much more embarrassing is forced upon us: How shall we most plausibly, and with least possible violence, break our faith."[234]

Theodore Frelinghuysen circa 1832[235]

His speech was covered in newspapers across the country. His allies included Senators Peleg Sprague of Maine and Asher Robbins of Rhode Island, who proposed to amend the Treaty to allow Cherokees the right to stay on their land until they chose to remove, meaning they would not be forced off, and to guarantee their legal rights going forward. There was robust debate on the two amendments. Frelinghuysen stated that President Jackson had usurped the powers of the judiciary and was acting as a one-man Supreme Court, having ignored the Court's ruling in the *Worcester* case. He asserted there were three fundamental and undeniable precepts about the relationship of the Indians to the United States: The Indians hold original and absolute title to their lands; they are sovereign political entities with their own governments; and the Indian treaty system based on the Trade and Intercourse Acts is the only recognized mode of interacting with the American Indians. "I insist that, by immemorial possession, as the original tenants of the soil, they hold a title beyond and superior to the British Crown and her colonies, and to all adverse pretensions of our confederation and subsequent Union."[236] But the two amendments were rejected by votes of 27 to 20 and 28 to 19, and the Senate confirmed the Removal Act by a vote of 28 to 19.[237]

Sam Houston, who became a friend of John Jolly at age fifteen when he ran away from home to join the Cherokees, was christened "Blackbird" by Jolly. Later he fought beside Andrew Jackson and the Cherokees against the Creeks. Determined to help the Cherokee in their hour of need, Blackbird wrote missive after missive to President Jackson and other officials about the immorality and illegality of kicking the Cherokees off their land. But despite his fame and close association with Jackson, his entreaties were ignored.

Sam Houston As a Young Congressman - 1826[238]

As the debate in the House neared its climax, those who supported Indians whose lives and lands were at stake seemed unable to overcome Jackson's venal politics. Would a last-minute passionate intervention on the floor of the House by Representative Davy Crockett turn the tide? He had become one of the most popular people in the country. A Jackson supporter, he was first elected to Congress in 1827 after serving two terms in the Tennessee legislature. At the time, he was quite poor and lacked the funds to travel to Washington, but friends helped him out. When asked who he was at the first tavern he visited, he replied: "I am . . . fresh from the backwoods, half horse, half alligator, a little touched with the snapping turtle. I can wade the Mississippi, leap the Ohio, ride upon a streak of lightning, and slip without a scratch down a honey-locust . . . I can hug a bear too close for comfort, and eat any man opposed to General Jackson."[239] He was reelected in 1829 with a large majority, but quickly decided he couldn't support Jackson's Indian Removal policy. "[I]t was expected of me that I would bow to the name of Andrew Jackson, and follow him all his motions and windings, and turning, even at the expense of my conscience and judgment. Such a thing was new to me, and a total stranger to my principles."[240] When he rose to speak, his eloquence was homespun and direct: "I have always viewed the native Indian tribes of this country as sovereign peoples. This has been recognized as such from the very foundation of our Government. The U.S. is bound by treaties to protect them, and it is our duty to do so. As for using the money of the American people to remove them, I will not do it. I will do only what I can answer to God for."[241]

The Removal Act was narrowly approved by the House of Representatives on May 26th by a vote of 102 to 97 and signed into law by President Jackson on May 28th. As a result of his vote against the bill, Crockett was defeated for reelection and returned home for two years. He won the next election by a slim majority. By then, Crockett had become enormously popular in most of the country, even as his speeches became more and more anti-Jackson. The Removal Act was a moral turning point in his life: "I voted for Andrew Jackson because I believed he possessed certain principles . . . when he left those principles . . . I considered myself justified in opposing him.

This thing of man-worship I am a stranger to; I don't like it; it taints every action of life...."²⁴² Jackson opposed him in the next election, and Crockett was defeated.

Davy Crockett circa 1835²⁴³

Following passage of the Removal Act, Georgia enacted a statute abrogating all Cherokee laws and punishing with jail any Indian who encouraged fellow Cherokees not to relocate.²⁴⁴ Did my ancestors know that this signaled the beginning of the end of their time on Cherokee ancestral lands? Undoubtedly it was a terrible omen, but my guess is that they reacted calmly. After all, the Cherokee Nation was sovereign, many treaties had been solemnly signed by previous US Presidents, and they had good lawyers. Chief Ross hired former US Attorney General William Wirt to file a lawsuit before the Supreme Court challenging Georgia's attempt to deny Cherokee sovereignty. He requested the Court to nullify Georgia's law on the ground that Cherokees are an independent, sovereign nation. While his role as their lawyer was a bit ironic given that he had argued Cherokees were *not* a sovereign nation while Attorney General in 1824, he became a close ally. Wirt also was the Anti-Masonic Party's presidential candidate in the upcoming election to unseat Jackson. Euphoria swept the Nation as they celebrated this step. How could they lose, given all the treaties? But days after oral argument in early 1831, and despite Wirt's being unopposed since Georgia hadn't deigned even to appear, the Supreme Court made a fateful decision in *Cherokee Nation v. Georgia*. Although Justice Marshall recognized Georgia's threat "to annihilate the Cherokees as a political society" he concluded: "If courts were permitted to indulge their sympathies, a case better calculated to excite them can scarcely be imagined . . . A people once numerous, powerful and truly independent, found by our ancestors in the quiet and uncontrolled possession of an ample domain, gradually sinking beneath our superior policy, our arts and our arms, have yielded their lands by successive treaties, each of which contains a solemn guarantee of the residue, until they retain no more of their formerly extensive territory than is deemed necessary for their comfortable subsistence."

Noting that the Constitution gives the Supreme Court the power to judge disputes between a state of the citizens thereof, and foreign states, citizens or subjects, Marshall ruled that the Cherokees are not a state or a foreign nation but a "domestic dependent nation". Hence, the Court lacked jurisdiction to rule.[245] Deciding that Indians were "dependent" meant they were not free sovereign peoples; thus, the states could do what they wanted. Annie's Uncle Crying Snake wrote a column for the *Phoenix* citing the minority opinion by Justices Thompson and Story that would have recognized their sovereignty based on the twelfth article of the Treaty of Hopewell, which contains a full recognition of the sovereign independent character of the Cherokee Nation.[246] The Supreme Court's decision elicited another long missive from the Cherokee National Council to the people of the US written by Lewis Ross and a committee of elders: "After the peace of

1783, the Cherokees were an independent people; absolutely so, as much as any people on earth . . . . We wish to remain on the land of our fathers. We have a perfect and original right to remain without interruption or molestation. . . . . On the soil which contains the ashes of our beloved men we wish to live—on this soil we wish to die . . . ."[247]

Whites living in Cherokee territory were required by another 1831 Georgia law to obtain residency licenses and swear an oath of loyalty to Georgia. If they refused, Georgia threatened to expel them and seize their lands. Eleven missionaries, among the Cherokees' best friends, refused to accept this, claiming that Georgia had no authority over the Cherokee Nation. The Georgia Guard began rounding up missionaries on July 7th, starting at Samuel Worcester's house on their way to Camp Gilmore, near Lawrenceville. Methodist minister James Trott was the next to be picked up, followed by his colleague Dickson McLeod. They stopped for the night at a private home, where the three men were shackled by the ankles. The next morning, the Georgia Guard added Elizur Butler, who was picked up separately and forced to walk for two days while chained to a guardsman's horse. They arrived at Camp Gilmore on July 10th where they joined several other missionaries and a couple of white men married to Cherokees who had refused to sign the oath.[248] On July 16th, they sent a letter to Colonel C. H. Nelson, in charge of the fort where they were locked up along with Samuel Mayes (Annie Spirit's future husband), who also had refused to sign the oath: [249] " . . . it would be a high gratification to some of your prisoners, if Mr. Trott and Mr. Worcester might be permitted to hold a prayer meeting tomorrow evening . . . If the favor can be granted, be so kind as to give us an answer as soon as convenient. We wish to be understood that we should all greatly desire the privilege of attending. S. A. Worcester, Elizur Butler, J. J. Trott, Samuel Mayes"

Their letter was rejected brusquely by Colonel Nelson: "We view the within request as an impertinent one. If your conduct be evidence of your character and the doctrines you wish to promulgate, we are sufficiently enlightened as to both. Our object is to restrain, not to facilitate their promulgation. If your object be true piety, you can enjoy it where you are."[250]

A writ of habeas corpus was issued on July 19th for them to be presented before the county court at Lawrenceville, which was brought to the prison by William Rogers in his capacity as agent for the Nation. Represented by the law firm Chester, Harris and Underwood, Mayes and the missionaries were tried in Lawrenceville on September 15th. They were convicted by the jury and sentenced by Judge Clayton to four years at hard labor in Milledgeville Prison. Governor Gilmore agreed to pardon all who agreed to sign the oath. Most did and were released, but Worcester and Butler refused and remained imprisoned.[251] Mayes wrote a letter to the Governor on September 17th requesting clemency. His appeal was successful, so he was freed, returning to his wife and family.[252]

William Reed, Chairman of the Prudential Committee of the American Board that oversaw the missions, appealed to President Jackson on November 3rd, citing the missionaries' years of work in the Cherokee Nation at the express invitation of the US government in 1816. Noting that the US had provided financial support for mission schools, his letter listed the numerous treaty provisions confirming Cherokee sovereignty. Reed asked Jackson to secure the missionaries' release and to file a lawsuit against the state for false imprisonment, but on November 14th Jackson instructed Secretary of War Cass to send this reply: "Sir: I am instructed by [the President] to inform you, that . . . he has no authority to interfere."[253]

Cherokees in both parts of the country were angry about their treatment. Whether they had left for the west or remained in their homeland, treaty commitments were not being met. Western Cherokees held a special Council meeting in November 1831 to confront the US about its failure to keep key promises in the 1828 treaty. Chief Jolly led a delegation to Washington, D.C. with Alex Saunders, Black Coat, Rain Crow, John Rogers and Andrew Vann to meet President Jackson. Their demands were to expand the size of the western territory, raise the annual annuity to encompass the thousands of people who had moved west, get rid of Osage reserves as was promised in the 1828 treaty, and be reimbursed for livestock killed and stolen in Arkansas. The delegation waited for several months for Jackson to respond. Secretary Cass finally agreed to pay for their lost and stolen property but refused to increase their territory, raise the annuity, or extinguish the Osage reserves.[254]

In the Cherokee homeland, threats against leaders escalated. A white Georgian named Harris confronted Chief Ross on November 30th as he rode home from visiting Major Ridge, shouting: "Ross, I have been for a long time wanting to kill you, and I'll be damned if I don't do it!" His shots missed Ross as he galloped away.[255] Chief Ross and Council members needed constant protection. To inform the larger public about the Cherokees' plight, Elias Boudinot began a fund-raising tour for the *Cherokee Phoenix* in several East Coast cities. His speeches always noted that Cherokees "reside on the land which God gave them . . . The promises of Washington and Jefferson have not been fulfilled. The policy of the United States on Indian affairs has taken a different direction, for no other reason than that the Cherokees have so far become civilized as to appreciate a regular form of Government."[256] Boudinot wanted to inform people in the US how developed the Cherokees had become, as a way to build alliances across political lines.

The Cherokees' lawyer William Wirt appealed Worcester's case to the US Supreme Court in early 1832 on the ground that Georgia was infringing their sovereignty. He wanted to give Chief Justice Marshall and the court another opportunity to rule on the heart of the matter. *Worcester v. Georgia* was argued from February 20th to the 23rd and the Court ruled quickly in favor of the Cherokee Nation by a vote of 5-1. Once again Georgia snubbed its nose at the Court and the Cherokees by refusing to participate. Stating that the missionaries' arrests and convictions violated federal law, Chief Justice John Marshall wrote for the Court:

> All these [Congressional] acts, and especially that of 1802, which is still in force, manifestly consider the several Indian nations as distinct political communities, having territorial boundaries, within which their authority is exclusive, and having a right to all the lands within those boundaries . . . .The Cherokee Nation, then, is a distinct community, occupying its own territory, with boundaries accurately described, in which the laws of Georgia can have no force . . . .The act of the State of Georgia under which the plaintiff in error was prosecuted is consequently void, and the judgment a nullity . . . The Acts of Georgia are repugnant to the Constitution, laws, and treaties of the United States."[257]

Based on this ruling, heir attorney in Georgia asked the Superior Court on March 7th to release the prisoners. The Superior Court refused, but Judge Clayton agreed to accept the Mandate. When Attorney Chester followed this by requesting the Governor to discharge the prisoners, he replied: "You got around Clayton, but you shall not get around me." The prisoners languished in jail. Despite this legal setback in Georgia, the Supreme Court's judgment filled Cherokees with optimism. Elijah Hicks and Elias Boudinot applauded it. Hicks wrote on March 24th "The arrival of this decision has been like a shower of rain on the thirsty vegetables of the earth."[258]

John Ridge was more circumspect about the Court's ruling, writing Stand Watie, an important Cherokee politician and Elias Boudinot's brother: "You . . . ought to advise our people that the contest is not over . . . the Chicken Snake General Jackson has time to crawl and hide in the luxuriant grass of his nefarious hypocrisy until his responsibility is fastened upon by an execution of the Supreme Court at their next session."²⁵⁹ He was in Philadelphia raising awareness about the Cherokees' plight the week that the court ruled in *Worcester v. Georgia*.

Elias Boudinot circa 1832

But President Jackson did nothing when Georgia ignored the Supreme Court's ruling. Denigrating the Court's ability to enforce its decision Jackson demanded: "Does the Supreme Court have an army?" The President wrote Ross to "Relocate or be ruled by Georgia law." A few days later John Ridge went to Washington to speak with the President, urging him to enforce the Supreme Court's decision. Jackson refused, saying that he should tell his people "their only hope of relief was in abandoning their country and removing to the West."²⁶⁰ Jackson continued pushing Cherokees to emigrate, working through his agents, Benjamin Curry and John Coffee. Coffee wrote to Georgia Governor Wilson Lumpkin on March 17th about the Supreme Court's decision, deploring it mainly for delaying the inevitable and comforting himself with the "determination of the President and Secretary of War [that] will I hope be a sufficient offset against the decision of the Supreme Court and enable us in a short time to have things going on as they were before the decision was made."²⁶¹

He also alerted Lumpkin about Chief White Path, perhaps the most famous traditional chief at that time, who was actively opposing emigration and urging his people to remain in their homes Coffee threatened that his men would "proceed to Ellijay (a Cherokee stronghold in the Georgian mountains) for the purpose of arresting and bringing to trial Whitepath and Sunday . . . These Chiefs have become very bold, and believe their mountains will protect them from our power."²⁶² Their mission was a failure, as they couldn't locate White Path or Chief Sunday. Coffee hoped that at least one thousand Indians would be relocated that April, but only 380 people were on the flatboats that left the Cherokee Agency at Calhoun on April 10ᵗʰ. Of that number, forty were white, 108 were black and most of the rest were mixed bloods. After navigating the Muscle Shoals rapids, they were transferred to the steamboat *Thomas Yeatman* at Waterloo for the voyage along the Mississippi, Ohio, and Arkansas Rivers. But the promised supplies and rations were not at their destination when they were put ashore, destitute and left to their own devices to survive.²⁶³

The Cherokee National Council met on July 23ʳᵈ at Red Clay, Tennessee, the most important gathering place after the New Echota government buildings were no longer safe to use. Georgia had made it clear that Cherokee tribal business could no longer take place there and the US supported Georgia. The sacred Blue Hole spring provided cool, clean water for everyone and the new Council house was plain compared to New Echota. Buffalofish and several of his brothers were there along with thousands of others for this very important gathering. Chief Ross opened the meeting in the normal way, saying "We have met again in General Council and greeted each other in friendship . . . we are peculiarly indebted to the dispensations of an all-wise Providence, whose omniscient power over the events of human affairs is supreme, and by whose judgments the fate of Nations is sealed."[264]

Reconstructed Council House at Red Clay[265]

Representative Elisha Chester presented Jackson's treaty to trade all Cherokee land for an equivalent amount west of the Mississippi as a *fait accompli*, implying there was nothing to negotiate. His proposal was soundly rebuffed by the Spirit family and everyone there except John Ridge, Elias Boudinot, William Hicks, James Starr, William Coodey, John Walker, and William Rogers—who thought the proposal worth considering. Their view was unanimously rejected by all the other Cherokees who attended. It was unclear what the US would try next.

White settlers continued to invade the Cherokee Nation in ever increasing numbers. In Georgia, new laws prevented Cherokees from protecting their rights by prohibiting them from testifying in court. Enrolling Agent Curry noted that hundreds of families wanted to leave but "although the Indian finds a market at his door for his stock, he cannot sell for cash, and to sell on credit is equal to giving it away."[266] Plaintive letters to the *Phoenix* from people in the west urged those in the east not to move, as the promised food and supplies hadn't materialized and the "new" land was occupied by other

Indian tribes. Reverend Jesse Bushyhead, Annie's third cousin, was one of those who returned east, telling everyone not to believe the US promises.[267] But her great-grandma Susannah believed they would be safer in Arkansas, remembering how much she and The Spirit had liked it after moving there years earlier.

Georgia's "Gold Lottery" began raffling off 40-acre plots of Cherokee land in October 1832. The gold rush that had begun in 1828 had flooded northern Georgia with prospectors. Dahlonega ("yellow metal" in Cherokee) was the focus of their interest. The estimated value of the gold extracted was already about $16,500,000, the second largest in the country.[268] The lottery continued for several months as parcel after parcel was essentially given away to bachelors at least eighteen years old, widows, families of orphans, and male heads of family who were three-year residents of Georgia. Winners in the lottery had to pay just $10 per lot.

As Jackson ran against Henry Clay for reelection in late 1832, the centerpiece of his campaign was expelling Indians. Once reelected, he ignored appeals from many in the Senate and Congress as well as esteemed writers and theologians, moving rapidly to force the Cherokees to leave their remaining lands in North Carolina, Tennessee, Alabama, and Georgia. His fifth annual message to Congress on December 3, 1833 was starkly racist: "Established in the midst of another and a superior race and without appreciating the causes of their inferiority or seeking to control them, they must necessarily yield to the force of circumstances and ere long disappear . . . .Surrounded by our settlements, they have neither the intelligence, the industry, the moral habits nor the desire of improvement which are essential to any favorable change in their condition."[269]

Were the Cherokees naive about retaining their sovereignty against the tides of prejudice? Of course. Were they wrong to believe in the words of the US Constitution and treaties solemnly signed by US Presidents? Of course not. They thought their strategy was sound and that there was a limit to Jackson's depravity; unfortunately, they were wrong on both counts. With the benefit of hindsight, it seems obvious that Annie's family should have moved west with her Uncle John Huss and his family in 1837. But such individual actions wouldn't have changed the fate of the Cherokee people overall given Jackson's overweening desire to rid the east of all Indians. His smug cruelty seeps through even a formal painting such as this one.[270] Even if the Cherokees had remained united in support of remaining in their homeland, it is doubtful that would have changed what happened. But they were not united, and a formal movement of supporters for a negotiated settlement gained momentum. What became the Treaty Party was born, with huge consequences for the Cherokees.

Andrew Jackson by Ralph Eleaser Whiteside Earl

13

The Treaty Party

In 1834, The Ridge and Elias Boudinot began a secret negotiation with senior US officials for a treaty that would sell all Cherokee land in the east and provide sufficient land in the west for the Cherokee Nation to be reconstituted. This was the beginning of what became known as "the treaty party." It was supported mainly by mixed-blood Cherokee and especially those who owned large numbers of slaves, but it never attracted large numbers of ordinary people. The Ridge acknowledged the irony that he had condemned Black Fox, principal chief of the Cherokee after the death of Little Turkey in 1802, thirty years earlier for doing the same thing. In 1808 The Ridge led a revolt of younger chiefs who deposed Black Fox.[271]

While the Cherokee Nation was being assaulted from outside, their internal situation was deteriorating. With their government outlawed by Georgia, more people began to leave under the pressure. An emigration party commanded by Lt. Joseph Harris departed on March 3rd from the Cherokee Agency with around 460 Indians. One of the most infamous of the early removals, trouble began immediately, with outbreaks of measles and cholera in the temporary camps built to hold the Indians until they got onto the boats. Harris described the departure scene this way: "I saw many a manly cheek suffused with tears. Parents were turning with sick hearts from children who were about to seek other homes in a far off and strange land; and brothers and sisters with heaving bosoms and brimful eyes were wringing each other's hands for the last time."²⁷²

Harris commissioned the steamboats *Blue Buck*, *Rainbow*, *Squeezer*, and *Moll Thompson* to descend the Hiwassee and Tennessee rivers with flatboats carrying the Cherokees and their possessions. After arriving at Waterloo on March 19th, they transferred to a larger steamboat, the *Thomas Yeatman*. As the trip progressed, some flat boats were lost with all the emigrants' belongings, a few people were washed overboard during storms and died, and there was increasing disease. Once onto the Arkansas River, low water forced the boats to stop at Cadron Creek, where they unloaded their possessions and made camp. Tending to the sick was the immediate priority, driven by the introduction of a malignant type of cholera that killed the wives of Black Fox and Charley McDaniel along with several others within twenty-four hours. Many others died in the next few days.²⁷³

A few days later the remaining ill and older Indians were transported in fourteen wagons pulled by oxen, while the majority had to walk. Harris forced them to leave behind most of the possessions they had brought with them to start their new lives, including looms, ovens, spinning wheels, farm equipment, and bedding. Their destination was Dwight Mission on Sallisaw Creek, where they arrived on May 10th. Eighty-one Cherokees were recorded as dying on the trip west, and by the end of the year about half of those who survived had also succumbed to illness and died.²⁷⁴ Although news of this horror was reported in the national press and the *Phoenix*, nothing stilled Jackson's zeal to rid Georgia, Tennessee, Alabama, and North Carolina of the Indians, and nothing could stop the waves of internal violence. While returning home from a meeting of the National Council, John Walker, Jr. (Sequaneyoho), a leading advocate of removal, was assassinated on June

24th by James Foreman and his half-brother Anderson Springston. That marked the beginning of internal civil war, with numerous killings in the following years.

Elijah Hicks presented a petition to the National Council in August charging Major Ridge, John Ridge, and David Vann with treason for negotiating with the US, calling for their impeachment and removal from office. Although they weren't tried, the charges were never dropped. The Treaty Party held a meeting on November 28th to continue discussing a treaty with the US. Held at Running Waters, the plantation of John Ridge not far from Oothcaloga (now Calhoun, Georgia), several members of Annie's extended family were there, including her great-uncle David Sconti, who signed the appeal to the US Senate and House of Representatives urging the US to set aside a large territory west of the Mississippi for the sole and perpetual use of the Cherokee Nation.[275]

Early in 1835, US government agents began carrying out a census of every inhabitant, including all property and household items, putting a dollar value on farms, homes, mills, ferries, orchards, animals and tools. All were grotesquely undervalued, while the enormous wealth inherent in their forests, rivers, streams, marshlands, prairies, and wildlife was not valued at all. It's painful to recall the abject reality of the Cherokee situation due to their dependency on the US to honor the promises they had made. Stripping Cherokees of their rights, the US imposed a ruthless bureaucratic system valuing—without any review or appeal—how much each household's improvements were worth. In Floyd County, local men were paid $4 per day to carry out surveys that typically valued a peach tree at eighty cents, an acre of cleared farmland at $3.00, and just $4.50 for a large shingle-roofed cabin with plank floors and a stone chimney. While the census was underway, Buffalofish was one of thirty-seven Cherokees who signed a letter requesting that US Indian Agent Major Benjamin Curry delay the census until after the corn crop could be harvested. He agreed and the census was completed in the autumn.[276]

```
            A CENSUS OF THE CHEROKEES WAS ORDERED THIS YEAR
Undated letter addressed to Majr. Benjamin F. Curry, U.S. Indian
Agent.
The Cherokees asked that the taking of the "sense" (census) of the
Cherokees be postponed until "the time when corn is in roasting
order when the people will have more leisure to attend."
This census was ordered by the Secretary of War "as to the mode of
paying their present years annuity and to whom.... We hope that you
will have the money on the ground that you may pay it over at once
as the tribe shall direct."
Signed in behalf of the voters by:
John Ridge                          Jas. A. Foreman
D.R. Coody                          C.F. Foreman
Saml. Ballard                       Tesah toaskee X  → wallengshee
Jacob West                          John Ratliffe X
Sar nah na X                        Charles Moore X
Alexander Brown X                   Bear Meat X
George West                         Yohncokilla X
Nelson West                         Rile X
Spirit Buffalofish Sour X           Hammer X
David Vann                          Watie X
David J. Hooks                      Ground Hole X
Jas. Johnson                        John Fields Sr. X
Henderson Harris X                  Archy Rome X
Jas. Fields X                       Paris Solurculla X
Ezekiel West                        Ground X
David Scoutahie                     Coou X
Major Ridge                         Itte cunnahee X  little aurvahe
George Chambers X                   Charles H. Vann X
(X = signed by mark)                John Fields, Jr. X
SOURCE: Cherokee Letters, page 569, Georgia Archives.
```

While he was away in January 1835 rallying for Cherokee rights in Washington, Chief Ross's home, ferry, and farm at Head of Coosa were seized by William Smith and John Lumpkin, who crossed the Oostanaula River to hand the property over to lottery winner William Bishop. Lumpkin demanded that Ross's wife Quatie and their children depart immediately. Initially she refused, but after the men started throwing furniture outdoors and threatened her and the children, she retreated to the second floor and signed a pledge to give up the house in ten days. On the final day, she gathered her children and left for their cabin in Tennessee. Bishop moved in.[277] When Ross returned from Washington late in the month, he found his home occupied by Bishop. Ross received about $20,000 for his 300-acre farm with a large two-story home, an overseer's house, houses for his twenty slaves, a blacksmith shop, large orchards and a US Post Office. The post office alone generated an income of $1000 each year.

Bishop's Claim to Ross's Property[278]

Ross and Quatie's Cabin on the Tennessee-Georgia Border[279]

US envoy John F. Schermerhorn offered the Ridge Treaty Party delegation $3,250,000 for the Cherokee Nation on March 14, 1835. Ross, who received excellent intelligence on what was happening, intervened, countering with a demand for $20,000,000. By this time Ross knew that Cherokees were unlikely to prevail, and as chief wanted to be involved in any deal. When that figure was rejected outright, Ross said he would accept an amount set by the US Senate, believing it would be a fair arbiter. The Senate almost immediately offered $5,000,000, and Ross backed away from his decision to allow the Senate to decide. John Ridge suggested to President Jackson that he write a letter to the Cherokee Nation outlining the deal and explaining why they must accept it. Jackson agreed, and on March 16th he wrote to Chief Ross, still in Washington. On April 7th Jackson's letter was printed in newspapers around the country: "You are now placed in the midst of a white population . . . How, under these circumstances, can you live in the country you now occupy? Your condition must become worse and worse, and you will ultimately disappear, as so many tribes have done before you . . . You have but one remedy within your reach. And that is, to remove to the West and join your countrymen, who are already established there . . . Deceive yourselves no longer."[280]

Predictably, Jackson's letter made little impact on Ross or the great majority of Cherokees. Annie's father, mother, grandfather Buffalofish, and grandmother Wo-de-yo-he attended a crucial meeting at Running Waters on July 20th to discuss the proposed New Echota Treaty. The assembly opened with a fine prayer by Reverend John Huss, and then everyone sang a hymn in Cherokee.[281] Schermerhorn was given as much time as he wished to explain the plan to buy all Cherokee land, ranting on for almost three hours while Reverend Jesse Bushyhead interpreted for him. Major Ridge's Treaty Party faction called for a vote on the US offer to trade the Nation for $5,000,000 in cash and 13 million acres in the west, plus relocation expenses and payment for the improvements to their farms. Buffalofish and his son voted with the pro-treaty group, finally accepting that moving was the best option under the circumstances. But Chief Ross won an overwhelming vote against the Echota Treaty on July 22nd, with just ninety-two people voting yes, while more than 2,000 others voted against the proposal. The voting took place as they listened to the Georgia Guard's band sounding out their rat-a-tat-tat drum patterns for hours, accompanied by the taut shrieks of fifes. After almost everyone, including Buffalofish and other family members, rejected Schermerhorn's and Archilla's proposal to give annuity payments to individuals rather than to Cherokee Treasurer Martin, Regional Agent Lieutenant Bateman turned over the regular payment to Martin.[282]

Ross reached out to the Ridge faction on July 31st by inviting twenty people from the Treaty Party to his home for the day. They spent it in conversation without interference from government agents, but nothing changed the entrenched views of the Treaty Party people. With no accord politically, the Treaty Party decided to seize the Cherokee Nation's printing press. Stand Watie, fully supporting the Treaty Party, was assistant editor of the *Phoenix* and had access to the printing press. Arriving with the Georgia Guard at Elijah Hicks's house in New Echota in late August, just hours before wagons sent by Ross arrived to take the press and type to Red Clay for protection, Watie confiscated the press, type, and copies of the paper. The printing press was never returned, and for the remainder of the time until removal, the Cherokee Nation had no newspaper. Ross called the seizure a "high-handed measure [that] could not have been sanctioned for any purpose than to stifle the voice of the Cherokee people."[283]

John Ridge held a Green Corn Dance on August 24th at his Running Waters plantation, attended by hundreds, to build support for the removal treaty. Chief Ross attempted to hold the traditional Green Corn celebration elsewhere to counter Ridge's, but the Georgia Guard dispersed everyone who came. The split continued to deepen. Ross seemed to be running out of options. He called for a full National Council meeting at Red Clay to discuss the proposed treaty on October 12th. John Howard Payne, a famous actor and one of the Cherokees' best friends, described the scene: "The woods echoed with the trampling of many feet: a long and orderly procession emerged from among the trees, the gorgeous autumnal tints of whose departing foliage seemed in sad harmony with the noble spirit now beaming in this departing race . . . here were a few aged men, and some few women, on horseback. The train halted at the humble gate of the principal chief: he stood ready to receive them. Everything was noiseless . . . The chief approached them. They formed diagonally in two lines, and each, in silence, drew near to give his hand."[284]

Again, Ridge's proposal was overwhelmingly rejected. Chief Ross ended the meeting with these words, "Let us be united and leave a character on the page of history that will never dishonor the name of the Cherokee nation."[285] But the Treaty Party faction stepped up their counter efforts, working closely with the infamous Georgia Guard. They raided Ross's home on November 7th as he and Payne were reviewing documents. With bayonets fixed, they arrested the two men, taking them in the driving rain to the prison at Spring Place, where they found Chief Going Snake, Speaker of the Council, chained to a table. They were held there until John Ridge arrived and obtained their release.[286]

Major Ridge and his core supporters met secretly with Schermerhorn on December 22nd in New Echota. As he was reading aloud the draft treaty, the roof caught on fire. Despite that sign of foreboding, a small group of Treaty Party supporters voted to submit the treaty to Jackson. The Ridge's view was that the ultimate safety of his people was paramount: "I am one of the native sons of these wild woods. I have hunted the deer and turkey here more than fifty years . . . The Georgians have shown a grasping spirit lately; they have extended their laws . . . which harass our braves and make the children suffer and cry . . . I know the Indians have an older title than theirs. We obtained the land from the living God above . . . Yet they are strong and we are weak. We are few, they are many . . . We can never forget these homes . . . but an unbending, iron necessity tells me we must leave them . . . There is but one path of safety . . . Give up these lands and go over beyond the great Father of Waters."[287]

After several days of editing, the Treaty Party invited around 500 people, who they hoped were supporters, to meet with US officials on December 29th at Elias Boudinot's home. Although Annie Spirit's father and grandfather were among the small number who initially had signaled their support, this time they refused to sign. Since 1829, when Buffalofish and Wo-de-ye-ho were forced to leave their home and sacred places near Lithia Springs, they had hoped their Nation would endure in its homeland. They thought that moving to a safer area near the Head of Coosa would protect their family. While vacillating in recent months about what to do, they decided to stick with the great majority of the people. The fates of 16,000 Cherokees were sealed by the signatures of a few members of the tribe that day.

Chief Ross and the National Council immediately wrote another appeal to the US Congress: "In truth, our cause is your own. It is the cause of liberty and justice . . . We have practiced [Washington and Jefferson's] precepts with success and the result is manifest. The wilderness of forest has given place to comfortable dwellings and cultivated fields . . . On your sentence our fate is suspended, on your kindness, on your humility, on your compassion, on your benevolence, we rest our hopes."[288]

Henry Clay, who had lost a close election to Jackson, termed the New Echota Treaty "unjust, dishonest, cruel and shortsighted in the extreme." Representative Henry Wise of Virginia said that Cherokees are "more advanced in civilization" than the rest of Georgia. Representative John

Quincy Adams called the treaty "infamous . . . it brings with it eternal disgrace upon the country." But none of those words had any impact on Jackson, who continued on his path, enshrouded in a vapor of hate, prejudice, and greed.

It is sobering to compare how much land Cherokees were forced or induced to cede to the US and various states over the decades to what they were promised in the west. Charles Royce prepared this chart in 1887 listing the number of square miles and acres lost in each cession: altogether over 81 million acres.[289]

Ross and the National Council never slackened their efforts to stop forced migration of their people. Demonstrating the enduring determination of the Cherokee people to remain on their ancestral homeland, Ross's leadership was unfaltering. If he couldn't stop the process, perhaps he could obtain more than the $5 million stipulated by the Treaty—if not the $20 million he had once hoped for, then at least a fairer number. Whatever that number, it was all they could count on to build a new Nation.

Date of treaty.	State where ceded lands are located.	Area in square miles.	Area in acres.
1721	South Carolina	2,623	1,678,720
Nov 24, 1755	South Carolina	8,635	5,526,400
Oct 14, 1768	Virginia	850	544,000
Oct 18, 1770	Virginia	4,500	2,880,000
	West Virginia	4,300	2,752,000
	Tennessee	150	96,000
	Kentucky	250	160,000
1772	Kentucky	10,135	6,486,400
	West Virginia	437	279,680
	Virginia	345	220,800
June 1, 1773	Georgia	1,050	672,000
March 17, 1775	Kentucky	22,600	14,464,000
	Virginia	1,800	1,152,000
	Tennessee	2,650	1,696,000
May 20, 1777	South Carolina	2,051	1,312,640
July 20, 1777	North Carolina	4,414	2,824,960
	Tennessee	1,760	1,126,400
May 31, 1783	Georgia	1,650	1,056,000
Nov 28, 1785	North Carolina	550	352,000
	Tennessee	4,914	3,144,960
	Kentucky	917	586,880
July 2, 1791	Tennessee	3,435	2,198,400
	North Carolina	722	462,080
Oct 2, 1798	Tennessee	952	609,280
	North Carolina	587	375,680
Oct 24, 1804	Georgia	135	86,400
Oct 25, 1805	Kentucky	1,086	695,040
	Tennessee	7,032	4,500,480
Oct 27, 1805	Tennessee	1	800
January 7, 1806	Tennessee	5,269	3,372,160
	Alabama	1,602	1,025,280
March 22, 1816	South Carolina	148	94,720
Sept 14, 1816	Alabama	3,129	2,194,560
	Mississippi	4	2,560
July 8, 1817	Georgia	583	373,120
	Tennessee	435	278,400
Feb 27, 1819	Georgia	837	535,680
	Alabama	1,154	738,560
	Tennessee	2,408	1,541,120
	North Carolina	1,542	986,880
May 6, 1828	Arkansas	4,720	3,020,800
Dec 29, 1835	Tennessee	1,484	949,760
	Georgia	7,202	4,609,280
	Alabama	2,518	1,611,520
	North Carolina	1,112	711,680
July 19, 1866	Kansas	1,928	1,233,920
Total		126,906	81,220,374

14

Chief Ross's Final Efforts

While Ross and his team were preparing to return to Washington in December 1835 to continue negotiations with the President, he received a letter from Secretary of War Cass and Commissioner of Indian Affairs Herring that it would be "utterly useless ... for the proposed delegation to come here, under any expectation of holding communications with this Department."[290] Hoping even at such a late date to convince the President to respect Cherokee rights, Ross wrote back asking again for a meeting: "We're not animals but sentient beings and we have much to offer, if the U.S. would only live up to its own ideals. We copied most of them into our Constitution!"[291] Ross and his delegation presented their credentials, requesting meetings with Cass and President Jackson. Cass deigned to meet them briefly on January 6, 1836, stating that the President was unmovable: "The amount to be paid for your land won't be increased, the old individual reservations won't be allowed, and payments will go to individuals, not the Cherokee Nation."

Jackson did meet for a few minutes with Ross the next day but had no interest in listening to any further words. A couple of days later when The Ridge arrived in Washington with the New Echota Treaty in his saddle bag,

Jackson met him and his associates at the White House to celebrate their mutual victory. As a last gesture of disdain, Jackson struck out the clause in the treaty as signed at New Echota allowing Cherokees who desired to remain to become US citizens of the states in which they resided. None of the Treaty Party demurred, and Jackson forwarded the Treaty to the Senate for ratification.[292] Ross sent a formal protest to Cass on January 13th. Amazingly, both Stand Watie and John Ridge signed it, but during the meeting with Cass, the younger Ridge made clear he was on Schermerhorn's side and supported the Treaty. Ross retorted, "this is your fourth entire revolution in politics within as many months, varying as often as the moon, without the excuse of lunacy . . . "[293] In February, Ross instructed Assistant Principal Chief George Lowrey to convene an Assembly regarding the New Echota treaty. It was bitterly cold that winter, but most members of the National Council convened at Red Clay, where they unanimously rejected the Treaty.

George Featherstonhaugh (the first US geologist) was invited by Special US Agent John Mason to attend the meeting and summarized the situation: "At the time of my visit, the Cherokees were almost incensed to desperation; they were yet about 18,000 in number, were brave, and had leaders of great ability . . . The proposition to abandon their native country was abhorrent to the Cherokees, with the exception of a very small minority of them . . . ."[294]

Senate debate opened on March 7, 1836. A day later, the Cherokee's appeal was circulated to every Senator, outlining the case against the New Echota treaty. Ross railed that "The alleged Treaty is false upon its face, and against the known wishes of the Nation."[295] He was assured by Henry Clay, Daniel Webster, and other senators that it would not be approved. But Senator Hugh White of Tennessee, who had spoken against it during the debate, changed his vote at the last minute after being pressured by Jackson. The treaty was approved 31-15 on May 18th, one vote above the constitutional requirement, despite impassioned pleas by Webster, Calhoun, and Clay.[296]

That was a bleak day. The Cherokees had many friends in Congress, just not quite enough. President Jackson signed the New Echota Treaty on May 23rd with a deadline of two years for all Cherokees to move or be arrested. But vacillating like thin reeds in a stiff wind, most still had not given up. Ross sent another "Memorial of Protest of the Cherokee Nation" to the House and Senate on June 22nd where, predictably, it fell on deaf ears.[297]

When John Ridge returned home in June, he found the Nation verging on chaos. He and his father immediately wrote President Jackson, expressing their grave concern about what was happening: "We found our plantations taken in whole or in part by the Georgians—suits instituted against us for back rents of our own farms . . . commenced in the lower courts, with the evident design that, when we are ready to remove, to arrest our people, and on these vile claims to induce us to compromise for our own release, to travel with our families. Thus our funds will be filched from our people, and we shall be compelled to leave our country as beggars and in want."[298] There was no respite even for Treaty Party leaders.

Not deigning to reply, the President appointed General John Wool to command the Army of East Tennessee and the Cherokee Nation to oversee removal. His mission was to prepare Cherokees to depart, providing food and preventing white depredation. That was a tall order to say the least, but he cared nothing about protecting Indians so that part of his mandate was largely ignored.[299] Ross decided to hold a large public meeting in Athens, Tennessee to inform the people about what was coming. Wool's troops were causing consternation by seizing rifles and pointedly questioning whether people accepted the Treaty. Thousands were in attendance waiting to see their leader. While standing on the platform waiting to speak, someone put an envelope in his hand: a letter from Wool confirming Jackson's decision that no alterations to the treaty would be made. Ross read the entire treaty to his people word by word.

Everyone sat silent and somber. When Ross asked if they were disposed to give their assent they unanimously answered "No!"[300]

General Wool treated Chief Ross as an obstructionist who was blocking him from successfully executing his mission. He stated that if the Cherokees didn't remove peacefully, he would make them "prisoners of war" and there would be "no halfway measures." He was proud of "destroying the influence of John Ross very fast."[301] To that end, Wool ordered Ross's arrest along with Elijah Hicks, Roman Nose, and White Path in late 1836, holding them overnight to convince them to stop resisting removal. When that failed, he released them, but the next day arrested Reverend Evan Jones, perhaps the most important of all the missionaries to the Cherokees, who he accused of instigating rebellion. Jones was born in Wales on May 11, 1788, emigrating to the US in 1821 with his wife and four children. He accepted the Baptist Foreign Mission's call to move to its new mission in the Cherokee Valley Towns, which began his exceptional service to the Cherokee Nation and its people.[302]

Wool's actions brought a reprimand from the acting Secretary of War Harris for exceeding his authority, but reprimands were far from sufficient to sway anyone in the US government or military at that point.[303] In response, the Cherokee National Council agreed on resolutions that were handed to General Wool and sent to the President, stating once again that the New Echota Treaty "is null and void, and can never in justice be enforced upon our nation; and we do hereby solemnly disclaim and utterly reject said instrument, in its principles and all its provisions."[304] Summarizing the Cherokee's rejection of the Treaty for the Senate and House on September 28th, Ross noted that those who negotiated it had no legal authority, stating: " . . . we are despoiled of our private possessions . . . We are stripped of every attribute of freedom. Our property may be plundered before our eyes; violence may be committed on our persons; even our lives may be taken away . . . We have neither land nor home, nor resting place that can be called our own."[305]

Home of Elias Boudinot and Harriet Gold[306]

Ross and key members of the National Council traveled to Arkansas in late November to meet with western Cherokee officials in Tahlonteeskee, the first capital of the early settlers. On the way, they stopped at Fort Gibson to meet US Agent Stokes, learning that an order for Ross' arrest had been made under the Intercourse Act of 1834, which ironically was designed to protect Indians from unscrupulous traders. From a legal perspective, the law certainly did not apply to Cherokees visiting Cherokees. Ignoring the threat, Ross led the meeting in early December without interference from US officials. The Western Cherokee Council passed a resolution of Cherokee solidarity in demanding recission of the illegal Echota Treaty,[307] but predictably nothing came of this. The economy of the Cherokee Nation was falling apart, as white lottery winners continued claiming homes and farms. The mood became ever darker, as the clock was ticking towards the date set for removal: June 1838. While more and more Cherokees were losing their farms and land to lottery winners, leaders of the Treaty Party were able to keep theirs. Elias Boudinot's property was withdrawn from the lottery process entirely by Georgian officials as a favor to him.

From November 1836 to the spring of 1838, Cherokees could pick up basic rations in New Echota. Government Commissioner Albert Lenoir oversaw the provision of corn, beef, bacon, and salt. Ration books kept at the fort show that Annie's father, her Uncle Poorbear Buffalofish (one of Buffalofish's sons), her mother's first husband George Vann, and other family members went there several times. This page from the 1836 handwritten ledger shows Poor Bear and George Vann receiving rations.[308]

Field agents Samuel Burns and Joseph Watters began valuing the Spirit family's farms at Dykes Bend on November 9, 1836. The records of those evaluations contain priceless details of the lives of individual Cherokees. Buffalofish's household was listed as containing ten full-bloods and three slaves, three weavers and two spinners.[309] Annie's family included ten full bloods, one reader of Cherokee, three weavers, and three spinners.[310] Her great-grandmother Susannah's farm lists just herself, while her Uncle Crying Snake's household consisted of four full bloods, including a farmer, a weaver, and a spinner, whose improvements included an eight-acre field and home valued at $158.50.[311] Buffalofish and Wo-de-yo-he owned two houses, one about eighteen by twenty feet and one-half stories high with a puncheon floor and brick chimney, the other about eighteen feet square with a wooden chimney. Their three slaves spoke English and were spinners, weavers, and gardeners, living in a new house about the same size as theirs. The household had a women's loom house, a hog pen, a stable, and two corn cribs. They tended a large garden, had a ten-acre field, and an orchard with 145 peach trees valued at eighty cents each and 75 apple trees valued at $1.50 each. Their farm included twenty acres of good bottomland. All of that was valued at just $934.25.[312]

Buffalofish's daughter Nakey and her husband Nitts owned a farm valued at $217.50; his daughter So-Wa-Chee and her husband Sawney Vann's large farm was appraised at $811; his son Alexander's (Oo-ta-lah-nah) farm was valued at $271.50; his son Eagle-on-the-Roost's (Wa-Lu-Kil-Lah) farm was valued at $193.[313] Annie's parents had no slaves, and their home and barn were smaller; they were allotted just $346.50 for everything, including their orchards and animals.[314] How ludicrously small those numbers were in light of the reality of their rich lands and lives there, and the long-term value had they been allowed to stay in their homeland. Moreover, most people didn't receive what was promised, partly because of the nefarious work of Wilson

Lumpkin, who approved white counterclaims against the Cherokees after they were no longer there. Whites typically charged "back rent" on farms that Cherokees had refused to hand over to lottery winners.[315]

Other family members' properties were valued about the same time. Annie's great-uncle Sconti's three farms on Town Creek included eleven full-blood Cherokees of which three were farmers, two were weavers, and two were spinners.[316] John Huss's home in Will's Valley contained five full-blood Cherokeess, four half-bloods, and two mixed-blood Catawbas. Among them were one weaver and three spinners, including two who were fluent in English and nine who could read and write Cherokee.[317] Charles Poor Bear owned two farms with a household of ten full-blood Cherokees, of whom two were weavers and three were spinners; one of them read Cherokee.[318] Caty Knightkiller and her husband's household in Will's Valley comprised thirteen full-blood Cherokees and five half-bloods, including three English speakers and five who were fluent in Cherokee.[319] Evaluation records exist for almost everyone in her extended family.

Black Watt Adair, half Cherokee, died of a heart attack after the lottery winner arrived to seize his properties on Two Run Creek near Oothcalooga, the "garden spot" of Cherokee country (now Kingston, Georgia). Black Watt and his wife Rachel Thompson owned 200 acres with a large home, guest house, barns, stables, and orchards valued at $4,207. They also owned a sawmill, grist mill, miller's house, and blacksmith shop in addition to the Elbert Adair farm and the Hand Place on the Etowah River. Altogether, their improvements were valued at $12,839.[320] One of their daughters, Nancy Adair, was Samuel Mayes' first wife, born on October 7, 1807. Her grandfather John W. Adair married Nancy Lightfoot, whose mother was Ga-ho-ga and father was Captain John Lightfoot. When I peer far back in time, it's clear that, while Annie's parents and grandparents weren't rich like Black Watt, they were well-off. Among their peers, they were seen as progressive and open-minded, yet still traditional. Their generation readily adopted the new written language, created courts, established an elected legislature and started a public education system. They were an optimistic and resilient people, proud of their heritage. Everyone wanted to learn to read and write in their own language.

The first group of 600 Treaty Party supporters left for the west with their belongings, tools, horses, oxen, and slaves on January 1, 1837. At the end of February, as his second term drew near to a close, President Jackson reviewed with satisfaction how he had forced almost all Indian tribes in the east and southeast to give up their lands and move west. The grotesque human misery caused by this seemed not to trouble him. After all, they were but savages, and the white people who had elected him needed that good land. He remained unconcerned about the conditions in which the Indians were being driven west. Serene in the knowledge that his hand-picked successor Martin Van Buren, who most called "Old Kinderhook" since he came from the Dutch town of Kinderhook, would be taking on his mission. Jackson looked forward to returning to the Hermitage, supported by his battalions of slaves at his plantation near Nashville. One of his final acts was to appoint the odious Georgia Governor William Lumpkin as Indian Commissioner, putting him in charge of valuing Cherokee property.

Major Ridge had become a distinguished and wealthy man, often dressed as though for a fancy ball. As one of the negotiators of the New Echota Treaty, he was treated well overall by US and Georgian officials before departing on the trip west. But not even the Ridges could avoid lottery winners seizing parts of their property before they left. The Ridge's ferry was seized along with a large section of his property on the other side of the Oostanaulah by a Georgian named Cox. One of John Ridge's large Alabama farms was seized by John Garrett. Although the terms of the New Echota Treaty were supposed to protect Cherokees from such acts, General Wool did nothing to enforce them. John Ridge's June letter to Jackson described the outrageous acts of violence: " . . . notwithstanding the cries of our people . . . the lowest classes of white people are flogging the Cherokees with cowhides, hickories and clubs. We are not safe in our houses, our people are assailed day and night by the rabble . . . This barbarous treatment is not confined to men, but the women are stripped also, and whipped without law or mercy."[321]

The Ridge, his wife Sehoya, their son Walter, granddaughter Clarinda, and a group of Treaty Party supporters moved west on March 3rd under the direction of Dr. John Young, their trip paid for by the US. Numbering 467 people, the group departed from Ross Landing on the steamboat *Knoxville*, pulling flatboats behind them. At Decatur, they transferred to the train down to Tuscumbia, where they boarded the *Newark* for the rest of the voyage by water. Physicians Clark Lillybridge and Samuel Doak traveled with them, and only four people died. Their trip was brief. They switched to the light steamboat *Revenue* on March 21st and reached Fort Smith on March 28th, but almost everyone was sick. Major Ridge, already weak, spent most of the trip in a cabin with his wife. After leaving the boat, they traveled with horses and wagons, looking for a place to settle. The Ridge chose Honey Creek as the place to rebuild his life.

At the end of September 1838 John Ridge and Elias Boudinot left on horseback with their families traveling in carriages while their slaves rode horses or walked. Buffalofish's daughter Nakey and her husband Nitts joined that group along with their five children.[322] They arrived in late November. The Ridge was eager to get to work in the family's new general store, already a success under his father, and build a new home.

By the time Van Buren assumed the Presidency, most Americans accepted the removal policy, having watched tribe after tribe depart their ancestral lands, which were scooped up by white families. Although Ross still held out hope that Van Buren would change US policy, that was quickly dashed when they met on March 16th. Ross plaintively asked the new President: "Will the government of the United States claim the right to enforce a contract thus assailed by the other nominal party to it?"[323] The President demurred, and the brief encounter was over. Secretary of War Poinsett drove in the knife on March 24th writing Ross that the President viewed the New Echota Treaty as "fully constitutional and binding."

Meanwhile, General Wool had issued his infamous "Address to the Cherokee Nation" on March 22nd outlining his advice: "Leave then this country . . . and remove to the country designated for your new homes, which is secured to you and your children forever; and where you may live under your own laws, and the customs of your fathers, without intrusion or molestation from the white man."[324]

General John E. Wool[325]

Wool was relieved of his command in July partly because of his public comments about the "dirty assignment" he'd been given and his comments on white intruders into the Cherokee Nation: "If I could . . . I would remove every Indian tomorrow beyond the reach of the white men, who, like vultures, are watching, ready to pounce upon their prey and strip them of everything they have or expect from the government of the United States. Yes, sir, nineteen-twentieths, if not ninety-nine out of every hundred, will go penniless to the west."[326] Armed with their winning lottery tickets, Georgians continued streaming in to take over Cherokee homes, farms, and ferries. Lust for Cherokee gold continued stoking tensions. There were many riches on their lands. While gold played only a tiny role in their culture, their land was so rich that the US began minting gold coins at Dahlonega on April 17, 1838, just before the remaining Cherokees were rounded up.[327] The gold was stolen along with everything else. Nearby were the communities of Frog Town, Chestatee Old Town, Bread Town, Amicalola, Tensawattee Town, and Big Savannah. Along the Etowah just west of Dahlonega were the farms of Daniel Davis and Silas Palmour, who had married Cherokees. Daniel's wife was Rachel Martin, one of Annie's second cousins.

In early August the final official National Council meeting was held at Red Clay, which had served as the capitol since Georgia turned New Echota into a garrison. More than 4,000 people attended, including Annie's parents, grandparents, and many aunts, uncles, and cousins. Federal troops were watching. Camped out in tents among kin and friends, they sang their favorite hymns loudly and in what some reported as "joyous harmony," but Daniel Butrick captured the sober mood as the singing ended: "Knowing the Cherokees well, I think they would choose death on the spot rather than leave their country. But . . . God has his eye upon all that is passing, and at his own time the Cherokees will be avenged."[328]

Reverend Bushyhead interpreted Reverand Evan Jones' discourse on Sunday (Jones was one of the most important missionaries in the Cherokee Nation and widely loved) and also preached his own sermon in Cherokee. Bushyhead was a large, noble-looking man, the best interpreter in the nation, and was physically agitated as he intoned: "But when to Calvary they turned, sending his Son to die for sinful man . . . ." A few times his emotions stopped him and he faltered for a minute, but then continued. George Featherstonhaugh recorded the scene on August 4th with painterly strokes: "One circumstance particularly struck my attention—the interesting and correct manner in which the music was conducted. Their hymns were all in Cherokee; the music was the common tunes we are accustomed to in our churches, and was performed with far more correctness, as regards time, enunciation and effect, than what is found among the white congregations . . . [differing] from them only in a browner complexion, and in being less vicious and more sober."[329]

Ross asked for the guidance of God and the Great Spirit in the opening prayer. Going Snake, one of the older chiefs who had led a large body of warriors supporting General Jackson against the Creeks, suddenly shouted, "We saved Jackson and his men at the battle of the Horse Shoe . . . nothing has stung more deeply than Jackson turning on us after we served him so well." That evoked thunderous acclaim, which spread like wildfire. White Path, who also was there at age seventy-six, walking well and alert, said: "I agree, Jackson is cursed for all time, just a little weasel whose neck should be wrung, and then wrung again to be sure!" The Council again unanimously rejected the New Echota Treaty, sending Ross back to Washington with a large delegation to try once more to negotiate with Van Buren. At first it seemed he had won a two-year reprieve from the new President, but under political pressure from Jackson, Van Buren reneged. He did agree to pay the annual annuities due under prior treaties without objection, the first time that had occurred in several years, and the total sum was increased a little. Meanwhile, Treaty Party supporters continued their exodus to the west.

Ross spoke at a large gathering on October 8th urging that crops be planted in the winter and spring as usual, but admonished everyone not to fight whites with arms: "I shall not cease my effort to prevail on the United

States government to turn aside from the ruin they would bring upon our native country . . . Have we done any wrong? We are not charged with any. We have a Country which others covet. This is the only offense we have yet been charged with." Some members of the Spirit family decided to leave, including Reverend John Huss and Caty Knightkiller and their families. John had become a supporter of the New Echota Treaty.

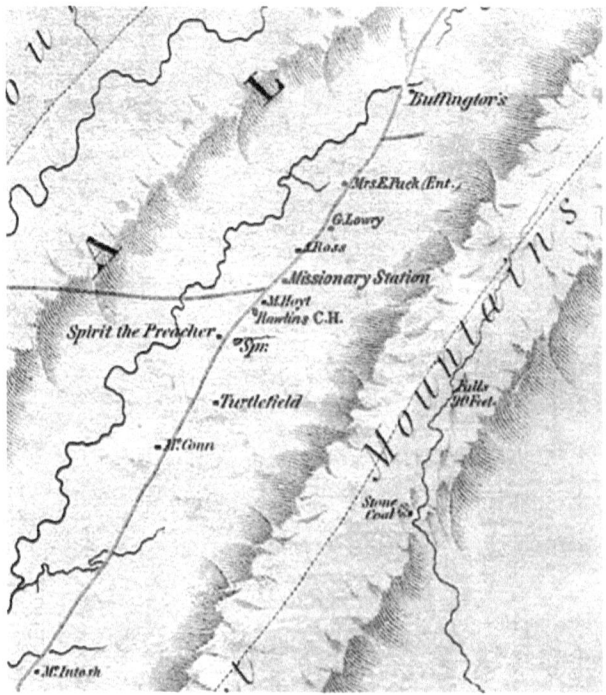

Reverend John Huss's (Spirit the Preacher) home along the Alabama-Georgia Border[330]

Huss and his wife Nancy led a group of seventy-four west on November 11th, including their children; Annie's Aunt Caty and her husband Knightkiller with their boys; Annie's great-uncle David Sconti and his wife Mary Buffington with their children; her great-aunt Betsy with her son with Sequoyah (Big Dollar George Guess) his wife Tianna, and Tessee Guess (another of Sequoyah's sons). Traveling overland, the trip took several months. They had good weather and arrived without a fatality. This is what John and Nancy Huss left behind, with the pitifully small values allotted them by the US agents:[331]

One dwelling house 19x18 feet, two-story, hewed logs, chinked and daubed, lined inside with boards, puncheon floor, board loft, shingled roof, one tight window, two doors cased and faced, good batten shutters, wooden chimney, rock back hearth and jambs	$100
One shed 19x10 feet, one story hewed logs, puncheon floor, board roof nailed on, lined with boards, one door cased & faced, batten shutters, wooden chimney, rock back hearth & jambs	$25
One house 18x16 feet, 1 and ½ story, hewed logs, puncheon floor, board loft, board roof, lined with boards, one board door, shutters, wooden chimney, rock back hearth and jambs	$50
One shed 16x12 feet, one story, skelped logs, puncheon floor, board roof, lined with boards, one door shutters and one window, wooden chimney, rock back hearth and jambs	$25
One smoke house 14x12 feet, skelped logs, board roof, lined with boards, shutters, dirt floor	$18
One hen house 10x8 feet, ½ story, round poles, board roof, dirt floor	$5
Yard enclosure, one acre, good fence	$12
One stable 14x14 feet, one story, round logs, board roof	$25
One stable 20x16 feet, 1 and ½ story, round logs, board roof	$25
One acre horse lot, good fence	$12
One garden, ¼ acre, post and rod fence	$10
39 apple trees, large and bearing, $3 each	$117

60 peach trees, bearing, $1 each	$60
1 and ½ acre field, common fence	$15
4 acre field, upland, common fence	$32
1 and ½ acre field, common fence	$12
4 acre field, good fence and land, $12/acre	$48
3 acres cleared land	$18
540 rails, on fence	$5.40
12 and ½ acre field, old land, ordinary fence, $7/acre	$89.24
6 peach trees, ordinary, old	$3
8 acre field, upland, ordinary fence, $7/acre	$56
11 peach trees, ordinary, old	$5
Total	$861.64

Huss departed as a matter of choice rather than at the point of a gun. In the hindsight of history, Cherokees didn't have a choice once the Senate, Congress and Supreme Court failed to prevent their demise at the hands of federal officials acting in concert with Georgia, Alabama, and Tennesse. No matter when Cherokees moved west, collectively they lost their ancestral homeland. Cherokee preachers, led by Annie's cousin Jesse Bushyhead and missionaries like Evan Jones, stayed in the homeland to give comfort to the thousands who remained. Bushyhead and Jones were particularly important as they preached regularly from 1836 to 1838 in Georgia, Tennessee, and North Carolina in the forty-two communities that were part of their circuit. They traveled this route of about 240 miles spreading the gospel, but perhaps more importantly, fostering optimism to help Cherokees ward off depression.[332] But nothing they did could stop the US government from taking over the Cherokee Nation and forcing them all to move west.

The capitol, New Echota, was fortified in early 1838 after some of its beautiful buildings had been destroyed. By March it had become Fort Wool. Annie's family passed the winter amid the gloom that had settled over everyone. Nonetheless, complying with Ross's request, they planted corn, beans, squash, potatoes, and tomatoes; tied up and thinned raspberry and blackberry canes; and prepared the kitchen gardens. The full Wolf moon that arose on January 10th was particularly luminous that year, seeming to hang over the land like a protective lantern. The last frost was in February, robins and warblers returned early, and the spring was the most beautiful anyone could remember. By late March, wildflowers, laurel, and white hawthorn were in full bloom, with azaleas not far behind. Redbuds and dogwoods were thick with blooms in April, and roses were blooming vibrantly in early May, their aromas suffusing the air. Bees were everywhere, and bats returned ravenous from hibernation with their uncanny navigation skills and zest for pollinating plants. Children played their normal games, reveling in the early warmth. Ball games among the older boys and adults occurred every evening in March and April, and afterwards, there often were dances. Story tellers were in demand. In the lodges *adawehis* retold the old tale of the earth's origin:

> The earth is a great island floating in a sea of water. It is suspended at each of the four cardinal points by a cord hanging down from its sky vault, which is of solid rock. When all was water, the animals were above in galun lati, beyond the arch; but it was very much crowded, and they were wanting some more room. They wondered what was below the water, and at last Dayunisi, "Beaver's Grandchild," the little water beetle, offered to go and see if he could learn. He darted in every direction over the surface of the water, but could find no place to rest. Then he dived to the bottom and came up with some soft mud, which began to grow and spread on every side until it became the island which we call the earth. It was thereafter fastened to the sky with four cords, but no one remembers who did this . . . .The world had been cold until the Thunders, who also lived in galun lati, sent their lightning and put fire into the bottom of a hollow sycamore tree that grew on an island. The animals knew it was there but were prevented from reaching it by the water. Raven tried to remove the fire but his feathers were scorched and turned black. Wa Huhu, the screech owl, got his eyes almost burned out. The eyes of Hooting Owl and Horned Owl became ringed with ashes they couldn't wipe away. Eventually the fire was captured by Water Spider, who from the secretions in her body spun a bowl in which to carry the fire. She brought a coal in the bowl, which she balanced on her back while she swam.[333]

Many important people continued to support the Cherokees' cause. Ralph Waldo Emerson (America's most famous poet and philosher) wrote to the President on April 23rd urging him not to inflict "so vast an outrage upon the Cherokee Nation."[334] He received no reply.

Ralph Waldo Emerson circa 1838

By early May, everyone in the Cherokee Nation was saying it would be the best harvest ever. There was a sense of hope about nature's bounties and a lulled sense of optimism, given that Chief Ross was still negotiating with President Van Buren about removal, despite all the warning signs to the contrary. Shortly before the May removal deadline, Ross was given a petition signed by 15,665 people, almost the entire Cherokee Nation. Elijah Hicks, Situwakee (an important and revered leader), and Chief White Path were tasked with presenting it to the Senate, but Georgia intervened with the President, demanding that it not be considered. The President agreed, and Congress adjourned without seeing the petition. Even then, Ross didn't give up in trying to get a better deal, writing Poinsett at the War Department: "You can expel us by force, we grant; but you cannot make us call it fairness." Poinsett, feeling that Ross wouldn't agree to leave unless he received a better offer, agreed on his own authority to increase the payment for the Cherokee homeland to six million dollars, to be paid directly to the Cherokee Government along with arrears on the annuities.[335] He also accepted Ross's proposal for the Cherokee Council to organize the move at government expense. Poinsett wrote General Scott on May 23rd regarding this change in plan, noting there was no need for a roundup; unfortunately, his letter arrived too late.

Poinsett wrote two additional letters expressing his concerns about the risk of disease in the stockades, stating it would be better to "consult the dictates of humanity as well as prudence" and assemble the Cherokees just a short time before removal but Wool didn't reply.[336] Perhaps he had no choice at that point, faced with hordes of white families pouring in to claim farms, houses, and ferries. The growing military presence was felt like ripples spreading on a pond, provoking deep fear. General Charles Floyd from the Georgia Militia arrived at Fort Wool on May 24th to take command of the Middle Military District. A West Point graduate and seasoned soldier, he maintained strict control of Georgia forces, reporting almost daily to General Winfield Scott in Tennessee. He led the first roundup in Georgia on May 26th and within days thousands had been captured and taken to stockades in New Echota, Fort Means, and Ross's Landing.[337]

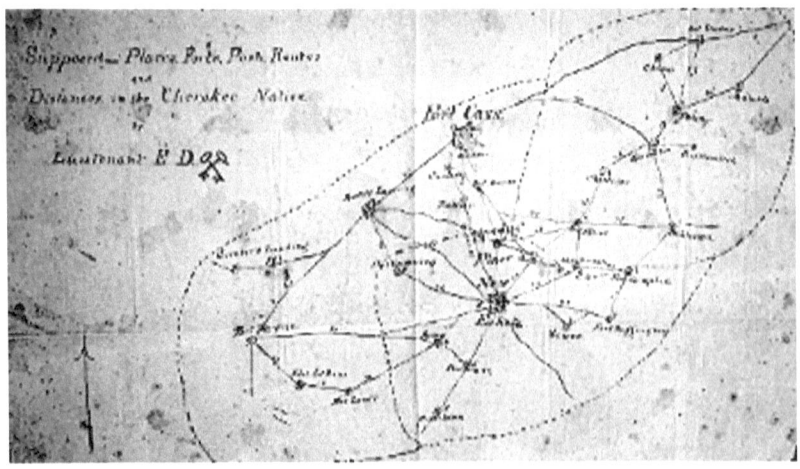

Main Forts and Roads in the Cherokee Nation 1837[338]

Still in Washington to make sure the new agreement would be honored, Ross received a payment of $25,000 for "arrears of annuities, per act 12th June, 1838" along with $7,000 for the delegation's travel expenses the past two years. On the way home, he picked up his daughter Jane from the Moravian School in Salem, North Carolina.[339] Some said Ross was a fool for making those last stands, but his steady hand at the helm of the Nation in those turbulent years and later was crucial for the Cherokees. He was a hero who dedicated his life to serving his people.

Chief John Ross in 1858[340]

15

The Roundup and Exodus

Chief Ross urged Cherokees to ignore the treaty as he remained in Washington trying to convince the government not to force them to leave. But many, including The Spirit, informed federal agents that they were ready to depart on one of the boats as soon as possible.[341] Although he and his brothers had planted their crops, danger was mounting, and the future was clear: Troops were coming to take them away. Agents paid The Spirit a portion of the valuation for the farm and he prepared to move with his wife and their children (Annie, Charles, Watt, Susan Scontie, Lydia Vann, and Annie Vann). A few days later they began loading their possessions onto wagons, leaving their dogs and animals with other family members who weren't ready to depart.

In the spring of 2019, historian Michael Wren sent me a fragment of a muster roll from Lieutenant Deas' April 1838 water detachment. The next to last line lists Annie's father and mother (Spirit and Chow-u-ka) with two males under age ten (Charles and Watt), one male between ten and twenty-five (it is uncertain who this was), one male under fifty (Spirit), three females under twenty-five (Annie Spirit, Annie Vann, and an unknown woman), one female between twenty-five and fifty (Elsie Vann), and one female under fifty (Annie's mother Chi-Wa-Yu-Ga).³⁴² David Knightkiller, one of Annie's first cousins, also was in the group, shown on another fragment and on the transcribed roster (Appendix 10), which is housed at the National Archives in Washington, DC.³⁴³ By moving early, Annie and her family didn't have to survive in a stockade that terrible summer.

This group of 250 Cherokees was marched from Ross's landing to Waterloo, departing from there on April 6th on the steamboat *Smelter*. Deas kept a detailed journal of the trip.³⁴⁴ They got underway about 10 a.m. and ran steadily all day covering one-hundred miles. They reached Paducah, Kentucky by evening the next day and arrived at Little Rock, Arkansas on April 11th where the group had to change to a smaller boat, the *Little Rock*, because of shallow water. Deas rented it with one towed flatboat from Phillip Pennywit for $1,650.³⁴⁵ They ran into a sand bar at Lewiston on the 14th, and everyone was ordered off the boat. They had to walk five miles up the south bank of the Arkansas River, where the lightened boats were waiting. But just two miles further on, another bar blocked their progress. Everyone and their baggage were unloaded, and they camped out for several days. It was raining hard, and as they had no tents, Deas rented a small house for them. They reboarded on the 17th and were able to run another fifty miles until Bolinger's Bar blocked them temporarily. They reached McLean's Bottom on the 20th, where Deas gave up on making further progress on the Arkansas River. He contracted for several wagons, and the group began the final stage of the trip overland on the 24th, arriving at Fort Smith on the 28th and crossing into Cherokee territory. Since they had no tents, Deas bought sufficient cotton for them to construct their own shelters. It was still raining hard.

Annie's parents hoped to make their new start near John Huss and his extended family on Honey Creek in the northeast part of the new Nation. But after arriving, they decided it was too far away and began farming in what became Flint District along the Going Snake border, where Spirit's Aunt Nakey and her husband Nitts settled when they arrived in November 1837. Since they were able to bring essential farming and household tools with them, they quickly built a new home and put in a garden with Nitts's help. They began their new lives there not knowing if they would ever see the rest of the family again.

As Annie's immediate family departed their homeland, 15,000 Cherokees remained in Georgia, Alabama, North Carolina, and Tennessee. General Winfield Scott arrived in Athens, Tennessee with 2,200 soldiers on May 8th. His initial order on May 10th specified the roundup of all Cherokees. Soldiers set out on that task with vigor, working day and night herding everyone at gunpoint into hastily built stockades.

General Winfield Scott by George Catlin[346]

Scott's infamous Order 25 issued on May 17th from the Cherokee Agency in Tennessee provided clarity about his plan to divide the Cherokee Nation into three military districts to facilitate the roundup of everyone.[347] His order included an admonition for soldiers to provide "every possible kindness" but stressed that no one would be allowed to escape: "Corn, oats and fodder, also beef cattle . . . will be taken . . . for the regular consumption of the Army . . . " Certificates were supposed to be filled out with details of grain and animals seized so that "owners may be paid for the same on their arrival at the depots . . . " That didn't happen. Few Cherokees received payments for their crops and livestock. Moreover, the General ordered that all "other moveable or personal property left or abandoned" should be collected and appraised by the Superintendent of Cherokee Emigration for the benefit of the Indian owners." Those orders also were not enforced. Most, if not all, Indians received nothing.[348] Reverend Stephen Foreman outlined his reasons for ignoring the authorities on May 31st: "My determination and the determination of a large majority of the Cherokees yet in the Nation is never to recognize this fraudulent instrument as a treaty nor remove under it until we are forced to do so at the point of the bayonet . . . "[349]

Fear spread rapidly as thirty-one stockades were quickly built in Tennessee, Alabama, North Carolina, and Georgia. Cherokees despaired at being prisoners in their own land, but they had no weapons to speak of nor any inclination to fight. In the end, they were powerless against the armed forces of the US, Georgia, Tennessee, Alabama, and North Carolina. The roundup in Georgia took place quickly and was essentially finished by mid-June. People were surprised in their homes by soldiers wielding rifles with sharp bayonets and revolvers. If children were out playing, or men were working in the fields, too bad, families were summarily separated. Evan Jones, who worked in the Valley Town district of North Carolina during the roundup, described his sorrow at seeing people "allowed no time to take anything with them, except the clothes they had on. Well-furnished houses were left a prey to plunderers who, like hungry wolves, follow in the train of the captors. These wretches rifle the houses, strip the helpless unoffending owners of all they have on earth."[350]

Etching of Reverend Evan Jones[351]

When their turns came, Annie's grandparents, aunts, and uncles no doubt were stoic. Her uncle Oo-cha-leh-neh, his wife A-toh-hee Cornsilk, and their family experienced the roundup like so many others, forced to leave wearing what they had on, not allowed to bring their dogs or horses. No doubt the soldiers surveyed their beautiful farm with envy, deeming it better than theirs or what they could aspire to. They were held at first in the newly constructed Fort Means near the Cass County-Floyd County line.[352] Soon, more than 500 Cherokees were there. They were moved to New Echota around June 1st, which had been turned into a large armed camp; shortly afterwards, they were marched to the Mouse Creek stockade near the Cherokee Agency.

The stockades were terrible, almost beyond comprehension. Built with split logs more than eight feet tall and sharpened to points at the top, most were 200 feet wide by 500 feet long. Life inside was harsh. There was no privacy. Most slept on the ground. For the most part, there was no roof, and whatever rough roofing materials were available were used to construct primitive protection from the rain and sun. Daily food rations consisted of flour and salt pork, often close to spoiled, a huge contrast to their normal diet of fish, meat, vegetables, nuts, and fruit. There was no way to be clean, as the early summer rains turned the earth to mud, and when the heat set in, dust was everywhere. They languished there in the hot and muggy summer weather. Eyewitnesses describe the appalling reality: "The medical aid was hopelessly, even criminally, inadequate and incompetent . . . No provision was made for sanitation and the camps were soon filthy and swarming with vermin. Fever and dysentery were rampant and infant mortality during the summer months was appalling . . . "[353] Reverend Daniel Butrick described how "in two or three days about 8000 people, many of whom were in good circumstances . . . were rendered homeless, houseless and penniless . . . .In driving them, a platoon of soldiers walked before and behind . . . armed with all the common appalling instruments of death; while the soldiers . . . would often use the same language as if driving hogs, and goad them forward with bayonets."[354]

General Floyd reported to General Scott on June 15th that no more Cherokees were free in Georgia.[355] During the preceding weeks, while soldiers scoured Cherokee country looking for fugitives, special agents were seizing their belongings to sell to white Georgians. James Hemphill and Joseph Watters oversaw this work in Floyd County, stripping homes and fields of tools, livestock, baskets, crockery, churns, fiddles, books, beds, and canoes. Beginning on May 30th it took them twenty-one days to pillage all the Indian homes in Floyd County. Their valuations were fairly detailed, providing another small window into the richness of Cherokee lives. (A fragment of their valuation book for that area survives and is Appendix 8.[356]) Buffalofish's belongings were valued at $107.68.[357] Buffalofish's daughter So-Wa-Chee and her husband Sawney Vann lived nearby; their personal possessions were valued at $187.25.

Cherokee leaders at the Fort Cass Aquohee camp petitioned General Scott on June 17th to stop the emigration during the summer: "We have been made prisoners by your men, but we do not fight against you . . . We are Indians . . . we have hearts that feel . . . we ask that you will not send us down the river at this time of year. If you do we shall die . . . "[355] That summer was the most oppressive in living memory and illness was high in the stockades, with whooping cough, dysentery, and cholera rampant. There's no way to know how many died in the stockades as no one was keeping track, but Daniel Butrick estimated that more than 2,000 people perished. Dr. J. W. Lide, who was contracted to work in the stockade camps, reported "a high grade of diarrhea, hazardous dysentery, and urgent remittent fever . . . Measles and whooping cough appeared epidemically among the Cherokees about the first of June."[358]

Some Cherokees escaped the dragnet. Each case depended to a large degree on the terrain, both physical and legal. It was harder for Scott's military to find small groups in the higher Appalachian Mountains, which enabled some to escape to North Carolina. A few Cherokee families in Georgia managed to remain on their lands and were rewarded on December 29, 1838 when the legislature granted them full citizenship.[359] Twenty-two families are mentioned specifically in the legislation, including twelve in the Cordery family and several members of the Waters and Rogers families who lived along the southeastern boundary of the Cherokee Nation next to the upper Chattahoochee River. But their right to remain in Georgia came at a price, as most had to re-purchase their farms, houses, and ferries from lottery winners.[360]

The US military was more concerned with how many they rounded up rather than those who died or were killed. One terrible incident involved Euchela, a local Cherokee leader who resisted along with a band of 100 followers in North Carolina, and Tsali, an old man captured with his wife, brother, and three sons. When Tsali's wife was prodded with a bayonet, he killed the soldier in anger, escaping with his family. Colonel W. H. Thomas tracked down Euchela and his warriors, promising that if they surrendered Tsali, they would be permitted to remain and be at peace. Euchela replied, "I cannot be at peace because it is now a whole year that your soldiers have hunted me like a wild deer. I have suffered more than I can bear. I had a wife and a little child, a bright-eyed boy and because I would not become your slave they were left to starve up on the mountains and I buried them with my own hands at midnight."[361] Tsali accepted his fate, turning himself in along with his brother and two sons. They were court-martialed and sentenced to be shot. Bound to a tree before being killed, Tsali calmly made his last statement: "I am not afraid to die, oh no, I want to die, for my heart is very heavy . . . But Euchela, there is one favor I wish to ask at your hands.

You know I have a little boy who was lost among the mountains. I want you to find that boy if he is not dead and tell him that the last words of his father were that he must never go beyond the Father of Waters, but die in the land of his birth. It is sweet to die in one's native land and be buried by the margin of one's native streams."[362] Tsali's youngest son Wasituna was found and pardoned, allowing him to remain in North Carolina, thus fulfilling his father's wish.

Some areas in North Carolina and Tennessee were transferred legally to Cherokee individuals through treaties signed from 1818 to 1828, usually parcels of 640 acres, and a few of those also escaped the Trail of Tears. But one can't generalize from those cases—most people lost everything in the end, whatever promises were made. It's impossible to overstate the waves of anguish they experienced at being forced off their ancestral lands and leaving everything they had created—the Supreme Court, legislature, public schools, farms, houses, barns, ferries, and boats. To be prisoners in their own land was torture. But the worst was yet to come as the remaining Cherokees were driven across the country during the ensuing months. Many more would die on the Trail of Tears.

16

Cherokee Genocide

The eminent Japanese-American historian Ronald Takaki described President Jackson as the nation's "confidence man" who developed "a metaphysics for genocide."[363] Some have used the word "holocaust" to describe Cherokee removal (Tlo Va Sa), but that should be reserved for happened under the Nazis in World War II. As Gail King noted in 2009, removal was "certainly a Holocaust-like event, and similarities to the Nazi-executed Holocaust are instructive, especially because they reveal patterns of intentionality—personal or organizational and . . . historical denial that such events ever took place . . . "[364]

After Chief Ross negotiated with General Scott to organize the remaining trips without any military involvement, planning began in earnest. Thirteen trips were organized by the Cherokee Council, paid for with government funds provided under Article 9 of the New Echota Treaty. Most took land routes later in the year, using commercial ferries to cross rivers. Though longer than the water route, they were initially thought to be safer. Divided into groups of about one thousand people. George Hicks and others assembled the wagons, horses, oxen, and supplies needed for their move west. But four detachments went by boat in June and July under government supervision.

Deas' second water detachment departed from Ross's landing on June 6th on the steamboat *George Guess* with prisoners from a stockade four miles away, including several members of Annie's extended family.[365] At Decatur, Alabama they disembarked and boarded a train on the Tuscumbia, Courtland and Decatur Railroad, traveling sixty-six miles to Tuscumbia Landing in order to avoid the dreaded Muscle Shoals. Built in 1833, the Decatur was the first railroad west of the Appalachian Mountains and the first train most Cherokees had ever seen. At Tuscumbia, Deas transferred the Cherokees to the steamboat *Smelter*, continuing along the Tennessee, Ohio, and Mississippi Rivers before turning north up the Arkansas River to Indian Territory. Arriving at Fort Coffee on the 19th, it was one of the most successful trips as no one died. Deas reported that the trip began with around 600 people, although the muster roll wasn't written until later. He arrived with 429 people. His journal succinctly describes the trip, including that at least 100 people deserted. Rations consisted mainly of flour corn meal and bacon as the beef purchased went bad in the warm weather. When they arrived at Fort Coffee on June 20th, the Indians began taking all their belongings to shore and the trip ended there. There were no deaths recorded.[366] History doesn't record where they went after getting off the boat, but like Deas' April detachment, they were left without supplies and had to depend on help from the Old Settlers. Deas again provided them material for tents "in consideration of their destitute condition."[367]

A second group of 846 people, including several of Annie's extended family, was forced onto boats on June 12th in the middle of the scorching summer. When they got to the Arkansas River, low water forced them to stop 100 miles from their destination. Without proper provisions and in searing heat, they traveled the final leg overland, arriving on August 5th. Seventy-three people died on that journey. A third contingent of 1,070 people left Ross Landing on June 17th, including several of Annie's family members, but low water forced them to go overland to Waterloo, Alabama where they took boats to the same place where the second group went aground. They had to make an unplanned and arduous trip overland, arriving at Ft. Coffee on September 7, 1838 having lost 146 people.

Annie's Uncle Poor Bear with his family of six, her Aunt Nelly Buffalofish with her two children, and her half-brother Weely Vann and his young son were on the July 10th detachment led by Captain G.S. Drane, departing from Waterloo on the Steamboat *Smelter*. The Drane muster roll was partially transcribed and is in Appendix 11.[368] It was an arduous trip with an estimated 289 desertions and at least 141 deaths, described in Drane's October 17th report to General Scott.[369] They had to abandon the boats on August 13th and travel overland until arriving on September 4th at a dispersal depot known as Mrs. Webber's plantation because it was owned by Akie Webber.[370] Today it is the site of the Stilwell, Oklahoma Cemetery.[371]

After those disasters, General Scott allowed Ross to supervise the remaining removals later in the year. A contract with US officials was agreed upon to cover the expenses for transport and provisions based on Ross's request of $65.88 per person. He was welcomed by hundreds of people on July 13th when he returned home. He immediately sent runners around the nation to inform everyone that the Cherokees must move. His brother Lewis was put in charge of this enormous task on July 21st at the Council meeting held at Red Clay.[372] The remaining Cherokees languished in stockades for the brutal summer months until the overland trips began in late summer:[373]

The Council published a Resolution of defiance on August 1st noting the Cherokee people's title "to their lands is the most ancient, pure, and absolute, known to man." Since the people's "free consent" had not been given, "the original title and ownership of said lands still rest in the Cherokee Nation, unimpaired and absolute . . . ". The Resolution declared that their "inherent sovereignty . . . together with the constitution, laws, and usages . . . [remain] in full force . . . and shall continue so to be in perpetuity . . . ."[374]

The 13 Contingents leaving under their own supervision:		
DETACHMENT	DEPARTED	ARRIVED
Hair Conrad	Aug 23, 1838	Jan 17, 1839
Elijah Hicks	Sep 1, 1838	Jan 4, 1839
Jesse Bushyhead	Sep 3, 1838	Feb 27, 1839
John Benge	Sep 28, 1838	Jan 17, 1839
Situwaki	Sep 7, 1838	Feb 2, 1839
Old Field	Sep 24, 1838	Feb 23, 1839
Moses Daniel	Sep 30, 1838	Mar 2, 1839
Tsuwaluka	Sep 14, 1838	Mar , 1839
James Brown	Sep 10, 1838	Mar 5, 1839
George Hicks	Sep 7, 1838	Mar 14, 1839
Richard Taylor	Sep 20, 1838	Mar 24, 1839
Peter Hildebrand	Oct 23, 1838	Mar 24, 1839
John Drew	Dec 5, 1838	Mar 18, 1839

Scott re-started the "emigration" process, as he'd taken to calling it, in late August. The last service held at the Brainerd Mission on August 18th was led by Evan Jones and Jesse Bushyhead. Brainerd was very important to the Cherokee Nation.

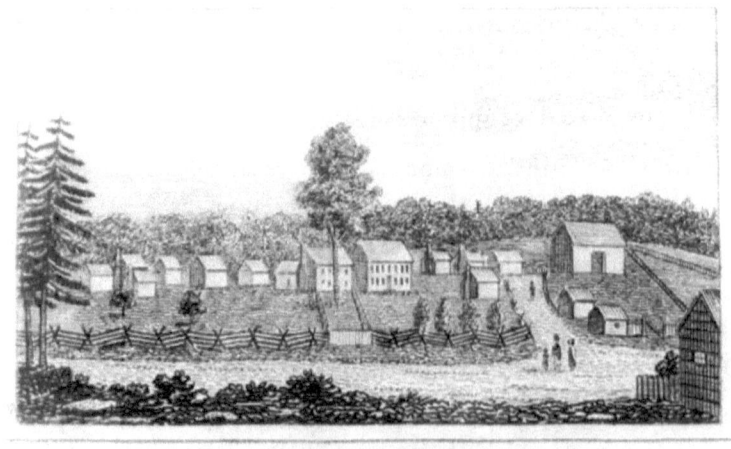

Engraving of Brainerd Community 1838[375]

Ross ensured that each group had physicians, interpreters, commissaries, wagonmasters, teamsters, and grave diggers. Hundreds of wagons with their teams pulled into position along the Hiwassee River near Charleston, Tennessee. Ross climbed onto a wagon and said a prayer asking for God's guidance, to a chorus of "Amen, Amen." Many wagons were small and too light for the conditions ahead. It's hard to imagine traveling in rough country over 1,000 miles in a Zuraw wagon just nine and a half feet long, lightly built and with primitive suspension. Its design dates to the late 1700s.[376]

One of Buffalofish's sons who was a teamster on George Hicks' September 7th detachment was paid $151.66 for his service.[377] That muster roll shows a Spirit and ten family members, including two males older than ten, five males younger than ten, two females older than ten, and two children younger than ten. A copy is in Appendix 12.[378] Buffalofish and Wo-de-yo-he were on one of the land detachments, but without complete rosters, it is impossible to know which one. Reverend Charles Walker drew this illustration in the 1970s based on his extensive research, listing them and several members of their family.[379]

Illustration by Charles O. Walker

Last Cherokee wagon leaving homeland.

Stitch: 10 fullbloods. One farmer. Four spinners.
Sucking: Two fullbloods. One farmer.
Robin: Two fullbloods. One farmer. One weaver and one spinner.
TAH TA LEE: Six fullbloods. One farmer. One weaver and one spinner.
Peggy: Four fullbloods. One weaver and one spinner. No farm nor farmer.
Cant Do It: 16 fullbloods. A farmer. One weaver and two spinners.
George: Five fullbloods. A farmer. One weaver and one spinner.
CHU QUA TA TA KEE: Nine fullbloods. Two farmers. One weaver and one spinner.
Eagle on the Roost: Seven fullbloods. One farmer. One reader of Cherokee. One weaver and one spinner.
Buffalo Fish: 10 fullbloods. Three slaves. Two farmers. Two readers of Cherokee. Three weavers and two spinners.
Water Hunter: Three fullbloods. One slave. One farmer. One mechanic. One reader of Cherokee. One weaver. One spinner.
Crying Snake: Four fullbloods and one -?-. One farmer. One weaver and one spinner.
Sawnee Vann: Seven fullbloods and one quarterblood. Two slaves. One farmer. One weaver and one spinner.
Jacob West: One halfbreed and five quarterbloods. One white intermarriage. Owned 13 slaves. Two farmers. Two mechanics. Seven readers of English. One weaver and one spinner.
Foggs: Seven fullbloods. No farm. A farmer. One reader of Cherokee. Four spinners.

As the first land detachments prepared to depart, Chief Hicks offered these words of hope: "We are now about to take our final leave and kind farewell to our native land, the country that the Great Spirit gave our Fathers . . . .it is with sorrow that we are forced by the authority of the white man to quit the scenes of our childhood . . . we bid farewell to it and all we hold dear . . . .we know that it is a laborious undertaking, but with firm resolution we think we will be able to accomplish it, if the white citizens will permit us."[380]

When the first group led by Hair Conrad started off, the day was clear. William Shorey Coodey described what happened next to John Howard Payne, a famous actor and playwright who was one of Ross's closest friends : "Going Snake, an aged and respected chief . . . mounted on his favorite pony passed before me . . . At this very moment, a low sound of distant thunder fell on my ear — in almost an exact western direction a dark spiral cloud was rising above the horizon and sent forth a murmur I almost thought a voice of divine indignation . . . The sun was unclouded—no rain fell— the thunder rolled away and seemed hushed in the distance."[381] Almost as quickly as it arrived, the cloud disappeared and the sky was once again clear: an omen, many said, portending great misfortune. The omen was correct. It would be a travail of epic misery and death, which Cherokees called "Nuna-Dat-Sun'Yi" or "The Trail Where They Cried." Conrad's detachment halted after just eighteen miles because of lack of water. The second detachment led by Elijah Hicks left on September 1st with White Path as assistant conductor. Instead of heading a party of his close friends and neighbors, Jesse Bushyhead volunteered to conduct people from a distant part of the nation in the North Carolina mountains who had no leader. His detachment left on September 3rd, Situawake departed early on September 7th, and later that day, a party of 1,118 started off with fifty-six wagons and 560 horses, led by George Hicks with Collins McDonald as assistant conductor. Their first major obstacle was the Tennessee River crossing at Blythe's Ferry just below the mouth of the Hiwassee River, where the detachments headed northwest to McMinnville, Murfreesboro, and Nashville.[382]

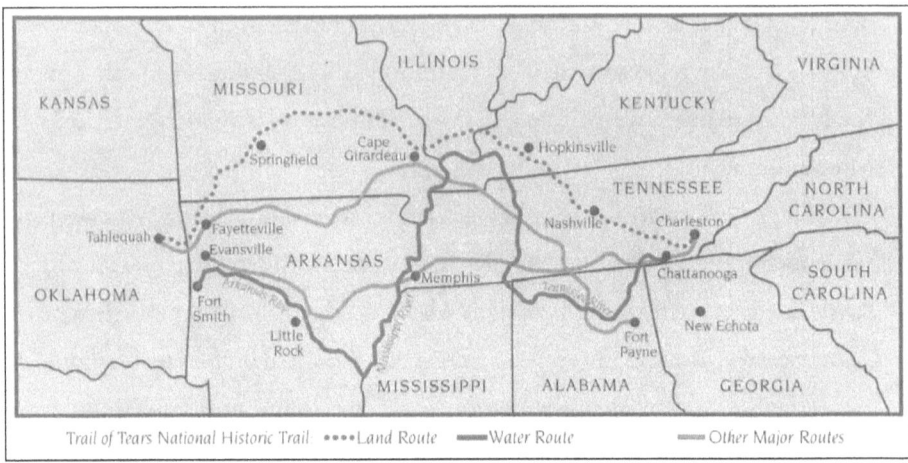

Main Routes of the Detachments[383]

Chief Ross, his family and other relatives and friends departed in mid-November, quickly catching up with the Hildebrand detachment. Rations purchased by Lewis Ross were waiting in Nashville—corn, oats and fodder, as well as thick boots, heavy socks, blankets, bearskins, cloaks, and overcoats that would be welcome later. They crossed the Cumberland River over a covered bridge and continued west. The drought was even worse now, and it was difficult to find sufficient water for their animals. Progress was slow; many were severely ill with dysentery, measles, whooping cough, and fevers from being locked up in the stockades so long without clean water.

Essentially, the detachments were villages on wheels, and as the journey progressed, patterns of daily life formed. The hunters were the first to leave each morning, armed with bows and arrows and blowguns, of which there were several types. The long blowgun was extremely effective in killing birds and squirrels. They usually hunted most of the day, joining the camp at night with what they had caught, sometimes a brace of turkeys or a deer. In the evenings, the detachments were often visited by missionaries and tradesmen bringing supplies. But sometimes, white people who were just curious would also come by to stare, as though Cherokees were forest animals. Sometimes commissary wagons with supplies were waiting when they reached the next camping spot. Occasionally, a mill nearby would grind their corn. but mainly their trusty mortars and pestles were used. Families tended to group themselves in informal lodges, the wagons pulled into a rough circle for the night. Men on horses would drag dry wood to each area, and fires would be started to prepare evening meals. It became a routine. Children often played games, usually stickball or 'chunky' where spears are thrown at moving targets. Some families were able to keep their dogs. Along the way, some Cherokees escaped. Lawlo, a Nottely headman, led a group of twenty people back to North Carolina, Cheesquaneetah took his family back to Georgia, and Junaluska guided fifty people to their homes in North Carolina.[384]

A Typical Detachment[385]

In December, President Van Buren cavalierly wrote Congress that everything had gone perfectly: "It affords me sincere pleasure to be able to apprise you of the entire removal of the Cherokee Nation of Indians to their new homes west of the Mississippi. The measures authorized by Congress . . . have had the happiest effects, and they have emigrated without any apparent reluctance . . . ."[386] His view was countered by many people and publications around the country, including this editorial in the Washington *National Intelligencer*: "Before we can claim for our Government the credit for having dealt 'justly' with Indians throughout, we must sponge from the tablet of memory . . . the refusal to fulfill our treaty stipulations with the Cherokees for ten years, and the final enforcement of a treaty to which they never assented . . . ."[387]

After harsh droughts early in the removal, dense rains began in the late autumn, and all the detachments experienced one of the coldest, most miserable winters of the century. As the weeks and months slid by, food was running short but attempts to buy more were routinely rebuffed, and when successful, they had to pay exorbitant prices. Toll roads charged absurd amounts for each wagon and horse. As Jesse Bushyhead aptly put it: "They fleeced us!"[388] Prices for provisions were doubled or tripled; the prices of ferry crossings were inflated: "Opportunists followed, like vultures picking at a corpse, presenting false claims by which to deprive the travelers of their horses or oxen, their wagons, even silver if they carried any."[389] A Cherokee boy named Samuel Cloud described his experience as a nine-year old, walking past white towns in the middle of winter, with people just staring at him and his family: "I hate the white people who lined the roads in their woolen clothes that kept them warm, watching us pass . . . None of them care about me or my people."[390]

Hick's detachment stopped for a few days in early December at Gray's Inn, just across the Kentucky state line in Guthrie, Todd County. It was a mirage of refuge, but at least there was warmth and good food, and most detachments lingered there.[391] Proceeding to Hopkinsville, they saw a tent over White Path's and Fly Smith's graves along the banks of the Little River.

Hicks heard from his brother Elijah that White Path had "been in the last stages of sickness for many days and has to be hauled and is helpless, who cannot last but a few days" when his party was near there earlier."[392] His name means "I dwell on the peaceful path—the white path." Born in 1761 near Ellijay, he was a wonderful speaker. Influenced by the teachings of Seneca prophet Handsome Lake, he rebeled against Christianity, wanting Cherokees to return to the old tribal laws. He helped the mountain Cherokees who lived around Ellijay fend off the intrusions of white Georgians. His death was a great loss just when they needed him most. This quote of White Path's sticks with me: "I will draw thorns from your feet. We will walk the White Path of Life together. Like a brother of my own blood, I will love you. I will wipe tears from your eyes. When you are sad, I will put your aching heart to rest." [393]

The Hicks detachment continued west, with people suffering grievously. No records exist showing how many people in the family died along the way, but a traveler from Maine who was in southern Kentucky late in the year wrote, "Even aged females, apparently nearly ready to drop into the grave, were traveling with heavy burdens . . . with no covering for the feet except what nature had given them . . . .We learned from the inhabitants on the road . . . that they buried fourteen or fifteen at every stopping place . . . "[394] Hicks learned that thousands of people were trapped ahead in Illinois waiting for ice flows on the Ohio and Mississippi Rivers to melt. Soon they had caught up, in the end waiting for two weeks for a ferry across the Ohio River to Golcanda, Illinois during the incessant blizzards. Daniel Butrick wrote in his journal that twenty-six people in his detachment had died since departure.[395] Around 3,000 Cherokees were trapped by the weather in terrible conditions, without adequate shelter, food, or fuel. Death stalked them daily. A tiny ray of light shined the day they heard that Reverend Jesse Bushyhead's wife Eliza had given birth to a girl on January 3rd after crossing the river into Missouri. Named Eliza Missouri Bushyhead, she was one of Annie's cousins, who shared her passion for education. In a few places, local people gave Cherokees food and clothes, but mostly they continued to be treated like animals in a zoo, with people just wanting a glimpse of the savages.

One aged Cherokee who fought with General Jackson during the Creek wars arrived in a little village in Kentucky and was approached by an old man who recognized him. "[W]ith a down-cast look and heavy sigh," the Cherokee said, "Ah! My life and the lives of my people were then at stake for you and your country. I then thought Jackson my best friend. But, ah! Jackson no serve me right. Your country no do me justice now . . . ."[396]

Although the initial plan had been to travel between ten and fifteen miles a day, that depended on the weather and condition of the roads, which were problematic to say the least. Once the drought broke, there was some relief, but only briefly as rain poured down for days. There was no shelter other than the wagons, and there were far too few of those. Some days, they just hunkered down waiting for a break in the weather. More people began to die, especially the old and very young. The snow and sleet started early that year, the cold beyond anything Cherokees had ever experienced.

Winter on the Trail of Tears[397]

When the ferry finally began service again, Cherokees had to pay eight times the normal fare. The trip across the Ohio River to Golcanda was wild and dangerous, with ice floes floating freely and animals crazed with fear. Afterwards, there was a brief respite as they moved through Jonesboro towards the Mississippi River, where they boarded a boat at Green's Ferry in Southern Illinois to cross over to Cape Girardeau, Missouri. As usual, they had to pay more than whites for the privilege. There were few good Samaritans.

Chief Ross's family continued traveling with the Hildebrand detachment as far as the banks of the Ohio River. Quatie was sick from the beginning of the trip; when she began to fail, Ross hired the small riverboat *Victoria* to carry his family the rest of the way. They arrived at Little Rock on February 1, 1839. She died that night and was buried there.

Money and supplies were running out as the detachments headed southwest towards Fayetteville. Many arrived at the Woodall Farm, one of five depots: Jesse Bushyhead (February 27th), Choowalooka (March 1st), Moses Daniel (March 2nd), James Brown (March 5th), Richard Taylor (March 24th), and Peter Hildebrand's (March 25th). Hicks' detachment arrived at Beattie's Prairie, southwest of Maysville, Arkansas. It was a welcoming place.[398] Around 1835, the James and Franklin Thompson families settled there near a spring along Hog Eye Creek, establishing large farms, a blacksmith shop and a store. Jim Thompson was married to Mary Patsy Lynch, another of Buffalo Fish's cousins. Martha's mother, Nannie Martin, was a daughter of Susannah Emory and John Martin.[399] They were a generous family, working hard to welcome new arrivals.[400] Annie's family probably were reunited with Buffalofish, Wode-yo-he, Crying Snake, Alexander, and Eagle-on-the-Roost in April 1839. Despite every cruelty they'd suffered, they had their freedom once again. As did Annie's little brother Watt, thousands died during removal. But no soldiers were guarding the Cherokees any longer, and they had a new home. Still, a deep sadness lay over everyone as they struggled to start new lives.

Supplies and basic materials for rebuilding were a major problem. Army Captain Collins signed a contract with Glasgow and Harrison on January 15th to supply emigrants with subsistence rations for the next year. The General Depot was at Mrs. Webber's in Stillwell. By early April, however, the promised rations were mostly just a mirage, and much of what was available was spoiled. It was nothing like the Cherokees' regular diet. Chief Ross wrote Cherokee Agent Montfort Stokes on April 5th about the poor rations but received no reply. He filed a detailed complaint with the area army commander, Brigadier General Matthew Arbuckle, requesting that Cherokees be allowed to take over their own subsistence as they had their removal. Arbuckle merely sent Ross's letters to William Armstrong, Indian superintendent for the western territory, who forwarded them to Washington, where they gathered dust. The rations remained beyond despicable. Most of the materials promised for rebuilding and farming hadn't been delivered, and many people had lost all their tools and farm implements along the way. The money they were to receive under the terms of the New Echota Treaty hadn't been transferred. It was a tough beginning.

If the Treaty of New Echota hadn't been signed by the small group in the Treaty Party in 1835, would Jackson have been able to dissolve the Cherokee Nation and drive them off their ancestral homeland? The answer is that raw power was all that mattered. Jackson would have found a way to get rid of all the Indians in the east no matter what. He didn't care what the Supreme Court said and brushed aside all the fine words of Sam Houston, Emerson, and the other luminaries who tried to give Cherokees solace. You can't push the river when the flow is powerfully against you. In 1835, at the Running Waters meeting, Annie's father and grandfather had agreed to support giving up their homes and moving even though all the Keetoowah voted no—a unanimous gesture of defiance to the Treaty Party. The fact that John Huss supported moving, and that Annie's grandfather Spirit and his wife had moved to Arkansas in 1819 as part of the Old Settlers group, were powerful forces. If Cherokees had remained fully united, it might have turned out differently, but I doubt it.

The Cherokee people shared a deep history as they tried to rebuild in a new land in the west, but they were still deeply divided as well. They would face many pitfalls and setbacks in the years ahead, but they came through it with heads high and spirits strong, their collective resilience more powerful than any obstacle.

17

Rebuilding

A few weeks after they arrived, Cherokee families were becoming more comfortable despite what they'd been through. Annie's family were among the luckiest, arriving in time to plant a garden and build a simple home. Most of their extended family weren't so fortunate, but whenever and wherever they arrived, provisions steadily improved through the help of the missionaries and families such as the James and Franklin Thompsons on Beattie's Prairie. Like everyone else, they had to decide where to live, without much information on which to base a decision. At their reunion in April 1839, Annie's parents urged everyone to join them in Flint District, hoping to recreate their family's prior life along the Etowah. But Buffalofish; his wife Wo-de-yo-he; and their sons Alexander, Crying Snake, and Eagle-on-the-Roost went their own ways. Buffalofish and Crying Snake headed south to a wild area along the Flint and Skin Bayou District line. Alexander and Eagle-on-the-Roost decided to try Going Snake District along its border with Flint. Records from the 1840s show them located in those areas.

Annie was growing up quickly, helping take care of her sister Susan and little brother Charles while her parents, her half-brother Weely Vann, and her half-sisters Annie and Elsie Vann concentrated on building houses and clearing land for their gardens, orchards, and crops. It was essential to plant quickly. Despite the hardships of their trips and the pain of losing family and friends, Cherokees were becoming more sanguine about the future. To improve morale, they sang "Guide Me O, Thou Great Jehovah" and "Amazing Grace" as translated into Cherokee by Samuel Worcester.

Amazing Grace

Oo nay tla na, he you way gee	ᎤᏁᎳ, ᎠᏓᏅᏧ
Ee ga goo yaw hay yee.	ᏥᎪᎯᎥ.
Na gwoo Jo saw, we you low say	ᎠᎩᎩᎤ, ᎤᎬᎦ
Ee ga goo yaw ho nu	ᏥᎪᎯᎦ

Most Cherokees arrived with few supplies or tools. Without proper storage facilities, their food often spoiled, but there was little choice; to survive, they had to eat the rotten meat and bug-infested flour provided by the United States. Initially sleeping in tents, they quickly built simple log homes, barns, and smokehouses while clearing land for crops. Although deeply shocked at what they'd been through, people recovered quickly, resiliently building homes and farms on virgin land. But their old local knowledge, once intuitive, was relatively useless. All sorts of practical effects flowed from not knowing enough about the weather, insects, plants, and wildlife and their habits. At summer's peak, it was muggy and oppressively hot, while during the depths of winter, there were snow and ice storms with a ferocity beyond anything they'd ever seen. But some of the land reminded them of home, especially the hard-wood forests, streams, rivers, and hilly land. Annie's curiosity and love of nature helped immerse her in the new homeland, and she became known for her knowledge of plants and trees.

Almost everyone was stymied by continuing US intransigence about compensation payments and supplies. The annuities due under the New

Echota Treaty and earlier agreements were not being paid. Cherokees would end up fighting with the US government for many years about those payments. White suppliers wanted sky-high prices for meat, grain, and corn when they were willing to sell, and often they were not. Happily, within a year, they began producing enough food to take care of basic needs.

The Old Settlers and those who were removed held a conclave on June 3rd in Takatokah (Double Springs), a few miles northwest of Tahlequah, which attracted more than 6,000 people. Chief Ross started off by calling for a peaceful union, citing the Bible's precept that "a house divided against each other cannot stand."[401] But the reality was that Cherokees remained badly split. The Old Settlers balked when Ross proposed new laws applying to everyone. The meeting broke up in disarray on June 20th. Sequoyah proved to be a crucial unifying force, joining Reverend Jesse Bushyhead in suggesting that a second conclave be held on July 1st.[402] But even his leadership couldn't contain the anger that many had against the Ridges, Boudinot, Stand Watie, John Bell, James Starr, and George Adair, leaders of the Treaty Party.

All seven were found guilty of treason for illegally selling the Nation's lands in the New Echota Treaty. Following up on the conviction, 300 men met at Double-Head Springs on June 20th to plan their assassinations.[403] According to custom, three men from the clan of each defendant put their numbers in a hat. Twelve had an X mark to indicate the designated executioners.

Elias Boudinot, Major Ridge, and his son John were executed in cold blood on June 22nd.

In the still western darkness, the executioners mounted their horses. The occasional cry of a whippoorwill and the beat of hooves broke the heavy silence. When the sun rose red and low in a June morning mist, the murder party reached John Ridge's house and surrounded it. Three of the men forced the lock of the front door and crept inside . . . They were interested in only one sleeper. When they found him, they swiftly fired a pistol at his head. The pistol failed to discharge . . . .is captors dragged him into the yard; two men held his arms and others held his body. The murderers stabbed him until blood poured from twenty-five wounds."[404]

Reverend Worcester alerted Stand Watie to his brother's death, and he was able to escape, using the missionary's horse for a quick getaway. Later, standing over Elias Boudinot's mutilated body, he offered a $10,000 reward for the names of the men "who made that mark on my brother's head."[405] He hated John Ross the rest of his life. But it was widely acknowledged that something would have to happen to the Echota Treaty signers. As John Ridge himself had written presciently, "You say John Ridge was prompted by a selfish ambition when he signed the treaty. It is not so. John Ridge signed his death warrant when he signed that treaty, and no one knows it better than he . . . Let it not be said that John Ridge acted from motives of ambition, for he acted for what he believed to be in the best interests of his people."[406]

This turn to blood vengeance was shocking. Yes, Treaty Party leaders had violated a sacred rule not to sell Cherokee land without tribal approval. True, the Ridges and Boudinots benefitted personally from the deal with their valuations boosted, their property protected by Georgia authorities until they emigrated, and all their expenses reimbursed. But assassination wasn't the right response. Without those, it is doubtful there would have been what amounted to an internal war.

Chief Ross and Sequoyah called for the second conclave to take place as planned on July 1st. In an effort to convince more Old Settlers and western chiefs to participate, Sequoyah sent a message urging everyone to gather to "talk matters over like friends and brothers . . . we have no doubt but we can have all things amicably and satisfactorily settled."[407] Sequoyah succeeded in convincing Chief John Looney to come, but several other important chiefs refused. Still, around 2,000 people were there. Ross began by encouraging all Cherokees to rekindle their social fire: "We are all a part of the household of the Cherokee family and of one blood." Ross granted pardons to the men who murdered Boudinot and the Ridges. After eleven days of discussion, the Old Settlers, Treaty Party, and Ross's National Party agreed to form one political body called simply "Cherokee." With Sequoyah serving as Western President and George Lowrey as President of the Eastern Cherokees, an Act of Union written by William Shorey Coodey was signed on July 12, 1839:[408]

> WHEREAS our Fathers have existed, as a separate and distinct Nation, in the possession and exercise of the essential and appropriate attributes of sovereignty, from a period extending into antiquity, beyond the records and memory of man;
>
> AND WHEREAS these attributes, with the rights and franchises which they involve, remain still in full force and virtue, as do also the national and social relations of the Cherokee people to each other and to the body politic, excepting in those particulars which have grown out of the provisions of the treaties of 1817 and 1819 between the United States and the Cherokee nation, under which a portion of our people removed to this country and became a separate community: But the force of circumstances having recently compelled the body of the Eastern Cherokees to remove to this country, thus bringing together again the two branches of the ancient Cherokee family, it has become essential to the general welfare that a union should be formed, and a system of government matured, adapted to their present condition, and

providing equally for the protection of each individual in the enjoyment of all his rights;

THEREFORE we, the people composing the Eastern and Western Cherokee Nation, in National Convention assembled, by virtue of our original and inalienable rights, do hereby solemnly and mutually agree to form ourselves into one body politic, under the style and title of the Cherokee Nation.

At the Council meeting held from September 6th to October 10th, Ross was elected principal chief, while David Vann from the Old Settlers was chosen as Assistant Chief and Treasurer. The court system was reestablished, and a constitution modeled closely on the original was approved. But US government agents kept meddling in Cherokee affairs, with continuous propaganda against Ross with whom they declined to deal with directly.

Commissioner of Indian Affairs Crawford didn't want Reverend Jones, one of the Cherokees' best missionary friends, to live in the new Cherokee Nation because he had helped North Carolina Cherokees avoid the Trail of Tears. Although Superintendent Armstrong was instructed by Crawford to expel Jones, the National Council protected him and Armstrong backed down. Near the end of September, General Arbuckle ordered Ross to turn over the assassins, threatening military action if he didn't comply, but Ross pointed out that the US lacked any jurisdiction in the Cherokee Nation. Despite that reality, US officials continued to press for the killers to be arrested.

Hoping to discuss these issues with President Van Buren, Ross led a delegation to Washington, D.C. late in 1839. The President refused to see them. The official US position was that only the Treaty Party could speak for the Cherokee Nation. Ross was persona non grata even though he had been re-elected Chief almost unanimously. How could the President treat Ross and the overwhelming majority of Cherokees this way? Once again, the solemn words of the US government meant little in the light of day. General Mathew Arbuckle, who was appointed Commissioner over the new Indian territory, requested that representatives of the three Cherokee factions gather at Fort Gibson while the Ross and Watie delegations were in Washington during the first half of 1840. After ten days of discussion, there was agreement to leave the Constitution as it was, but the Act of Union was changed to allow Old Settlers to receive their share of per-capita payments.

The going was harder in Washington where the three factions were working at cross purposes. Ross applied for the annual annuity to be paid normally, but that was rejected by the President. Ross learned later that Treaty Party members had already been paid over $3,000 in annuities and that Watie was pushing for a divided Cherokee Nation with Old Settlers and Treaty Party members living in one area and all payments divided. That was too much for Secretary of War Poinsett to accept, but he didn't care a whit for Ross either. At this point, Ross wrote his old friend John Howard Payne, the famous actor, poet and playwrite, for help: "The bar of the Executive door, which has been bolted against my admission into the presence of His transitory Highness of the White House, is still closed, but I do not despair of yet finding entrance through the Legislative Hall." With Payne's help, Ross was able to convince the House Committee on Indian Affairs to review the matter, which sided with him. When the full House refused to release the hearing record, it was leaked to the press by Representative John Bell of Tennessee. Many fine words were written about the situation in newspapers, which changed nothing. After Ross returned home in the early autumn, a general assembly was held on October 28, 1840. Reporting that the annuities hadn't been paid and his position still wasn't recognized by the Government, Ross appealed for solidarity. The stalemate was broken in November when Secretary Poinsett decided to release the annuities, instructing Superintendent Armstrong to inform Ross that the US was ready to pay all arrears. Sadly, that didn't happen before President William Henry Harrison took office.

Vice-President John Tyler and Secretary of War John Bell were friendly to Cherokees, and the new Harrison Administration agreed to support Ross. Cherokee optimism rose briefly. But by the time Harrison died suddenly in April 1842, the money still hadn't been transferred. No one knew what that would mean politically, but Secretary Bell continued being supportive. Newly sworn in President Tyler told Ross at their first meeting, "You may assure your people that not justice merely shall be done them, but a liberal and generous policy will be adopted toward them."[409] By the end of the year, however, the US still hadn't signed an agreement with the Cherokee Nation. Although Ross's negotiations had generated the payments desperately needed for tools, farm equipment, and materials, the funds promised in the New Echota Treaty were needed to fund their schools and administration of the Nation. At the Council meeting in November, Ross presented a long report in English, interpreted word for word into Cherokee by Jesse Bushyhead. Ross read out a portion of President Tyler's letter promising to negotiate a new treaty "which shall give to the Cherokee nation full indemnity for all wrongs which they may have suffered,,, [and]guaranty their lands in absolute fee simple . . . ."

That year, the Nation began focusing on schooling, with ambitious plans. Eleven public schools were provided for in an act of Council on November 16th, and Joseph Foreman was chosen as the first Superintendent of Education. He played many important roles in the Nation, before and after the Trail of Tears. As Assistant Editor of the *Phoenix* in 1829, he helped translate documents from English into Cherokee, often serving on delegations to Washington. He was a delegate in 1836 trying to reverse the New Echota Treaty. After removal he helped Samuel Worcester and John Huss translate the New Testament into Cherokee and served as an

Associate Justice on the Supreme Court. Foreman was clear that without the six million dollars promised in the Echota Treaty, the new schools couldn't be operated properly. The Council was anxious to invest in new roads and ferries to connect their country. But US officials continued to refuse to transfer the money.

Out of desperation, families began filing claims against the US government in 1842 for their lost farms, homes, livestock and personal possessions. Those personal testaments to what Annie's family and so many lost, written down in their own words and sworn under oath, are moving. Annie's great-uncle Crying Snake filed the first claim on March 23rd before George W. Adair, Clerk of Flint District. Stating that his former residence was on the Etowah River where he was forced to abandon improvements in 1838, and earlier had lost twenty-three acres and his all his improvements at Buzzard Roost on the Chattahoochee River, he requested compensation of $2,075.25.[410] Relating that white Georgians "stole and destroyed his property at such a rate he was forced to abandon" the Buzzard Roost farm, he moved first to "The Sixes" on the Etowah, establishing a six-acre farm, but soon lost that to other white Georgians and relocated south of the Etowah where the rest of his family had moved. There he built up a farm with six acres in corn, one acre of sweet potatoes, a half-acre of Irish potatoes, and a half-acre of beans. His claim relates that he was rounded up by US troops in 1838 and forced to leave behind everything.[411] Crying Snake's signed and attested submissions are in Appendix 13.

It was a welcome surprise to unearth these original claims documents, which bring alive my ancestors' realities. Since there are no letters from that period, these documents provide the only substantive record of what they owned, and what they lost.

The same day Crying Snake's paternal grandmother Susannah (Tsah'wah'u'gah) filed a claim for her large farm with two houses at Buzzard's

Roost, having been driven off in 1829; her twelve-acre farm on Crawfish Creek (Che-so-no-wy) where she moved next, building a new house and planting fifty fruit trees, from where she was forcibly removed by white Georgians in 1832; and her last home on the Etowah River, lost in 1838. For Buzzard's Roost and Crawfish Creek, she asked for $1,027, while her separate claim for the large farm on the Etowah River was for $528.25, both witnessed by Crying Snake.[412] Her claim is in Appendix 14. There is no record of her ever receiving compensation.

Buffalfish's wife Wo-de-yo-he (War-Te-Yoh-He) filed a detailed claim on April 5th for $4,252. Reading her itemized list of what was stolen at Buzzard's Roost in 1829 and along the Etowah River in 1838 is sobering. She and Buffalofish were well off, owning sixteen horses; more than 100 cows; three breeding hogs; several acres planted in corn, cotton, beans, and potatoes; three spinning wheels; and many farm implements and household items itemized with specificity. Her claim is in Appendix 15. There is no record of her ever receiving compensation.

Eagle Buffalofish, one of Buffalofish's and Wo-de-yo-he's six sons, also known as Eagle-on-the-Roost, Wa-Lu-Kil-Lah and Chualukiller, had a large family. His claim for $3,299.50 covered their land, home, and animals stolen in 1829 at Buzzard's Roost and their large farm along the Etowah. It provides many details about the family's life, including their nine horses, twenty cows, and dozens of household items. Attested to by Walking Stick, it is heartbreaking in its detail: four pewter bowls, twelve white plates, twelve cups and saucers, a set of silverware for twelve, a loom and spinning wheel. His signed and attested claim is in Appendix 16. There is no record of him ever receiving compensation.

One of Buffalofish and Wo-de-yo-he's daughters, So-Wa-Chee, married Sawney Vann, who filed a claim for their family of ten living along the Etowah River in 1838 when they were arrested and taken three miles to a fort. Besides their home, Vann listed fifteen acres of growing corn, two acres of potatoes, fifteen head of cattle, fifty hogs, twenty sheep, 100 chickens, three horses, three plows, spinning wheels, household furniture, and three good rifles. His claim totaled $1,250, which was attested to by Alex Brown. His claim is in Appendix 17. He eventually received partial reimbursement.

Annie's future husband Sam Mayes also filed a claim. Among his possessions recorded in 1836 were a ferry landing at Bolton's Creek; a fishery with extensive weirs valued at $150; and the Ka'nan'sausky, Squel'look, and Miller farms. Altogether, he owned 269 acres of improved land and 200 acres of fenced woodland. His public ferry was lost in the lottery to Thomas Paloch of Harris County. According to the agents, he was entitled to be paid $11,935 for everything; like most others, though, he didn't end up receiving all of that.[413] His April 11th supplemental claim was "for use of 329 acres of bottom land in 1837 at $4/acre, $1316; for the ferry's use for 1835-37, $600; for false imprisonment, $5000."[414] Mayes recovered nothing.

Annie's Uncle John Huss filed and witnessed claims for the children of his deceased wife Nancy Gourd to her 640-acre reservation and ferry at the mouth of Battle Creek, where it enters the Tennessee River. The first was submitted on September 13, 1837, before departing the homeland, on behalf of his son William Huss and his wife's son Jefferson Blaylock.[415] His affidavit regarding the ferry with the second claim was filed on April 24, 1842, stating that it was "valuable being on a very public road."[416] Pigeon's affidavit supporting the claim estimated the ferry was worth "at least one-thousand dollars."[417] John McCloy's claim for the lost 640-acre farm filed on February 11, 1842 requested compensation of $8,787, to be shared with his siblings William Huss and Jefferson Blaylock. It was mostly rich bottomland, with a large orchard and several buildings.[418] As was the case with most claims filed by Cherokees, these were dismissed by the US Court of Claims on the flimsy ground that Nancy Gourd didn't repossess the farm and ferry after it was seized by white men, but that was impossible. American justice of the day wasn't worth much to Indians.

Considering the detailed claims process with records dating back to 1836, one might think that the US government would finally be willing to pay them what they were owed. But you would be wrong. They were not paid. Many people passed away while awaiting justice. A new Board of Commissioners was established on July 23, 1846 to deal with the old claims, once again requiring individuals to submit detailed claims along with supporting evidence. The deadline was December 31st, and while that was just a short time away, 1,229 Cherokee families filed. Only twenty-eight people received a positive decision, including Sawney Vann, who requested $655 and was awarded $600 and Rachel Buffalofish, who requested $102 and received seventy. John Buffalofish requested $765 but was awarded zero; Nelly Buffalofish requested $2,050 but was awarded zero; Rider Fields, one of Annie's third cousins, requested $2,114 but was awarded zero. The claims process proved to be extremely disappointing to everyone as reasons for denial were rarely given. At that point Cherokees gave up on ever receiving compensation for their claims.[419]

No evidence exists of Annie's mother and father receiving anything for themselves and their children. Like most Cherokees, they were busy just trying to live and support their families. In Georgia, they lived close to Chowyouka's first husband, George Vann, and his first wife Ailsey Ratt, and their daughter Lydia. But in the new Nation, they were separated geographically and rarely saw each other. Chowyouka's children with George—Annie, Elsie, and Weely Vann—lived with Annie's family. Late in 1842 when she was nineteen, Annie Vann[420] married Andrew "Raven" Adair. He was more than twenty years older, a handsome man with a roving eye, and many in the extended family thought the marriage ill-advised, but it lasted until he was killed along with one of his sons in 1855. They had three children—Edward Sylvester in 1851, Rosella in 1853, and Lydia just before her father died. Andrew had at least two other wives and many children. Back in the homeland, he had been well-off, with a large farm (Big Spring Place) in the Oothcaloga Valley that was valued at $3,683.50.

Annie rarely got to see her Uncle John Huss, who lived up north on Honey Creek near his sister Caty Spirit and her husband Knightkiller. Reverend John was even more important to the Nation after removal, when he resumed preaching in late 1840. There was something about the way he spoke and sang that touched people, and he lived his ideals as father, husband, and minister transparently. His mixture of intellect, thoughtfulness, and common sense was widely admired. His preaching focused on healing the rifts in the Cherokee Nation, which were profound and deep. But bad blood between Treaty Party members and the rest of the Nation led them to kill people they thought were behind the murders of their leaders in 1839. Stand Watie knifed James Foreman to death in a bar just over the Arkansas line on May 14, 1842. Foreman died of his knife wound within an hour. Watie was charged with murder but went free in an Arkansas court on a claim of self-defense. After his brother was assassinated in 1839, Watie became increasingly militant, fomenting a low-grade civil war that continued over the next few years. One notorious incident took place in the Saline District, where David Vann and Isaac Bushyhead were election superintendents. They were attacked by George West, a white man married into the tribe, who stabbed Isaac to death while West's father Jacob and brother John almost beat David to death, shouting "kill him, kill him!" George escaped; Jacob and John were tried and convicted for murder, and Jacob was executed. Several others who were counting ballots were attacked, and some ballots were destroyed.

The venom coursing through Cherokee veins was ruinous, but no one seemed capable of stopping the violence and healing the wounds. Still, John

Ross was re-elected principal chief, with George Lowrey as his running mate. Their opponents were two Old Settlers, Joe Vann and W. S. Adair. Everyone hoped that the election would bring peace, but violence, murders and robberies persisted. The "Starr Gang" was at the center of the trouble, carrying out a reign of terror targeting Ross Party members and blacks. Led by Tom Starr and his brothers Bean and Ellis, the gang included James McDaniels, Sewell Rider, and Ezekiel West. The passions unleashed over the last decade didn't die out quickly, but eventually, a sense of community re-emerged. People were building homes, mills, farms, and towns. Schools continued to be a major preoccupation. The Council appropriated $5,800 to support schools in 1843, and many were quickly built.

Annie's parents' farm was doing well, but they missed the close family life along the Etowah River. They were able to get together occasionally with Buffalofish's and Wo-de-yo-he's children Crying Snake and his wife Alcie Vann; Alexander Buffalofish, his wife A-toh-hee Cornsilk, and their son Ben; Charlie Buffalofish and his wife Sallie Wool Tail; Nakey, her husband Nitts, and their seven children: and So-Wah-Chee, her husband Sawney Vann, and their seven children. Periodically, Annie also saw her maternal uncles Jess and Jim Swimmer and her paternal great-grandmother Wo-De-Yo-He. She especially enjoyed visiting her half-sisters, Annie and Elsie Vann, and her stepsister, Lydia Vann, who married Ti-es-kee Fields prior to removal. Jane Jennie, their first child, was born in 1839.[421] Occasionally, the family traveled north to visit Buffalofish's siblings along Honey Creek: David Sconti Spirit; his wife Mary Buffington; and their three children David, Susie, and Peggy; Caty Spirit, her husband Knightkiller, and their two children David and Henry; Reverend John Huss and his large family; and Betsy Spirit and the family of her son with George Guess, Big Dollar George's wife Tianna and their four children Robert, Nancy, William, and Moses. Family was crucial to their healing and ability to move forward with their lives.

Annie's grandparents Buffalofish and Wo-de-ye-ho apparently moved back to Georgia in late 1841, as others were doing, most likely living with Rachel Martin, one of his second cousins, Susannah Emory's and John Martin's daughter.[422] Rachel married Daniel Davis in 1808,[423] who avoided the Trail of Tears by signing the loyalty oath. They'd made many improvements to their property along the Etowah River in Lumpkin County, including a large two-story house with eight rooms; seven cabins for their twenty-three slaves; an orchard of more than 900 peach, apple, and pear trees; forty acres of fenced woods; and 150 acres of bottomland on the river. Despite having signed the oath and being white, he was forced to re-purchase 212 acres of his own land because he had a Cherokee family.[424] Among the few Georgians who qualified for a reservation of 640 acres under the 1819 Treaty, he sold it to Georgia in 1823 for $4,000 and moved to the Etowah.[425] His fortuitous appointment as Justice of the Peace for the 830th District Company of Militia in 1835 helped protect his family. He was one of only a few Georgian men married to Cherokees who wasn't forced to leave.[426] Buffalofish died in 1842.[427] His wife is thought to have remained for some time but eventually returned west. Given the politics, it seems surprising that two elderly Indians could just be absorbed into the Georgia countryside, but there were many Indians and mixed people around. Daniel was an important member of the community and could protect relatives and friends as a Justice of the Peace.

Another important Cherokee who returned to the homeland in that period was Chief Junaluskee. He made two attempts to escape during the Trail, finally returning home to the mountains of North Carolina in 1843. He is said to have walked the entire way alone, his wife and children having died in the west. Prior to 1838, he lived on a 640-acre reservation from the 1819 Treaty, in Deep Gap, and had two 300-acre farms at Yularka and Cheoah. He filed a claim in 1843 about the loss of those properties but received no compensation. Junaluska was honored with a special law on January 2, 1847 making him a citizen and protecting his land in perpetuity:

> Whereas the Cherokee Chief Junoluskee, who distinguished himself in the service of the United States at the battle of the 'Horse-Shoe,' as commander of a body of Cherokees . . . since his removal west of the Mississippi, returned to the State, and expressed a wish to remain and become a citizen thereof: Sec. 1. Be it enacted by the General Assembly . . . That the said Junoluskee be, and he is hereby declared a citizen of the State of North Carolina, and entitled to all the rights, privileges and immunities consequent thereon. Sec. 2. Be it further enacted, That the Secretary of State . . . is hereby authorized and directed to convey unto the said Junoluskee, in fee simple, the tract of land in Cherokee county, in district 9, tract No. 19, containing three hundred and thirty-seven acres, which said land the said Junoluskee shall be empowered to hold and enjoy . . . .[428]

Chief Ross returned to Washington in April 1844 accompanied by Elijah Hicks, John Benge, and David Vann to negotiate the treaty that President Tyler had promised in 1841. They met the new War Secretary, William Wilkins, presenting him with key points for the treaty, but Wilkins surprised them by asking their response to the proposal of Old Settlers and the Treaty Party to divide Cherokee territory and split the annuities. The Cherokees remained divided. Parts of the US government were only too happy to continue playing off the factions, no progress was made, and the negotiators returned home empty-handed. David served as Treasurer of the Cherokee Nation from 1839-1853, doing an admirable job. He was married to Martha McNair and had seven children, two of whom married Sam Mayes' boys, Joel and Samuel, Jr., both future chiefs. Mary Delilah married

Joel while Martha Elizabeth wed Samuel. This painting captures David Vann's taste for colorful clothes. His finger-woven sash and shoulder strap were common in those years. He was a key advocate for a national newspaper to help bring Cherokees back together.

Charles Bird King Portrait of David Vann in 1825[429]

Annie's third cousin Reverend Jesse Bushyhead suddenly passed away on July 17, 1844, a terrible blow, as he was one of the key peacemakers who brokered agreements to solve the deep political divides. Born on November 4, 1804, he was one of the few Cherokees who could read, write, and speak Cherokee and English with equal facility, and his gentleness was legendary. In 1829, he attended a white school in Tennessee for a time, then began preaching in Amohee, his hometown. He formed the first Indian Christian church in the Cherokee Nation in 1832.[430] Elected to the Cherokee Supreme Court in 1840, Jesse was an exemplary judge with a distinct philosophy about crime and punishment. The American Baptist Magazine's 1844 tribute captures his wisdom in one of his charges to a jury before it began to deliberate in a case in which Stand Watie represented the defendant:

> I trust none of you have any prejudice against the accused, and that you will all of you bear in mind that you break your solemn oath if you permit yourselves to consider anything in forming your judgment, but these facts which you conscientiously believe to have been unquestionably proven. There appears to me much in the evidence that bears heavily against Archilla Smith; and much too, of a suspicious complexion. I would beg you most scrupulously to separate the doubtful from the less doubtful; and not to permit anything unsure to operate upon your verdict. It is a maxim, in these cases, of all good men, that it is better for ten guilty to escape than for one who is innocent to suffer. Bear this in mind, and if you feel in the slightest degree as if the accused has been accused wrongfully, let him be acquitted.[431]

William Gammell viewed Bushyhead as " . . . the ablest and most successful of the native preachers and one of the ablest and most energetic men of the nation to which he belonged . . . one of the noblest exemplifications of Christian character it has ever produced."[432] Son of Oo-no-du-tu (Cherokee for Bushyhead) and Nancy Gourd Foreman, he married Eliza Wilkerson. They had four children, including Eliza Missouri on the Trail of Tears in 1839, and Dennis Wolfe Bushyhead, who later served as Principal Chief.

Reverend Jesse Bushyhead - 1842[433]

The *Cherokee Advocate* resumed publication on September 26, 1844, an important development welcomed by everyone. Its first editor was William P. Ross, the chief's nephew and an honor graduate from Princeton University. Like the original paper, it was published weekly, printed in both Cherokee and English. Having their own paper again gave the Nation an important focal point and helped them heal. The new Supreme Court building in Tahlequah also opened in 1844, a good year for the Cherokees with much to celebrate.

Meanwhile, Chief Ross had fallen for a young Quaker girl, Mary Bryan Stapler. Thomas McKenney introduced them in 1841 when she was studying at a Pennsylvania boarding school. He was so in love that he promised to give up his job as Chief for her. They were married in Philadelphia, and she moved west with him to Park Hill, where he had built a beautiful home. But he didn't keep his promise to give up being Principal Chief!

As 1844 ended Secretary Wilkins appointed Brigadier General Roger Jones, Lieutenant Colonel R. B. Mason and Pierce Butler, the Cherokee agent, to investigate what was still dividing the Old Settlers, the Treaty Party, and the Ross administration. They arrived in Tahlonteeskee on November 15th and met separately with each group. Ross's delegation argued that all sides had accepted the 1839 Constitution giving Old Settlers and Treaty Party members the special representation they requested, but the former repeated their list of grievances. The Commissioners' report on January 17, 1845 rejected the Old Settler and Treaty Party claims, recommending against dividing the Cherokee Nation, and urging that the vexed issue of money be dealt with quickly. They endorsed a new treaty based on the 1841 letter from President Tyler, but no one knew if, and when, that would prevail in Washington. The years were sliding by, and since most of the money owed under the New Echota Treaty still hadn't been paid, the Nation was forced to borrow against the promise of those funds.

The new President, James Polk, continued the government's policy of not recognizing Ross as Chief, but did agree to start working on the new treaty. Ross and a small delegation spent most of 1845 in Washington lobbying for immediate payment of the annuities and money due under the New Echota Treaty and finalizing details of the new treaty. In late summer a breakthrough came when the annuities were partly paid, although there still wasn't closure on a new treaty or payment of the six-million dollars for the Cherokee homeland. Ross returned home, not knowing that Stand Watie and other Treaty Party representatives had stayed in Washington to continue lobbying against him.[434] By March 1846 Polk had succumbed to the Treaty Party's entreaties, and supported by the new Commissioner of Indian Affairs, William Medill, asked Congress on June 2nd to pass legislation splitting the Cherokee Nation.[435] Luckily, Indian Superintendent Armstrong supported the Cherokees and convinced the President to establish another Commission to review everything. Based on its recommendations, the President presented the Senate with a new Treaty on August 7th providing full payment of arrears. The Cherokee Nation finally came together. Article 1 provided for Cherokee rights to the land in perpetuity: "That the land now occupied by the Cherokee Nation shall be secured to the whole Cherokee people for their common use and benefit; and a patent shall be issued for the same, including the eight hundred thousand acres purchased, together with the outlet west, promised by the United States . . . in the third article of the treaty of 1835."[436]

Article 9 provided for a "fair and just settlement" of all money due the Cherokees under the Treaty of 1835, calculated to be $6,647,647, to be paid in equal per capita amounts to all the Cherokees who remained in their homeland in 1835.[437] The sums previously paid for improvements, ferries, spoilation, removal and subsistence after arrival in the west were deducted from that amount. The Treaty also provided a broad amnesty for crimes committed on both sides and abolished the Lighthorse Brigades, which were controlled by Ross and detested by Treaty Party supporters. The Old Settlers received a guarantee for part of the annual annuity payments, while the Treaty Party was awarded $100,000, including $5000 for the heirs of the dead Ridges.[438] John Ross and Stand Watie stood together shaking hands celebrating the agreement.[439] The violence quickly subsided. A new day dawned for the Cherokee Nation, and more broadly for all the Indian nations, which wanted to work together to protect their land and their rights.

# 18

John Huss Spirit and
The International Indian Council

After moving west in 1838 and settling on Honey Creek, John Huss established a church there. He carried on a robust correspondence with the help of translators, including with John Mix Stanley. One of the best painters of Indian life, Stanley's portraits were extremely popular. Many were obtained by the Smithsonian Institution. Sadly, most were lost in an 1865 fire, including his portrait of Huss (Plate 26 with the name "We-cha-lah-nae-he or The Spirit"), but a few are left. These are my favorites:[440]

Buffalo Hunt on the Southwestern Prairies (J.M. Stanley)

Osage Scalping (J.M. Stanley)

Indian Telegraph (J.M. Stanley)

Huss outlined the successes of Christian proselytizing in a letter to Stanley on January 30, 1844: "My Friend, you wish that I should tell you something about the Cherokees living on Honey Creek . . . .I will write to you in Cherokee, it being the only language which I can write . . . When we came to this country . . . there were but few who emigrated from east of the Mississippi, that formerly were connected with the church . . . but now there are a great many, and we have built a house of God . . . ."[441]

Stanley described the creation of the International Indian Council in June 1843 as an important Cherokee initiative, and also painted portraits there. Ross, Lowrey and Huss invited representatives of all Indian tribes living nearby to gather in Tahlequah to discuss jointly governing their new tribal lands.[442] The meeting was well-organized, and the mood among the ten-thousand delegates from twenty-one tribes was jovial. A "Great Council Fire" was kindled in the capitol square.[443] There was much information to share as they discussed their visions for the future. At the closing of the Great Council on July 3rd Assistant Chief Major George Lowrey presented the history of wampum as a symbol of peace among tribes.[444] "As a closing part of the ceremony the "Path of Peace," a broad belt of black and white wampum beads, was spread upon the ground and all the representatives of the various tribes and nations walked over it, signifying that from thenceforth their footsteps should follow in the pathway of peace and progress."[445]

Lowrey's knowledge of Cherokee customs was beyond that of anyone else at the time and his long speech closed with this passage from his wampum history: "You Cherokees are placed now under the center of the sun; this talk I leave with you for the different tribes, and when you talk it, our voice shall be loud enough to be heard over this island. This is all I have to say."[446] There was a general murmuring of approval as his words spread and were discussed in small groups. Reverend Huss was happy the story had been told so well. This painting shows George Lowrey in his turban at the event, wearing large earrings and a nose ring. He was one of the last to give up those traditions.

George Lowrey (J.M. Stanley 1844)[447]

Chief Ross rose to present his address to the delegates: "Brothers . . . You have also smoked the pipe of peace, and shaken the right hand of friendship around the Great Council fire, newly kindled at Tahlequah . . . .let us so then act that the peace and friendship which so happily existed between our forefathers, may be forever preserved and that we may always live as brothers of the same family."[448] He presented the proposed compact among the tribes: "Peace and friendship shall be forever maintained between the parties to this compact, and between their respective citizens," and "no nation, party to this compact, shall, without the consent of all the other parties, cede, or in any manner alienate to the United States any part of their present territory."[449] That was the strongest statement of solidarity yet agreed among the tribes. Although the Compact was signed initially by only a few Indian Nations, the gathering generated good will that furthered better connections for years to come. There were many similar meetings over the next few decades. Stanley captured the event in this painting, which is sufficiently detailed that some individuals can be identified, including General Zachery Taylor:[450]

International Indian Council, Tahlequah 1843 (J.M. Stanley)

Following the International Indian Council meeting, they turned their attention to the burning matter of completing a new Treaty with the US so that they could finally be paid for their ancestral homeland. Although John Huss had never been very political, he was an important bridge between the factions and agreed to serve on the delegation to Washington in 1846 to sign the new treaty with the US, which finally solved the issues that had lingered since removal. A period of calm settled over the Cherokee Nation and their progress speeded up. Reverend Huss continued to play a healing role in the Nation.

When Huss passed away suddenly in 1858, the entire Cherokee Nation mourned his passing. His wise counsel would be sorely missed in the harrowing years that followed. Always a strong supporter of education at all levels, he lived long enough to see the Female and Male Seminaries constructed and beginning to flower, but there were troubling signs on the horizon.

19

Female and Male Seminaries

The highest priority of the Cherokees was always education. After a prolonged debate about building a higher education system, the Council finally agreed on November 26, 1846 to allocate $80,000 for construction of institutions of higher learning for men and women for "improvement of the moral and intellectual condition of our people." As contemplated by their Constitution, the Nation had sufficient means to educate their youth, a shared value of all parts of the body politic.

The cornerstone of the Male Seminary was laid by Chief Ross on October 28, 1847. During the following two years, Council members visited Yale University, Mount Holyoke College, and Newton Theological Seminary searching for teachers and developing a curriculum. The Male Seminary opened on May 6, 1851, with the military band from Fort Gibson playing for the large crowd and Chief Ross speaking about the importance of education for the Cherokee Nation's future. The Female Seminary in Park Hill opened the next morning. They each cost about $60,000. It would be hard to overstate the Cherokees' pride at these accomplishments. Augustus W. Loomis, a missionary, recorded his impression in the early 1850s: "We visited the Female Academy, a large handsome, well-finished brick building.

One almost wonders what such a noble edifice is doing away out there. From the top of it we saw the Seminary for young men, two miles distant."[451]

Subjects taught included English grammar, composition, elocution, math, astronomy, botany, economics, geology, geography, history, philosophy, and zoology. Language classes were offered in Greek, Latin, French, and German. Students read Thucydides, Livy, Homer, Virgil, Ovid, Cicero, Moliere, and Goethe, as well as Watt's *Improvement of the Mind* and Paley's *Natural Theology*.[452] Cherokee students were better educated than most in the US at that time. Applicants had to pass a tough two-day test in reading, spelling, grammar, arithmetic and geography. Those who passed were educated at tribal expense, while boarders paid five dollars per month for lodging, food, laundry, fuel, textbooks, and all necessary supplies. Pupils had to furnish only blankets, linens, and toilet articles. The Council provided free education to fifty pupils whose parents couldn't pay the fees. The Female Academy employed a full-time Steward who managed the kitchen, laundry, building maintenance, and the grounds. Dr. Elizur Butler was the first person to hold this position.[453] Annie's husband Samuel Mayes and his wife Nannie Adair sent several of their children to the Seminaries, and many of Annie's grandchildren were educated there.

Female Seminary in 1851

Male Seminary in 1851

The daily schedule at the Female Seminary was rigorous: Students rose at 5:30 am and had to be in Study Hall by 6:00 to study before breakfast at 7:00. There was a half hour of chapel every morning. The second retiring bell rang at 9:15 pm announcing bedtime. There were tennis and basketball courts. Twice a month the girls went to Tahlequah to visit art galleries, see an opera, go ice-skating, or visit relatives. There were spelling bees every Friday. Students could invite a friend to a fancy dinner once a semester, for which everyone dressed up. The older classes put on an annual play at the Opera House in Tahlequah, always an event not to be missed. None of the girls appreciated demerits for being late, passing notes, whispering during study hall, leaving a light on after 9:00 pm, or sending a letter to a boy, which meant losing home visits and shopping trips in town. Chief Ross and his wife Mary Stapler normally came to the Female Seminary every Sunday to attend church.

In early August 1852, the first public examinations were conducted at Park Hill for forty-six seminary girls. "Dressed in white with pink sashes, the students demonstrated their mastery of the subjects they had studied in a daylong series of oral examinations."[454] Students at the Female Seminary began publishing *Cherokee Rose Buds* on August 2, 1854. This is the second issue:[455]

CHEROKEE ROSE BUDS.

VOL. I.   Devoted to "The Good, the Beautiful and the True."   NO. 2

FEMALE SEMINARY, CHEROKEE NATION, WEDNESDAY, AUGUST 2, 1854.

THE CHEROKEE ROSE BUDS
Is published at stated periods
BY THE
CO-EDITRESSES,
CATHARINE GUNTER,
NANCY E. HICKS.

TERMS.
The terms of subscription, as regulated by the committee, are 10 cents per copy.

ORIGINAL POETRY.

Our Wreath of Rose Buds.

I.
We offer you a wreath of flowers
Culled in recreation hours,
Which will not wither, droop, or die,
Even when days and months pass by.

II.
Ask you where these flowers are found?
Not on sunny slope, or mound;
Not on prairies bright and fair
Growing without thought or care.

III.
No, our simple wreath is twined
From the garden of the mind;
Where bright thoughts like rivers flow
And ideas like roses grow.

IV.
The tiny buds which here you see
Ask your kindly sympathy;
View them with a lenient eye,
Pass each fault, each blemish by.

V.
Warmed by the sunshine of your eyes,
Perhaps you'll find to your surprise,
Their petals fair will soon unclose,
And every bud become—a Rose.

VI.
Then take our wreath, and let it stand
An emblem of our happy band;
The *Seminary*, our garden fair,
And we, the *flowers* planted there.

VII.
Like roses bright we hope to grow,
And o'er our home such beauty throw
In future years—that all may see
Loveliest of lands,—the Cherokee.

CORRINNE.

Report of the Secretary.

It having been proposed to elect new Editresses for our paper, a meeting was convened for the purpose; it, however, proved ineffectual, and a second meeting was called, at which, after being called to order,

Miss Catharine Gunter and Nancy E. Hicks were chosen as Editresses of the Paper.

The meeting then adjourned.

Students at the Male Seminary also organized a literary magazine, *The Sequoyah Memorial*, dedicated to "Truth, Justice, Freedom of Speech and Cherokee Improvement." Both magazines were printed side-by-side in

English and Cherokee and made available to the whole Nation. The first graduates received their degrees in February 1855. Among them was Joel Bryan Mayes (Tsa-Wa-Gak-Ski), Sam and Nannie Mayes' eldest child and a future chief. The two families attended the graduation ceremony together, united in their pride. Joel decided to continue his studies another year and on January 29, 1856 wrote his close friend Victoria Hicks about the future: "The past with all its joys and sorrows is gone, with it alone fond memory can converse. The present is busy working its many changes. Yet 'tis to the future that these thoughts will most naturally fly . . . But since our human life hangs over accident and misfortune, and since the future must know us ever, the great question is, how shall we meet it . . . Then, I would say to meet it calmly, and boldly and with pleasure."[456]

While the Male and Female Seminaries were the pinnacles of the educational system, around 1,100 students were enrolled in twenty-one regular Cherokee schools in 1852.[457] During the next forty years, almost 3,000 young women were educated at the Female Seminary,[458] including the hiatus of ten years because of the Civil War. After the War, the Seminaries were run somewhat differently because of financial realities. Students had to pay for their room and board, which meant lower enrollment—fewer than fifty women applied in the first two years after reopening.[459] But by 1876, both the Cherokee Nation and the seminaries had recovered, with 167 students enrolled at the Female Seminary that autumn. During the next twenty years, support for the seminaries remained strong, and the composition of the student body gradually changed to better reflect the demographics of the population as children from poorer families received more scholarhips. However, the Seminaries continued to be used mainly by mixed-blood students.

They enjoyed regular events that helped structure each week of studies, and there was intense competition for good grades: "At the end of each semester, the names of all students with at least a 90 percent average in all classes . . . were listed on the honor roll in the *Cherokee Advocate*."[460] The seminaries continued to develop as the years went by, with the girls putting on annual plays at Tahlequah's Opera House and the men holding an annual oratory contest there. In 1907, the Female Seminary put on "A Midnight Summer's Dream" with all the sets, props, and costumes made by the students. More than 1,000 Choctaw and Cherokee Indians attended the production.[461] That year Charles Haskell came to Tahlequah during the race for Oklahoma's governor and was invited to dinner at the Female Seminary. The girls greeted him with a chant: "Haskell, Haskell, he's our man; If I can't vote, my sweetheart can."[462] At that time, women had not been given the right to vote in the US.

The library was a key feature of both the original and rebuilt Female Seminaries, with an extensive literature and history collection, thirty-two regular periodicals, and the St. Louis daily newspapers. It included a large reading room where every student had to spend a prescribed number of hours each week studying or reading:[463]

The dining room was formal as well as functional:[464]

Charlotte Mayes and William Houston Ballard's daughter Sarah (Annie Spirit's granddaughter) graduated from the Female Seminary on May 28, 1902 and was chosen to deliver the Class Prophecy. The program reveals an interesting ceremony, featuring vocal and instrumental music, recitations of essays, and a class history.

PROGRAM

INVOCATION

Instrumental Solo, "Grillen" (Schuman) . . . VIRGIE LINDSEY
Class History . . . . GOLDA BARKER
The Alamo, a Story . . . . LOLA WARD
Vocal Trio, "Lullaby" (Emerson)
　ELIZABETH MCSPADDEN, SALLIE PARRIS, and SUSIE SEVIER
Oration, "Our Alma Mater" . . . . BULA EDMONSON
Recitation, "Jack Hall's Boat Race" . . . GENOBIA WARD
Instrumental Solo, "Carmen, Fantaisie Brillante" (J. Leybach)
　　　　　　　　　　　　　　　　ELIZABETH MCSPADDEN
Eulogy, "Li Hung Chang" . . . . . LIZZIE ROSS
Oration, "The World's Exposition" . . . LUCY STARR
Vocal Solo, a. "Soupir" (Leo Stern)
　　　　　b. "Flower Tragedy" (H. Lemmel) . CLARA COUCH
Biography, "Empress Josephine" . . . BIRD PAULKNER
Recitation, "The Prisoner's Plea" . . . SUSIE SEVIER
Oration, "Our Golden Inheritance" . . . MARY RIDER
Instrumental Solo, "Novellette Op. 99" (Schuman) LULU MORGAN
Class Prophecy . . . . . . SARAH BALLARD
Oration, "Uncrowned Kings" . . . . CLARA TYLER

CLASS SONG

PRESENTATION OF DIPLOMAS
BY PRESIDENT OF BOARD

BENEDICTION

Program of 1902 Female
Seminary Graduating Class

208 | Female and Male Seminaries

1902 Graduating Class Female Seminary[165]

1903 Female Seminary Graduates

Annie Spirit's granddaughter Janana Ballard and some of her friends were photographed in 1903 when she was teaching primary grades at the Female Seminary:

Teachers and Preachers in Tahlequah, c. 1903. Seated, from left to right, are Will Scott and L. M. Logan, teachers at the Cherokee Male Seminary; Will's sister Susie Scott, Methodist minister James Parks; and Janana Ballard, teacher at the Cherokee Female Seminary[466]

Two of Annie Spirit's other grandchildren graduated in 1904 and 1906 —William Houston Ballard on June 2, 1904 and Ruth Ballard on May 31, 1906. Each graduation in the family was cause for a big celebration. There were ten teachers at the Female Academy in 1906, including Janana Ballard, who taught primary students. Her photo is on this faculty card from that period.

Teachers at Female Seminary - 1906[467]

Four of the School Rooms - Female Seminary 1906[468]

Grant Foreman published two books listing all the students who attended the Male Seminary from 1876 to 1909 and the Female Seminary from 1876 to 1904, based on the original records of the Superintendent of Education. Each book provides the names of teachers for each term.[469] The demise of the Male and Female Seminaries is discussed in Chapter 32, End of the Dream.

20

Annie Spirit and Samuel Mayes

Annie's and Samuel's paths possibly crossed when she was growing up, given how close his farm on the north side of the Etowah was to her family on the south, and the importance of his ferry at Bolton's Creek. In those days, everyone knew each other, given family and clan connections and their relatively small population. But history does not record when they first met.

After removal, Samuel and his wife Nannie Adair settled at Muddy Springs, about three miles from Stilwell, where a Cherokee school was soon established. In the 1850s, his eldest son, Joel Bryan Mayes, was a teacher there along with Sophia Vann, William Penn Adair, William Fields, Carrie Bushyhead, and Warren Adair—a stellar group. His farm wasn't far from Annie's parents' place, and there was a fair amount of socializing among various communities. It's unclear how they got together, but one story goes that when Annie was 21, Sam knocked on the door one day and asked her to take a walk. In any event, his courting and marrying her was a surprising development, considering the difference in ages and the reality of his large family with Nannie. But at that time, Cherokees didn't believe marriage was forever. Chowyouka had married George Vann before marrying The Spirit, and also had a child with David Sconti after removal. Her uncle John Huss and Aunt Caty Knightkiller are said to have helped Annie find some land, and the family pitched in to build a small house with a stone fireplace and a barn. As a traditionalist, Annie likely wove Sam a marriage belt of river-reed fibers dyed red and black, which served much the same function as a wedding ring. By September, she was pregnant, and their first child, Sarah, arrived on May 10, 1849. Annie's mother Chowyouka helped her a lot in those early days, as did her maternal grandmother, Chi-Wa-Yu-Ga. Wanting Sarah to be bi-lingual, Annie spoke Cherokee to her most of the time, while Sam spoke English, although his basic Cherokee was adequate. We know he continued spending time with Nannie at Muddy Springs because she had their last child, Noel, in 1850, overlapping his new family.

Several months later, Sam announced that he had a plan to get rich out west. Stories of the gold rush in California were all the rage, motivating many Cherokees to join the rush. He had tried his hand at gold mining in Georgia prior to removal. Sam outfitted a group for the trip using stock from the trading post he owned with John Thompson Adair at Adair's home six miles east of Stilwell. Adair served on the Supreme Court from 1843-1859. The party included Sam's sons George and Tip, William and George Adair, Captain Richard Fields, Ben Cross, Robert Paden, Starr Bean, Will Goss, William and Charley Holt, and Dennis Bushyhead. Taking the Upper California Trail north of the Arkansas River by way of Salina in the summer of 1850, they intercepted the old Santa Fe Trail somewhere in No-Man's-Land and joined a larger group. It proved to be a harsh trip, with water said to cost $1.00 a gallon. It was reported that one man gave a dollar for the water, took one swallow and gave the rest to his horse, knowing that otherwise it would die. Sam and several in the group were recorded on the Federal Census that year as living on Mathenias Creek on October 4th working as miners. That is near El Dorado. Sam was forty-six years old.[470]

Charlotte, Annie and Sam's second child, arrived on October 6th while Sam was away. A few months later, he and the gang returned with gold, full of boisterous stories and even more enthusiastic about California. It wouldn't be his last trip west. In mid-1852, Sam announced that he wanted to try California again, this time with cattle. In early September, he returned to California with his sons Tip and Francis and several other men. To raise funds for the trip, he pledged one of his slaves, who was an excellent blacksmith, to John Murrell for a loan of $1,500. Callis, another of Sam's slaves, wanted to go west with him, and they agreed he would be freed in return for his work on the expedition. Driving a herd of 1,000 cattle, they took the Marcy Trail by the way of Taos, New Mexico to California, establishing a ranch in the Sacramento Valley. Sam's son Frank and Callis were left to run it while the others did some gold mining before returning home in early 1853. Sam presented Murrell with $1,500 in gold from their successful mining. As the story goes, Frank and Callis operated the California ranch successfully until 1863, selling it for a bag of gold. Frank started back home along with a Cherokee named Lige Terrell and a white man called Campo. Terrell and Campo reported that Frank was robbed and murdered halfway back, but they escaped. Most people assumed they'd killed Frank and stolen the gold, but nothing was ever proven.[471] Callis returned home in 1865 after the Civil War ended, a free man. He loved California, making periodic trips there the remainder of his life.

Annie's half-sister Annie Vann Adair had her first child, Edward Sylvester,[472] in 1851 and her second, Rosella in 1853. They lived close by, and their children grew up together. Her stepsister Lydia sometimes brought her children, Jennie, born in 1839 on the Trail of Tears, and Thomas, born in 1846, over to play. Annie Spirit's brother Charles died early in 1854, just twenty-two years old. He'd never married, had no children, and never got over the trauma of moving when he was just four years old. Annie and Sam's third child, Elmira, was born September 10, 1854. Their family seemed destined to be composed only of girls, but William Penn Mayes, my great-grandfather, arrived on Christmas day in 1856. For the next two years, their lives moved at a fast pace with the children growing up during the Cherokee Nation's economic and political renaissance. Their married life came to an abrupt end when Sam passed away on December 30, 1858, leaving Annie to raise their four young children. But she wasn't alone. Her mother Chikuyu and grandmother Chi-wa-yu-ga helped with the children, ensuring they learned the old rituals. Her great-great-grandmother Susannah lived near John Huss on Honey Creek and came down to visit from time to time. Born around 1760, she carried the history of the Cherokees in her stories. Annie's Uncle Charles Poorbear Buffalofish regularly visited his son Hunter (Canahelage), born in 1849, and stopped in to see Annie. Annie's half-brother Weely Vann lived close by with his son Tee-saw-yuh-hi. Their families were growing up together. Sam's sister Lucy and her husband George Ward brought several of their children and grandkids to help with farm chores, and their daughter Sabrina came by occasionally with her grandson George Monroe Ward.

Tentacles of past events emerged periodically, stupefying everybody. During the 1853 election, Andrew Adair and his son George were killed on September 10th by seventy-five armed men because of Andrew and George's alleged involvement in the murder of Isaac Proctor. They were seized from Andrew's house and riddled with bullets. The culprits were caught, convicted, and some were hung; nevertheless, a pall lay over the family. Andrew had four wives and more than twenty children, which meant a lot of mourning. Annie Vann Adair couldn't get over her husband's death and never remarried, raising her children alone.

My great-grandfather Billy Mayes especially needed a father figure, settling on his half-brother Joel, whose wife, Martha Candy, had died the previous year. After Joel graduated from the Male Seminary in 1855, he began teaching at the Muddy Springs school and started Billy off with the Cherokee alphabet while helping the girls with their lessons. His brother Samuel Houston Mayes was thirteen when Sam died and became another father figure for the children. Years later, Joel and Samuel would both serve as Chiefs of the Cherokee Nation, while Billy worked closely with them as Interpreter for the Senate. Wash Mayes, another of Sam's boys, and his wife Charlotte Bushyhead owned a large ranch near Locust Grove, and sometimes they invited the children over to ride. Charlotte, one of Reverend Jesse Bushyhead's daughters, was Annie's fourth cousin.[473] George Vann's daughter Lydia and her husband Ti-es-kee Fields had a daughter named Jane Jennie, born in 1839 just after removal. She married Rufus Bell Adair in 1858 and had Susan (Wut) in 1859. As sisters, she and Annie were close. Despite occasional brutal shocks, optimism was rising both in the Cherokee Nation and the Spirit Family during the 1850s.

21

The 1850s in the Cherokee Nation

The Nation showed great optimism as they invested deeply in education and built a modern country. In 1850, the Council appropriated $7,000 per year for free public schools. It was an exciting time to be Cherokee, their pride rising as they developed towns, farms, ranches, orchards, mills, roads, and ferries across the Nation. But occasional political melodramas seared their collective consciousness. Senator Robert M. Johnson of Arkansas introduced a bill in February 1854 to end Indian sovereignty by creating three large territories to be called Chelokee, Muscogee, and Chatah. His idea was to have capitals in Tahlequah, the Creek Agency, and Doaksville in a single Indian area that would have its own Federal Court. The US would take over large portions of Indian Territory not already inhabited, opening it to white settlers, along with the huge Cherokee Outlet which was to be divided for individual farms for whites. At the same time, the Kansas-Nebraska Act was under consideration in Congress. When it was approved in 1854, more Cherokee Territory, the Neutral Lands in southeast Kansas, was seized. Chief Ross protested strongly against both proposals. Later that year, the Senate Committee on Territories reported favorably on Johnson's bill, but it never came up for a vote and died in committee. Although a positive result, it was clear the US was moving to override Indian treaties and sovereignty in order to promote a white takeover of Indian Country.[474] The news stories died down, but Ross continued to worry about US intentions, telling his people on October 5, 1857: "Years of trial and anxiety, danger and struggle have alone maintained the existence of the Cherokee people as a distinct community and such must continue to be the case if we would live as men."[475]

The Cherokee Nation continued to develop quickly. During the summer of 1857, Ross made a grand tour of the countryside, presenting a report of his findings to the Council that autumn, noting the "well cultivated farms . . . well filled public schools, large and orderly assemblages, and quiet neighborhoods, which . . . furnish a sure indication of the susceptibility of all classes among the Cherokee people for a thorough civilization."[476] As the decade ended, Cherokees had made amazing progress. The mood in the Nation remained upbeat. According to the census, the total population was around 21,000, and their children were being educated in thirty public schools. But the Nation was in poor financial shape because the US still owed them millions of dollars. The Council was distressed at having to close the Male and Female Seminaries because of lack of funds. But slavery was becoming divisive. Already in the mid-1850s there was talk about whether there would be war over slavery. Members of Annie's extended family—including her Uncle John Huss and her grandfather Buffalofish—had owned a few slaves. She may have inherited one of Samuel Mayes' slaves when he died in 1858, although they all may have stayed with his first wife Nannie Adair. Like many, the family divided into those following the Keetoowah Society's teaching and the pro-slavery side led by Stand Watie and the Knights of the Golden Circle.

Amid all this, the rumblings of war began to pulsate. The warning signs were ominous. For several years, there had been debates about slavery among the Cherokees and their neighbors in the Choctaw, Chickasaw, Seminole, and other tribes, and also about the position of free negroes in their nations. The missionary societies that helped with schools were increasingly divided while great debates were ongoing in the US Congress about the political development of the west, focusing on whether new states would be free or slave holding. George Butler, the US agent for the Cherokees, was a state rights man and a strong supporter of slavery, going so far as to describe Cherokee progress as being based on slave holding. That was preposterous, but at least he didn't try to impose his political views on the Cherokees. His successor, Robert J. Cowart of Georgia, was different. Starkly racist, he began trying to remove missionaries who opposed slavery immediately after assuming his new position in April 1859.[477]

Equally upsetting was that the US government had decided to leave Indian Territory virtually undefended, ignoring its treaty commitments that Indians would always be protected. Fort Gibson had essentially been abandoned. To top it off, the worst drought in memory was afflicting Kansas, Missouri and the whole of Indian Territory, causing serious crop failures. As the US election campaign unfolded, Seward proposed this radical idea, about which Lincoln was silent; no one knew if he supported it or not: "The Indian territory . . . south of Kansas, must be vacated by the Indians" to make room for white settlers.[478]

As the rumbles of war percolated, Cherokees were vulnerable on many levels, yet at the time it seemed unlikely that whatever was happening between the northern and southern states would affect them. They had their own sovereign Nation, with clear boundaries. They didn't know that the Confederacy would be so duplicitous or that the US government would use the Civil War as an excuse to attack Indians generally after the War, to the eternal detriment of First Peoples.[479] The Civil War would sweep away everything built up so hopefully during the prior thirty years.

Although Cherokees and other tribes were unaware of this at the time, almost all Indian trust funds totaling $3.5 million were invested in southern states' bonds, including $796,000 in Virginia, $562,000 in North Carolina, and $482,000 in Missouri. Only a tiny amount was invested in northern securities, which meant their annual payments would be greatly reduced if not eliminated entirely during the war.[480] The issue of slavery was a driving force in the Civil War both in the US and in Indian Territory as people split over slavery's future. Although the Cherokees owned a relatively small number of slaves and more than ninety percent owned none, those who did mostly sided with the Confederacy because their mutual interest was the same.

22

Slavery

It wasn't uncommon among mixed-blood Cherokees to have slaves, but the tiny percent who did had only a few each, except for a handful of "plantation" owners. By 1835, 207 Cherokees owned a total of 1,600 slaves, the great majority with ten or fewer.[481] To put this into context, the number of slaves owned by white Georgians in 1840 was around 286,000.[482] The richest Cherokee in the mid-1830s was Joseph Vann, son of the notorious James Vann, who had more than 150 slaves at his large plantation near Spring Place, Georgia. In contrast, Annie's grandfather Buffalofish had three slaves, John Huss Spirit also had three, and Annie's first husband, Samuel Mayes, had five or six. We know this from the detailed evaluation records prepared prior to removal. Everyone in the Cherokee Nation would have known of Vann, given his wide-ranging influence as a member of the Council and his wealth. His mansion, constructed of bricks made by slaves from the local red clay, was as elegant as any home in the US at the time.[483]

But Vann's wealth and high percentage of white blood did not save him. Colonel Bishop and the Georgia Guard evicted Joe and his family in 1834, converting their home into their local headquarters. Later, Joe sued the US, winning $19,605 in compensation, a fortune at the time although though still a fraction of its value.[484]

Articles in *The Cherokee Advocate* regularly spoke out against the slave trade and the realities of slavery, making an impression on many people. Moravian, Presbyterian, and Baptist schools in the Nation invited children of slaves to attend along with Cherokee children. Cherokees allowed their slaves to be educated and to participate in all social and religious activities. In some mission schools, there were more black students than Cherokee. But in early 1824, the Council began enacting laws against interracial marriage and stripped black people from owning horses, cattle, and hogs.[485] Later that year, a law declared than any free negro entering the Nation "shall not be allowed to reside . . . without a permit from the council." It also discouraged free black people from moving into the Nation: "All free negroes coming into the Cherokee Nation under any pretense whatsoever, shall be viewed and treated, in every respect as intruders, and shall not be allowed to reside in the Cherokee Nation without a permit."[486] The 1827, Cherokee Constitution excluded African Americans from the vote and public office: "No person who is of negro or mulatto parentage, either by the father or mother's side, shall be eligible to hold any office or trust under this Government."[487]

Extra burdens were placed on slaves during the removals in 1837 and 1838. There was so much work to be done in the new homeland that distinctions meant little. Most all survivors slaved together side by side and many died, Cherokee and black, but clearly slaves remained a subservient group without basic rights.[488] In the west, Cherokee courts upheld property rights in slaves essentially the same way that northern non-slave states did. Slavery changed Cherokee society overall in profound and negative ways, including "demeaning the traditional labor of women" as growers of corn while discouraging men from farming.[489] The larger plantation owners, all from the Treaty Party, built new farms using even more slaves than they had had in the east. Joe Vann was the worst. After having his slaves build a replica of his Georgia mansion at record speed, he beat some of them for "poor work". Twenty-five revolted on November 15, 1842, escaping the Webber's Falls area. After robbing a few stores for supplies and ammunition, they headed for Mexico, which had abolished slavery in 1836. The Cherokee Council voted on November 17th to empower Captain John Drew to raise a posse of 100 men to "pursue, arrest, and deliver the African Slaves to Fort Gibson." A few miles north of the Red River, they were caught and returned, but their exploit generated other slave revolts. Vann permanently assigned the men to work on his fleet of steamboats. He died along with several of them the next year on the *Lucy Walker* when it blew up during a race on the Ohio River.[490]

The Cherokee National Council approved An Act to Prevent Amalgamation with Colored Persons on September 19, 1839: "That it shall not be lawful for any free negro or mulatto, not of Cherokee blood, to hold or own any improvement within the limits of this Nation; neither shall it be lawful for slaves to own any property . . . "[491] It took the extraordinary step of outlawing their education in 1840: "That from and after the passage of this act, it shall not be lawful for any person or persons whatever, to teach any free negro or negroes not of Cherokee blood, or any slave belonging to any citizen or citizens of the Nation, to read or write."[492] The Council went further in 1842, making it unlawful for any free negro to help slaves escape: "[S]hould any free negro or negroes be found guilty of aiding, abetting or decoying any slave or slaves, to leave his or their owner or employer, such free negro or negroes, shall receive for each and every such offence, one hundred lashes on the bare back, and be immediately removed from this Nation."[493]

But most Cherokees, especially full bloods, did not support slavery. The Keetoowah Society helped bring the issue into public discussion in the 1850s. Even so, we don't know what happened to Annie's grandfather's and husband's slaves. No evidence exists of Buffalofish's slaves remaining with his children after he died in 1842, but some think that Sam Mayes continued to own a few until his death in 1858. In 1861 as the Civil War began, the political power of the great majority of Cherokees who didn't own slaves was relatively weak. Thus, it's easy to fathom why the Confederacy attracted as much support as it did among the wealthier class, who in a broad sense led "Southern" lives. If the US government hadn't abandoned the Cherokee Nation and other tribes militarily at the beginning of the war and had continued paying their annuities, the Cherokees likely would have either stayed neutral or supported the Union. If that had happened, Stand Watie probably would still have organized some troops to support the Confederacy, but the anti-slavery feelings among the majority probably would have prevailed.

During the War, the Cherokees' pro-union Government freed all slaves, allowing them to decide if they wished to be Cherokee or not. An Act Providing for the Abolition of Slavery in the Cherokee Nation was passed on February 18, 1863; two days later, An Act Emancipating the Slaves in the Cherokee Nation was passed on February 20th. The latter reads: "That all negro and other slaves within the lands of the Cherokee Nation be and they are hereby emancipated from slavery, and any person or persons who may have been held in slavery are hereby declared to be forever free."[494] The Treaty signed with the US on July 19, 1866 gave "all the rights of native Cherokees" to freed black slaves residing within the Nation. The revised Cherokee Constitution is clear:

> All native born Cherokees, all Indians, and whites legally members of the Nation by adoption, and all freedmen as well as free colored persons who were in the country at the commencement of the rebellion, and are now residents therein, or who may return within six months from the 19th of July, 1866, and their descendants, who reside within the limits of the Cherokee Nation, shall be taken and deemed to be citizens of the Cherokee Nation.

In the 1890s, freed slaves who had some Cherokee blood were placed on the Dawes Roll, while those who were thought not to have Cherokee blood were put on the Freedmen Roll. They retained citizenship and voting rights in the tribe until 1983, when the Council changed the law to require citizens to have a certificate of their degree of Indian blood, which Freedmen didn't have, as neither the Dawes Roll nor Freedmen Roll asked for that information. That led to a legal saga that played out for years. In 2001, the Cherokee Supreme Court ruled in *Riggs v. Ummerteskee* that the 1983 law was constitutional. Lucy Allen, descendant of a freed slave, sued the Tribal Council, challenging the tribe's authority to strip citizenship from descendants of Dawes enrollees. On March 7, 2006, the Cherokee Supreme Court ruled 2-1 for Allen, but a 2007 referendum overruled that decision and litigation continued. Federal Judge Thomas F. Hogan put the matter to rest in *Cherokee Nation v. Nash* on August 20, 2017: "The Cherokee

Nation can continue to define itself as it sees fit but must do so equally and evenhandedly with respect to native Cherokees and the descendants of Cherokee freedmen . . . .In accordance with Article 9 of the 1866 Treaty, the Cherokee Freedmen have a present right to citizenship in the Cherokee Nation that is coextensive with the rights of native Cherokees."[495]

From the time of the Civil War, the Keetoowah were the main political and cultural force opposing slavery. The Golden Circle, composed solely of slave owners, was formed in the late 1850s to counter the Keetoowah and support the Confederacy. There were Masons in both groups.

23

Keetoowah, Masons, and the Golden Circle

In the 1840s and 1850s, a man's position on slavery played a role in his choices about which Masonic lodges and churches to join. Lodges associated with Northern Baptists and Keetoowahs were anti-slavery and pro-Union, while those linked to Southern Baptists and Southern Methodist churches were generally sympathetic to slavery. Many people in my family were affiliated with Masonic Lodges, and I've wondered about the links between various churches and the Keetoowahs. The Keetoowah (Anikituhwagi or "people of the Kituwah") were attracted by the harmony of the Masonic ideals of wisdom, strength, and beauty.[496] The name Kituwah refers to one of the seven Cherokee mother towns located on the Tuckasegee River just above Bryson City in Swain County, North Carolina.[497] Even before removal, some Cherokee leaders were inducted into the Masonic Society. John Ross, for example, was initiated in 1827 at the Olive Branch Lodge of the Free and Accepted Masons in Jasper, Tennessee.

In 1848, Grand Master R.H. Pulliam of the Grand Lodge in Arkansas helped create a new lodge in Tahlequah. Officers were sworn in at Supreme Court Headquarters on Keetoowah Street on July 12, 1849. Fort Gibson Masonic Lodge 35 opened on November 6, 1850, Choctaw Lodge 52 near

Fort Washita was chartered on November 5, 1852, Flint Lodge #74 started at Peavine on November 9, 1853, and Muskogee Lodge 93 began operating on November 9, 1855. In 1852, the Cherokee National Council donated several lots in Tahlequah to be used jointly by the Masonic Lodge and the Sons of Temperance, paying for construction of a building to house the two organizations. Erected in 1853 and owned jointly, Cherokee Lodge #21 occupied the second floor.[498] In 1855, the Grand Master of Arkansas commented that "All over the length and breadth of our state the Masonic Order is flourishing, and amongst our red Brethren, in the Indian Territory, it is taking deep hold . . . The members of these Lodges compare very favorably with their pale-face neighbors . . . ."[499]

In 1855, Chief Ross and Reverend Evan Jones took steps to counter a secret society organized in Delaware and Saline Districts that promoted slavery and removal of abolitionists from the Nation. At the core of that plot were people from some Freemason "Blue Lodges" established by Arkansas Masonic officers affiliated with the Southern Methodist Church and the Knights of the Golden Circle.[500] Stand Watie was the leader of the Knights, and a Freemason. Their inner circle included John Rollin Ridge, Elias Boudinot, William Penn Adair, James Bell, Joseph Scales, and Josiah

Washbourne. But it's important to note that not all the members of Blue Lodges were pro-slavery. Lodge 21, for example, included Keetoowahs who supported Chief Ross and also Golden Circle men.

Reflecting these deepening fissures, the 1855 election for Principal Chief and the National Council was hard-fought, and the Council ended up being slightly pro-slavery. Many of the wealthier class wished to continue owning slaves and supported the new "Southern Rights" party created by larger slave holders. However, most Cherokees did not. Still, immediately after the election, the new Council, reflecting its changed composition, enacted a bill declaring the Cherokee to be "a slaveholding people." Although only a tiny minority owned even a single slave, ordinary Cherokees were not well-represented on the National Council.

In 1857, like everyone else, Cherokees read about the US Supreme Court's *Dred Scott* decision that black people are not equal to whites.[501] Ironically, Chief Justice Taney used the status of Indians to explain why blacks were not entitled to citizenship: "The situation of this population was altogether unlike that of the Indian race . . . [I]f an individual should leave his nation or tribe, and take up his abode among the white population, he would be entitled to all the rights and privileges which would belong to an emigrant from any other foreign people."[502]

The Keetoowah Society was anti-slavery as part of its commitment to equality. A group of Keetoowahs gathered at Peavine Baptist Church on April 15, 1858, to formalize their political and religious movement to fully protect Cherokee sovereignty and renew the old traditions. First, they prepared the sacred fire—*atsi-la gulunkw'tiyu*.[503] Cherokees venerated fire, which played an important role in igniting Kituwah spirit. In older days, before a Council meeting began, the Fire Keepers started the fire before the sun started to rise. They built earthen mounds about three feet tall to hold four logs pointing in cardinal directions, representing the four men originally chosen to hold the sacred fire. Around the fire were seven arbors for the seven clans.[504] Those present danced around it as their ancestors did. The opening pipe ritual, with everyone taking seven puffs, then a sacrifice to the Sacred Fire—a rabbit or chicken—led to deep discussions, and sometimes there were stomp dances that were exciting both for participants and spectators. Each of the seven clans were called up separately to dance around the fire and smoke from the sacred pipe. Many women wore rattles made of turtle shells around their legs and moved along in time to the men's drumming, creating sounds that seemed to give each person a second heart. Annie Spirit owned a classically beautiful pipe.

Annie Spirit's Smoking Pipe[505]

Originally known as the Amohee Church after its mother church in eastern Tennessee, Peavine was founded by Reverend Jesse Bushyhead. Lewis Downing became its pastor after Jesse's death in 1844. Born in eastern

Tennessee in 1823 to Samuel Downing and Susan Daugherty, both from distinguished Cherokee families, Lewis attended school at the Valley Town Mission and later at the Baptist Mission under the tutelage of Reverend Evan Jones. Early in life, he became a convert and was ordained to the Baptist ministry. Lewis was a strong Ross supporter, first elected Senator from Going Snake District on August 4, 1845, and re-elected in 1851 and 1859. On the evening of April 20, 1858, the modern Keetoowah Society was formed. Those present approved the Constitution drafted by Bud Gritts and Lewis Downing, agreeing that "Our secret society shall be named Keetoowah. All the members of the Keetoowah Society shall be like one family. It should be our intention that we must abide with each other in love . . . We must lead one another by the hand with all our strength. Our government is being destroyed. We must resort to bravery to stop it."[506]

The Keetoowah Constitution of April 29th noted that in the struggle between North and South, the latter "are the people who took our lands away from us . . . Their greed was the worst kind; they had no love and they are still following us to put their feet on us to get the last land we have."[507] Having a written constitution based on timeless Kituwah beliefs was an important step for all those who weren't slave owners. The Head Captains were Levi Gritts, Smith Christie (Gasannee) and Lewis Downing, all Baptist ministers. The Constitution provided for a general welfare fund to take care of sick, distressed, and poor full bloods.[508] A key part of the Keetoowah Society was the militant group of "Pin" members, who were anti-slavery. They chose the US flag as their symbol and wore crossed straight pins or a single straight pin on the left lapel of their hunting jackets, using secret signs such as touching the hat when they met or taking their left lapel and drawing it forward and rightward across the heart.[509] When two Pins met and wanted to verify their identity, one would ask "Who are you?" The reply was "Tahlequah, who are you?" The password response was "I am Keetoowah's son."[510] By 1861, there were about three-thousand Pins, a sizable force, and they had majorities in both houses of the Cherokee legislature.

In contrast, the 1860 Constitution of the Knights of the Golden Circle stressed their pro-slavery beliefs: "We . . . in order to form a more perfect union and protect ourselves and property against the works of Abolitionists do establish this Constitution for the government of the Knights of the Golden Circle in this Nation . . . No person shall become a member . . . who is not a proslavery man . . . "[511] Based on this provision, Stand Watie and William Penn Adair circulated a petition to evict Reverend John B. Jones from the Nation as an "intruder" who "is scattering his principles of Abolitionism like fire brands throughout the country . . . ."[512] Watie and the Knights believed that if the missionaries were expelled, the Cherokee people would side with the South, but they were seriously mistaken, in large part because they didn't understand the strong feelings of the Keetoowah against slavery. It was impossible for them to support the people who stole the original Cherokee lands. The die was cast for civil war within the Cherokee Nation.

24

The Civil War in Indian Territory

An Intertribal Council was convened at Creek Agency (just north of Muskogee) on February 17, 1861 to discuss the war-like signals coming from the Southern states. Chief Ross's nephew William P. Ross represented the Cherokees. No Chickasaw or Choctaws attended, having already decided to side with the Southern States if the Union dissolved.[513] Most delegates were from the Creek, Cherokee, and Seminole tribes. Creek Chief O-Pothle-Yohola was the leading voice favoring all the tribes sticking together as neutrals. He would play a major role in the next few years. But like many tribes, the Creeks were divided, with Daniel McIntosh siding with the Confederacy.[514]

Chief Ross's instructions to the Cherokee delegation were clear: "We have only to adhere firmly to our respective Treaties. By them we have placed ourselves under the protection of the United States, and of no other sovereign whatever . . . The parties holding the responsibilities of the Federal Government will always be bound to us."[515] He didn't want the Cherokees to align with the Confederacy but to be neutral in the conflict so as to protect their lives and lands.

But all federal Indian agents in Indian Territory were Southern men, actively engaged in influencing the tribes to side with the South. Most had already left their official posts, including the most influential of them all, Douglas Cooper; he was actively raising troops for the Confederacy in April, May, and June while continuing to be paid by the US government. Cooper became the key assistant to General Pike in negotiating Confederate treaties with the tribes.[516] There was no response from the US, which seemed largely unaware of what was going on. Moreover, the US had stopped paying the annuities due under the various treaties, which undermined Ross's position and proved to be a tragically short-sided decision. The absence of US troops in Indian territory left Union-supporting Indians in the lurch.[517]

Stand Watie was working with the Arkansas Secession Convention in March 1861, organizing local chapters of the Knights of the Golden Circle (also known as the Southern Rights Party). When Arkansas voted for secession and union with the Confederacy on May 8th, Elias Cornelius Boudinot was Secretary of the Convention, having moved there after his father's murder in 1839. As the war started, Cherokees turned against each other, with most Treaty Party members choosing the Confederacy. But even after the fall of Fort Sumter on April 13th, Chief Ross still felt the best course was neutrality. Stressing Cherokee obligations to the United States, he issued a Neutrality Proclamation on May 17th: "They should not be alarmed by false reports thrown into circulation by designing men, but cultivate harmony among themselves and observe in good faith strict neutrality between the States threatening civil war . . . There has been no declaration of war between the opposing parties, and the conflict may yet be averted by compromise or a peaceful separation."[518]

Confederate General Ben McCullough wrote to Ross on June 17th requesting that Watie's troops be accorded volunteer status with the Confederacy. Ross was unswayed: "Your demand that those people of the Nation who are in favor of joining the Confederacy be allowed to organize into military companies as home guards for the purpose of defending themselves in case of invasion from the North is most respectfully declined. I cannot give my consent to any such organization . . . it would be a palpable violation of my position as a neutral . . . ."[519] Although a majority of the tribe endorsed that policy, Watie organized the First Cherokee Mounted Volunteers regiment on July 12th in support of the Confederacy, ignoring the official neutrality proclamation. That was an illegal act under prevailing Cherokee law. Shortly afterwards, he was promoted to Colonel by the Confederacy, with command of twelve companies composed of a small number of Cherokees and a much larger contingent of Creeks. They quickly joined the Confederate Army in Missouri along the northeastern border of the Cherokee Nation.

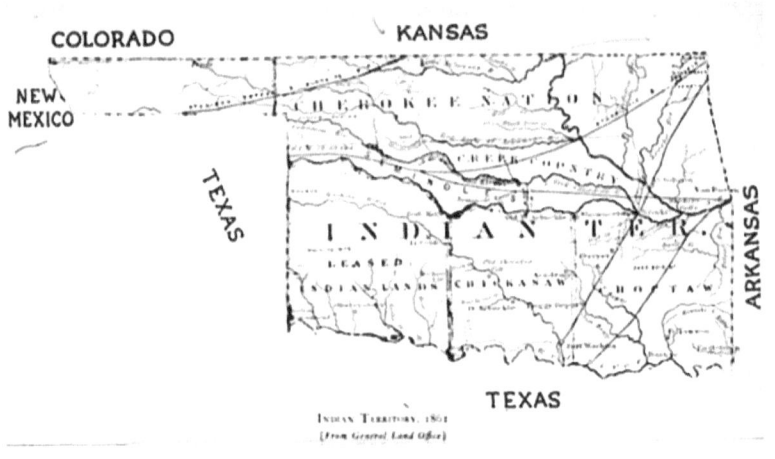

Map of Indian Territory in 1861[520]

Several of Sam's and Nannie's sons enlisted on the Confederate side, serving in the First Cherokee Mounted Volunteer (Watie's Regiment), Cherokee Mounted Volunteers (Holt's Squadron), and other units. Joel Bryan Mayes was a Captain in one company of scouts for Watie, participating in an important Confederate victory on August 10th at Wilson's Creek, Missouri. Around 1,000 Choctaws and Cherokees along with General

McCulloch's troops took on General Lyon's Second Kansas Volunteer Infantry and Colonel Franz Sigel's German/American troops. Mayes' company had moved unseen into the bushes next to the Union line, and their first volley knocked Lyon from his saddle, the first Union General killed in action. The Federal troops retreated to Springfield. Many scalps were taken by Mayes' men. Some compare this to the Battle of Bull Run in Virginia on July 10, 1861.[521]

Stand Watie in 1865[522]

After Chief Ross learned the details of the Union defeat at Wilson's Creek, he began to change his mind about neutrality, given that the tribes had been abandoned militarily by the US and their annuity payments had stopped. Having decided that Indian Territory wasn't a priority, the US withdrew the small Federal garrison forces, leaving the Cherokees and other Indian Nations undefended. Union-leaning Cherokees felt betrayed. Ross convened a general assembly in Tahlequah on August 21, 1861 and around 4,000 people attended. They were divided on whether to remain neutral or to support the North or South. Amid this swirling brew of discontent, Ross gave this address: "The great object with me has been to have the Cherokee people harmonious and united in the full and free exercise and enjoyment of all their rights . . . . Union is strength; dissension is weakness, misery, ruin . . . . [I]n view of all the circumstances of our situation . . . in my opinion the time has now come when you should signify your consent for the authorities of the nation to adopt preliminary steps for an alliance with the Confederate States . . . ."[523] Ross had changed direction, going against what he'd stood for publicly and privately for years, but under the circumstances, with no protection from the US and no longer receiving the money promised under various treaties, he had little choice.[524] Ross wrote to General McCulloch on August 24th: "We are authorized to form an alliance with the Confederate States . . . as early as practicable . . . we have deemed it prudent . . . to organize a regiment of mounted men and tender them for service.[525]

McCulloch wrote back on September 1st thanking Ross, but he also wrote confidentially to Confederate War Secretary Walker about the reality on the ground as he saw it: "Colonel Stand Watie belongs to the true Southern party. I hope our government will continue this gallant man and true friend of our country in our service, and attach him and his men (some 300) to my command. It might be well to give him a battalion separate from the Cherokee regiment under Colonel Drew. Colonel Drew's regiment will be mostly composed of full-bloods, whilst those with Colonel Stand Watie will be half-breeds, who are educated men, and good soldiers anywhere, in or out of the Nation."[526]

Confederate representatives promised that Indians would control their own destinies if the South won the war and that they would pay the lapsed annuities starting immediately. After what Cherokees had suffered at the hands of the US government the past thirty years, that was nectar to many. After heated speeches pro and con, the vote narrowly supported the Confederacy, although the decision was murky and there were differing interpretations of what happened since several inconsistent resolutions were passed. Most Cherokees departed thinking that neutrality would be maintained, while Treaty Party people perceived a green light to support the Confederacy. The First Resolution stated, "We fully approve the neutrality recommended by the Principal Chief in the war pending between the United States and the Confederate states." But the final Resolution read, " . . . reposing full confidence in the authorities of the Cherokee Nation, we submit to their wisdom in the management . . . of the relation between the United and Confederate States of America and which may render an alliance on our part with the latter states expedient and desirable."[527]

Ross agreed that a new Regiment called the First Cherokee Mounted Rifles, to distinguish it from Watie's regiment, would be formed under the command of John Drew, a wealthy salt works owner who was married to one of Ross' nieces. Most of the new troops were full bloods belonging to the Keetoowah Society and therefore were not Watie's natural allies. Ross named Lewis Downing chaplain of the new Regiment, Robert D. Ross as surgeon, and his nephew, William Potter Ross, as Lieutenant Colonel. Thomas Pegg was named Major, and the Captains included Richard Fields, John Porum Davis, James McDaniel, and Lewis Ross. The regiment consisted of eleven companies from the various districts.

The old Creek Chief O-Pothle-Yohola took a different approach on August 15th, writing President Lincoln this heartfelt letter: " . . . you said that in our new homes we should be defended from all interference from any person and that no white people in the whole world would ever molest us . . . . But now the wolf has come . . . . Now White people are trying to take our people away to fight against us and you . . . ."[528] But the President did not reply. Although O-Pothle-Yohola no longer had an official role, he was widely admired and still respected. He had many supporters. The Creek Nation was divided. A wealthy landowner, Christian convert and Freemason, he always tried to protect the sovereignty of his people. In 1836, he had led 8,000 Upper Creeks out of Alabama and along the Trail of Tears west to Indian Territory. He had hoped to reconcile all his people, but the Lower Creeks were supporting the Confederacy. As in the other Indian nations, that meant brother against brother.

The Confederacy began paying the annuities owed to Cherokees, Seminoles, Creeks, Choctaws and Chickasaws. Most everyone hoped the fighting would take place in neighboring Arkansas, Missouri, Texas and Kansas rather than on Indian territory. For his part, O-Pothle-Yoholo started a pan-Indian rebellion in support of the Union against the Confederacy with people from fifteen tribes. They freed all their slaves, inviting them to join their army amd around 500 did so.[529] By early September, O-Pothle-Yoholo raised the Union flag and was ready for battle with around 3,000 warriors.[530] The Cherokee Council, prodded by Watie, declared war on the US government on October 28th. In hindsight, that was a tragic mistake.

Following Confederate victories in Missouri, a Treaty with the Confederacy was signed with General Albert Pike on October 7th at the Murrell home in Park Hill, and a Confederate flag was raised over the courthouse in Tahlequah, a sad, fateful day.[531] The Council issued this Declaration about the new alliance on October 28th: "The Cherokee people had its origin in the South; its institutions are similar to those of the Southern States, and their interests identical with theirs . . . .Whatever causes the Cherokee people may have had in the past to complain of some of the Southern states, they cannot but feel that their interests and destiny are inseparably connected with those of the south. The war now waging, is a war of Northern cupidity and fanaticism against the institution of African servitude; against the commercial freedom of the South, and against the political freedom of the states, and its objects are to annihilate the sovereignty of those states and utterly change the nature of the general government."[532]

Neutrality was over. Stand Watie and Ross shook hands as Ross looked him in the eye and expressed "his warm desire for union and the harmony of the nation." Watie replied that "there now existed a party in the nation known as the pin party, and as long as they held their political organization there could be no peace."[533] But the die was cast: the two camps were in it together.

The first important battle took place on November 19, 1861 at Round Mountain, sometimes called Red Forks, north of the Red Fork River near present-day Keystone, Oklahoma. O-Pothle-Yoholo was camped with a large group of warriors from many Indian nations. Besides Creeks there were Choctaws, Chickasaws, Seminoles, Comanches, Delawares, Kickapoos, Wichitas, and Shawnees. By actively courting freed slaves and freedmen, his force was swelled with hundreds of men who desired freedom. Colonel Douglas Cooper led the Confederate forces, including Texas fighters commanded by Colonel William Quayle. O-Pothle-Yoholo had sent most of his people north towards Kansas, keeping intact his fighting force of several thousand men. Approaching Round Mountain, he ordered fires to be lit in a semicircular fashion and waited for the Confederates to arrive. Taken by surprise, Captain Brinson's Company D Texas Cavalry troops met a hail of bullets. Under cover of darkness, Cooper attempted to locate the Texas Cavalry and O-Pothle-Yoholo but was met by fierce fire. After taking many casualties, they decided to pull back for the night. O-Pothle-Yoholo's forces moved north during the night, his goal being to reach Bird Creek to join pro-Union Cherokees. As his forces moved north, they lit the prairies on fire to ensure Confederate forces had no hay for their horses, or many other provisions either.[534]

The Battle of Bird Creek in the Cherokee Nation (Chusto-Talasah) commenced on December 8th with the Confederates holding a large advantage in men and firepower. But O-Pothle-Yoholo was a clever strategist, and after a short time in Cherokee territory, he had already convinced the Keetoowah full-bloods to support him. The Confederate forces were separated. O-Pothle-Yoholo's large force of about 2,000 men surrounded Drew's Regiment of 480 Indian troops, while Cooper's larger force was a few miles away. Most of Drew's full bloods deserted during the night, taking their horses with them, leaving him with just sixty men. They marched to join General Cooper the next morning. Cooper, Quayle, Drew, and McIntosh's Creeks intended to attack O-Pothle-Yoholo the next day but were surprised in the morning by 200 warriors attacking from the rear. Quick action by Captain Young and his Chickasaw-Choctaw squadron diverted that attack. Resuming his direct assault, Cooper drove O-Pothle-Yoholo from the prairie back to the woods with fierce hand-to-hand combat. But after several hours of fighting, as evening fell and a rain began to pour, it was a stalemate. Cooper decided to pull back for the night. When he tried to find O-Pothle-Yoholo the next morning, all his warriors had vanished with their horses and supplies. Fifteen Confederates were killed, forty-seven were wounded, and they had exhausted their gunpowder. Although some say Cooper won this battle, his main objective of crushing O-Pothle-Yoholo's rebellion had failed.[535]

Confederate President Davis transmitted to the Provisional Congress all the Indian treaties Pike had negotiated on December 12th, requesting their approval while at the same time removing Pike's promises about a form of sovereignty and payments of annuities.[536] The tribes weren't informed about the changes, information that might well have changed their minds about the alliance.

O-Pothle-Yoholo was camped at Shoal Creek, a stream running from the Verdigris River in the Patriot Hills on December 26th facing Cooper's and Colonel McIntosh's formidable forces. They included the Second

Arkansas Mounted Rifles, a battalion of 1,400 men drawn from the Third, Sixth, and Eleventh Texas Cavalry, and Watie's battalion. The Confederates felt confident of crushing O-Pothle-Yoholo this time, but Cooper's large force was delayed because most of his teamsters deserted when he was two days away. Watie's forces also hadn't arrived yet, but McIntosh decided to make his move without them on December 26th. O-Pothle-Yoholo's forces were well-positioned and waiting for them. After several volleys, the Texas cavalry units led the charge, overwhelming the Union Indians. The Confederates killed about 250 of O-Pothle-Yoholo's forces, capturing 160 women and children, thirty wagons, 500 horses, oxen, cows, sheep, and many dogs.[537]

Charles Bird King Painting of O-Pothle-Yoholo[538]

O-Pothle-Yoholo and the survivors abandoned everything and fled for Kansas. It was snowing hard and extremely cold. Watie chased them, following their trail for twenty-five miles. Major Elias Boudinot and Captain Joel Mayes led the charge, killing about fifteen fighters and taking more women and children captive. The Creek and Seminole forces were destroyed. By the time the survivors reached Leroy, Kansas, they were a spent force, joining about 6,000 people from the Indian Nations along the border, only to find that the Union promise of help, supplies, and support would not be kept. While Kansas provided a safe haven for the loyal Indians against direct Confederate assault, there were virtually no provisions. Many people froze to death during that bleak winter and around 2,000 ponies perished.[539]

Map of Loyal Indians' Retreat to Kansas[540]

Whether they fled their Nation or not, life for all Cherokees became very hard. Annie didn't want to move to Kansas, deciding to stick it out at home in Flint District. Near the end of December that bleak year, her mother fell ill and died.[541] She was more alone than ever. Thousands of loyal Indians retreated to Kansas during the harsh winter of 1861.

A few months earlier, Annie's close friend and companion Simon Snell had joined the pro-Union Cherokee forces and was fighting. He was a full-blood Cherokee and a strong supporter of the Keetoowah. The Cherokee Nation was more fractured than ever. By early 1862, more than 2,000 members of the tribe had fled to Kansas, taking refuge with thousands of Creeks, Seminoles, and other tribes. The Cherokee Indian Home Guards were formally organized there, fighting for the rest of the War on the Union side with other tribes and freed black troops. The First Indian Home Guard regiment was principally Creek, while the Second and Third regiments were mainly Cherokee. The Second Regiment had sixty-six officers and 1,800 privates, while the Third Regiment had fifty-two officers and around 1,400 privates.[542]

Pro-Union Indians Signing Up to Fight[543]

The next major battle took place in miserable weather from March 6-8 at Pea Ridge, sometimes called Elkhorn Tavern, in northwest Arkansas on the edge of the Cherokee Nation. Union divisions commanded by Major General Samuel Curtis had about 1,100 men, excellent artillery, and adequate provisions. Facing them were more than 1,600 Confederate troops led by General Albert Pike, General Earl Van Dorn, General McCullough, and Stand Watie. That was the largest Confederate force mobilized west of the Mississippi during the War. Pike integrated his force with Watie's and John Drew's fighters, and McCulloch's men joined them. They encountered a small Union battery supported by cavalry on March 7th, quickly overwhelming them and seizing their guns, but were too disorganized to capitalize on their minor victory.

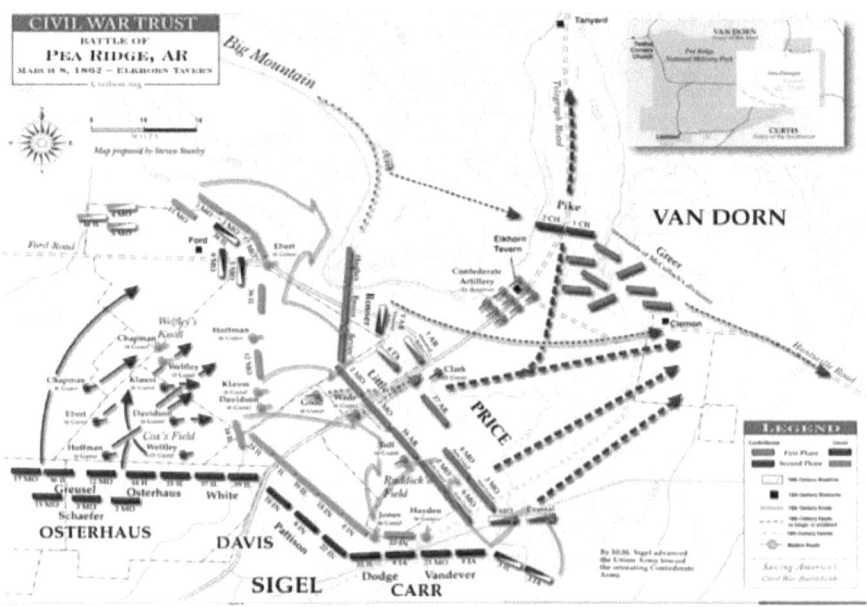

Map of Union and Confederate Troop Positions in March 1862[544]

The Confederate Military History summarized the battle: "Snow fell during the night, and clothed both hill and valley in a mantle of white. The hills are high on both sides; the valley deep, about half a mile in width ... General McCulloch, in person, directed the movement against the enemy's front and center, near Leetown, up the valley and along its sides. For this the enemy was prepared, and resisted with a storm of shot and shell from his batteries in position, and with infantry behind his breastworks ... Four times the Confederates repulsed the enemy's lines ... with great slaughter of men and horses ... [545] Colonel Mcintosh led a cavalry charge with five regiments across a field and was shot dead. That wing of the army was paralyzed.

Illustration of the Battle of Pea Ridge in Progress[546]

How much the deaths of McCulloch, Hébert, and Mcintosh affected the battle has been debated ever since, but clearly they were important losses. The final battle took place around Elkhorn tavern on the morning of March 8, 1862 when Curtis's artillery opened fire against the Confederates on Pea Ridge. After several hours of shelling back and forth, Curtis succeeded in silencing the Confederate guns, and the Southern troops began fleeing the Ridge. Federal riflemen took a harsh toll with their superior firepower. Many Confederate troops were armed only with shotguns or pistols and were low on ammunition. Having lost their two best commanders, their organization and morale were poor; the Confederate Army was routed, losing many more men in a decisive defeat. Watie retreated to Camp Stephens. One of the best accounts was written by Major-General Franz Sigel, a German immigrant. His full report to Brigadier General Samuel Curtis is in Appendix 20.

Portrait of Sigel Drawn During the War[547]

But the Union's grievous mistake of pulling most troops out of Indian territory continued to leave Cherokees vulnerable to Watie's raids as guerrilla warfare raged throughout the Cherokee Nation. Homes were burned, crops destroyed, livestock killed, and innocent people were slaughtered. Watie's depleted force of 400 men was camped on Cowskin Prairie not far from his sawmill in early June. Union Colonel Doubleday decided to try and finish him off, marching with over 1,000 soldiers down the Spring River to surprise him. Doubleday's artillery began pounding Watie's position on the evening of June 6, 1862. Union troops quickly took the camp, capturing Colonel William Penn Adair. The remaining Confederate troops abandoned their camp along with hundreds of horses and cattle. Watie was at the sawmill and missed the action.[548]

Final Hour of the Battle of Pea Ridge - Painted by Hunt Wilson[549]

Colonel J.J. Clarkson was promoted to commander of all Confederate troops in Indian Territory on June 26th, with Colonels Watie and Drew in charge of the Indian regiments. Meanwhile, the Union commanders finally decided to mount a major action to stop Confederate activity in the Cherokee Nation. They were hoping for Chief Ross's full support, even though the Indian Home Guard's forces hadn't been paid or provided the promised arms, clothing, and supplies. Lieutenant James Phillips wrote Ross on June 26th outlining a proposal: "I have learned . . . that you and your people are truly loyal to the government of the United States . . . .my purpose is your protection and to . . . give you and all your friends an opportunity to show their loyalty to the United States Government."[550]

Clarkson's Confederate troops were camped near Locust Grove on July 3rd while Watie's' men were nearby at Spavinaw Creek. Union troops led by Colonel Weer arrived at their Locust Grove camp around daybreak, surrounding his camp and launching withering fire as they woke up. By the end of the day, Clarkson surrendered more than 100 troops and sixty wagons of supplies. Drew's regiment was camped at Flat Rock Creek not far away; after the news of Clarkson's capture reached them, virtually all remaining Cherokees defected to the Union side. Lewis Downing and his 200 men also joined the Union force.[551] On July 4th, there was a big celebration at the greatly enlarged Union camp on Cabin Creek.

Following these victories, Captain Harris Greeno of the Sixth Kansas Calvary captured Tahlequah on July 15th without firing a shot. He formally arrested Chief Ross and the officers guarding him at Park Hill, including William P. Ross, Thomas Pegg, Anderson Benge, Joseph Chooie, Lacy Hawkins, Archibald Scraper, Joseph Cornsilk, and John Shell. All volunteered to join the Union army. A few weeks later, Ross and his family were taken to Pennsylvania where a Cherokee Government in Exile was established. Ross was never to return to the Cherokee Nation.[552] Later that summer, Annie married Simon Snell (or 'Snail' as 'A-la-gua' is often translated), a young Cherokee captain in the Indian Home Guards who fought on the Union side from the beginning. By then, he was in the Third Regiment formed in July 1862 under the command of Colonel William Phillips. Most of the Regiment were Pins, as was Simon. His father, Nickajack, died during the war shortly before Simon and Annie were married. Simon's siblings Akey and E-yah-te-whe-ske were killed in 1863, but Le-La-Tah, his mother, survived.

Simon and Annie's Wedding Photo

Chief Ross and his family moved to Pennsylvania in August. While in exile he established a pro-Union Cherokee government. Soon after, he traveled to Washington to explain the Cherokees' situation to President Lincoln. Ross requested more Federal troops to protect them and payment of the annuities that had lapsed since 1861. The President listened intently but didn't commit himself. Instead, the three Union Indian regiments and the Kansas artillery were ordered to withdraw to Kansas. Although Indian Commissioner Dole requested that the troops be returned immediately, Union generals vacillated; Lincoln wasn't focused on Indian country and gave no instructions. That left a large opening for Watie to continue his campaigns in Indian territory on behalf of the Confederacy. He illegally appointed himself principal chief on August 21st. His troops continued marauding, killing many people and stealing everything he could carry. That led many pro-Union Cherokee families to flee back to Kansas and the refugee camps they'd only recently left.

The next important battle was fought at Fort Wayne on October 22nd on the edge of Beattie's Prairie. That fort, never completed and abandoned in 1842, served as a temporary base for Watie's regiment. About 7am, Brigadier General James G. Blunt, a Kansas physician turned soldier, and his mixed Cherokee, Indian, and Kansas troops from the First Division of the Army of the Frontier made a surprise attack on Cooper's and Watie's troops. The Third Indian Home Guard helped avert a flanking operation by Cooper, pushing Confederate forces back seven miles and capturing their battle flag and four artillery pieces. Blunt routed the Confederates from the field, driving them from the old fort after just a half-hour battle. They fled to the Canadian River, leaving their artillery, ammunition and equipment behind.[553]

The Confederates were again soundly defeated on December 7th at the Battle of Prairie Grove in northwest Arkansas, after which Union forces finally swept back into Cherokee territory. Colonel William Phillips' troops attacked the Confederate stronghold at Fort Davis just across the river from Fort Gibson on December 27th. In the face of the superior Union artillery and pressure of the Indian Home Guard troops, the Confederates retreated, and Phillips ordered the fort burned to the ground. His troops chased Watie and Cooper south, burning homes along the way as the Confederates withdrew to Honey Springs in the far south along the borders with the Creek and Choctaw Nations.

Many of Annie's relatives and friends fought on the Union Side. The list of those involved in the Home Guards on the Union side is impressive—more than 2,000 Cherokee men.[554] Their overall mission was to occupy the frontline along the Arkansas River, with the main base being Fort Gibson, and they were involved in numerous battles. In 1862, Simon Snell's regiment fought on July 28th at Bayou Bernard; Neosho and Spring River from September 1-6; Shirley's Ford on September 20th; Newtonia from

September 30th to October 4th; Fort Gibson on October 15th; Cane Hill on November 28th; Salem on December 2nd; Prairie Grove and Rhea's Mills on December 7th; Neosho again on December 15th; and December 20th at Cane Hill. The Home Guards played a determinative role in the Civil War in Indian Territory, strongly supported by the Keetoowah Society, whose political aim was to maintain Cherokee sovereignty. Keetoowah men and women visited Cherokee soldiers in their tents and hospitals, maintaining vital social connections.

As 1863 began, Brigadier General William Steele was named commander of Confederate troops in Indian Territory but was still forced to serve under his bitter rival, Colonel Cooper. Watie's men tried to break up a Keetoowah Council meeting on Cowskin Prairie in January, but Phillips' troops stopped him. After a three-day Council meeting on Cowskin Prairie on February 20th, Major Thomas Pegg was elected Council President in Ross's absence. The Keetoowah Cherokee government voted to overturn the 1861 Treaty with the Confederacy, declaring Watie and his troops outlaws. An emancipation law was enacted on February 21st abolishing slavery in the Cherokee Nation. Pegg and his compatriots, including Lewis Downing, served as the official government of the Cherokee Nation during the rest of the war. Cherokees who had been driven out of their homes began returning. By April 8th, the First, Second and Third Indian Home Guards, along with Kansas cavalry, numbered more than 3,000 men based in Fort Gibson, an excellent spot on a bluff overlooking the Grand River and near both the Arkansas River and Texas Road. This was the key part of Colonel Phillips' plan to advance in force into Indian Territory to protect Cherokees and other tribes.

But Watie responded by calling a meeting at Webber's Falls on April 24th, demanding that he be elected Principal Chief of the Confederate Cherokees. He was duly chosen by acclamation. The same day, Colonel

Phillips, having been informed about the meeting, marched 600 men all night to launch a surprise attack early the next morning. Watie's men were totally unprepared, with many not even dressed, and they were soundly routed, losing most of their equipment and animals to the Union forces. Barely a shot was fired. The Battle of Cabin Creek on July 2nd proved to be crucial for the Union. A large wagon train of supplies headed for Fort Gibson was desperately needed by the Union, and Watie was determined to stop it. This was the first battle where former slaves played a major role. The First Kansas Colored Infantry under Colonel James Williams bravely crossed the creek in the face of withering fire, bearing down on Watie's troops, who turned and fled to the river, which was at flood stage. Many died as they tried to cross. On July 5th, the Union supply wagons reached Fort Gibson.

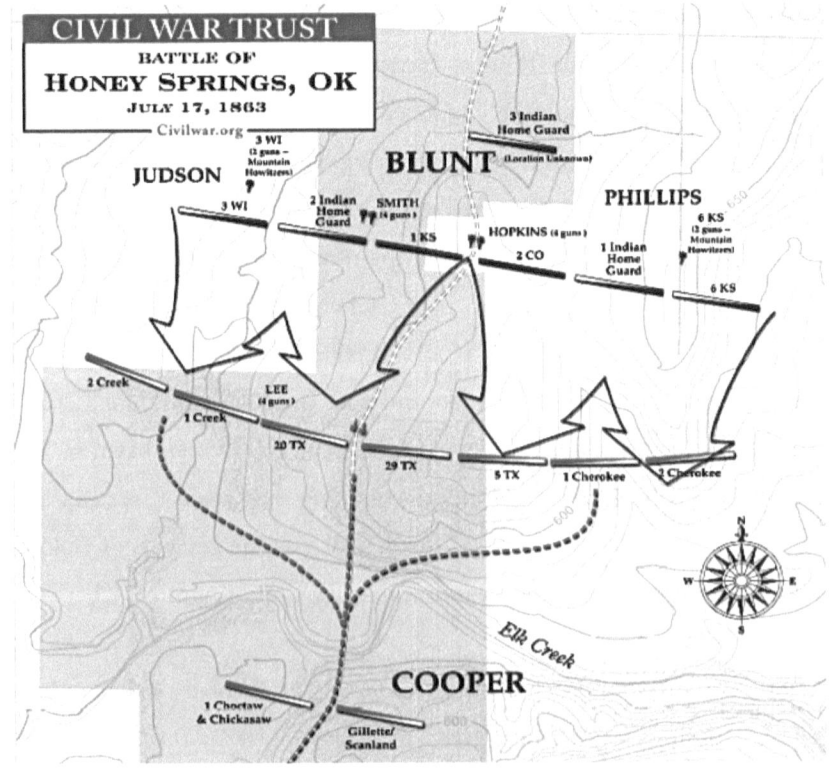

Map of Union and Confederate Forces at Honey Springs[555]

The Battle of Honey Springs on July 17th—sometimes called the Battle of Elk Creek—was the decisive confrontation between Confederate and Federal forces in Indian Territory. It took place in McIntosh County about four and one-half miles northeast of Checotah and fifteen miles south of Muskogee, along the Creek border. The battle became famous and has been discussed and debated ever since. The supply depot at Honey Springs, about twenty miles southwest of Fort Gibson, was the principal operations base for Confederate General Douglas Cooper, who had around 5,000 soldiers in the area. The 1st and 2nd Cherokee Mounted Rifles fought for the Confederates in the battle. Joel Mayes, Samuel Mayes' eldest son, served with the Second Mounted Regiment along with his seventeen-year-old brother Samuel. Joel's brothers John Thomas Mayes was a Captain and Commander of Company H in Stand Watie's regiment, while Wash Mayes served with Captain Adair's Second Cherokee Mounted Rifles.

Major General Blunt decided to launch a surprise attack with Companies C, F, and H of the Sixth Kansas infantry, along with the 2nd Indian Home Guard and First Kansas Colored Infantry. They marched at night along the Texas Road towards Honey Springs. Their weapons were far superior to the Confederates, including six Napoleon cannons that fired twelve-pound shells, and unlike the Confederates, they had dry powder. Many of the Confederates guns wouldn't fire because of inferior Mexican gunpowder and the dense rains of the preceding days and were forced to retreat under fire. As one commentator concluded, the Union's victory "prevented the Confederates from controlling Indian Territory north of the Arkansas River," opening the path for Blunt to take Fort Smith two months later in September: "Combined with the Union advance under Major General Frederick Steele west from Helena, Arkansas, the base established there seriously compromised Confederate efforts to maintain control of that state."[556] It was the largest battle fought in Indian Territory and proved to be the turning point, often termed the "Gettysburg" of the war in Indian Territory.[557]

The First Kansas Colored Infantry played a key role, destroying almost the entire first line of Texans early in the battle. The fighting turned into a rout after a few hours as the Confederates' defensive line collapsed. Union forces killed or wounded more than 130 Confederates and took forty-seven prisoners, while losing only seventeen men. Cooper retreated down the Texas Road towards Honey Springs and then south of the Canadian River. Blunt followed the Confederates to their camp on the Canadian but found it abandoned, as Cooper pulled his forces further south towards Perryville. By August 26th, Cooper and Watie were reportedly only twenty-five miles away, and Blunt continued to move his forces quickly towards them. His artillery decimated the Confederates' exhausted and ill-equipped forces, as they fled towards the Red River. Around half the Confederate losses were borne by the Texas Cavalry. Blunt seized or burned all the Confederate supplies in Perryville. A detailed report on the Battle of Honey Springs is in Appendix 19.

Sketch by James R. O'Neil Drawn During the Battle of Honey Springs[558]

Unbowed, Watie returned to Tahlequah on October 28th to burn down the Capitol, as well as Chief Ross's home at Park Hill for good measure. Watie continued to bedevil the Cherokees in smaller ways for the next two years, but normal life slowly returned. Simon and his unit were involved in many battles that year, fighting near Maysville in late January, at Fort Gibson in late February, on Greenleaf Prairie from March 12-15, Fort Gibson on March 27th, Tahlequah on March 30th, Maysville on May 6th, Fort Gibson from May 20th to late June, Cabin Creek on July 1st, Honey Springs on July 17th, and Fourteen-Mile Creek on October 30th.

As 1864 began, Union forces controlled most of Indian Territory. President Lincoln issued a proclamation in early January offering pardons to all Indians who stopped fighting for the Confederacy. Colonel William Phillips was his emissary, who began a scorched-earth campaign south on February 1st with his 1,500 troops from the First and Third Indian Home Guards and the Fourteenth Kansas regiment. They marched almost to the Texas border, burning Confederate farms and homes, killing livestock, and taking no prisoners during their month-long campaign. They didn't lose a single man.

Elias Cornelius Boudinot, serving in the Confederate House of Representatives in Richmond, confirmed to his uncle Stand Watie on May 7th that Watie's promotion to Brigadier General had been approved. Watie had been waiting a long time for that news.[559] Flush with that success, Watie and his gang kept going, capturing the steamboat *J.R. Williams* on the Arkansas River on June 1st as it headed for Fort Gibson laden with Union supplies. No one seemed able to stop Watie's attacks, which included successful raids at Massard's Prairie in Arkansas on July 27th and Gunter's Prairie in August. In mid-September, he made his most audacious move yet, taking a force of about 2,000 troops, including General Richard Gano's Texas brigade and a six-gun artillery battery, up the Grand River

Valley fifteen miles north of Fort Gibson. Watie attacked a Union supply train at Cabin Creek on the night of September 19th that was headed for Fort Gibson with 300 wagons of food, clothing, ammunition, and supplies. Watie's forces were much larger than the Union troops guarding the train, mainly the first Kansas colored volunteers. After hours of fierce fighting, the remaining Union forces escaped towards Fort Gibson while the Confederates seized more than 100 wagons and around 700 mules, burning all the other wagons and thousands of tons of hay. Simon's regiment fought there. Watie slaughtered the black troops, most of whom were cutting hay, taunting them as he departed by shouting "Where is the First Kansas [racial slur] now?" The Second Battle of Cabin Creek was the worst Union defeat in Indian Territory, allowing Watie's forces to continue their raids.

Amid the fighting in 1864, Annie learned that her half-brother Weely Vann, his wife, and their only son, Tee-saw-yuh-hi, had been killed. They'd fled to Kansas earlier in the war, and Annie had lost touch with them, another bitter blow from the war. Many family members and friends were killed or wounded. Simon's unit was engaged in another fight at Cow Creek in November, their last serious battle of the War.

In late 1864, representatives of the Cherokee, Creek, and Seminoles met to discuss how best to negotiate with Washington about their future and that of all the Indians in the region. Lewis Downing wrote to President Lincoln on December 20th with this proposal, noting the precedent of the 1843 International Indian Council: "[W]e propose that the nations, who are fighting under the banner of the Union, invite all the tribes of the Southwest and as many others as possible to meet in general convention and re-establish their league of amity and re-assert . . . their loyalty to the Federal Government . . . Let them there league together to crush out the rebellion and put an end to the war throughout the country. We propose that the said convention of tribes be held near Claremore's Mound, on the Verdigris River . . . in the early part of next June . . . to smoke the pipe of peace."[560]

That was an inspired initiative, but Downing didn't receive a reply from the President; consequently, the proposed conclave didn't take place. That lost opportunity would have prevented some of the tragedies lying ahead for Indians. In early 1865, hostilities began winding down in Cherokee country. Simon's Regiment was involved in just two small fights, from Fort Gibson to Little River and Hillabee the last half of March and a skirmish at Snake River, Arkansas on April 28th. Annie and most Cherokees read with joy that General Robert E. Lee surrendered to General Ulysses S. Grant at Appomattox on April 9th to formally end the War, although Confederate President Jefferson Davis resisted. With General Grant at Lee's surrender was a Seneca Lt. Colonel named Ely Samuel Parker, whose Seneca name was Hasanoanda, the only Native American to hold a high rank in the Union Army.

Hasanoanda (Sitting on the Left)[561]

Hasanoanda wrote the final draft of the surrender terms signed by Lee. He had a distinguished military career, serving as Grant's military secretary and writing most of Grant's correspondence. At the surrender, Lee said: "I am glad to see one real American here." Hasanoanda replied: "We are all Americans."[562] He was promoted to Brigadier General on April 9, 1865. President Grant named him Commissioner of Indian Affairs in 1870, the first Native American to hold that position. Earlier in life he studied for the Bar in New York but wasn't permitted to take the exam as Indians were excluded until 1924. He trained as an engineer instead, which led to his being commissioned as a captain in Grant's army in 1863. Parker served as Chief Engineer of the 7th Division during the siege of Vicksburg and was named military secretary to Grant following the siege of Petersburg. During 1866, he was a member of the Commission that renegotiated treaties with the Cherokees and other tribes.

Hasanoanda (leaning on a chair fifth from the right)[563]

Cherokees and the whole nation learned the shocking news on April 15th that President Lincoln had been assassinated. Although the War was almost over then, his death would have profound consequences for the nation, including Indians and African Americans, given Vice-President Andrew Johnson's sympathy for the South.

Portrait of Lincoln Drawn During the War[564]

When Jefferson Davis was captured on May 10th, the war was over for most people. On May 31st all Union Cherokee troops were mustered out of service—including Annie's beloved Simon. The ordeal was over. They could begin their lives anew, but they would pay for what Watie and his supporters had done. And he wasn't quite finished yet. Refusing to give up, he was fighting on with his small band of followers. Watie finally surrendered his sword to US Lieutenant Colonel Asa Matthews on June 23rd at Doaksville, near Fort Towson in the Choctaw Nation, the last Confederate General to lay down arms. One can't deny he was a brilliant strategist who inspired his men, but it's easy to imagine how different the war would have been had he died decades before for his role in the New Echota Treaty. He was the main instigator for supporting the South at every stage of the conflict, starting with the initial negotiation with the Confederacy to form an alliance and concluding with the manic attacks launched during the last year of the war.

Watie's role was a burr in the Cherokees' public and private discourse for a long time afterward. Why was he so motivated to fight on? I think it was a matter of pride coupled with his inflated ego, but slavery was an important factor as he owned more than one-hundred slaves at his plantation on Spavinaw Creek. He also saw himself as a traditional warrior with time-honored attributes and traits from the past. Historically, war was the "beloved occupation" of Cherokee men: warfare "was an institution that expressed spiritual power, honor and communal and clan values."[565] In earlier days most Cherokee men expressed their manhood through warfare, and war "was not only a passage for Cherokee males into manhood, but a way to rise in warrior rank and become great."[566] Perhaps he saw himself as a descendant of Dragging Canoe and other great warriors of the past, but well before removal in 1838, Cherokee men had given up their attachment to war and its rituals. In that sense, Watie was a throwback to an earlier generation. Whatever the mix of factors that led him to continue fighting, no one can deny that he was a great soldier. Whether that made him a great man is open to debate.

The Civil War in Indian Territory was devastating for all the tribes. At least one-fourth of the 2,200 Cherokees who fought on the Union side died in battle from wounds or from disease. No one knows how many died fighting for the Confederacy, but probably that number was even higher. I think nobody suffered a harsher war than the supposedly independent and sovereign Indian nations. One-third of Cherokee women lost their husbands, quite a few women were killed in the fighting, and many children were orphaned. Nearly 60% of the native people in the Five Civilized Nations were destitute refugees.[567] Lewis Ross and the Council agreed on July 14th to provide amnesty for those who fought for the Confederacy but banned Stand Watie and a few other leaders from any future political role in the Nation. Everyone pardoned had to sign this oath, which was preserved with the clerk of the Supreme Court: "I do solemnly swear . . . in the presence of Almighty God, that I will hereafter faithfully abide by, support and defend the Constitution and Laws of the Cherokee Nation." The full document is in Appendix 21. It would take a herculean effort to rebuild the Cherokee Nation in the ensuing years and establish rapport with the US. That required a new Treaty.

25

Aftermath of War

Elections were held after Chief Ross returned home from Washington on September 1, 1865. He won easily. His first task was to negotiate a new treaty with the United States. A preliminary intertribal "peace council" began at Fort Smith, Arkansas on September 8th, a far cry from what Downing had proposed to President Lincoln in 1864. President Johnson cared little about Indians, and his Administration chose people to represent the US who were more interested in commerce and exploitation than in healing the wounds of war. Dennis Cooley, President Johnson's newly appointed Commissioner of Indian Affairs, was perhaps an unavoidable choice, but a poor one from the Indian perspective. The other members of the Southern Treaty Commission were Southern Superintendent Elijah Sells, Brigadier General William Harney, Colonel Ely Parker and Thomas Wistar, a Quaker. Their assigned mission was to implement newly proposed legislation to completely reorganize Indian territory, the so-called Harlan Bill, which would strip away Indian sovereignty.

Cooley began the meeting by asking Downing to offer a prayer in Cherokee. That was a nice touch, and at first Cherokees were optimistic. Most of the tribes were represented except for the Wichitas and those from the Leased District. None had received any information about the purpose of the gathering and had no way of knowing that the government's real desire was to move all tribes living in Kansas south into Indian Territory and to collapse all the tribal governments into one large Indian Territory under the control of the United States. Setting the stage to reveal that draconian US proposal, Cooley criticized what he termed "the great crime of secession" and concluded that Indians deserved the "rightful forfeiture of all annuities and interests in the lands in the Indian Territory."[568] He didn't mention the reality that the US had abandoned its wards from the beginning of the war, or that the majority loyally fought on the Union side. That was a sobering beginning.

The next day things only got worse. Cooley had prepared a long document containing provisions for a new treaty, including these stark paragraphs: "It is the policy of the government . . . that all the nations and tribes in the Indian territory be formed into one consolidated government, after the plan proposed by the Senate of the United States, in a bill for organizing the Indian territory."[569] That came as an enormous shock to all the Indian participants. Ross, Downing, and other Indian leaders resisted even discussing the document, stating they weren't empowered to negotiate. They all expressed dismay at the take it or leave it deal. None had ever seen the Harlan Bill. But Cooley had his instructions from the White House and continued berating the Indians for their disloyalty.

Ross was a particular focus of his contempt. For the first few days, the Council hadn't included representatives from any of the secession leaders of the various tribes, but on the fifth day E.C. Boudinot and several others arrived. Cooley presented what he termed a "Treaty of Peace" that was filled with lies and half-truths about what the Indian tribes allegedly had done, insisting that it be signed on the spot. A few did so under protest, with formal, written reservations stating they weren't guilty of disloyalty.

As for Ross, Cooley insisted on this astounding provision: "Whereas, we believe him still at heart an enemy of the United States . . . and that he does not represent the will and wishes of the loyal Cherokees, and is not the choice of any considerable portion of the Cherokee nation . . . [we] refuse as Commissioners in any way or manner to recognize said Ross as chief of the Cherokee nation."[570] Lewis Downing immediately filed a formal protest requesting recission of the decision, noting that the sanction "destroys at once the right of the people of the Cherokee nation to choose their own rulers" and that John Ross "is principal chief in law and fact, having been elected to that position without opposition . . . ."[571] But the US representatives refused to budge, and on September 21st the ill-named peace council broke up in disarray.

The anger as the tribes departed was palpable. After returning home, they quickly learned the details of S. 459, the infamous Harlan Bill, which would create a new Territory encompassing all Indian land, with a governor appointed by the President for a four-year term. All the tribes would have to give up their sovereignty. Any law passed by the Legislative Council could be vetoed by the governor, and the US would retain complete supervisory power over finances. Only males could be members of the legislature. The entire territory would have just a single non-voting representative in the US House of Representative. The bill wasn't even debated in the House, but the Senate tried to rush its passage. Fortunately, Senator Lafayette Foster, a Republican from Connecticut, exposed the perfidy of the proposal when it was discussed in late February 1865: "The Indian bill . . . changes our whole Indian policy. It violates the plighted faith of the United States . . . [and] will cast great dishonor on the United States if we pass it."[572] Amazingly, Harlan brought the bill back for debate on March 2nd, leading Foster to make these observations: "It changes . . . radically our whole Indian policy. It violates our treaties . . . it will be a stain upon the national honor, a breach of the national faith. . . . [promising that Cherokees] in no future time without their consent be included within the territorial limits or jurisdiction of any State or Territory."[573]

Although few Indians even knew this debate was taking place, it was watched closely by Reverend John Buttrick Jones, son of Evan Jones, who played a key role in informing Senators about its implications. Senator Foster continued to stand up for Indians throughout the debate; nevertheless, in the end, the bill was approved in the Senate. Since it wasn't considered by the House, however, it didn't become law. That was a respite of sorts, but also a clear signal of the continuing desire of white men to control Indian destiny. The Harlan Bill was a travesty so grave that it made dialogue about a future relationship with the US government almost impossible, yet because each of the tribes depended on the US to honor its prior commitments to pay annuities, they had to negotiate.

After the war, some Confederate Cherokee homes were confiscated and sold to the highest bidders. Simon and Annie bought the old Johnson Downing farm on Spring Creek, and in early June, they moved in. But Lewis Downing intervened and legally restored the property to the Downing family. Simon and Annie's money was refunded, and they left in November 1865, moving to the north side of Honey Creek not far from where her Uncle John Huss had built his home in 1837. A small spring-fed creek winds downhill there, feeding Honey Creek. Its water is pure and runs fast. The mouth of Honey Creek became Annie's home, her refuge and solace for the rest of her life. Annie's son, my great-grandfather William P. Mayes, recalled: "We moved there in June 1865 and left there in November. When we located on Honey Creek . . . Delaware District was a wilderness at that time. Very little fencing and not so many houses left from the ravages of the so-called Civil War."[574]

Births surged across the Nation following the War, and there was renewed energy about rebuilding what had been lost. Annie's half-sister

Susan Sconti married William Wirt Miller in 1860 just before the War. He had enlisted in Stand Watie's regiment on July 4, 1862 and served as a private in Company K until being taken prisoner on January 15, 1863. Their first child, Sarah Annie, was born on August 9, 1865.[575]

A Cherokee delegation arrived in Washington, D.C. on January 18, 1866 to negotiate the new treaty, including White Catcher, Daniel Ross, Sam Benge, Smith Christie, Thomas Pegg, Reverend John Jones, and James McDaniel. They brought two detailed documents explaining the Civil War from the Cherokee point of view. The first, termed a "Memorial of the Delegates of the Cherokee Nation to the President of the United States and the Senate and House of Representatives," outlined how the Civil War occurred on their land. Emphasizing the key role played by the Keetoowah Society for the "great mass of the men of the Cherokee Nation" who supported the Union side, it characterized the Knights of the Golden Circle as a "disloyal element" backed by the Confederacy. Requesting that the legal rights of Cherokees under past treaties be respected in negotiating an updated treaty, the document stated: "We boldly claim that we have done our duty . . . as the friends and allies of the Federal Government . . . We fought to the end of the war, and when the last rebel was whipped, we were honorably mustered out of the service. The graves of eight hundred Cherokee warriors, fallen by our side in your service, testify that we have done our duty. Now . . . all we ask is that the Government do its duty to us . . . ."[576]

True to form, the Confederate Cherokees also insisted on participating, led by E.C. Boudinot, who had insinuated himself with Harlan by agreeing to one of his pet projects, a railroad through Indian land from St. Louis to Galveston. More importantly, Boudinot was open to the idea of one Indian Territory for all the tribes. He wrote Cooley that the Cherokee Memorial was "but a tissue of misrepresentations and falsehoods from beginning to end" and argued again for dividing the Cherokee Nation in half.[577]

John Rollin Ridge, Saladin Watie, Richard Fields, E.C. Boudinot, William P. Adair (left to right)[578]

Douglas Cooper, a former Federal Indian Agent who sided with the Confederacy and became an officer on that side, and General Pike, who negotiated all the Confederate treaties with Indian tribes, had returned to favor with US President Johnson. The amnesty rules should have banned their involvement, but they were useful to politicians like Harlan and Cooley. Stand Watie participated actively with Boudinot. Cooley gave the two Cherokee delegations equal status but preferred negotiating with Watie and Boudinot. Ross still was persona non grata.[579] To his credit, Cooley eventually refused to divide Cherokee Territory, but the Treaty signed on July 19th required these major concessions:

- The Neutral Lands in Kansas and the Cherokee Strip were ceded to the United States.
- All remaining Cherokee land in Arkansas was surrendered to the United States.

- Beyond the ninety-sixth parallel in the Outlet, Cherokees had to allow the US to settle Kaw, Osage, Pawnee, Ponca, and Tonkawa tribes, and to allow white settlers to enter.
- They had to allow telegraph, railway, and other rights of way through their lands.
- All slaves had to be freed, which the pro-Union Cherokee Government had done in 1863 so that condition applied only to those who had sided with the Confederacy.

Acting Chief Lewis Downing called the National Council to session on July 13th. Having thought through the many negative aspects and future costs of a divided Cherokee Nation, he proposed to remove the barriers that had been put in place. Noting that while the Canadian District had been set apart as a refuge for those who sided with the Confederate States, most had already returned to their old homes and were living there in peace. He believed that Cherokee laws should be uniform in every part of the Nation, and he managed to outsmart the Southern Party's goal of dividing the nation. As late as June 1st, they believed the US would agree to their proposal and, indeed, had begun planning to govern their area as an independent entity. Watie and his faction promised to give the railroad companies unfettered access to all Cherokee territory, with alternating blocks on each side—which alone would have given away more than one million acres—and to accept a territorial government for all Indians supervised by white officials appointed by the Interior Secretary. For various reasons, President Johnson didn't go along with the treaty drafted by Watie and Cooley. Downing and Ross proved to be the better negotiators, gaining approval for a single treaty for all Cherokees and neutralizing the dangerous demand for territorial Indian government. At Downing's request, that provision was made conditional on all Indian tribes in the territory agreeing to accept it, which of course never happened. The Indian negotiators didn't fare as well on the railroad question. They were forced to accept two railways running through their lands, one north-south and one east-west. Although William Penn Adair, James Bell, Watie, and other Southern Party leaders argued the new treaty wasn't binding on them, without support from President Johnson, they gave in. Cherokees were ready for a new start.

Lewis Downing in 1868[580]

26

New Start

Shortly after the new treaty with the US came into effect, Chief Ross died while in Washington on August 1, 1866. He was initially buried in the Stapler family plot in Wilmington, Delaware next to his wife Mary; however, in early May of 1867, Jesse Bushyhead, William P. Ross, and Riley Keyes returned the coffin to the Cherokee Nation. It lay in state at the Male Seminary until the formal burial on June 1st. William honored him with these words: "It is proper, that here, should his dust mingle with kindred dust, and that a suitable memorial should arise, to mark the spot where repose the bones of our greatest chieftain."[581] Only one-eighth Cherokee, Ross devoted his entire life to his people's well-being.

After Ross's death, Lewis Downing served as Chief until the October 19th election. He supported equal rights for all Cherokees and formed a new political party bringing together both pro-Confederate and pro-Union people, a crucial step in healing the Nation. He had every reason to expect that he would be elected Principal Chief and was deep in preparations with Keetoowah colleagues for the next few years of tribal work. In a surprise vote, however, the National Council chose William Potter Ross, John Ross's uncle, a Mason in Lodge 21 and a well-respected lawyer and businessman.

Educated at Princeton, where he graduated first in his class, he was bilingual and served as the first editor of the successor to the *Phoenix*, the *Cherokee Advocate*. Elected to the Cherokee Senate in 1849, he served four two-year terms, and when the Male and Female Seminaries were built, he was chosen as their first director. Although, as William McGloughlin puts it, the Keetoowahs "had to accept as chief one of the most haughty, elitist, and acculturated of the mixed-bloods,"[582] there was no love lost between him and the Southern Party, and he was a good negotiator. Perhaps a key factor in the election was that Downing didn't read or speak English.

Chief John Ross circa 1865[583]

There was a long way to go to catch up to where Cherokees were before the War. As a result of deaths and emigrations, the population had dropped from 21,000 in 1860 to around 14,000. It would take years to get over that huge loss. But everyone got to work, sharing the pride of re-building their institutions, homes, farms, and infrastructure. Running the Nation required many different jobs, local to national, and Cherokees were up to it. They continued building their country on their own terms, creating new farms from prairies along with hamlets, towns, and cities. Doctors, lawyers, and teachers were educated mostly in Cherokee schools. Land and water transport was developed to link the growing population together.

The first deal they made regarding railroad construction was handled well. Cherokees were to become shareholders in the new southern branch of the Union Pacific—putting up $500,000 from the planned sale of the Cherokee Outlet—and would hold two seats on the board. In contrast to the giveaway promised by the Southern Party, the right of way would be restricted to 100 feet with no gifts of large parcels of adjoining land. The Bureau of Indian Affairs, however, refused to countenance sale of the Outlet to buy stock in the railway company, and the contract lapsed.[584] Meanwhile the Atlantic and Pacific Railroad was negotiating to buy the Neutral Lands for its right of way. There were thousands of white, black, and Indian squatters on the land already, who also had to be satisfied with any deal. The Neutral Lands were sold for one million dollars, beginning with a down payment of $75,000 and regular payments thereafter. Although it took four years for all the details to be agreed upon and the payments to begin, it proved to be a decent deal for the Cherokees.[585] However, the new rail lines would have major impacts on the control of their nations. Old tribal towns vanished as new towns were built along railroad routes. Whites now had easy access to Indian Territory, and by 1890, there were more than 140,000 living in Indian country. Clearly, the railroads brought some benefits to the Cherokees and other tribes, but they had difficulty managing such change so quickly.

The Spirit family was doing its part to help the revival. Simon's and Annie's son, Charles Ewing Snell, was born on January 17, 1867, growing up with his four half-siblings, all of whom survived and were thriving. Sarah was nineteen, ready to attend the Female Seminary; Charlotte was sixteen, waiting for her local school to re-open; Elmira was thirteen; and William was eleven, almost as tall as a grown man. The Cherokee public-school system reopened on March 1st with thirty-two schools, including two for freedmen in Tahlequah and Fourteen Mile Creek. All schools were free and fully under Cherokee control.[586] But many Cherokees were struggling to recover from the War. The winter of 1865-66 had been severe, and some planting seeds had to be used for feed. Much of their farmland had been lost temporarily during the War; thus, the 1866 harvest was small. As always, however, the Cherokees were committed and resilient, and things improved steadily after that.

Sam Mayes' sister Lucy Mayes Ward died in Delaware District on November 11, 1867. Following Sam's death in 1858, she and her husband George were helpful to Annie and her children, especially their daughter Sabrina. Early in 1868, Charlotte told Annie she was in love with George Monroe Ward, Annie's second cousin, one of Lucy Mayes and George Ward's grandchildren. They'd known each other forever, but Annie opposed the marriage because he'd been a strong supporter of Stand Watie, fighting with him at the Battle of Pea Ridge, among others. Charlotte was strong-willed, and they eloped. A few months later she returned, having decided not to follow through with the marriage. Later in the year, Annie's eldest daughter Sarah married William England, whose family came west as part of a voluntary removal in 1834. That emigration resulted in many deaths at Cadron Creek, including his grandfather William England. He served on the Union side during the Civil War in Company G of the Sixth Kansas Volunteer Cavalry. He and Sarah had three children in the next few years:

Joseph in 1870, Lucy Ann in 1873, and George in 1875. They were Annie's first grandchildren. She loved visiting their elegant home, which featured beautiful wood moldings and large stone fireplaces.[587]

Annie's great aunt Caty Knightkiller passed away at her farm on Honey Creek in 1869.[588] One of her great-grandfather Spirit's children with Susannah, her husband Knightkiller was a fine man, and their children, David and Henry, were part of Annie's constellation of cousins. Born in 1790, Caty experienced a lot of history and was a connector among the generations. In the late 1860s, Sam's sons Joel and Samuel Mayes were courting two of David Vann's and Martha Price McNair's daughters, Mary Delilah and Martha Elizabeth. David was assassinated by Pin Indians during the Civil War in 1863. He served as Cherokee Nation Treasurer from 1839-1853 and was a key member of the negotiating team for the 1846 treaty signed with the US after removal. Annie remained close to most of Sam's and Nannie's children, having buried her feelings about the Civil War. Joel married Mary on September 15, 1869. In the summer of 1870, Rosella Adair, Annie's half-sister Annie Vann's daughter, and her husband, George Brewer Downing, had their first child, Mary. Like clockwork every year for the next few years, they welcomed Elizabeth, Joel Mayes, and Lafayette into the family.[589] Samuel Mayes, Jr. married Martha Elizabeth Vann on September 9, 1871, another big event for the family. They had a son named William Lucullus Mayes on February 6, 1874. Cullus, as they all called him, was a good friend of Will Rogers when he grew up, taking him to Springfield, Missouri to compete in his first rodeo.[590]

During the election campaign in the summer of 1867, Reverend John Jones drew on his influence among the full bloods to support Lewis Downing's political movement, which promised to rehabilitate the Southern Cherokees and bury the hatchet with those who had supported the Union. Drawing strong support from both factions, Downing was elected chief on August 5th.

Thereafter, the Downing party played a major role in the political affairs of the Cherokee Nation until statehood. One of his greatest early successes was the 1868 updating of the 1866 Treaty, a landmark agreement that settled the internal affairs of the Nation while resolving myriad ambiguities and obscure provisions in the original. It required the US to pay $3,500,000 for the Cherokee Strip in Kansas, to begin paying 5% interest on the $500,000 promised earlier for the Neutral Lands, and to settle all arrears promptly.[591] The Cherokee Nation was in desperate need of cash.

The new Capitol was opened on Tahlequah's Courthouse Square in 1869. A classic design in red brick on the site of the original wooden building, it took only two years to build, with every brick made on site. Much of the Cherokee Nation was there to celebrate.

Cherokee Capitol circa 1880[592]

Back east in their old homeland, Cherokees who had escaped the Trail of Tears were thriving in the mountains of Georgia, Tennessee, and North Carolina.[593] Their attempt to organize a government began in December 1868 at a meeting in Cheowa, where they created a Council and resolved to elect a chief. That Council met at Qualla Town on November 26, 1870.

The 1872 census showed seventeen hundred Cherokees living in North Carolina, Tennessee, and Georgia. Their efforts finally bore fruit in 1889 when the Eastern Cherokees were formally incorporated.

Despite the 1868 Treaty, Congress continued to meddle in the Cherokee Nation's affairs. In early 1870, it began writing legislation to replace all tribal governments in Indian Territory with a new territorial regime under the full control of the United States. That had been the US goal in the 1866 Treaty negotiation, but perhaps no one imagined Cherokees would be so successful at running their own country. This proposed abrogation of Indian sovereignty and treaty rights brought a swift response. Lewis Downing wrote Congress on March 8th: " . . . all we ask is that [you] not forget that we hold our lands in fee simple, by letters patent from the President of the United States; that those lands were bought and paid for in cash and in exchange for lands deemed more desirable by the United States; and that our national character is recognized and confirmed again and again by the highest laws known to political societies, namely, treaties; which guarantee that the jurisdiction of no State or Territory of the Governing State shall ever be placed over us without our consent."[594]

The letter was signed by scores of Cherokee leaders, who enclosed petitions against the proposal. The proposal was withdrawn after a few months. Indians had won another round with the United States.[595] But the US Supreme Court took a serious step to limit Cherokee sovereignty in *The Cherokee Tobacco* case decided on May 1, 1871. The court ruled 4-2 that an 1868 law expanding the federal tobacco tax overruled the express language of the 1866 Treaty that farmers "shall have the right to sell any products of his farm . . . without . . . paying any tax thereon . . . ." The Court ruled that the 1868 law implicitly abrogated that provision of the treaty.[596] That was a terrible and obviously erroneous conclusion, but power determined the result, as usual.

This map by Charles Royce shows the land originally assigned to the Cherokees.[597] Over time much of that land was lost, including the large parcels in Arkansas and Kansas. What was left had to be shared with other first peoples driven from their homes and crammed artificially within these lines. Tribes were strewn about on the map as if a huge windstorm had dumped them there. The Cherokee Outlet (47 in the map) covered eight million acres designated in perpetuity for them. The Neutral Lands in Kansas (38 on the map) were taken away in the revised treaty forced on the Cherokees following the Civil War. The large area in Arkansas (37 on the map) was taken from them in the 1840s.[598]

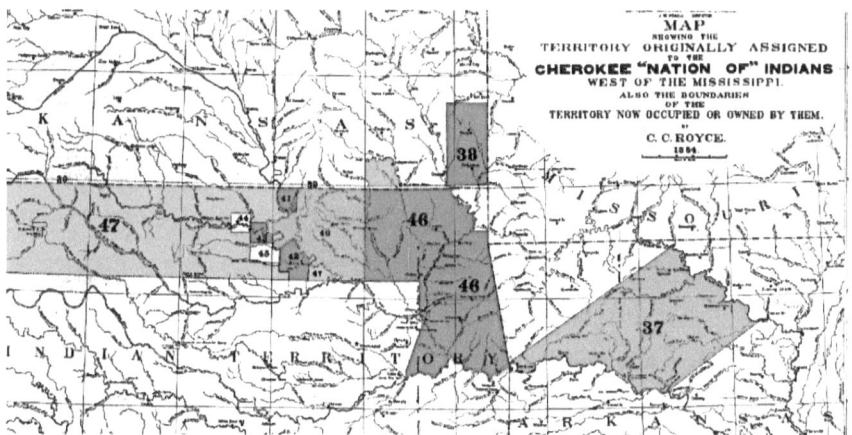

Cherokee ingenuity proved capable of using the natural attributes of the land and water, with numerous sawmills and gristmills built and timber, salt, coal, copper, and zinc exploited. Cattle ranches spread into every area. The lingering feuds of the Civil War largely evaporated as the people chose unity. The election of 1871 solidified the Nation's path, with Lewis Downing reelected Principal Chief on August 7th by an overwhelming margin. Annie's cousin Hunter Poorbear Buffalofish (Canahelage) was elected to the Council that year.[599] His father, Charles Poorbear, connected Annie to her great-grandparents.[600] A reminder of the fractious internecine past and how that flame was put out came when Stand Watie died on September 9th. To most, he had been a nightmare, although he remained a hero to some. A statue in his honor was erected in Tahlequah's courthouse square in 1921 by the Daughters of the Confederacy, near a general memorial to the Confederacy installed in 1917. They were both removed in June 2020.[601]

The first General Council of the Indian Territory convened in Okmulgee on September 27, 1871, composed of elected delegates all the tribes under the terms of Article 12 of the 1866 treaties. William P. Ross represented the Cherokees, along with delegates from the Muskogee, Ottawa, Osage, Seminole, Choctaw, Chickasaw, Shawnee, Quapaw, Seneca, Wyandotte, Peoria, Sac, and Fox nations. They decided in December to establish a permanent General Council to protect their collective rights, agreeing to oppose any move by the US to set up a territorial government in Indian Territory. The Cherokee National Council took several steps towards creating an Indian government for the region, including writing a constitution: "It should be Republican in form, with its powers clearly defined, and full guarantees give for all the powers, rights and privileges respectively, now reserved to them by their treaties."[602] The draft constitution was debated for several days in mid-December and approved on December 20th by an overwhelming vote. It protected individual rights and freedom of religion and was progressive in many other respects. No one could be jailed because of debt, for example. It would have created an Indian State with its own governor, senate, legislature, and judiciary. Since the US opposed the constitution, however, it wasn't allowed to become a reality. There is resonance between this initiative and their later effort to create an Indian state in parallel with Oklahoma in the early 1900s.In the 1871 Indian Appropriations Act Congress declared that American Indians were no longer considered members of "sovereign nations" and forbade the US government from establishing treaties with them.[603]

Annie's daughter Charlotte married William Houston Ballard, a 3/4 Cherokee from Echo, Delaware District on December 26, 1871. His father, Archibald Ballard, was born in Tennessee in 1832, and his mother was Annie's fourth cousin, Annie Fields, born in 1834. Annie Fields' parents were Jane Jennie Huss and Rider Fields. Annie Spirit and Annie Fields were kindred spirits and became life-long friends.

Annie Fields   *Willian Houston Ballard circa 1880*

William's grandfather Samuel and grandmother Diana Otterlifter brought the family west in 1832 after selling their farms in Red Clay County, Tennessee and Shoemaker, Georgia.[604] William and Charlotte's first child, Jane Anna (Janana), was born on January 1, 1875 and others followed every couple of years: Anna May (1877), Lucinda (1879), Sarah Eleanor (1881), Zoe Wyly (1882), William Houston (1884), Ruth May (1887), and Ethyl Savilla (1890).[605]

Near the end of 1872, Annie's daughter Elmira married Daniel Finn. The wedding was a modest affair, but most of the family were there. Elmira's and

Daniel's daughter Cynthia Ellen arrived on March 23, 1874 in Southwest City, Missouri, where they were living not far away from Annie. But their marriage didn't last another year, and Elmira moved back home with the baby. She married William Gladney in 1876. His father, Jackson Gladney, was born in Belfast, Ireland in 1809 and arrived in New Orleans with his two brothers when he was about sixteen. William's mother was Mary Arminda Post from an old Cherokee family. Her mother, Elizabeth Pettit, was born in 1790 and died in 1837 just before removal. Her father, William Post, born in 1794, was one of the old settlers in Arkansas in the same period as Annie's great-grandfather Spirit. Mary Aminda's and Jackson's other children became closely interwoven with the family in the following years. Elmira and William lived in the Fourteen Mile Creek area near Hulbert. They had eight children: Joseph (1878), Annie (1881), Mary (1883), Henry (1886), Minnie Bell (1888), Charlotte (1890), Elizabeth (1893), and John Rogers (1897). Elmira became a renowned midwife, helping deliver hundreds of babies in the district.

Chief Downing died in office in Tahlequah on November 9, 1872. He was buried in the Ned Adair cemetery southeast of Choteau near his farm on Spring Creek. Simon and Annie were there with hundreds of Lewis's friends and his third wife, a white woman named Mary Eyre, whom he met in Washington. She had moved to Tahlequah before his second wife died. Lewis fostered a new flowering of the Nation. Everyone loved to hear him speak—especially in Cherokee—his calm, sober eloquence about what is right and wrong bringing people together. Before his death, Downing had led the planning for a new orphans' home. In 1873, the Council purchased Louis Ross's farm near Salina including its mansion, barns and 300 acres of fertile bottom land, mixed timber, and pasture for the orphans.

Orphans Home circa 1873[606]

The first asylum in the region for what was then called insane, deaf, dumb, and blind people was established outside Tahlequah the same year, operated jointly by the Cherokees and Choctaws.

Cherokee Asylum[607]

Annie's half-sister Susan Sconti Miller passed away after a short illness on September 26, 1876, leaving three young children, Sarah, Rosa, and

Nannie.[608] Annie was close to her younger sister. Her husband William Miller found it difficult to take care of three young girls. Annie along with her half-sister Annie Vann Adair stepped in to help with him with their nieces.[609] William Miller eventually remarried and had several other children.

Annie suffered a grievous blow on May 1, 1877 when her beloved Simon suddenly passed away. Although he'd been wounded several times in the War, it seemed that he had put those injuries behind him. His cause of death is unknown. He was buried in the Snell graveyard. Annie was alone once again, not even twenty years after Sam died, but that didn't slow her down. Her son Billy was courting William Gladney's sister, Annie Harper Gladney, of whom she was particularly fond. She liked the prospect of further intertwining the two families.[610] While Annie Harper was teaching at Silver Lake school south of Bartlesville before their wedding, Billy wrote beautiful love letters. His penmanship was excellent, as was his flair for words:[611]

Billy and Annie Harper Gladney were married on August 16, 1877. Their ornate wedding certificate was kept in the Mayes family bible.[612]

The Nation was fully back on its feet, and Annie had a big family to look after. Billy and Annie's first child, Maggie May, arrived in 1878, and Nellie Maude, my grandmother, followed in 1880; Claude was born in 1882, Joel Bryan in 1884, Lizzie Bell in 1885, Ridge Parker in 1888, and Mary Hazel in 1894. We will learn more about them later but suffice it to say here that they were the artists and wanderers in the family. Maude loved to paint and play music with her sisters Hazel and Lizzie. Each had a penchant for adventure, reminding Annie of their grandfather Sam Mayes. Joel struck out to see the world at age seventeen, working on ships that took him around the world. He ended up living in Modoc, California.

On Christmas day 1877, Sarah's husband William England passed away suddenly, devastating the family. Joseph, Lucy Ann, and George were just seven, five, and two respectively. Sarah was miserable as a widow and struggled to keep up with the children. Enter Charles F. McGinnis, a dashing young businessman who swept her off her feet. He proposed, and she sponsored him for membership in the Cherokee Nation before their wedding on January 16, 1879. Annie was happy that her grandkids had a father again, and the family continued growing with William arriving in 1881, Charlotte Elizabeth in 1883, and Cleveland in 1885. They remained in the big house William had built earlier, where the extended family often got together for dinner. It was a quietly elegant home, and the large table in the walnut-paneled dining room could easily seat twenty people. Annie's children wrote letters to each other almost weekly.[613]

Annie had a lot to keep up with, given her growing brood of grandchildren, and there was always politics. In mid-1879, Dennis Wolfe Bushyhead, her 4th cousin, was nominated to head the new Independent Party formed by supporters of John Ross's National Party. He was elected Principal Chief by a small majority of 400 votes on October 4th shortly after marrying Elizabeth Alabama Schrimsher.[614] Born in 1826 at Mouse Creek in Tennessee, Dennis first attended school in 1833 at the Candy Creek Mission School directed by Reverend Holland. After moving west in his father's detachment in 1838, Dennis attended the mission school at Park Hill run by Reverend Worcester. In 1841, he was sent to Lawrenceville in New Jersey, graduating in 1844 and entering Princeton University as a sophomore. He returned after his father passed away; a few months later, he joined Lewis Ross's general mercantile business. He worked there until 1849, when he joined Annie's first husband Sam Mayes in joining the California gold rush. He struck gold, staying there for eighteen years, avoiding the tragedy of the Civil War. He returned to take over his brother Jesse's mercantile business in Fort Gibson in 1868, following Jesse's murder on December 24, 1867. Becoming interested in politics, he was elected Treasurer in 1871, serving for eight years.[615]

Dennis's campaign for Principal Chief stressed more transparent accounting and wiser use of tribal funds. Probably the best choice for the time, he was able to work with all political factions. As Chief, Dennis dramatically reduced the Nation's debt and brought its currency on par with the US dollar, putting the Nation on a firmer economic footing. The population was 19,720 when he assumed office, about the same as in 1850, but there was a 9 to 5 ratio of women to men, reflecting how many men were lost in the War.[616] White intruders who were not subject to the jurisdiction of Cherokee courts were a major problem from the beginning of his tenure, reflecting a serious flaw in the 1866 Treaty. The Chief developed a working relationship with Judge Isaac C. Parker on the Federal Court at Fort Smith, Arkansas, who stopped some of the white interlopers, but ultimately there were too many. Without US support to protect the borders, the number continued to mount.

Chief Dennis Wolfe Bushyhead in the early 1880s[617]

Dennis helped lead the Intertribal Council meeting in Eufaula in late 1879, with thirty-two tribes participating. It had come a long way since John Lowrey and John Huss launched the group in 1843. The Council's main job was fending off continuing US efforts to create a new state to absorb all the Indian nations and undermine their sovereignty. Once again, the Cherokee Nation exhibited deep resilience as it found ways to get things done.

27

Life Goes On

Just when Cherokee lives had fully recovered from the ravages of the Civil War, Senator Henry L Dawes of Massachusetts, chair of the Committee on Indian Affairs, toured Indian country to study how Indians were living and how to convince them to accept individual ownership of land. H Indians owned their land in common, is meetings with Chief Bushyhead and other leaders were cordial and business-like on the surface, but nothing changed his mind about what he perceived Indians needed. Noting that every Cherokee family owned its home, that the fruits of labor were shared and there was no debt, he somehow concluded it was essential to get rid of land held in common and promote individual land ownership. Indians across the US had the same approach as the Cherokees but that didn't matter to Dawes, who was quite public about the rationale for his mission: "They have gone far as they can go because they own their land in common. There is no enterprise to make your home any better than that of your neighbors. There is no selfishness, which is the bottom of civilization."[618]

Fighting off this political assault became Chief Bushyhead's focus. Speaking about the importance of common land to the fabric of Cherokee society on January 17, 1881, he noted "There is no doubt but this is the true system of government for the protection of the poor and helpless in the continued possession of their homes—hence we have no paupers."[619] Cherokees joined with the Chickasaw and Creek nations in a letter to President Garfield: "Ownership of lands in common has been a part of tribal policy of the Indian since time immemorial. It is with them a religion as well as a law of property. It . . . cannot be ignored without the gravest perils to the people . . . Ownership in severalty [individually] must necessarily result in the acquisition of the great body of the lands by a few strong and unscrupulous hands, with poverty and misery for the masses of the people."[620]

Although most Cherokees felt this latest attack on their sovereignty by forced forms of property ownership would come to naught, as had so many similar initiatives through the years, this time was different. Senator Dawes had a one-track mind about forcing all Indians to adopt a white lifestyle, bedeviling them for the next twenty years while gradually building political support in Washington for the final take-over of Indian lands and sovereignty.

Senator Henry Dawes circa 1885[621]

The Cherokees didn't give in easily or quickly. As in the 1830s, they employed good lawyers and lobbied hard on their own behalf. In late 1886. the *Advocate* reported that Dawes had introduced the legislation he'd been threatening to extinguish tribal governments, distribute part of their common lands to individual tribal members as "allotments," and make the "surplus" available to white settlers. Those allotments were to be much smaller than what most people were actually using, thus creating a "surplus." Despite every inconvenient truth about the legal roots of Cherokee sovereignty in all the treaties signed, the US Congress decided to support Senator Dawes's proposal to destroy Indian governments, courts, legislatures, and schools, and to take away their common lands. To see this written down and learn how seriously and effectively it was pursued is like gazing into a dark and haunted world. Chief Bushyhead and Joel Bryan Mayes, who was running for Principal Chief, declared that Dawes would be stopped in his tracks, calling the proposal unconstitutional on its face and a violation of all Cherokee treaties with the United States. But the US Congress approved the Dawes Act, which was signed by President Grover Cleveland on February 8, 1887, dealing a death knell to Indian tribes everywhere by dividing Indian reservations into individual tracts.[622] It was a historic strike against Indian culture, political rights, and economic self-sufficiency. Ironically, Dawes saw himself as a friend of Indians and worked closely with white reformers on his plan, most of whom were probably well-meaning but couldn't see past their own prejudices.[623]

The House of Representatives Minority Report on the legislation had a starkly different conclusion: "The real aim of the bill is to get land out of Indian hands and into the hands of white settlers . . . If this were done in the name of Greed, it would be bad enough, but to do it in the name of Humanity, and under the cloak of an ardent desire to promote the Indian's welfare by making him like ourselves, whether he will or not, is infinitely worse."[624] That feeling was echoed by President Grover Cleveland after signing the legislation into law: "Hunger and thirst of the white man for Indians' land is almost equal to his hunger and thirst after righteousness."[625] Still, none of those feelings interfered with the ongoing political realities. The Indians were slated to lose once again.

Another pressing issue for Bushyhead was Cherokee ownership of the Cherokee Outlet or Strip, where vast herds of longhorn cattle from Texas were moved over the Chisholm trail. A detached parcel belonging to the Cherokees under the New Echota Treaty approximately ninety miles wide, it encompassed around six million acres that Cherokees used for grazing and hunting. Texas cattlemen initially had refused to pay for use of the Outlet, but after two years of negotiation, Bushyhead signed a five-year lease with the Live Stock Association headquartered in Kansas on July 5, 1883. The cattlemen agreed to pay $100,000 per year for grazing rights, which covered the Cherokee education budget and then some, while protecting their sovereignty over the Outlet. But the US was unhappy about the situation, tying it to the issue of holding property in common, and signaling their desire to undercut the contract.

Bushyhead was easily re-elected to a second term as Principal Chief on October 6, 1883. He did a superb job overall, including his leadership on the freedmen issue. He supervised a detailed census of Cherokees by blood and adoption, including all freedmen, which constituted the basis for sharing tribal income from the Outlet rents. But some believed freed slaves shouldn't be sharing with Cherokees, which led to a Cherokee Senate bill excluding them. Bushyhead forcefully reminded everyone that by the terms of the 1866 treaty, *all* freedmen remaining in the Nation were full citizens, and he vetoed the Senate bill. On that basis, the US authorized an additional $300,000 payment that year. Sadly, the Cherokee National Council overrode his veto. That was hotly debated, but in the end, the freedmen didn't receive equal compensation, and discrimination settled more deeply into the fabric of Cherokee society.

During the 1880s, Annie welcomed more grandchildren. Sarah and Bill England had three children: Joseph (born in 1870), Lucy Ann (1872) and George (1875). William and Charlotte Ballard had Janana in 1875, Anna Mae in 1877 and Lucinda in 1879. William had become an important man, elected as Councilor from Delaware District in 1881, and he shared something with Annie: their grandparents all returned to Georgia. His great-grandfather Samuel Ballard also had moved back to Georgia in the early 1840s, passing away there in early 1863, a victim of the Civil War. No one was keeping records about how many people managed to return to the homeland, but it was substantial. Emira's and William Gladney's children, Joseph Foreman and Annie, were born in 1878 and 1881, respectively. Charlotte and William's daughters Janana, Anna Mae, Lucinda, and Sarah Eleanore visited Annie often on Honey Creek. Their last child, William Houston, Jr., arrived in 1884. Billy's first children, Maggie May and my grandmother, Nellie Maude, were born in 1878 and 1880, respectively. Claude was born in 1882, and Joel Bryan arrived in 1884. The Spirit-Mayes family continued to grow.

My great-grandfather William Penn (Billy) Mayes began his political career on December 30, 1885 when he was appointed Olympus postmaster by President Grover Cleveland. He operated the post office in a one-room building with his wife Annie Gladney, who taught at the local school. The mail was brought by horse-drawn carriage from Vinita to Southwest City three times a week, serving several small towns along the way. Sometimes the mud was so deep that four horses were needed to get through. A friend wrote that when "they were on trips Elizabeth Cox Alexander kept office for them. The mail carrier would come by Mayes' and bring a gallon jug every day and get it full of buttermilk at the Mayes farm and take it home. He also carried passengers if he had room.[626] Billy served as chief interpreter for the Senate for twelve years, working closely with his half-brothers Joel and Samuel Mayes while they were Chiefs.[627] He improved 400 acres of land and always loved farming and hunting. Reminiscing about his childhood, he was nostalgic:

> When we located on Honey Creek... Delaware District was a wilderness at that time. Very little fencing and not so many houses were left from the ravages of the so-called Civil War. There were lots of wild hogs in the country, also lots of game of all kinds that inhabited this country at that time. Us Indians had a good time in those days. Oh! If we could just recall those days how happy we could be once more. When we would not wonder where we were going to get the money to pay our taxes with.[628]

The first Olympus school was east of the cemetery. Both Annie Mayes and John Cox taught there. It is uncertain what year it burned down, but it was re-established on the Cox farm, on a branch of Honey Creek. Soon afterwards, a new schoolhouse was built on the north side of the branch, where Annie Mayes was the head teacher. Others who taught there over the years included John Parks, Eugene Thompson, Lon and Mary Hampton, George Cox, Owen and George Fields, and Lola Ward.

In August 1884, Annie's Uncle Charles Poorbear Buffalofish died in Southwest City, where he'd gone for treatment, the last of that generation. She was close to his son Hunter, who was married to Aggy Tail, and Charles' funeral brought together family members from around the Nation. When Hunter was arrested by US authorities in 1887 for an alleged offense against another Cherokee, convicted, and sentenced to prison, Chief Bushyhead retained Cornelius Boudinot to fight this attempt by the US to exercise jurisdiction. Boudinot asked President Cleveland to give Hunter a full pardon and to leave the Cherokees in full control of their courts. His efforts were successful and Hunter was released.[629]

The pride and joy of the Nation, the Female Seminary, burned to the ground on Easter Sunday, April 10, 1887. The people's shock was visceral. Many turned up there that day weeping, so much of the Cherokees' hopes and pride were tied up with the Seminary. Following the pattern of tragedy followed by hope, rebuilding and resilience, the National Council decided to rebuild quickly. Construction commenced at the new site near Hendricks Springs north of Tahlequah within a few months. At the dedication ceremony for the new building on May 7, 1889, Tahlequah's brass band led a procession of more than 2,000 citizens through town to the new school, where Chief Joel Mayes spoke.[630]

CHEROKEE NATIONAL FEMALE SEMINARY, TAHLEQUAH, I. T.

The Spirit family was immensely proud of Joel although the election aftermath was fraught. Voting returns showed clearly that he'd won, but his opponent, Rabbit Bunch from the National Party, declined to concede. With the National Party holding a majority in the Senate, the Council postponed announcing the election results and adjourned, leaving Dennis Bushyhead in place for the time being. The situation became tense as armed members of the rival factions began to arrive in Tahlequah. In January 1888, supporters of the Downing party invaded the executive offices, publicly counted the ballots, and based on the results, installed Joel as chief. Chief Bushyhead gracefully retired, and bloodshed was averted. Joel faced an enormous task, as the US government was moving quickly to implement the Dawes Act legislation that would dismember the Cherokee Nation.

Born in Georgia on October 2, 1833, Joel came west with his father, Annie's first husband, Samuel Mayes, in 1838. After attending public school in Muddy Springs, he was in the first class to graduate from the Male Seminary in 1856, returning to teach after graduation. He also edited a literary publication, *The Sequoyah Memorial*, whose motto was "Truth, Justice, Freedom of Speech and Cherokee Improvement." This is the masthead of the first issue:[631]

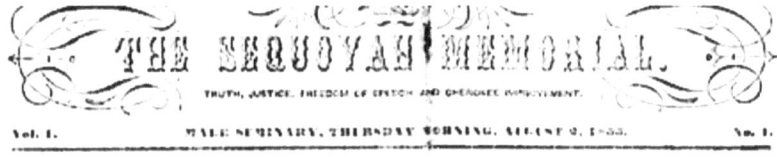

Joel moved to Rush County, Texas at the beginning of the Civil War but returned in 1862, enlisting on the Confederate side with his brothers. He served as paymaster and quartermaster in Bryant's Battalion of Cherokee Partisan Rangers and was elevated to Lieutenant Colonel near the end of the war. Joel started his political career as Clerk of the District Court in 1868 and was elected Judge of the Northern Circuit in 1873. In 1878, he was asked to Chair the Commission on Citizenship and elected Clerk of the National Council. Soon afterward, he was elected to the Supreme Court, where he served as Chief Justice for two years. He was a master Mason in Lodge 10. He and his wife Mary Delilah Vann—daughter of David Vann and Martha McNair—lived in a two-story frame home with a staircase of wild cherry and walnut woodwork. They had 300 acres in cultivation with more than 500 head of cattle, seventy-five horses, 500 sheep, and 150 hogs. He also was a renowned cider maker.

Chief Joel Byran Mayes[632]

When the Cherokee Outlet lease with the Texas cattlemen expired in 1888, Joel and the "Immortal Fourteen" successfully negotiated a renewal for twice the amount of the first lease: $200,000 per year for five years. One of the fourteen who played a major role was William D. Mitchell, a blacksmith elected to the Council from Going Snake District in 1887.[633] That was more than enough to continue funding all the schools, and the Cherokees were jubilant about the deal. But the federal government intervened, stating that the lease was invalid, though providing no justification. In 1889, President Benjamin Harrison ordered that no cattle would be allowed to graze in the Outlet, by decree without any legal rationale. Once again, just money and power counted. To their credit, the cattlemen and Livestock Association continued to honor the lease up to 1890, but then Federal troops invaded Cherokee territory to oust the cattlemen, and the payments stopped. The Government insisted on buying the entire Outlet for $1.25 per acre. Chief Mayes resisted but was forced to give in under the continuing pressure, even though that was a direct violation of their treaty rights. The Cherokee Nation received $10.2 million, dedicating those funds to education. At the same time, the US continued pushing to open the Unassigned Cherokee Lands to white settlement, but Joel and the Council were staunchly opposed. At one point he was offered a $25,000 bribe to go along but refused, thundering: "We don't have to sell the Cherokee Nation!" Congress introduced legislation to open the Unassigned Lands to white settlement, and in February 1889, Mayes led a delegation to Washington, D.C. to lobby against the takeover: "We have come to protest any action on your part to extend your territorial jurisdiction over any part of our country. We refer you to the treaties in which you solemnly agreed not to extend your territorial rights over us without our consent."[634]

But the Springer Amendment to the Indian Appropriation Bill gave the President power to open the region by proclamation, and newly-elected President Harrison did so on March 23, 1889. So much for democracy. On April 22nd, white settlers swarmed across the border of the Unassigned Lands and into the Cherokee Nation. They were called "Sooners." The name stuck, and Oklahoma today is often called "the Sooner State." It is difficult to imagine today how Congress and the White House could be so removed from Indian reality, but the grim truth is they always cared only about getting more land. Indians had no army; the US government had all the power. Mayes and the National Council fought hard against the proposed Dawes legislation that would end Cherokee sovereignty. At a general tribal meeting attended by hundreds of people, Mayes shouted:

This is wrong, it's a violation of every Treaty we've made with the US We will fight this to the finish. Consider these words in the New Echota Treaty: 'The lands ceded to the Cherokee Nation . . . shall in no future time, without their consent, be included within the territorial limits of any State or Territory. But they shall secure to the Cherokee nation the right, by their national councils, to make and carry into effect all such laws as they may deem necessary for the government . . . within their own country . . . ' Can any words be clearer than those?

Not that law and logic ever meant much to the US government in its dealings with Indians, but of course he was correct. After all that had occurred, most Cherokees remained hopeful, wanting to see the best in America. They couldn't believe the US would try to steal their country a second time. The Cherokees fended them off for many years, hiring competent lawyers to defend their rights. But except for a few preachers, they had no lobbyists, while the other side was well-funded and politically motivated.

Annie's younger son, Charles Ewing Snell, was elected Solicitor from Delaware District that year at age twenty-two, and Wash Mayes was elected Sheriff. Charles' first term was served with distinction, and the family had high hopes for his political career. Thomas M. Buffington, Annie's third cousin and good friend, was elected circuit judge for the Northern District, comprising Delaware, Cooweescoowee, and Saline Districts. At that time Annie Spirit Snell (commonly known as "Grandma Snell") operated a boarding house near her home on Honey Creek. In 1937, Buffington reminisced about those days: "I held court in each one of the districts alternately. Each district had its own courthouse. The Delaware and Saline Courthouses were built right out in the woods. The Delaware courthouse was on Honey Creek, a few miles south of Grove, near Grandma Snell's [Annie Spirit] place. She was a full blood Cherokee woman and kept a boarding house where all attending court would eat and sleep and I remember we were well fed."[635]

Delaware Courthouse in the 1890s[636]

Annie Spirit Snell kept the boarding house going until the Court closed in 1898 when the US terminated tribal courts. She had a large brass dinner bell to announce lunch and dinner. Nan Quahlate helped her run the place and did a lot of the cooking. Nan loved that bell, and Annie gave it to her when the boarding house closed. Jess Fields recalled that the Delaware District Courthouse was built about five miles southwest of Grove: " . . . a large two-story frame structure that stood on the hill just above the springs that fed the Courthouse Hollow creek. During meetings and at court sessions a little store was maintained and operated near the grounds."[637]

Annie always had a soft heart for full-blood Cherokees in distress, and her abiding interest in the welfare of Cherokees led her to many interesting people often outside the mainstream. In the late 1880s, she helped Jack Grasshopper, an old friend, build a one-room log cabin on a corner of her farm. He had fallen on hard times, and she wanted to make sure that he had a home and proper meals. According to the 1835 census, the Grasshopper farms were on Talking Rock Creek and Quenhulla Creek in Georgia. His parents and the rest of the family in the two households could read and write Cherokee.[638] Jack was born in 1843 shortly after his parents arrived in the west. His father, Grasshopper or To-la-tsu-qua, and mother, Che-yer-ner-ner, started their new life in McDonald County, Missouri. His maternal grandfather Wa-ja-lun-ty and grandmother Wat-ty moved with them. His one sibling, a brother named Se-ne-ka-naw-he-na, died in 1858. Jack's paternal grandfather Ja-lu-na-hy and grandmother Saw-ka-ne also came on the Trail of Tears in a different detachment, passing away a few years after they arrived. During the Civil War, Jack served as a private in the Third Regiment of the Indian Home Guards on the Union side, fighting in some battles with Annie's husband Simon. One of his cousins, Captain Daniel Grasshopper of the Third Indian Home Guards, was killed in action on October 3, 1862. Jack occasionally complained that he and others in the Home Guards had never been paid what they were promised by the Federal Government for fighting on the Union side. He and many others were awarded $100 on October 30, 1868, hardly a fair sum, but that was the standard amount the US government had decided Indian fighters should receive. He appeared before De Witt Lipe, Clerk of the Cherokee District Court on December 7th to sign for his allotment. This is his payment voucher:[639]

Jack's father passed away in 1866 just after the war ended; his mother died in 1870, and he was left alone. Perhaps because he had fought beside her husband Simon, Annie essentially adopted him. He was a loner by nature and liked living alone. Not everyone approved of her letting him live on her land, but the Keetowahs and the church provided a moral compass to help her decide between right and wrong. Jess Fields, who was born on Honey Creek in the early 1880s, recorded his memories of people there: "Another prominent Cherokee woman of those early days was Annie Snail

[Snell], who lived down toward the mouth of Honey Creek . . . another of the people devoted to the welfare of the Indians . . . a very old Cherokee by the name of Jack Grasshopper lived on the Snail [Snell] farm in a little one-room log house, and Annie Snail [Snell] looked out for him. . . . [he was] one of the strongest Indians he ever saw. He wore long hair that he kept braided. He could pick up two of the biggest fireplace logs and carry them in the house, one under each arm."[640]

CHEROKEE NATION, *Indian Territory*, ss :

Know all men by these presents that I, Jack Grasshopper, do hereby make, constitute, and appoint John W. Wright, of Washington City, my attorney, to sell, transfer, and assign a draft drawn in my favor for $100 and —— cents by C. Holmes, paymaster of United States Army, on United States Assistant Treasurer at New York City, dated the 30th of October, A. D. 1868, with full powers of substitution.

his
JACK + GRASSHOPPER, [SEAL.]
mark.
Company H, Third Regiment.

Attest:
GEO. O. SANDERS.
FRANK J. NASH.

I, De Witt Lipe, clerk of the district court of the Cherokee Nation, do hereby certify that Jack Grasshopper, who signed the above, personally appeared before me and acknowledged it to be his act and deed. I further certify that at the time of making such acknowledgment I read and fully explained such warrant of attorney to the party executing the same.

Witness my hand and seal of court this 7th day of December, A. D. 1868.
[L. S.]
DE WITT LIPE,
Clerk of the District Court.

When the allocations began, Jack needed help in registering even though he'd been on the 1880 and 1896 rolls. He couldn't understand why he was having difficulty, and Annie asked Billy to help. Jack appeared before the Interior Department's Commission to the Five Civilized Tribes in Needmore on May 6, 1902, and Billy verified his claim. It was accepted, and after that, he was part of the regular process. In the 1906 Guion Miller Roll census for allocations, Joe Fox Raven and Annie were his witnesses before H.R. Crawford on November 10th, and he received his share as a full-blood Cherokee duly enrolled beginning with the 1851 Drennen Roll.[641]

Annie appreciated all Keetowahs, especially those who stood up firmly for Cherokee sovereignty. One such man was Ned Christie, whom she knew from his service on the National Council as well as his official work on tribal issues over many years with her son Billy.

28

Outlaws and Heroes – Ned Christie Revealed

Nede Wade Christie (Ne-De-Wa-De) was an interesting and important character in Cherokee history, although there have been so many erroneous books and articles written about him over the years that the truth is difficult to ascertain. Nede was always known as "Ned." My grandmother told me stories about him when I was a boy visiting her in Tahlequah. She always said not to believe the bad things written about him, that he was a hero who stood up for the best values of the Cherokees.

Ned's paternal grandmother Quatse (or Betsy) was a daughter of Hiketiyah and a Dutch trader named John Christie. His maternal grandfather, Wakigu Dalasini, was the son of Tsatsi Dalasini, also known as Sugar Tree and Step-a-long.[642] They lived in the Smoky Mountains of North Carolina in Turtletown. His father, Watt Christie, was born in 1817, and his mother, Skyaheta, was from the same area, a member of the Bird Clan.[643] His white great-grandfather fully endorsed the matrilineal approach of the Cherokees.[644] The Christie family was in one of the thirteen Cherokee-led detachments that left their homeland in late 1838. His great-grandmother Betsy died along the way. After arriving in 1839, Watt and his first wife Wadaya settled the family on the banks of the Barren Fork in the community they called Wauhillau. This area became part of Going Snake District in 1840. Wadaya died in 1842, and Watt married Lydia Thrower (Skyaheta Tecorhurtuski) in 1849.[645] Ned was an excellent blacksmith and gunsmith and soon built up a thriving business. The *Phoenix* reported that people preferred taking their hoes and plows to him as " . . . he never fails to put them in order, no odds how rough they may be, and rough they are, as everyone knows who has ever been in their district."[646] Ned was born at home on December 14, 1852 and grew up speaking mostly Cherokee with his seven brothers and sisters. They attended the Caney School, learning to read and write both Cherokee and English. His father and grandfather served as chiefs of the Keetoowah ceremonial ground located in Wauhillau, which gave him a strong foundation in Cherokee traditions and ceremonies.

When the Civil War began in 1861, Watt and his brother Arch joined the Union as soldiers in Cherokee company E, along with Arch's son James. They fought alongside Annie Spirit's husband Simon. When they returned home in 1865, they found their district almost destroyed and began to rebuild. Ned bought a fiddle by mail order, quickly becoming a good musician and often playing at dances. He also was well known for his prowess playing marbles (known as digadayosdi in Cherokee*)*. As a young man, he loved guns and was proficient in both gunsmithing and shooting. His father gave him two 44-caliber cap and ball pistols when he returned home from the Civil War, which he converted into shell-percussion five-shot pistols, his favorite guns the rest of his life.[647]

Ned met his first wife, Nannie Dick at a dance when he was nineteen, and they had their first child, Mary (known as Mele or Wali), the next year. The marriage didn't last; Nannie decided to move in with Watt, which apparently didn't cause any trouble, even if strange. In 1874, Ned met Peggy Tucker, and they married in 1876. That year they had a son, James. Peggy died in early 1881, leaving him to take care of James. Ned then married

Jennie Scraper, a daughter of his friends Otter and Sallie Scraper later that year, and they had one daughter, Annie. But Jennie couldn't tolerate Ned's drinking and divorced him the next year. In 1886, he got married for the last time, to Nusi Goie Grease, known to most people as Nancy.[648]

Elected to the Cherokee National Council on November 11, 1885 as a member of the Keetoowah Society, Ned attended his first session on December 16th. Devon Mihesuah notes that to serve as a Councilor, "he had to be literate and informed about the Constitution, laws and happenings in not only the Cherokee Nation but also in other Indian Territory tribal nations and in the United States. Lengthy written transcripts of National Council meetings reveal that meetings took up much of his time and the seriousness of the agendas required his full attention. He had to be punctual and to understand the formal protocol of the meetings, which included drafting acts and laws." [649] His father, Watt, also served on the tribal council for decades, and his half-brother Jim was a senator.

Ned supported all proposals to protect Cherokee sovereignty, strongly opposing the Allotment Act of 1887 sponsored by Massachusetts Senator Henry Dawes. Ned was instrumental in stopping fraudulent marriages by white men to Cherokee women solely to gain access to their land and assets. Working closely with Chief Dennis Bushyhead, he opposed railroads being built across Cherokee land, helping to block the Southern Kansas Railway from building a new line.[650]

Ned traveled to Tahlequah to attend a special Council meeting on April 14th after the Cherokee National Female Seminary burned down on April 10, 1887. Ned was a strong supporter of education and urged rebuilding the Seminary quickly. The Council agreed unanimously but had to wait for a few weeks to get proposals and prepare the budget. While back in town on May 5th to prepare for the next Council session, Ned was said to have been seen where US Marshal Dan Maples was killed at Town Branch Creek.

Maples was investigating illegal whiskey sales and had decided to target Bub Trainer, who was notorious for his illegal stills. Ned was accused of being the shooter by John Parris, a member of Trainor's gang. After learning about the accusation, Christie proclaimed his innocence and returned home to prepare his defense, gathering evidence with the help of his father Watt. Thus, he wasn't present when the Council voted on May 9th to rebuild the Seminary. Ned never attended another Council meeting.[651]

Ned Christie National Council Portrait 1885[652]

The Federal Court for the Western District of Arkansas in Fort Smith had jurisdiction over the murder case since a US Marshal was killed. Judge Isaac C. Parker, who had a fearsome reputation as a hanging judge, was assigned to the case. Some sources say that Ned wrote to Judge Parker stating his innocence, requesting bail so he could find the killer and that Parker refused, but if that occurred, the letter is no longer in evidence. Parker's Grand Jury charged Bub Trainor, John Parris, Charley Bobtail, and Ned Christie for Maples' murder on July 23, 1887. Ned was supposed to attend the next Council meeting on August 22nd but decided to submit his resignation to Chief Bushyhead and remain at home. Fearing it would be impossible to receive a fair trial in Parker's courtroom, he refused to turn himself in and continued to maintain his innocence, saying "I would rather die at home, in my own Nation, with my people. I won't die in the white man's country."[653]

John Parris pled not guilty to the charge on October 5th, listing witnesses he said would exonerate him. Bub Trainor pled not guilty, also listing witnesses. But they failed to appear at court sessions on February 23 and May 1, 1888. Charley Bobcat said that Parris had killed Maples but there was no follow-up by Judge Parker or the prosecutor. Trainor's white father argued that he couldn't have killed Maples; perhaps because he was well-connected politically, his son was let go. Parris was arrested for another crime and sentenced to jail for a year, leaving the jurisdiction after he got out in 1890. Ned Christie became Parker's sole target.[654] Because he hadn't appeared in court to contest the murder indictment, he was charged and a new court date was set for September 26, 1889. A $500 reward was offered for his capture. Ned didn't appear. During the next year, he was protected at times by Keetoowah Society members, but mainly he and his wife went about their normal lives. Ned hunted, dried meat, kept the brush cleared on the farm, and took care of their horses and milk cows. Nancy maintained the large garden and continued selling surplus eggs and vegetables to neighbors. Their four watchdogs helped look out for strangers. His father Watt remained engaged in politics and was nominated for the Grand Council of the National Party, while his half-brother Jim continued serving as a Senator from Flint District.

Hoping to arrest him and get the reward money, a posse led by Marshal L. P. Isbell went to his home on September 26, 1889. A firefight ensued, wounding Ned and his cousin Arch Wolfe, along with Marshal Isbell, and the house was badly damaged by fire. The posse withdrew. Ned's injuries were serious, including some loss of vision in one eye, but he recovered. He decided to construct a new house west of Bitting Creek next to Thornton Spring, not a fortress as many reports have it, but a well-protected stone structure about ten feet square.[655] The US increased the reward for his arrest to $1000. Then the case went silent for several years. Around that time, Ned had this photo taken with a rifle propped on a chair and a pistol in his right hand, but it wasn't published and came to light only after his death.[656]

A posse of nine men led by Milo Creekmore attacked Ned's home on October 11, 1892 while he was eating breakfast with Nancy, her son Albert, Ned's daughter Mary, Arch, and Charles Hair, a 12-year-old boy who helped Ned on the farm. When Creekmore demanded his surrender, Ned replied by shooting two men in the posse. They tried to set fire to the house and planted sticks of dynamite, but the fuses failed to light. At that point, Creekmore sent a telegram to Marshall Yoes for help: "Send deputies to Ned Christie's. We have him surrounded, but have not enough men. Joe Bowers and John Fields, of our part, are wounded." Yoes replied: "Have wired everywhere for deputies. You will have lots of help tonight. Hold the fort by all means and get him this time."[657]

A larger posse led by Deputy Gideon S. White, a former captain in the US Cavalry during the Civil War, attacked Ned's home at 4am on November 3rd. As before, his wife Nancy, her son Albert, his daughter Mary, Arch Wolfe, and Charles Hair were there, along with Mary's daughter Charlotte and Ned's son Jim. There was sporadic gunfire for a few hours; then, the posse tried a small cannon, which failed to knock down the door. As the day ended, the stalemate continued. Around 4am the following morning, dynamite was placed next to the house, blowing out part of the wall and starting a fire. Christie emerged from the burning house and was shot dead. No one knows by whom, but there are many colorful stories about it. The only male found in the house was young Charles Hair. The others had fled through the root cellar and out the back of the house.[658] Ned's body was taken to Fort Smith and displayed at the federal courthouse strapped to a door for a day before being shipped to Ft. Gibson, where his brother James and his father claimed the body. Newspapers across the country had a field day with the story of the violent outlaw who met his proper demise. The lies about Ned Christie being an outlaw and murderer picked up steam from there on, continuing to this day in some publications.

Ned's wife Nancy tried to pick up the pieces of her shattered life by marrying Ned's brother Jack, with whom she had five children.[659] By all accounts they had a happy life together. But her seventeen-year-old stepson Jim, Ned's child with Peggy Tucker, was murdered and mutilated on July 4, 1893. Newspapers called him a killer just like his father, another lie and slur on the family. An investigation revealed that Tallow Mayes' son Sam murdered him for no reason at all. Sam was convicted and hung for the crime.

Assassinating Ned Christie wasn't sufficient revenge for the US Marshals. They indicted Arch Wolfe and Charles Hair (who was just twelve years old) for attempting to murder deputy Gideon S. White the day that Ned Christie was assassinated. Hair was convicted on March 21, 1893. Sentenced to three years of hard labor at the Illinois State Reformatory, he was a broken young man after returning home, dying in 1907 aged twenty-seven. Arch was convicted by Judge Parker of assault with intent to kill and liquor violations in early 1894 and sentenced to five years of hard labor at the Kings County Penitentiary in Brooklyn, New York. His grandfather and other family members wrote repeatedly to learn how he was, asking for his sentence to be served in the Cherokee Nation. They received no replies. For unknown reasons, Arch was moved to the Government Hospital for the Insane in Washington, D.C. on August 29, 1895. His case files do not reveal what form of mental illness he allegedly had, but his health was recorded as normal until 1903, when he was transferred to the newly-opened Canton Asylum for Insane Indians in South Dakota.[660] His family continued writing letters to the doctors requesting information and asking for him to be returned home to the Cherokee Nation. The files show no replies to those letters. Arch died at the Canton Asylum on July 2, 1912.[661]

What is the truth about the murder of Marshal Dan Maples? In the 1920s, several stories were printed in Oklahoma newspapers alleging that someone other than Ned Christie did it. In one version, Richard A. Humphrey, a former slave adopted into the Cherokee Nation, said that, on his way home from work, he saw Bud Trainor stooped over Maples with a pistol in his hand. That story hasn't been fully documented. After exhaustive research on the case, historian Devon Mihesuah concludes:

> Parris is the more likely culprit. Bobtail had immediately accused him of being the shooter after the men were taken to Fort Smith. Unlike Trainor, who continued to live in the area and behave badly, Parris made himself scarce after he left the Little Rock penitentiary in 1890. His

brothers stayed in Indian Territory but there are no more mentions of John [Parris] in the documents. Bud [Trainor] had the confidence to continue his wayward life. Parris may also have done so, but he lived it elsewhere, away from any possibility that attention might turn toward him as the killer of Dan Maples.[662]

Ned was a Cherokee patriot and a martyr. His life demonstrates the layers of cruelty and prejudice that Cherokees faced after removal, which brought untimely death and dishonor to many. His treatment was typical of what Cherokees faced during the 1890s, as the US resolutely continued its quest to strip Indians of their sovereignty despite the treaties signed so solemnly that protected the Nation in perpetuity. Ned Christie's leadership and passion would have been valuable for the Nation as they faced the decline of their sovereignty during the next decade.

29

The 1890s – Decline of Sovereignty

While united in trying to protect their sovereignty, the Cherokees couldn't stand up to the continuous US pressure and grudgingly agreed to sell the Cherokee Outlet in 1890. Retired Chief Bushyhead was as one of three commissioners who negotiated the sale. My great-grandfather Billy Mayes was serving the Nation as the principal interpreter for the Senate at that time, standing on the far left in this 1890 photo of Cherokee Senators:[663]

Joel Mayes was reelected in the election for Chief held on August 3, 1891, running with Stephen Teehee on the Downing Party ticket against George Benge and Henry Chambers. Chambers was elected Assistant Chief.

Mayes had done a good job trying to stave off the latest US attempts to undermine Cherokee sovereignty and had grown in the job. Everyone looked forward to his second term. Billy Mayes was a close confidante of his half-brother Joel and continued helping with interpretation and translations.[664] In spite of the ill winds blowing, the Nation still had a sense of optimism about being able to defend its rights. As Thanksgiving drew near, President Harrison released a Proclamation, which Joel mirrored in his, using it as a vehicle to refer to Cherokee sovereignty:

Thanksgiving Proclamation.

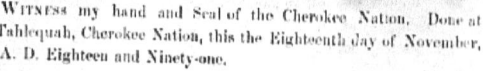

Whereas,

Benjamin Harrison, our great father, the President of the United States, has issued a Proclamation setting apart the 26 inst. as a day of joyful thanksgiving, in which to thank God "for the bounties of His providence; for the peace in which we are permitted to enjoy them, and for the preservation of those institutions of civil and religious liberties." It is proper that the Cherokee People should participate in this joyful praise, and thanks to God for the peace and prosperity they now enjoy, and ask Him to continue to the Cherokee People that civil liberty they have enjoyed from time immemorial, and ask that they may continue in the peaceful possession of their land and homes, to a time without end. Now, Therefore, I, J. B. Mayes, Principal Chief of the Cherokee Nation, do hereby appoint

Thursday, November the 26th, 1891

to be a day of Thanksgiving and Praise to God, that He still permits the Cherokee Nation of Indians to live in the enjoyment of this civil and religious liberty, and in this struggle for the right of soil and self-government, ask Him to shield us from all danger.

It is proper at this time for the Cherokees to gather themselves in close friendship and cease from toil and assemble in public worship also, give comfort and consolation the afflicted, performing acts of charity for the needy in a spirit that is good for him who gives, as well as for him who receives.

WITNESS my hand and Seal of the Cherokee Nation. Done at Tahlequah, Cherokee Nation, this the Eighteenth day of November, A. D. Eighteen and Ninety-one.

J. B. MAYES,
Principal Chief.

But Joel died suddenly on December 14th just four days after Henry Chambers passed away, both from influenza. That was a grievous loss at a time when the political situation required experienced leadership. As Chair of the Senate, Thomas Buffington took Joel's place until the Council could elect a successor. On December 23rd, Johnson Harris, a long-time Senator, was elected Principal Chief and Stephen Teehee was chosen as Assistant Chief. Billy Mayes continued to serve as chief interpreter for the Senate.

In spite of the politics, the 1890s proved to be a generally positive time for the Spirit family, although Annie's eldest child Sarah died of consumption (known today as tuberculosis) on May 26, 1890. Each of her six children came to her bedside to say goodbye as she counseled them to walk uprightly in life. The older ones with her first husband William—Joseph, Lucy Ann, and George—were grown up, but Annie helped take care of her younger children with Charles McGinnis—William, who was eleven; Charlotte, who was seven; and Cleveland, just six years old. The past was swept downstream like a river as she focused on the future. On a happier note, her family continued to grow. Her granddaughter Lucy Ann England married Thomas Chitwood in 1890 shortly after Sarah passed away, and her first great-grandson, Walter Newton Chitwood, arrived in 1891. Walter's sister Mamie Josephine, her first great-granddaughter, arrived in 1894. A new generation was coming along.[665]

Around 1891, Annie took in two young children—Joe Fox Raven, who was nine, and his two-year-old brother John; they were left homeless after their mother Sallie Tarpin disappeared and their father Eaw-Luh-Nuh Raven died. Their grandmother was Annie's half-sister Annie Vann Adair, who had been married to Andrew Raven Adair.[666] She'd been ill for a few months and told Annie that she didn't have the energy to take care of young children. Annie welcomed them into her home, formally adopting them in 1897. Perhaps she was foolish taking on young boys at her age, but she loved them dearly, and it all worked out well under the circumstances. This is her 1900 Dawes filing (an essential requirement for every Cherokee to receive an allocation of property) on their behalf.

```
                    Department of the Interior,
              Commission to the Five Civilized Tribes,
                     Vinita, I.T., September 22, 1900.

     In the matter of the application of Annie Snell for the enroll-
ment of two orphan children, Fox Raven and Johnnie Raven as Cher-
okee citizens; being sworn and examined by Commissioner Needles
she testified as follows:

Q  What is your name?        A   Annie Snell.
Q  How old are you?          A   Seventy-one.
Q  What is your post-office address?    A    South-west City.
Q  What are the names of these boys?    A    Fox Raven and Johnnie
Raven.
Q  How old is Fox Raven.     A   He is going on 20.
And the other one is going on ten.
Q  What was the name of their father?   A    Hisname was Raven; I
don't know his first name.
Q  What was the name of their mother?   A    She was named Sallie.
Q  Was it Sallie Raven?      A   Yes sir
Q  Their father and mother both dead?   A    They are both dead.

     Examined by Cherokee Rep've Hastings:

Q  They are brothers are they?    A    Yes sir
Q  Same mother and same father?   A    Yes sir.  They are full-bloods
I took them at two years old, and I have raised them.  I took
both boys, they are with me yet.
Their mother's name was Sallie; I don't think they put the Raven
down, I think it was Tarrepin.    I changed the name of the
oldest one to Joe; he was Fox when I got him.
Q  Do you want it put down as Joe?    A   I guess it would be
better to go as Fox.

     1880 roll page 657 #886 Fox Raven Saline District;
     1880 roll for mother page 668 #1131 as Sallie Tarpin, Saline;
     1896 roll page 523 #2602 Fox Raven Delaware District;
     1896 roll page 523 #2603 John Raven Delaware District.

     Com'r Needles:  The names of Fox Raven and John Raven appear
upon the census roll of 1896; the name of Fox Raven also appears
upon the authenticated roll of 1880; these children are averred to
be the children and descendants of one Sallie Raven whose name ap-
pears on the authenticated roll of 1880 as Sallie Tarpin, and they
are duly identified as such; they all being duly identified ac-
cording to page and number of the rolls as indicated in the testimony,
and having made satisfactory proof as to their residence, said
John and Fox Raven will be duly listed for enrollment by this Com-
mission as Cherokee citizens by blood.


     M D. Green, being first duly sworn, states that as stenographer to
the Commission to the Five Civilized Tribes he correctly recorded
the testimony and proceedings in this case and that the above and
foregoing is a true and complete transcript of his stenographic
notes thereof.

     Subscribed and sworn to before me this 24 day of September 1900.
                                                    Commissioner.
```

My great-grandmother Annie Harper Gladney Mayes began teaching at the Cherokee Orphans Home, located on the banks of the Grand River in

Salina, in the late 1880s along with five others under the supervision of Superintendent W.A. Duncan. This photo was taken on the front porch in the early 1890s.

Left to right: Cynthia Davis, Annie Mayes, Unidentified, W.A. Duncan, Jane Ross Nave, Andy Norwood, Unidentified[667]

Joel's brother George Wash Mayes (known as "Wash") was elected High Sheriff of the Cherokee Nation in November 1891, another family member serving in an important role. Born on November 5, 1824, Wash moved west with his family in 1837. In 1846, he married Charlotte Bushyhead, daughter of Reverend Jesse Bushyhead and Eliza Wilkerson, becoming a successful farmer and rancher near Locust Grove in Saline District. He supported the Confederacy in the Civil War, fighting with Captain Adair's Second Cherokee Mounted Rifles, and was a member of the Cherokee Confederate Council from Going Snake District between 1862 and 1865. Wash and Charlotte had eight children, one of whom was named after his father, Samuel Houston Mayes. Wash's term was five years and would have expired in 1896, but he died on October 24, 1894. Thus, he didn't live to see the Supreme Court decision in *Talton v. Mayes*, which upheld Cherokee jurisdiction over its criminal justice system. I'll return to that seminal case below.

Chief Harris completed negotiations for sale of the Cherokee Outlet, which Mayes had begun under duress. An agreement in principle was reached in January 1892, and Harris signed the contract for $8,595,736 for the estimated six and a half million acres on May 17, 1893. The Outlet was opened to white settlement on September 16th and torrents of people poured in. Harris was almost impeached for selling the land, with the lower house voting twenty-two to ten in favor, but he was cleared by the Senate.[668] Whether it would have turned out differently had Joel not died is unclear, but many people felt that Harris was too easy on the US and feared the precedent that was set. Feelings were running especially high among the Keetoowah.

The Dawes Commission arrived later in 1893 and began lobbying Cherokee citizens to support receiving individual allotments. The traditionalists, including the Nighthawk Keetwoowah Society, were adamantly opposed, as were most other Cherokees. Chief Harris did his best to fend off the Commission, but their joint lobbying in Washington with the Creeks, Choctaws, Seminoles, and other tribes lacked political traction. The fact that oil had been discovered on Indian land worsened their situation. The collective fear about losing their sovereignty once again was palpable. This map shows the Indian Territories in 1890.[669]

But like most Cherokee citizens, Annie had to keep looking to the future while living in the present. She began operating a boarding house in 1894 for merchants and businessmen from Southwest City who came regularly to collect on their loans to Cherokees to buy merchandise. Much of this trade was based on the promise of payments people would receive for the Cherokee Strip. She spoke about this a few years later: "I hired Dora Givens (later Crayton) to help cook for the boarders. Our table could seat up to twenty-five guests. I was fond of Dora, and hoped she'd marry my grandson Joe England, one of Sarah's children."[670] Joe was twenty-four, and with both his parents gone, Annie always looked out for him and his siblings Lucy Ann and George. They did go on a few dates, but that came to nothing. Grandchildren and great-grandchildren continued to arrive. Billy and Annie had another girl on January 28, 1894—my great-aunt Mary Hazel. The end of the year was shaping up to be a good one with everyone in the family doing well. But Annie's younger son Charles died on Christmas day in 1894 at his good friend Buffington Wyly's home, a hard blow.

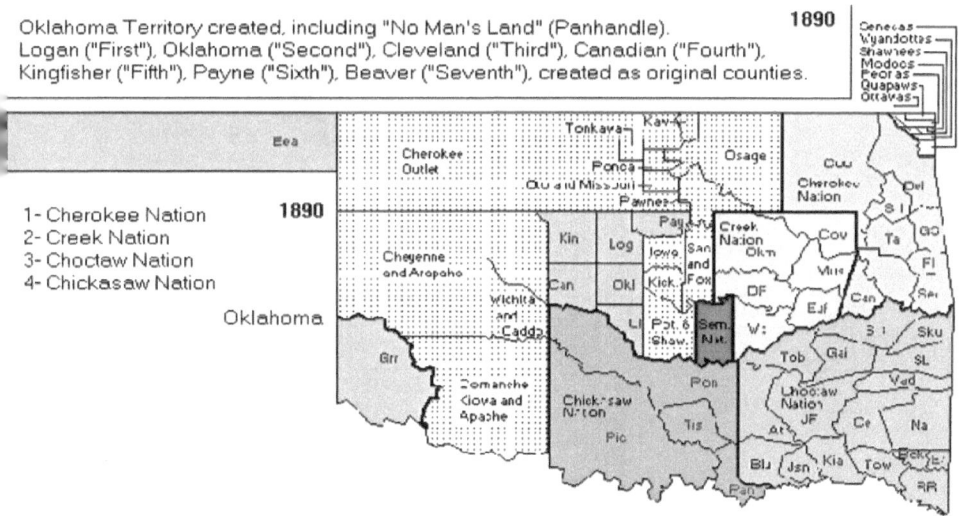

In the tribal election for Chief on August 5, 1895, Samuel Mayes' and Nannie Adair's son Samuel Houston Mayes, Jr. (Tsa-wa-gak-ski) was elected on the Downing Ticket.[671] He is one of my great-great uncles. Born May 11, 1845 at the family's Muddy Springs farm, he enlisted in the Confederate Army at sixteen, serving under Captain Ben Carter in the Second Regiment of Company K, First Cherokee Mounted Volunteers. He was involved in numerous battles fighting beside Stand Watie. Following the Civil War, Samuel moved to Rush County, Texas and attended school there for a time before returning home. He married Martha Elizabeth Vann, David Vann's and Martha McNair's daughter, in 1871. They built a large house he called Snowdale Farm on the site of his father's home. They had three children—William Lucullus in 1874, Joseph Francis in 1877, and Martha Carrie in 1880. Samuel was elected Sheriff of Cooweescoowee District in 1881 and served as a Senator from 1885 to 1895. He also owned an important ferry on the Grand River near Salina for many years and founded a major mercantile company in 1906.

Chief Samuel Houston Mayes - 1895[672]

As Chief, Samuel did his best against insurmountable odds as the US continued pressing Cherokees to give up their communal lands, courts, schools, press, and sovereignty. The Dawes Commission filed its first report on November 24, 1894. Arguing that Cherokee and other leaders of the Five Civilized Tribes had failed to negotiate in good faith and were corrupt, it recommended that the US should ignore the treaties, dissolve their governments, and allocate all their land. Immediately, representatives of the five tribes went to Washington to protest the report. Chief Mayes called the report "a lie, false as hell."[673] But their protests made no difference, and the Dawes Commission returned to Indian Territory in 1895 to survey tribal lands. Its second report on November 18, 1895 recommended that Congress establish a formal Territory covering what eventually became Oklahoma to govern the region, concluding that the tribes lacked the capacity for self-governance. Chief Mayes countered that Cherokees were "contented with their condition" and cited the treaty provisions guaranteeing their sovereignty.[674]

Some Cherokees became so disheartened by Dawes' allotment scheme that they considered moving to other countries. In 1895, Bird Harris brought to the Council a proposal to buy a large parcel of about 30,000 square miles in Mexico and relocate the Cherokee Nation there. E.C. Boudinot went to Washington, D.C. to discuss the idea with the Mexican Foreign Minister. Although that didn't lead anywhere, it reflected the strong feelings of many Cherokees about remaining masters of their own fate. My grandfather Billy thought the idea worth considering and, indeed, went to Mexico shortly afterward to check out a farmstead there. But he didn't act on the idea until 1908, when he bought a farm there. As usual, the Cherokees were resilient. Amid all this political turmoil, the lives of Annie's family became richer, with a deep focus on education. Her daughter Charlotte and her husband William Ballard sent more of their children to the Male and Female Seminaries than any other family. Their daughter Janana and Annie's grandson Joseph Foreman Gladney led the way, graduating from the Female and Male Seminaries on June 26, 1896. Elmira, Charlotte, and Annie threw a celebration party for the cousins, who were close friends. Janana's sister Anna graduated the next June, Lucinda followed on June 29, 1899, Sarah Elanor graduated on May 29, 1902, and Ruth was in the class that graduated on May 31, 1906.

CHARLOTTE & WILLIAM H BALLARD'S CHILDREN

JANE ANNA (TOP)

LUCINDA BALLARD HARLAN

SARA BALLARD WOOD

WILLIAM HOUSTON BALLARD

ANNA BALLARD CONNER

RUTH BALLARD

COUSIN HOMER GIBSON

Photo of Ballard Children and Cousin Homer Gibson[675]

Janana, Charlotte and Annie in 1900[676]

William and Annie's children were the artists in the family. Maggie and Maude went to the Female Seminary for some of their studies, where they learned to paint and play music. Maude could play anything on the piano, and both became good painters. Hazel, their youngest, was two years old and one of Annie's favorites. Hazel was one of my favorite aunts, and as a boy, I loved her paintings.

US politics continued its fateful trajectory against Indian sovereignty. Chief Mayes submitted a formal protest to the US Congress regarding House Bill 6309 on March 9, 1896, another in a long skein of elegant appeals to their erstwhile protectors. The protest argued that the Dawes Commission was illegally constituted and its actions to remove Cherokee sovereignty and control over its land and courts were illegal, concluding that the US was confiscating Cherokee land without any legal rationale or due process. The Cherokees' enduring faith that the US would ultimately live up to its Treaty commitments and the US Constitution is moving. One of the Cherokees most important documents, the protest is in Appendix

24. Written by Johnson Harris, George Benge, Roach Young, and Joseph Smallwood, it began by citing Article 5 of the New Echota Treaty:

> The United States hereby covenant and agree that the lands ceded to the Cherokee Nation . . . shall in no future time, without their consent, be included within the territorial limits or jurisdiction of any State or Territory. But they shall secure to the Cherokee Nation the right by their National Councils to make and carry into effect all such laws as they deem necessary for the Government and protection of the persons and property within their own country belonging to their people.[677]

But that entreaty didn't induce Congress to change anything: The Dawes Commission's recommendations would be implemented over their objections.

About the same time, an important US Supreme Court criminal case confirmed Cherokee sovereignty despite what the US Congress was doing to annul it. Like the 1833 Supreme Court decision in Worcester v. Georgia that Andrew Jackson ignored, *Talton v. Mayes* (May 18, 1896) made no difference to the politicians in Washington, D.C. But it's an important part of history. A murder conviction under the Cherokee legal system was challenged by a writ of habeas corpus on the ground that the grand jury was composed of only five people.[678] There was no dispute that Bob Talton, a half-blood Cherokee, had killed a Cherokee lawyer named Elliott at Catoosa in early November 1892. It was a brutal murder. Talton cut Elliott's throat from behind at the City Hotel following a fight at the pool hall and later cut off his head. Talton walked leisurely out of town afterwards and was located and arrested later. He was indicted on December 1st and convicted of first-degree murder on December 31st in a special session of the Cherokee Supreme Court with Judge John Wickliff presiding, and sentenced to hang on February 28, 1893.

In a first-ever claim, Talton's lawyer filed a writ of habeas corpus against Wash Mayes, High Sheriff of the Cherokee Nation, before US District Court Judge Parker in Ft. Smith, Arkansas on February 15, 1893. The writ contested the composition of the Grand Jury as not meeting the US Constitution's requirement of twelve jurors and claimed that Talton didn't receive a fair trial in the Cherokee court. Judge Parker denied the claim, stating that Cherokee law prevailed.

Talton appealed to the US Supreme Court on April 24, 1893, which ruled that the murder was an offense against the local laws of the Cherokee Nation, not an offense against the US and that, given the status of the Cherokee Nation under the 1835 New Echota Treaty, the Constitution's fifth amendment didn't apply. The Court found "the determination of what is the existing law of the Cherokee Nation . . . is a matter solely within the jurisdiction of the courts of that Nation." [679] In reaching that result, the Court noted that Section 30 of the Act of May 2, 1890, providing a temporary government of the Oklahoma Territory, states that "the judicial tribunals of the Indian nations shall retain exclusive jurisdiction in all civil and criminal cases arising in the country in which members of the Nation by nativity or by adoption shall be the only parties . . . ."[680]

Frank Josiah Boudinot (Kaw-la-nah or Raven) was one of the principal Cherokee attorneys during the struggles with the Dawes Commission. Son of William Penn Boudinot and great nephew of General Stand Watie, he was appointed in August 1896 in Cherokee Senate Bill Number 1, along with William T. Hutchings, Albert Z. English, D.W. Duncan, and W.W. Hastings.[681] Born on August 20, 1866 just after the Civil War ended, Boudinot attended high school in Flint, Michigan and graduated from the Baptist Indian University in Muskogee.[682] He served as Clerk of the Supreme Court of the Cherokee Nation in 1888 and 1889, as well as being assistant editor of the *Cherokee Advocate*, founded by his grandfather Elias

Boudinot. From 1890 to 1894, his legal practice before Cherokee courts brought him into contact with many different people. Boudinot loved being a lawyer but also found time to serve as Clerk of the Senate. Having decided to become a full-fledged attorney to better protect Cherokee legal interests, he was admitted to the University of Michigan Law School in 1894, where he studied until March 1895 when he was forced to return home because of ill health.[683] Boudinot never returned and didn't graduate but is listed in the Law School's records as being in the class of 1896. While studying at Michigan, he was an active member of the New York and California Club Courts, student organizations that complemented the Moot Court, where he sharpened his skills as an advocate.[684] In 1897, he married Anna S. Meigs, a granddaughter of Chief John Ross, with whom he had two children: Frank J. Boudinot, Jr. in 1899 and Henry Meigs Boudinot in 1907. Frank served as General Counsel to the Keetoowah Society in 1898 and 1899, a position that he never relinquished during the next forty-five years as he filed case after case on behalf of Cherokees generally and Keetoowah in particular. We'll learn more about Frank later.

Ex-Chief Bushyhead chaired the Cherokee delegation to an inter-tribal meeting held at McAlester on November 12, 1896, which agreed to take concerted action against the allotment of tribal lands and the US plan to extinguish tribal governments. The Indians were fully in the right and never gave up, but the US government remained impervious to the plain language of its numerous treaties with the tribes. The political rollercoaster continued apace, and there seemed to be nothing the Cherokees or the other tribes could do about it.

Women were very active in this seemingly futile struggle to protect the Cherokee Nation's sovereignty, particularly traditional women from the Keetoowah Society. Joining with women from the Creek, Choctaw, and Chickasaw tribes, they founded the Four Mothers Society at Illinois

Springs, which had more than 24,000 members at its peak, including Annie Spirit. Their goal was to restore women's power and place, as descendants of Selu the Corn Mother. The Green Corn and New Moon ceremonies were restored under their leadership, and stomp dances came back into fashion among full bloods, with women establishing the rhythm and beginning the dance while the men sang.[685]

There are many detestable aspects of the Dawes and Curtis Acts.[686] The Curtis Act, approved by Congress on June 28, 1898, applied Dawes Act provisions to the five Civilized Tribes.[687] Overnight, it abolished the Cherokee Tribal Court system, causing legal confusion that lasted for years, and required that membership rolls be prepared to allocate the surface rights of all tribal lands among the Cherokees and other tribes. The US announced that it would begin choosing all tribal chiefs, acting through the Bureau of Indian Affairs, which was completely unconstitutional. There was no Indian support at all for individual allocations, but the US simply exercised its will, creating new facts on the ground by determining who were citizens of the various tribes and forcing the allocations. On one level, it's difficult to imagine that Cherokees could accept this but, as so often over the past century, there was no way out of the dilemma. What could they do? They were powerless.

One repercussion not often discussed is how the Dawes and Curtis legislation enshrined in statute that Indian men were the heads of households. Thus, allotments went mainly to men, which undermined the traditional matrilineal approach, drastically reducing the economic and political power of women. Moreover, many states enacted statutes prohibiting Indian men from voting, further destroying how Indians had managed their politics and governance. Allotment commodified Indians' relationship with the land. Its privatization "forced many to choose between maintaining a traditional relationship with their lands or being able to feed their families by selling their allotments to white settlers." The Report of the Commissioner of Indian Affairs on October 1, 1898 made perfectly clear what lay ahead: "The Indians must conform to 'the white man's ways,' peaceably if they will, forcibly if they must. They must adjust themselves to their environment, and conform their mode of living substantially to our civilization . . . They cannot escape it, and must either conform to it or be crushed by it."[688]

Chief Mayes appointed seven Cherokee delegates for the Dawes Commission negotiations on January 7, 1899.

Cherokee Delegation to the Dawes Commission (Chief Mayes standing on left)[689]

Not seeing a way out of the dilemma, Mayes supported a "yes" vote, which shocked many, but he had no choice. Led by Redbird Smith, the Nighthawk Keeetoowahs worked hard to oppose the proposal. They lost the vote on the Dawes Commission treaty on January 31, 1899 by 2,015 votes but continued to oppose the tribe's loss of sovereignty in every way possible short of armed insurrection. As the symbol of the opposition, Redbird was arrested and imprisoned. Thomas Buffington was elected Principal Chief in September 1899 on a platform of concluding the negations and winding down the Cherokee Nation, running against Wolfe Coon. Wolfe was a full-blood Keetoowah, President of the Senate. He spoke no English, which made it difficult for him politically vis-à-vis US officials. It was a sad campaign, carried out under a pall of gloom. Wolfe had a lot of support, but many Keetoowah had become so disillusioned with politics that they didn't vote.

Buffington was a decent man but arguably wasn't up to the job of leading the Cherokee Nation at that critical time. Perhaps nobody was. Most likely, nothing would have changed had Wolfe Coon been elected, but it's clear the US would have had a fight on its hands trying to strip away Cherokee sovereignty. He was Annie's third cousin through his great-great grandfather Ezekiel's marriage to Mary Emory, another of Ludovic Grant's many legacies.[690]

Thomas Buffington - 1899[691]

In spite of losing the election, Wolfe asked to be included on the Cherokee delegation with other Keetoowah leaders: "We earnestly solicit your consideration of the fact . . . that the end of the Cherokee Nation and final division of property close at hand strikes closer and deeper into the hearts and lives of the Keetoowah or fullblood Cherokees than to any other people . . . ."[692] He was rejected by Buffington, who chose not to even submit the request to the National Council. The Keetoowah were shut out of the dialogue.

The Dawes Commission released its regulation limiting individual allotments to eighty acres on December 24th without considering the quality, features, and value of the land. Just eighty acres, take it or leave it. Freedman received only forty acres from the Dawes Commission. The Government's stated intention was to make all the "excess" land available to white settlers. That drove another nail into the Cherokees' coffin, provoking years of disputes and court battles.[693]

The Mayes family, like many others, owned large farms with acreage well above the limit. Retired chief Samuel Houston Mayes' Snowdale Farm was a large property of several hundred acres, with cattle herds, hayfields, and forests. Annie Spirit's property along Honey Creek also was large, but probably less than eighty acres. My great-grandfather Billy Mayes had hundreds of acres under cultivation and pasturage, as well as extensive woodlands. In the words of the Dawes Commission, all the "excess" was declared surplus and made available to white settlers. Loss of so much communal land was a harsh blow to him and the Nation. No longer would it be possible for each generation to have land on which to build new houses and farms. Billy was angry about how the Cherokees were treated, but he had numerous other interests and businesses by then on which to focus his attention, including the Hotel Hazel.

Muscogee, I.T.
December 24, 1899

CHEROKEE LANDS

Excess Holdings Over Eighty Acres to Become Public Domain on March 28.

Muscogee, I.T., December 24--Regarding the disposition of excessive holdings of lands in the Cherokee Nation the Dawes commission has issued the following letter:

In reply to your questions we beg leave to say that in accordance with the provisions of the rules and regulations promulgated by the Secretary of the Interior, it is proper for each individual Cherokee to file upon not to exceed eighty acres of land. All excess of holdings over this amount will become public domain upon March 28, 1899, and citizens have the right to sell their improvements prior to that time.

In the matter of the selections, the Secretary has made no distinctions relative to the different grades of values of lands. Citizens having bought the improvements of intruders or tendered the money therefor will be entitled to possession thereof, whether voluntarily given or not by the intruder, upon January 1, 1899. It will not be the duty of the commission at that time to place citizens in possession of lands upon which the title is in dispute.

Dawes Commission Regulation Converting Cherokee Land to the Public Domain

30

A Note on the Hotel Hazel

Billy Mayes was named Olympus postmaster by President Grover Cleveland in 1885. In the early 1890s, the US Government decided that Olympus (Indian Territory) no longer needed a postmaster, so the post office was closed. He and his wife Annie bought land in Grove, including lots eight and nine filled with hundreds of peach and apple trees, two lots in block sixteen as well as two box houses and a barn in block fifteen. They continued to manage their large farm on Cowskin Prairie near Olympus. Annie Spirit had a house with a small barn and well in block twenty-seven as well as her large farm on Honey Creek.

Grove was incorporated in 1895. In the spring of 1896, Billy and Annie built the sixteen-room Hotel Hazel with stables and a feed barn on lots one and two of block sixteen at the corner of Second and Hazel.[694] It was named after their youngest daughter, my great-aunt Mary Hazel, who was born on January 28, 1894.

The family agreed that the Hazel would strive to be the best hotel in the region. Annie Harper Mayes was firmly in command of the dining room, which featured seasonal fruits and vegetables, the finest beef, lamb, pork, poultry, and fresh fish. It was a great success, described as " . . . the leading hotel in this section of the territory and is a first-class hostelry in every respect. Neatness characterizes the place, the table is supplied with all the delicacies of the season and everything possible is done for the comfort and convenience of the guests."[695] In her old age, Annie Spirit participated actively in this venture, which brought many interesting people into the dining room and hotel. Here's a typical notice in the local newspaper of the time, the *Grove Sun*: "Mrs. W.P. Mayes, proprietress of Hotel Hazel, left an order with the Sun Tuesday for more of our up-to-now commercial printing. The Hotel Hazel is a first-class hostelry and offers special rates and attention to commercial men."[696]

Hotel Hazel around 1910[697]

Around 1900, Billy and Annie began renting a few rooms to longer-term boarders, and the stables, named the Red Front Livery Barn, were moved to 6 East Third Street between Main and Hazel. The stables burned down in 1913. In 1900, the boarders included Ed Paulding, Henry Thompson, Robert Pickens, Hugh Guthrie, David and Lilian Fink, and Oliver Mason.

In 1910, the year that Annie died, Hazel boarders included Walter Ross (an oil producer), Dr. Robert Caldwell, Judge Wilson Smith, and John Austin (a lawyer), a stellar group. Annie's granddaughter Hazel was assistant manager. The hotel had a large display room on the ground floor where traveling salesmen displayed their merchandise for local businessmen to buy. The Arkansas and Oklahoma Railroad laid tracks to Grove from Rogers, Arkansas in 1900; the next year, investors sold the line to the St. Louis and San Francisco Railway system. That brought many visitors to Grove, some of whom stayed at the Hazel, which sent a wagon to the depot to pick up passengers and luggage. In 1932 a doctor set up an office to fit eyeglasses. The hotel remained the headquarters for traveling businessmen up to the day it burned down in October 1933.[698] Billy became a politician, elected to four terms on the Grove City Council and Mayor in 1912 and 1916. Annie and Billy used the hotel as their home until she died on November 10, 1929.

Annie Harper Gladney Mayes circa 1925

My great aunt Hazel was a good painter, and especially liked iris, my favorite flower. I've grown iris all my life in honor of her and my grandmother, treasuring our visits to Tahlequah when I was a boy. Hazel's painting of iris blooming at my grandmother's home in Tahlequah has hung in my homes for the past forty years.

31

A New Century

The US continued to meddle more deeply into Cherokee affairs, even about education. President McKinley overturned the Cherokee National Council's decision to offer lifetime tenure to the principal of the Female Seminary, Ann Florence Wilson, on December 28, 1900. She was a superbly qualified woman who had served the school since being elected Principal in 1875. As she celebrated her 58th birthday that year, all the teachers at the Seminary were Cherokee, including two graduates she had taught earlier. Wilson had been supported by each of the seven chiefs under whom she had served and was beloved among the alumni and students.[699] McKinley gave no reason for his decision; even though there was no legal basis for his veto, it stood. Clearly, the US government wanted to swiftly close all Cherokee institutions.[700]

MISS A. FLORENCE WILSON,
FOR TWENTY-SIX YEARS PRINCIPAL OF C. N. F. S.

Florence Wilson about 1905[701]

As Chief Buffington and the delegates he had chosen were in Washington on April 19, 1901 negotiating the details of surrendering Cherokee sovereignty, the Keetoowahs published this appeal in the *Wagoner Record* newspaper:

> The full-blood Cherokee will never submit to such an agreement, which violates nearly every right held near and dear to full-blood Indians. We would rather submit to the Curtis Bill than to the new agreement; in the first place, Chief Buffington and his delegates had no authority to make such an agreement. The delegates were not chosen by the Cherokee people, neither by the Cherokee Council, but were appointed by Chief Buffington on his own responsibility, without consulting the full-bloods or real Indians. No, we will never submit to this kind of agreement.[702]

But Buffington continued on that path, and his address to the Council in November 1901 was direct: "Who of you desires to remain in the confused condition that prevails in the country now? . . . While the government we love so well and to which we have clung so tenaciously is fast going, let us give personal support to each other so that it may be said the Cherokee people are keeping abreast of the times and apace with the onward march of civilization."[703] Those were terrible days as Cherokees watched what they had fought for so long being dissolved before their eyes, one blow after another. Tom Buffington can be remembered as a realist, but when the Council voted to approve the deal demanded by the US, it was a sad day for most. Negotiations on details continued until 1902. Early that year, Buffington traveled to Washington, with Wolfe Coon and Redbird Smith representing the Keetoowahs, appearing before a Congressional committee arguing for larger allotments than eighty acres per household. The various political forces in the Cherokee Nation finally came together on this, but it was too late, and their effort failed. That year, there were around 42,000 citizens of the Cherokee Nation and 5,000 freedmen. All were essentially prisoners of the US. The final treaty was signed on July 2, 1902; the Cherokees' tribal government was to end on March 4, 1906 shortly before Wolfe passed away at his home a few miles north of Stilwell on April 20th. He left behind his wife Sarah Cornsilk and their five children. Born in 1851, Wolfe served as a Councilor from Going Snake District starting in 1883 and as a Senator from 1897 until his death. A Baptist minister and Keetoowah leader, he was a major force in the Cherokee community.

The Four Mothers Society to which Annie belonged didn't give up, continuing to agitate for fairness and equity. After operating informally for years, it was formally founded by Cherokee, Creek, Choctaw, and Natchez women in 1895, headquartered in Sulphur Springs. The Society was a strong supporter of an Indian state and maintained the old traditions of stomp dances stickball games, and feast days. It continued to be active until at least 1915.

Commissioner W. A. Jones transmitted a report to the Secretary of Interior on how to value eighteen different types of land for allotment from the calculated total of 4,420,070 acres on September 13, 1901. The most valuable at $6.50 per acre were "natural open bottom land" (11,646 acres), "best black prairie land" (1623 acres), and "bottom land covered with timber and thickets" (143,836 acres). At the bottom of the list were "rough and rocky mountain land" (220,341 acres) and "flint hills" (469,330 acres) valued at fifty cents per acre. The complete list is in Appendix 25.[704] Despite the terrible political situation, life went on. The resilience of Cherokees remained strong. As the Nation's legal existence was coming to an end, Billy and Annie focused on the Hotel Hazel and livery business in Grove while continuing to manage their farm. Their children all remained in the vicinity, raising their families. Politics was local, with Billy deeply involved in managing Grove's development and expansion as a member of the City Council.

William P. Mayes and Daughter Maggie (1928)

One solace for Annie was Billy's farm, a favorite retreat when she was feeling blue. My grandmother Maude's painting of the farm captures its peaceful ambience. It's been hanging in my bedroom for the past forty years, reminding me of the times I spent with her as a boy:

Maude and Hazel also painted porcelin and ceramics. This platter of Maude's remains in the family:[705]

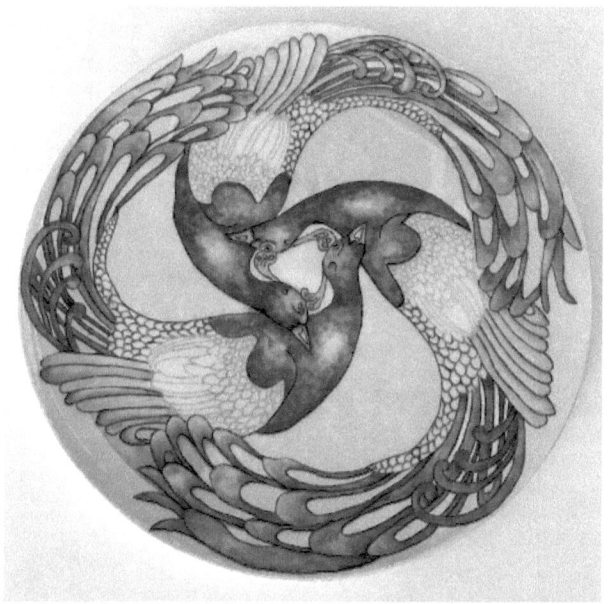

Hazel painted this salt and pepper set with a Dutch theme on German porcelin:[706]

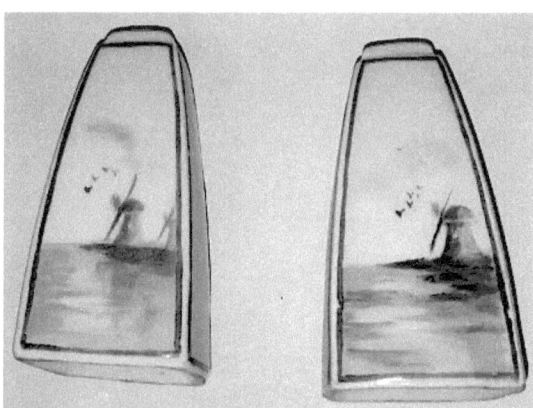

Maude painted this cloisonné toiletry set around 1915:[707]

32

End of the Dream

Frank Boudinot filed two important lawsuits against the US government in 1900 on behalf of the Keetoowah Society and the Cherokee Emigrant Council headed by Dave Muskrat. The first was for $5,000,000 on behalf of all emigrant Cherokees for their lost lands in the East; the second challenged the enrollment of more than 3,000 intermarried white persons to receive allotments of Cherokee lands. Even though no one else had much hope for a positive result, Frank was optimistic. It would take several years for the cases to wind their way through the courts.

Cherokees had to suffer through one more election before the charade of sovereignty was ripped away entirely. In 1903, Senator William C. Rogers from the Downing Party was elected Principal Chief, defeating E. L. Cookson. Known as the "merchant prince"[708] due to his trading posts in Talala, Skiatook, Vera, and Oologah, his term saw the final liquidation of the independent Cherokee government and the establishment of the state of Oklahoma in 1907.[709] All Cherokee institutions were closed, their newspapers were shut down, and every vestige of sovereignty erased. He was the last elected chief recognized by the US government, that power having been given up as a condition of becoming part of Oklahoma. Rogers remained thereafter as titular Chief, performing ceremonial functions for the tribe.

William C. Rogers - 1900[710]

But the Four Mothers Society and Keetoowah Society never gave up. An editorial in the *Nowata Advertiser* endorsed their campaign on November 25, 1904: "The women of the Cherokee nation are demanding that there be no forgotten past. When the rush of home seekers from the north and east reach [our] Territory and a new government reigns, the Cherokee women do not want their nation to be forgotten. They would have the past remembered and revered."[711] As the new land allotment process began in 1905, many Keetoowah traditionalists, including Redbird Smith, were imprisoned for protesting and were involuntarily assigned allotments. He was born to Pig Smith and Lizzie Hildebrand on July 19, 1850, learning about the ancient customs and ceremonies as a boy. He was instrumental in the work of the Nighthawk branch of the Keetoowahs, playing a crucial role in the attempt to preserve Cherokee sovereignty. He never faltered under the blows rained on him as he was imprisoned, tortured, and enrolled against his will; nevertheless, upon his release from jail, he urged his followers to stop the resistance. He described his mission this way:

I have always believed that the Great Creator had a great design for my people, the Cherokees. I have been taught that from my childhood up and now in my mature manhood I recognize it as a great truth. Our forces have been dissipated by the external forces, perhaps it has been just a training, but we must now get together as a race and render our contribution to mankind. We are endowed with intelligence, we are industrious, we are loyal, and we are spiritual, but we are overlooking the Cherokee mission on earth, for no man nor race is endowed with these qualifications without a designed purpose. Work and right training is the solution of my following. We as a group are still groping in darkness in many things, but this we know, we must work. A kindly man cannot help his neighbor in need unless he has a surplus and he cannot have a surplus unless he works . . . Our mixed-bloods should not be overlooked in this program of a racial awakening. Our pride in our ancestral heritage is our great incentive for handing something worthwhile to our posterity. It is this pride in ancestry that makes men strong and loyal . . . It is this same pride that makes men give up their all for their Government."[712]

Redbird Smith (right) and Dick Scott around 1910[713]

Nighthawk Keetoowah - Early 1900s

Despite intense US pressure for them to give up control of their lands, Indians hoped to have their own state. The five civilized tribes organized a Convention on August 21, 1905 to press for an Indian state alongside the proposed new state of Oklahoma. It was to be called Sequoyah. The call for the convention was issued by Chief Rogers and Green McCurtain, the Choctaw chief, and all residents in Indian Territory were invited to participate, the first formal political cooperation between whites and Indians there. The largest Indian meeting ever convened, the Five Civilized Tribes unanimously supported an Indian State, arguing "that owing to peculiar conditions existing in the territory it cannot be joined to Oklahoma without doing injustice to the citizens of the former [Indian] territory."[714] Indian hopes momentarily surged as energy rippled among the participants. A Constitution was drafted and submitted for a vote by everyone living in Indian Territory, similar to their effort in 1871. Annie's family was a strong supporter of this initiative. The proposed new State of Sequoyah and its Constitution were approved by large majorities of Indians.[715]

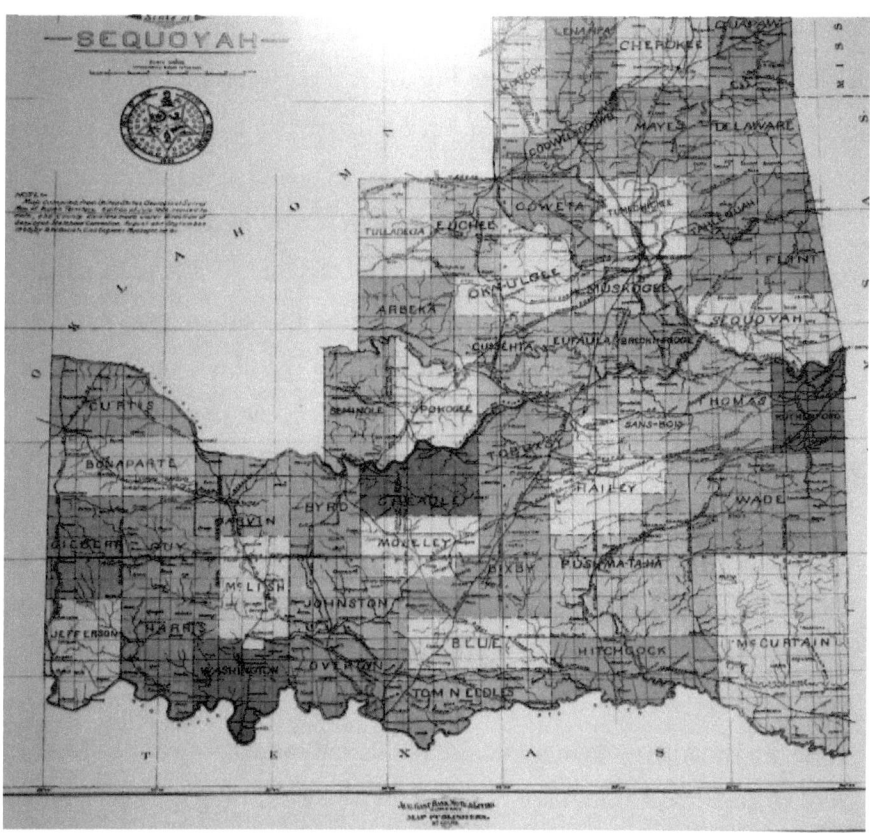

This initiative was exciting at the beginning because it seemed there really was a chance for an Indian State to be created. As usual, however, the US Congress ignored the vote and forced all the Indian Nations into white-dominated Oklahoma. They would be under white boots once again. Cherokees and other tribes responded with resilience and grit, taking their allotments and making the best of the new political situation. Indians had the largest population in many of the new counties, which provided some protection. The hardest things for Cherokees to accept were losing the Seminaries, the courts, and their beloved newspaper. The new *Oklahoma Constitution* borrowed just a few items from the proposed Sequoyah State Constitution. It granted the people a form of legislative power through referendums and included mandates for schools, courts, roads, electricity, water, and wildlife management. But only men were allowed to vote, disenfranchising Indian women, and it treated Freedmen like black people in the rest of the US. It also forbade anyone to openly carry a sword!

Considering the political circumstances, Chief Rogers decided not to call an election for Chief during the summer of 1905, which caused consternation among the Keetoowahs. Wanting to maintain a traditional base of tribal government, they instructed Frank Boudinot on September 20th to incorporate the Keetoowah Society under US law. In accordance with the Cherokee laws still in force, Frank was elected Chief along with a new Council on November 21st and took the oath of office in the Senate Chamber of the Cherokee National Council. But his election wasn't recognized by Chief Rogers. Both sides appealed to US Interior Secretary Hitchcock, who, of course, sided with Rogers.[716] Against the low expectations of many, Frank won the two Court of Claims lawsuits filed against the US in 1903 and 1905; however, they were appealed. He was admitted to practice before the US Supreme Court in 1906 to argue the cases, which upheld both judgments. Including interest, they totaled $11,000,000.[717] He was a hero in the Cherokee Nation, which honored his success:

> The United States Court of Claims rendered its decree in this case May 28, 1905, and the money was paid in 1910, and the Cherokee people today owe a debt of gratitude to Mr. Boudinot and the Society, and especially to Mr. Boudinot, for the collection of that old claim of four million dollars of seventy-five years' standing. It arose under the treaty of 1835, under which the Cherokees moved west. Every Cherokee who participated in that payment, to the remotest corners of the nation, should always be Boudinot's friend for this one gigantic act. . . . [718]

Boudinot described his situation and motivation in a memoir: "Because of my active opposition to the Cherokee National authorities and to the Dawes Commission, I was persona non grata, and was never recognized as Principal Chief by the United States Government. I have been, and am now the representative of my people, the Cherokees by blood, before the authorities of the United States government, including the Court of Claims and the Supreme Court . . . ."[719]

The Dawes Commission finally succeeded in breaking the Cherokees' tribal land up into individual allotments in 1906 when Congress passed an "Act to Provide for the Final Disposition of the Affairs of the five Civilized Tribes in Oklahoma" that gave the Interior Department authority to take over Cherokee courts, schools, and tribal government buildings. Like most everyone else, except for some of the most traditional Keetoowah who wouldn't register for the allotments and thus lost their land, Annie's family received their shares.[720] Descendants of many Keetoowah who refused to be recorded on the Dawes Roll were not allowed to be officially enrolled as members of the Cherokee Nation. Redbird was elected Chief of the Nighthawk Keetwoowah Council in 1908. Always concentrating on improving the lives of his people, he held that position until his death on November 8, 1918. Redbird's son Sam succeeded him as Chief of the Nighthawk Keetoowahs on April 7, 1919. Sam and the Nighthawk Council designated Levi Gritts as Chief of the Cherokees on December 9, 1920, an honorary title since they had no political power. Keetoowah spirit remained strong as the US crippled the tribe by reducing its land base by more than half and suppressing the Cherokee Nation financially and operationally. The US promoted white access to the newly open Indian land with advertisements like this one.[721]

Under Boudinot's leadership, the Keetoowah Society continued to hold meetings and maintain community associations according to the traditional rules. I admire him for his leadership and the Keetoowahs for their eternal pride in the Cherokee people. Frank was a serious, even stern, man who even so always maintained a sense of humor as he pursued his personal mission of obtaining recompense for the Cherokees' stolen lands in the southeast. A 1937 interview outlines his illustrious career representing Cherokee interests. As a young man, he attended Bacone University in Tahlequah from 1882 to 1886 and the University of Michigan Law School in 1886-1887. He served as Clerk of the Cherokee Supreme Court in 1888-1889 while working as Assistant Editor of the *Cherokee Phoenix*. He also started an independent paper called the *Tahlequah Capital* about that time. Boudinot moved to Washington, D.C. in 1916 to pursue court cases that benefitted Cherokees, after W. C. Rogers gave him a broad power of attorney.[722] Rogers continued conducting some Cherokee business in his continuing role as elected chief until he died. Boudinot brought another successful case in the Court of Claims in 1932 and also represented Choctaw,

Chippewa, Sioux, and Klamath tribes to obtain compensation. He helped write the law providing Emancipated Citizenship for American Indians approved June 2, 1924[723] and continued pressing the US Congress to implement it properly. But not all Indians wanted to be citizens, feeling citizenship had been imposed on them.[724] He played a major role in developing the first revision and codification of statutes affecting Indians. Frank died September 19, 1945 and is buried in Washington, D.C., another Cherokee hero. Pursuant to the Indian Reorganization Act of 1934, the Keetoowahs were formally recognized as the United Keetoowah Band of Cherokees on October 3, 1950. Its members are principally full blood Cherokees living in Northeastern Oklahoma.

Frank J. Boudinot - 1925[725]

Given the political upheaval in the Cherokee Nation, many people decided to explore other places. Annie's son Billy surprised her on March 12, 1908 by buying a fifty-acre farm and town lot in the Landon and Warner Colony in San Luis Potosi, Mexico, eighty-six miles west of Taupico on the Mexican-Central Railroad line. In letters to her and others in the family, he was enthusiastic about what could be raised there: "[P]ara grass, alfalfa, oranges, coffee, sugar cane, rice, cotton or almost anything," he wrote to Jim Thompson on April 12th on Hotel Hazel stationary. He wanted to move there, hoping to buy more land and mentioned getting a nine-month train ticket to give him sufficient time to decide whether to move permanently.[726] However, his wife didn't want to leave their children and grandchildren, so they remained in Grove while he managed the Mexican farm at a distance.

Receipt for Application and First Payment

GENERAL OFFICES OF
THE MEXICO-UNITED STATES LAND & IMMIGRATION CORPORATION
SHAWNEE, OKLAHOMA U S A

MEXICO OFFICE
VALLES STATE OF SAN LUIS POTOSI MEXICO

Mar 12-09

T. P. Mayes,

Grove, Okla.

DEAR SIR:

Your application for one farm, and one town lot, together with ××××× in the amount of Ten Dollars ($10.00) each, and a cash remittance of $ $10.00 have been received, and when your notes have all been paid in full you will be entitled to and will receive a "Clearance Receipt" entitling you to one farm, and one lot, in the final distribution of the 3497 farms and 3497 town lots in the LANDON & WARNER COLONY, in the State of San Luis Potosi, Mexico, according to the rules as advertised in the "HOMESEEKERS' AND INVESTORS' GUIDE."

Very respectfully,

Mexico-United States Land and Immigration Corporation

Per _____

IN REMITTING PLEASE SEND P. O.
MONEY ORDER OR ××× ×× ××××××××
REGISTERED MAIL. ×× ×××× ×× ×××××× ××

Annie Gladney Mayes continued teaching at the Olympus school for many years; she moved the old Cherokee School House in northeast Grove to her farm, about a mile northwest of town in November 1908, which was covered in the local press: "It being moved marks the passing of an old landmark in Grove, and calls to memory the days when the young Cherokees studied within its walls. May it stand in its new location undisturbed until time ceases to exist."[727] Annie's granddaughter Maude Mayes, my grandmother, also was a teacher in the local schools, a good painter, and an excellent pianist. She was one of Annie's favorite granddaughters, and the two often wrote letters to each other, some of which I received from Betty Lou Dealy. Maude was a major presence in my life. It was a great loss when she passed away in 1954 just after my tenth birthday.

Maude Mayes - 1900

Maude Mayes and husband William Harvey Barnes - 1909

Maude Mayes Barnes - 1912

Annie lost her half-sister Annie Vann Adair on January 20, 1909. The two old ladies had shared many experiences in life and were close. She never remarried after Andrew Raven Adair was killed in 1855. Her funeral was held in Locust Grove in Saline District. Annie's niece Rosella was there with her husband, George Downing, and their children, Mary, Edward, Elizabeth, Joel Mayes, and Lafayette. The old guard in Annie's extended family was flying away, and she must have known that her time was drawing near.

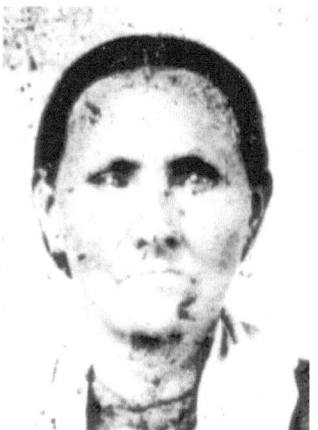

Annie Vann Adair - 1900

The Female Seminary held its final graduation ceremony on May 27, 1909 after a week of celebrations, including a baccalaureate service at the Lyric Theater in Tahlequah, performance of a German play, "A Treasure for the House," by the Junior Class, and instrumental recitals of pieces by Chopin and Schumann by several students. Mrs. R.L. Fite, a graduate of the class of 1880, expressed the feeling of most: "The sun has set forever on the Cherokee National Female Seminary."

Final Graduating Class of Cherokee Female Seminary

The commencement brochure concluded with these words:

> A sacred burden is this life ye bear,
> Look on it, lift it, bear it solemnly,
> Stand up and walk beneath it steadfastly,
> Fail not for sorrow, falter not for sin,
> But onward, upward, till the goal ye win.[728]

George Wright, Commissioner of the Five Civilized Tribes, offered the Cherokee Female Seminary Building and forty acres of adjacent land to the new Northeastern Normal School for $45,000. Governor Haskell accepted the offer, emphasizing it would "justly recognize and commemorate the history of such commendable educational effort as was put forth by the Cherokee Nation in the days when they were such an important part of the small lamp of enlightenment surrounded by a wilderness of darkness." Eliza Missouri Bushyhead Alberty, an 1856 graduate and Annie's 4th cousin, made a moving speech: "The State of Oklahoma has recognized its merit and perpetuated its history by adopting it as one of the permanent educational institutions of the State." The Governor replied: "If the people of Oklahoma continue the proper spirit that inspired the Cherokee Nation to create this institution, it will be through all the future as it has been during the past, a benefit to humanity and of the greatest credit to the State."[729] This photo of Eliza wearing a pendant of the Arabic Order of the Nobles of the Mystic Shrine was taken in 1913.[730] She and her husband David Rowe Vann served as stewards of the Male Seminary and for a time managed the Cherokee Insane Hospital. They also owned the National Hotel near the Council House in Tahlequah. She was a daughter of Reverend Jesse Bushyhead, born in 1839 while on the Trail of Tears in Cape Girardeau, Missouri.

Eliza Bushyhead Alberty[731]

The Oklahoma Legislature passed an act on March 6, 1909 to create Northeastern State Normal School in Tahlequah, purchasing the building, land, and equipment of the Cherokee Female Seminary from the Cherokee Government. Because they wanted there still to be a Cherokee school, even if under public administration in the new State of Oklahoma, the Cherokee Council merged the Male and Female Seminary classes into a coeducational school, which opened on September 14, 1909. Janana Ballard was one of the teachers, known for following the precepts of her mentor Florence Wilson. Janana "was a stickler for punctuality and cleanliness . . . [O]nce a week Ballard lined up the primary-grade students and made them remove their shoes and socks. Any girls with "stinky feet" had to perform chores in the kitchen or classrooms."[732]

Loss of Cherokee control over the education of their citizens was a huge blow, with many reflecting it was one of the saddest days of their lives. That was close to the last item on the US government's list of steps to shut down the Cherokee Nation. Losing their Female and Male Seminaries was truly the end of the dream for many. Yet beyond any government decree or unjust law, they knew their people well enough to have confidence that Cherokees are a resilient people and that the Cherokee Nation will exist forever. And they were right.

32

Epilogue

The Grove Press printed Annie's obituary:

Mrs. Anna Wake Snell, more familiarly known as Grandma Snell, died at her home on Honey Creek, eight miles southeast of Grove, on Sunday night, February 20, 1910, at the ripe old age of about 86 years. The deceased is the mother of our townsman, W.P. Mayes, also the mother of Mrs. Wm. Ballard of Needmore, and Mrs. John Gladney of Tahlequah. Grandma Snell was widely known throughout the Eastern part of Oklahoma, she conducting a boarding house for a number of years at the old Cherokee Court House south of Grove five miles. She has made her home for more than forty years on Honey Creek, and her friends abound in scores throughout Delaware County. Deceased was a member of the South Methodist church, and she always lived a Christian life. The community loses a good woman, a woman that was a mother to each one she was in contact with, and her departure has cast a gloom over Cowskin prairie . . . . The remains of the grand old lady were laid to rest in the family graveyard near her old home, Tuesday afternoon.[733]

Annie left 31 grandchildren and 32 great-grandchildren.[734] She is buried in the Snell family cemetery in Row 11 next to her husband Simon, with her name spelled using Sequoyah's syllabary—*a nu we gi   i la qui*.

Claude Hanna evokes a clear vision of Grandma Snell at one of the periodic revival meetings her church organized:

> The women would get up and start breakfast at daybreak and, after all had eaten, they would assemble in the schoolhouse and start song services, then prayer and preaching services afterwards. I shall never forget Grandma Snell's prayers. If you never heard Grandma Snell pray, you have missed something. I can remember many times seeing her kneel and turn her face toward heaven and start her prayer with, '*Oh gi do da, ga lu la dee ha hee,*' or as we might say, 'Our Father, who art in Heaven.' Of course, her prayers were all in Cherokee and I could not understand all the words, but one could easily tell that her prayers

were getting through. I just wish I could hear her pray again. At noon, another big meal would be ready, then afterwards more singing and preaching. Sometimes there would be an evening service after supper also. It seemed to me that the women were always cooking and there was always plenty of food for everyone, and oh, how good it was—all cooked outdoors and mingled with hickory smoke and sprinkled with a few ashes. We had hot biscuits for breakfast and hot cornbread for dinner and supper. I just wonder if they still have those meetings anywhere nowadays.[735]

Annie's life was honored at the Snell Family Cemetery on October 28, 2017, when the Oklahoma Chapter of the Trail of Tears Association held a grave-marking ceremony for her and two others.[736] As Trail of Tears Survivors, this plaque was attached to each grave.

My cousin LeeAnn Dreadfulwater at the Marking Ceremony

Since the 1970s, there has been a new day for the Cherokee Nation, following decisions by Presidents Johnson and Nixon to reaffirm Indian rights to self-determination. In 1971, the Cherokee Nation elected its first Principal Chief since 1902, and a new constitution was approved on June 26, 1976, replacing the one dating from 1866. It states that tribal membership will be determined with reference to the Dawes Commission Rolls. Thus, there is no minimum blood requirement. The 2010 federal census listed more than 300,000 people identifying themselves as Cherokees, the largest of any American Indian group. The modern Cherokee Nation, headquartered in Tahlequah, is managing its affairs with wisdom and prudence. It operates the largest Indian health service in the country. Its enduring existence honors the sacrifices made by their ancestors.

In recent years the Cherokee Nation has pressed for one of the commitments in Article 6 of the 1835 New Echota Treaty to be honored by the United States, a representative in Congress: " . . . it is stipulated that they shall be entitled to a delegate in the House of Representatives of the United States whenever Congress shall make provision for the same." Since the Supreme Court has ruled that the Treaty retains viability, there is no reason for Congress not to seat the designated Representative. In 2019 the Cherokees named Kimberly Teehee as their delegate. They are still awaiting a decision by the House of Representatives. "For two centuries, Congress has failed to honor that promise," Principal Chief Chuck Hoskin Jr. said. "However, the Treaty of New Echota has no expiration date. The obligation to seat a Cherokee Nation delegate is as binding today as it was in 1835."[737] It would be exciting, and exceedingly just, if the Cherokees win the right to be represented in Congress.

Acknowledgements

I am thankful for the inspiration provided by my paternal grandmother, Nellie Maude Mayes Barnes, who lived in Tahlequah when I was a boy. My family's home was in Tulsa; we visited her and other family members in northeast Oklahoma several times a year until she died when I was ten. I have fond memories of listening to stories at their homes in Muskogee, Tahlequah and at Lake Tenkiller. I especially enjoyed my grandmother's conversations with her siblings Hazel, Maggie and Ridge, which brought Cherokee history to life. One of her treasures was an early printing of the New Testament translated into Cherokee. She had walnut, pecan and chestnut trees in her yard. Each autumn we harvested and stored the nuts in large burlap sacks, to be opened in front of the fireplace during the winter. Grandma and her sisters showed us how important chestnuts were to Cherokees, preparing traditional dishes that were different from anything my mother fixed for dinner. I especially liked chestnut soup, a delicacy that I still prepare. They all were artists, painting landscapes, flowers and scenes from family farms, as well as decorating porcelain.

My Aunt Maggie married another Cherokee, James Polk Thompson, after whom I'm named. They lived in Tahlequah at Hill Crest, a beautiful two-story house with fine wood moldings. Jim served as mayor of Tahlequah for ten years and held numerous civic offices, including county treasurer. He opened the Sequoyah Theater in Tahlequah, and later the Thompson Theater across the street. My brother Glenn Mayes Barnes and I often watched the latest Western serials and cartoons on Saturday mornings there when we were visiting. They had two sons, James Mayes Thompson and Claud Elmo Thompson. Claud continued to run the Thompson Theater after his father's death. Mayes attended dental school in Chicago and began a thriving practice in Muskogee, perhaps the first Cherokee man to graduate from an accredited dental school. Mayes and his wife, Louise Pearson, had two children—Betty Lou and Pearson—who my parents stayed in touch with over the years. Betty Lou married Harold Dealy and lived in Muskogee until the end of her life. On one of my research trips to Oklahoma in the 1990s she gave me love letters written by my great-grandfather, his will, and details about his farm in Mexico. James Pearson Thompson married Patty Jean Paul, and their daughter, LeeAnn Dreadfulwater, who has worked for the Cherokee Nation for many years, helped induce me to learn enough to write this book. Thank you, LeeAnn.

I am thankful for the advice of librarians, curators and historians in Oklahoma, Georgia and Tennessee beginning with Rose Stauber in Grove, who helped when I was stumbling around looking for what to look for. Researchers at the Georgia Historical Society and the Trail of Tears Association located documents about Annie's grandfather, Buffalofish Spirit, and his family. I'd like to especially thank Michael Wren and Leslie Thomas of the Georgia Trail of Tears Association and Georgia Historical Society for unearthing key documents. Renee Harvey, Head Librarian at the Gilcrease Institute of American History and Art, provided a scan of the muster roll for the detachment on which some of Annie's relatives traveled west in June 1838. Archivist Kevin Cason at the Tennessee State

Library & Archives provided scans of claims filed in 1842 by Annie's great-grandmother, grandparents, uncles and aunts. Will Chavez, Assistant Editor of *The Cherokee Phoenix*, was helpful in verifying many details. The University of Michigan Law School provided important information about Frank Boudinot, who attended the Law School in 1894-95 and was a great advocate for the Cherokees. I especially thank Seth Quidachay-Swan, Head of the Collection Development and Access Services, and Mathew Fletcher, a professor in charge of preparing the Restatement of American Indian Law. Mathew brought to my attention an important 1896 US Supreme Court case that confirmed Cherokee sovereignty even as the US government was moving swiftly to take it away.

I greatly appreciate Charley Cope, Catherine Cotter, Carol Karasik and my cousins Justine Baker, Mary Ann Cassem (who produced the color version of Annie's portrait for the cover), Daryl Crotts, LeeAnn Dreadfulwater, Lee Fleming and Winona Ward for providing valuable suggestions and edits on the draft manuscript. Rachel Donaghe, wife of my cousin Denver, helped track down Samuel Houston Mayes' ancestors, solving a mystery that had lingered for years. I especially want to salute Corey Parson and Ariana Adams, my editors at the University of North Georgia Press who took the original manuscript and turned it into this book, and the copy editor Molly Lathem. Without their unstinting help, I wouldn't have finished the book. Thanks also to all the historians who recorded details about Cherokee families and their lives, a rich trove on which to draw. When sources disagree, I have chosen those that make most sense given the specific context. Any mistakes are my own.

Villamblard, France 2023

Appendices

To view the appendices, please visit:
https://ung.edu/university-press/books/cherokee-history-and-the-spirit-family.php

Notes

1. Elias Boudinot, *Cherokee Editor: The Writings of Elias Boudinot*, ed. Theda Perdue (Athens: University of Georgia Press, Brown Thrasher Book, 1996).
2. Emmett Starr, *History of the Cherokee Indians and Their Legends and Folklore* (Oklahoma Yesterday Publications 1979), plate 2, p. 12.
3. Pinterest. https://www.pinterest.fr/pin/407435716026620471/.
4. His obituary in the *Grove Sun* on November 24, 1945, p.1 noted that he knew "more early day history than any other citizen" and extolled his life: "He was a brother to ex-Chief Sam Mayes of Mayes County, who has been dead for a number of years, was active in Cherokee Tribal Affairs, serving as National Interpreter for the Cherokee National for a number of years. He lived a very useful and active life, and loved Nature. He enjoyed fishing and hunting, and though his eyesight became poor several years ago, he continued to go afield and enjoy himself…Hundreds of our citizens will miss Mr. Mayes' appearance on our streets and in the stores, the editor included, but we can cherish his memory and never forget the friendship he had for us. We feel that he has gone to that 'Happy Hunting Ground' from which no traveler returns…."

5. Annie's Eastern Cherokee Claim (hereinafter "ECA") #4924 was filed on December 10, 1906. It is a sparse document that doesn't list all her siblings, estimates her birth date as 1828 (her gravestone and other records show it was 1826), and lists her grandparents' names as unknown. She was very old when she filled out that form, which probably explains this, as well as saying her Uncle Weely Vann was known as "Poorbear", which isn't correct. One of her great-uncles was Charles Poorbear, and his son Hunter also was known as Poorbear. Her ECA contains important details about her second husband Simon Snell's family. In reconstructing Annie's family I've found other ECAs to be more informative, especially her half-sister Annie Vann's (#5585), Hunter Poorbear Buffalofish (#13231), Sarah Annie Miller (#5885), and Edward Sylvester Adair (#(5586).

6. One of the more informative texts about older customs and traditions was written by Lucy Lowrey Hoyt (Wah-Ne-Nau-Hi) in 1889, published as *The Wahnenauhi Manuscript: Historical Sketches of the Cherokees* (The Smithsonian Institution, Bureau of American Ethnology, Bulletin 196, edited by Jack Frederick Kilpatrick). Hoyt was one of twelve in the first graduating class at the Cherokee Female Seminary in 1855. The Cherokee Male Seminary also graduated its first class that year, including Monroe Calvin Keys, Lucy's future husband. One of his classmates was Joel Bryan Mayes.

7. Annie's extended family details are in Appendix 28.

8. A family chart is in Appendix 27. Don L. Shadburn with John D. Strange, III, *Upon Our Ruins: A Study in Cherokee History and Genealogy* (The Cottonpatch Press, Cumming Georgia 2011), p. 481: "Mary Grant, half-blood daughter of Ludovic, was born about 1726 at Great Tellico in Tennessee and died circa 1782. She first married to William Emory; her second marriage was to Old Sconti or Old Spirit. They had two daughters and one son: Peggy Spirit, born circa 1756, married William Shorey, Jr.

and Lydia, born circa 1758. The Spirit, son of Mary and Old Spirit, was born circa 1760 and died about 1828 in Arkansas. He llved for many years near Creekpath, Alabama, in the neighborhood of Major George Lowrey, and was a close associate of George Guess, or Sequoyah. The Spirit first married to Mary Blaylock and lived on Mouse Creek in Tennessee. Mary was a half-blood daughter of John Blaylock, a white captive among the Cherokees, and Nancy Gourd, a full-blood." See also p. 523, footnote 75 noting that White Horse wrote an article in the *Cherokee Advocate* on May 26, 1880 stating that Mary Grant had a son named Spirit.

9. In various documents her name is written in different ways, including Tsi-yu-ka, Chi-Yu-Ka, Chiyuka, Chowucah, Chiouke, Chowyouka and Chow-e-you-ka. The last one is how Annie Spirit wrote her mother's name on her Dawes and Miller Roll documents.

10. The lineage and relationships among the various Vann families are notoriously difficult to unravel. Some sources conclude that George Vann's father was John Cherokee Vann, but based on Annie Vann Adair's 1906 ECA #5585, he was Ducauligeeski Vann. I believe Polly Terrapin also was married to John Cherokee Vann, who died of smallpox at Hightower, with whom she had at least one child named Edith Kona Vann. The dates for Polly Terrapin and her parents are from: https://fabpedigree.com/s071/f562697.htm. One of Annie Vann's and Andrew Adair's children, Edward Sylvester, submitted ECA #5586, which contains many important details about both sides of his family. Both of these ECAs are in Appendix 26.

11. Susan Sconti Miller's daughter Sarah A. Burrow states in her 1906 Miller Roll ECA #5885 that her grandparents were David Sconti and Chiouke and that Charles Spirit was her uncle. Her ECA is in Appendix 26. Susan married William Wirt Miller (Dee-sto-stoak), with whom she had two other daughters, Rosa and Nancy. Rosa filed ECA #10739 under her married name Cheek, confirming those details. Nancy filed ECA

#10740 under her married name Baldridge.

12. A chart showing Annie Vann's ancestors is in Appendix 27.

13. I reconstructed Buffalofish and Wo-de-yo-he's family with the assistance of Michael Wren and by using Miller Roll applications filed in 1906. Two of the most important are Hunter Buffalofish's ECAs, #13231 and #6280, which list Buffalofish Spirit's and Wo-de-yo-he's children along with his uncles and aunts. These are included in Appendix 26 along with other selected ECAs.

14. Don L. Shadburn, *Cherokee Planters in Georgia, 1832-1838* (The Cottonpatch Press, Pioneer-Cherokee Heritage Series, Vol. 2 (1989), p. 93.

15. Ibid. p. 96.

16. McLoughlin, *Cherokee Renasence in the New Republic* (Princeton University Press, Princeton, New Jersey 1986), pp. 200-203. In principle, the US re-ceded the lands that Jackson and Coffee seized, in a treaty approved by President Madison in 1816 exchanging a large parcel in South Carolina plus indemnities of $25,500 as well as full pay and pensions for the Cherokee soldiers who'd helped Jackson at the Battle of the Horseshoe, but that came too late for many Cherokees. White families had already poured in, and Jackson used his power and influence to reverse Madison's decision.

17. Shadburn and Strange, *Upon Our Ruins: A Study in Cherokee History and Genealogy*, p. 118: John Huss Spirit "was a Cherokee minister and son of Old Spirit and Mary Blaylock, a half-blood." I have concluded that Susannah was the mother of Buffalofish's other children, and that John Huss Spirit's mother was Mary. Also note that John Lowrey testified in support of Nancy Gourd's heirs' claim to a reservation at the mouth of Battle Creek, that John Huss was "a Spirit". See RG75 E250 013. Nancy Gourd was one of John Huss's wives. Michael Wren has expressed doubt

that John Huss Spirit was a brother of Buffalofish, but the fact that he was known as "Captain Spirit" both before and after his ordination and that there was no other Cherokee family named "Spirit" – addition to the other evidence, led me to conclude that he was Buffalofish's half-brother. In this book I've recorded Mary Blaylock as his mother, and Susannah as the mother of his half-siblings.

18. Shadburn and Strange, pp. 482-484.

19. Ibid. p.482.

20. I discuss Cherokee slaves in several parts of this book, including Chapter 22. Less than ten percent of Cherokees owned a slave, and only a few of those operated plantations on a scale similar to southern plantation owners. There is no information about Buffalofish's three other than that they lived in a house similar to the family.

21. This is partly based on Sarah A. Burrows' Application No. 5885 on December 19, 1906 for a share of the funds appropriated by Congress on June 30, 1906. It provides details of the Sconti relationship, listing her paternal grandparents as Avery Miller and Nancy Ward and her maternal grandparents as David and Chiouke Sconti. Chiouke is one of several spellings for Annie's mother, Tsi-Yu-Ka, including Chouyouka, Chiyuka and Chah-wah-you-kah. Her sisters Rosa Miller Cheek and Annie Miller Baldridge also submitted ECAs that confirm these facts, as did their father, William Wirt Miller. The latter record gives her birth as 1843, which would mean that her mother was about fifty-three.

22. See Appendix 29. A number of additional great-grandchildren were born after Annie's death.

23. Sarah H. Hill, *All Roads Led From Rome: Facing the History of Cherokee Expulsion*, in Southern Spaces, February 20, 2017. Map of Cherokee County, Section 3, District 23 (1832) by surveyor John Harvey, showing plot numbers for the lottery. Georgia Archives. Map published by

William Philllips. Courtesy of County Maps collection, Georgia Archives, University System of Georgia. See https://southernspaces.org/sites/default/files/images/2016/hill_013_cherokee_co_land_lottery.jpg.

24. See Sid Chatfield, *The Cedar Tree*, in Appendix 1. He was a mentor to me on this project, and wrote a regular web page about Cherokee history and culture for many years.

25. I took this photo at the Cherokee Nation cultural center in February 2020.

26. Painting by Cecil Dick, "Stickball Players". Courtesy of the Cherokee Museum in Tahlequah, Oklahoma. I took this photo in February 2020.

27. See *Cherokee Marbles Still on a Roll Almost 1,200 Years Into the Game*, Letter From Oklahoma, Washington Post November 26, 1993, p. A4.

28. https://commons.m.wikimedia.org/wiki/File:Cherokee_Heritage_Center_-_Ancient_Village_5.jpg.

29. Hill, *All Roads Led From Rome*, Courtesy of Chieftains Museum/Major Ridge Home, image by Sarah H. Hill.

30. http://snowwowl.com/swolfstorycher1.html.

31. George Catlin, *Shut Your Mouth and Save Your Life* (N. Truebner & Co., London 1870). Catlin, who was a skilled painter and engraver, also carried out years of research about Indian health and their breathing techniques in both North and South America. Applying the basic precept of not breathing through his mouth even while asleep, he self-treated his long affliction of lung disease and reported that the health of his teeth also improved.

32. Jerry A. Maddox, *The Legacy of Ludovic Grant* (Author House 2007), p. 54.

33. Although there is no doubt that Ludovic Grant's wife was Cherokee, there are disputes about exactly who she was. Emmet Starr came to no conclusion about her name. Some think she was Elizabeth Tassel, but

based on everything I've read, my conclusion is that she was Eughioote. However, in order not to spread more potentially misleading information, I've not recorded her in my Reunion database, nor does she appear in the family charts in Appendix 27.

34. Maddox, p. 50.

35. Samuel Carter III, *Cherokee Sunset: A Nation Betrayed: A Narrative of Travail and Triumph, Persecution and Exile* (Doubleday & Company, Garden City NY 1976), p. 7.

36. Engraving by Issac Basire based on a painting by Markham. Courtesy of the British Museum. See https://www.geni.com/photo/view?album_type=project&photo_id=6000000020775330007&project_id=14699.

37. Rachel Caroline Eaton, *John Ross and the Cherokee Indians* (George Banta Publishing Company, Menasha, Wisconsin 1914), p. 12.

38. Ibid. p. 61. See also The South Carolina Historical and Genealogical Magazine, Vol. 10, No. 1, pp. 54-68 (South Carolina Historical Society, Jan. 1909. https://www.jstor.org/stable/27575222?seq=1 - metadata_info_tab_contents.

39. See https://sites.rootsweb.com/~tnpolk2/grant.htm.

40. Memoirs of Henry Timberlake (London in 1765). He died of smallpox before it was published. He sponsored the trip of Cherokee chiefs to England in 1764 to meet King George, but Lord Halifax, Secretary of State for the Southern Department, refused an audience with the King. Timberlake was arrested and imprisoned for failing to pay the debt incurred for lodging the Cherokee delegation. See https://mesda.org/item/collections/a-draught-of-the-cherokee-country/20600/. See also https://commons.wikimedia.org/wiki/File:Draught_of_the_Cherokee_Country.jpg.

41. Shadburn and Strange, pp. 481-82: "Mary Grant, half-blood daughter of Ludovic, was born about 1726 at Great Tellico in Tennessee

and died circa 1782. She first married to William Emory; her second marriage was to Old Sconti or Old Spirit. They had two daughters and one son: Peggy Spirit, born circa 1756, married William Shorey, Jr., and Lydia, born circa 1758. The Spirit, son of Mary and Old Spirit, was born circa 1760 and died about 1828 in Arkansas. He lived for many years near Creekpath, Alabama, in the neighborhood of Major George Lowrey, and was a close associate of George Guess, or Sequoyah." Shadburn and Strange cite an article in the Cherokee Advocate on May 26, 1880 by White Horse that Mary Grant had a son named Spirit. P. 523, fn 75.

42. Elizabeth married John Hellfire Rogers; Mary married Joseph L. Martin, William Rim Fawling and Ezekiel Buffington; and William, a close associate of Dragging Canoe known as Captain Will, had numerous liaisons. These relationships are outlined in Appendix 28, Annie Spirit's Family.

43. A chart of his ancestors is included in Appendix 27.

44. Colin G. Calloway, *The Indian World of George Washington: The First President, the First Americans, and the Birth of the Nation* (Oxford University Press 2018, Kindle Edition), p. 21.

45. Map drawn by Jeffrey L. Ward (2017) in Calloway, p. 128.

46. Calloway, p. 128.

47. Stanley W. Hoig, *Night of the Cruel Moon: Cherokee Removal and the Trail of Tears* (Facts on File, New York, NY 1996), p. 7.

48. A New Map of the Cherokee Nation with the Names of the Towns and Rivers, Thomas Kitchin, courtesy of the Thomas Gilcrease Institute of American History and Art, Tulsa, Oklahoma.

49. Courtesy of the British Museum and Thomas Gilcrease Institute of American History and Art, Tulsa, Oklahoma. See also https://pocketsights.com/tours/place/Ostenaco-and-the-Cherokee-1762-%28The-King%27s-Arms%29-23071:2827.

50. Ostenaco was also known as Outacite and Judd's Friend. Courtesy of the Smithsonian Institution, Washington, D.C. and the Thomas Gilcrease Institute of American History and Art, Tulsa, Oklahoma.

51. Calloway, p. 180.

52. See generally Calloway pp. 210-212.

53. See http://appalachiansummit.tripod.com/ and http://discoverkingsport.com/h-chief-dragging-canoe.shtml.

54. See https://www.aaanativearts.com/cherokee/dragging-canoe.htm.

55. My brother Robert Barnes owns an original of this map, which I photographed in 2018. Royce named it "Map of the Former Territorial Limits of the Cherokee Nation of Indians". It is housed at the Library of Congress Geography and Map Division located in Washington, DC. See http://www.loc.gov/item/99446145/. Royce also wrote an important manuscript for the Bureau of Ethnology of the Smithsonian Institution in 1883, *The Cherokee Nation of Indians: A Narrative of their Official Relations with the Colonial and Federal Governments*, which was published as the Fifth Annual Report of the Bureau of Ethnology in 1887 by the Government Printing Office in Washington, D.C., pp. 121-378. This is an extremely valuable document, which includes the full text of all treaties the Cherokees ever signed along with detailed commentary on the historical context, letters, Congressional and State actions. It is copiously footnoted and indexed. The report is provided on line by Project Guttenberg: https://www.gutenberg.org/files/46493/46493-h/46493-h.htm#INTRODUCTORY.

56. Calloway, p. 211.

57. Ibid. p. 232.

58. Hoig, *Night of the Cruel Moon*, p. 11.

59. Susan Marie Abram, *"Souls In The Treetops:" Cherokee War, Masculinity, and Community, 1760-1820*, PhD Dissertation Auburn

University 2009), p. 55.

60. Ibid., pp. 55-56.

61. Thomas L. McKenney, *History of the Indian Tribes of North America, With Biographical Sketches and Anecdotes* (D. Rice and Co. Philadelphia 1837-44), p. 413.

62. Calloway, p. 234.

63. Ibid. p. 247.

64. Ibid. p. 248.

65. Ibid. p.249.

66. Ibid. p. 250.

67. Ibid. pp. 254-255.

68. Ibid. pp. 275-278.

69. Ibid. p. 279

70. Ibid. pp. 257-258.

71. Abram, p. 56.

72. Brown Map of the Lower Towns, Figure 2.7, p. 22, Lamar Marshall, Larry Smith, and Michael Wren, Gail King Project Director. *Alabama Collection Camps, Forts, Emigrating Depots and Travel Routes Used During the Cherokee Removal of 1838-1839* (Southeastern Anthropological Institute Northwest Shoals Community College, Muscle Shoals, Alabama and National Park Service 2009). This is one of the more important publications by the National Park Service about Cherokee history, containing rare maps and removal details. See https://www.nps.gov/trte/learn/historyculture/upload/Alabama-Collections-Camps-Forts-Depots-and-Routes-508.pdf.

73. Carolyn Thomas Foreman, *An Early Account Of The Cherokees*, Chronicles of Oklahoma, p. 143.

74. Calloway, pp. 337-338.

75. Ibid., p. 340. Sevier served as Governor of Tennessee for two terms

beginning in 1796.

76. Daniel Blake Smith, *An American Betrayal – Cherokee Patriots and the Trail of Tears* (Henry Holt and Company, New York 2011), p. 13.

77. The 7th Essay of William Penn (Jeremiah Evarts) commented extensively on that provision as showing conclusively that the Cherokee Nation was not within the jurisdiction of the US or any state: "Within what jurisdiction is it, then? Doubtless within Cherokee jurisdiction; for this territory is described as 'belonging to the Cherokees." See George Barrel Cheever, *The Removal of the Indians: An Article from the American Monthly Magazine: An Examination of an Article in the North American Review: And an Exhibition of the Advancement of the Southern Tribes, in Civilization and Christianity* (Pierce and Williams, Boston, 1830), p. 52. For a copy of this interesting book, see https://ia800301.us.archive.org/6/items/removalofindians00evar/removalofindians00evar.pdf.

78. Ibid. p. 425.

79. See http://www.nativehistoryassociation.org/dragging_canoe.php.

80. Courtesy of Don Rankin.

81. https://www.goodreads.com/quotes/8909397-a-poem-by-tecumseh-so-live-your-life-that-the - :~:text="So live your life that the fear of death can,all things in your life.

82. Pinterest. See https://www.pinterest.com/pin/490822059367308088/.

83. See generally Calloway, who brings together a wide range of historical materials about Washington's involvement with Indians from his youth to his presidency.

84. Ibid. p. 3.

85. Ibid. pp. 6-7.

86. Ibid. pp. 12-13.

87. Stephens, p. 10.

88. Ibid p. 14.

89. Ibid. p. 2. See generally *The Journal of the Proceedings of the President, 1793-1797*, Dorothy Twohig, ed. (Charlottesville, University of Virginia Press 1981).

90. Cheever, p. 57.

91. Stephens, p. 19.

92. Ibid. p. 20. See also Anthony F. C. Wallace, *Jefferson and the Indians: The Tragic Fate of the First Americans* (Cambridge: Harvard University Press, 1999), pp. 206-240.

93. Calloway, pp. 329-330. See generally Smith, *An American Betrayal*, pp. 16-19.

94. Benjamin C. Nance, *The Trail of Tears in Tennessee: A Study of the Routes Used During the Cherokee Removal of 1838*, Tennessee Department of Environment and Conservation (2001), p. 17.

95. Grant Foreman, *Indians and Pioneers* (Norman: University of Oklahoma, 1936), p. 43.

96. McKenney, frontispiece. In 1821 he commissioned Charles Bird King to paint portraits of Indian leaders who came to his office. During the next twenty years King painted more than one hundred and forty elegant portraits. In 1836 James Hall began gathering material for the text, spending eight years on biographies and stories about each person. The books were published in 1837 to wide acclaim, but the financial panic and depression later in the year stopped the new venture for several years. McKenney published the third volume in 1844. Altogether one hundred and twenty portraits were included in the three volumes. This information is courtesy of Sean Samuels at Bauman Rare Books: See https://www.baumanrarebooks.com/blog/indian-tribes-of-north-america-by-thomas-mckenney-and-james-hall/.

97. Stephens, p. 63. See Jackson Papers, 4: 126.

98. Stephens, p. 64.

99. Wikimedia Commons. https://en.wikipedia.org/wiki/John_Jolly. Courtesy of the Smithsonian American Art Museum, Washington, D.C. Catlin was born in 1796 in Wilkes-Barre, Pennsylvania. Trained as a lawyer, he decided to become a painter, building a reputation for his portraits and engravings of American Indians. In 1841 he published *Illustrations of the Manners, Customs, and Condition of the North American Indians* and thereafter several other collections and books. He hoped to sell his painting collection to the US government, but they never reached agreement, eventually giving his Indian Collection to the Smithsonian American Art Museum.

100. 21 U.S. 543, 8 Wheat. 543, 5 L. Ed. 681 (1823).

101. Painted by Francis Alexander in 1835. Courtesy of the National Portrait Gallery and Smithsonian Museum, Washington, DC.

102. Letter from a Cherokee delegation to Secretary of War John C. Calhoun during President James Monroe's Administration. See http://www.teachushistory.org/indian-removal/resources/cherokee-indians-speak-us-government.

103. Nance, p. 13.

104. Stanley W. Hoig, *The Cherokee and Their Chiefs*, p. 139.

105. Stephens, p. 97.

106. Ibid. p. 102. See James D. Richardson, editor, A Compilation of the Messages and Papers of the Presidents, 2: 234-7. See http://onlinebooks.library.upenn.edu/webbin/metabook?id=mppresidents.

107. Stephens, pp. 108-109. Richardson, Messages and Papers, 280-3.

108. Benny Smith, *The Keetoowah Society of Cherokee Indians*, Masters Dissertation (Northwestern State College, Alva, Oklahoma, 1967). Cited by Lee Standing Bear Moore and Takatoka, *History of the Kituwah People*.

109. See Pat Alderman, Nancy Ward: Cherokee Chieftainess: Her Cry was

All for Peace; Dragging Canoe: Cherokee-Chickamauga War Chief: We Are Not Yet Conquered (Overmountain Press, Johnson City, Tennessee, 1978).

110. See generally Nancy Ward: American patriot or Cherokee Nationalist (University of Nebraska Press 2014), https://www.thefreelibrary.com/Nancy+Ward%3A+American+patriot+or+Cherokee+nationalist%3F-a0365982483.

111. There are numerous legends about her, and there isn't agreement on some basic facts including her birthdate and mother's name. Some sources call her Tame Doe but that stemmed from a history written in 1895 by E. Sterling King, *The Wild Rose of the Cherokee*. Dr. Emmett Starr wrote a study of her life in the 1890s, concluding that her birthdate was 1695 but other evidence puts it later, probably 1716. Starr recorded details about her husband, children, and their partners and children but David Hampton's Biography is the most reliable, and he has served as President of the Association of Descendants of Nancy Ward. See http://www.nancyward.org/bio.htm. For additional sources and references see Kathie Forbes, *Indian Reservations: Where History, Genealogy and Myth Collide*, https://www.indianreservations.net/2017/10/nanyehi-nancy-ward-beloved-woman-of.html 2017.

112. John P. Brown, Old Frontiers: The Story of the Cherokee Indians from Earliest Times to the Date of Their Removal to the West, 1838 (Southern Publishers Inc., Kingsport Tennessee 1938), pp. 148-149. Sometimes the drink is referred to as "black". It is strongly caffeinated, several times stronger than a cup of coffee today.

113. Barbara R. Duncan, ed., *Living Stories of the Cherokee* (University of North Carolina Press, Chapel Hill: 1998), pp. 202-203.

114. Miles, Tiya. *Dispossession*, Chapter 5, *The 1619 Project: A New Origin Story*, edited by Nikole Hannah-Jones (New York Times Company 2021),

pp. 136-137.

115. Ibid. p. 138. Quoted from Calloway, p. 307.

116. Ibid.

117. Theda Perdue and Michael D. Green, *The Cherokee Removal: A Brief History with Documents (*Bedford Books of St. Martin's Press, Boston and New York, 1995), pp, 124-125.

118. Ibid. pp. 125-126.

119. See https://accessgenealogy.com/alabama/tahchee-a-cherokee-chief.htm

120. James Batson, Tahchee and His Knife. See https://www.crazycrow.com/site/tahchee-and-his-knife/.

121. Ibid. August Pierre Chouteau owned a trading post at the Three Forks of the Arkansas River above Fort Gibson.

122. Ibid.

123. McKenney, p. 251. The Newsam lithograph is at the Library of Congress, see http://hdl.loc.gov/loc.pnp/pp.print. See also https://commons.wikimedia.org/wiki/File:Tah-Chee,_A_Cherokee_Chief._(15683665390).jpg.

124. A compilation of Cherokee Muster rolls from the battle is available at: https://cherokeeregistry.com/battle-of-horseshoe-bend-muster-roll/. They include R. Spirit (uncle); Shoeboot Swimmer (uncle); Turtle Fields (second cousin); (Archy Fields (3rd cousin); George Guess (Sequoyah, husband of Annie's great Aunt Caty Huss Spirit); and John Lowrey (wife of Annie's first cousin Elizabeth Shorey).

125. https://en.wikipedia.org/wiki/Battle_of_Horseshoe_Bend_(1814).

126. Ibid.

127. Abram, p. 145.

128. McKenney, pp. 419-421.

129. The Whale to Gov. P.M. Butler, 18 February 1843, Letters Received,

Office of Indian Affairs, 1824-1881, Cherokee Agency, 1843, M-234, Roll 87, reprinted in Brad Agnew, "The Whale's Rifle," in "Notes and Documents," Chronicles of Oklahoma 56 (Winter 1978-1979), pp. 472-73.

130. Meigs to Secretary of War, 4 June 1814, CIART, roll 6. See Abram, p. 152.

131. McLoughlin, *Cherokee Renaissance in the New Republic*, p. 194.

132. Courtesy of Horseshoe Bend National Military Park, Tallapoosa, Alabama and the National Park Service. See also https://americanlongrifles.org/forum/index.php?topic=46438.0

133. Gloria Jahoda, *The Trail of Tears: The Story of the American Indian Removals 1813-1855* ((Wings Books, New York 1975) p.224. See also Eaton, p. 26.

134. Kenneth K. Krakow, Georgia Place-Names: Their History and Origins (Winship Press, Macon, Georgia 1975), p. 217.

135. Michael Wren has done extensive research on the children, on which I've relied. Personal communication 2019.

136. Lisa Land Cooper, Every Now and Then - The Amazing Stories of Douglas County. See https://douglascountyhistory.blogspot.com/2012/07/buzzards-roost.html

137. Shadburn, Cherokee Planters in Georgia 1832-1838, pp. 91-92. This is from a report by Major James M. C. Montgomery in connection with the 1830 census in Cobb, Cherokee and Cass counties, noting that long before Cobb country was created, there were four large Indian towns in the area, including Buffalo Fish Town, Sweetwater Town and Buzzard Roost Village on the Chattahoochee River above above the mouth of Sweetwater Creek.

138. Personal communication from Michael Wren, 2019 regarding decisions on their 1837 Valuation Claims. This file is from Record Group

75, entry 232.

139. Cherokee Phoenix, June 12, 1830, p. 4. See https://www.wcu.edu/library/DigitalCollections/CherokeePhoenix/Vol3/no08/documents-page-4-column-1a-3b.html

140. Personal communication from Michael Wren, 2019 regarding decisions on their 1837 Valuation Claims. This file is from Record Group 75, entry 232.

141. NARA Microfilm A18, which comes from RG75 Entry 224 (Valuations of Property): Shaw & McMillan's Miscellaneous Valuations Book #1.

142. Shadburn, Cherokee Planters in Georgia 1832-1838, p. 93.

143. See https://sevenspringsmuseum.org/the-seven-springs-of-powder-springs/.

144. <?> See http://wakinguponturtleisland.blogspot.com/2013/02/lithia-springs-ga.html.

145. See http://sweetwatercreek.weebly.com/pre-civil-war.html.

146. See https://www.lithiaspringwater.com/index-2a.html.

147. After considering several sources, and the fact that there was no other Spirit family in the Cherokee Nation at the time he was born and growing up, I have concluded that John's father was The Spirit and that his mother was Mary Blaylock. Michael Wren isn't sure that is correct. My conclusion is buttressed by the fact that he was widely known as Captain Spirit, sometimes hosting elections at his farm near Wills Creek, and also supported by letters and affidavits from Samuel Worcester, John Lowrey and John McCloy. Worcester wrote a letter in 1849 outlining the names of his wives and adopted children, stating that "his wife Mary" was baptized with him and other family members. One of his wives, Nancy Gourd, married John Blaylock, born about 1790, and it is likely he had a sister named Mary. John Lowrey testified in support of Nancy Gourd's

heirs' claim regarding her reservation at the mouth of Battle Creek, that John Huss was "a Spirit". See RG75 E250 013. John McCloy's affidavit regarding Nancy's heirs' Battle Creek reservation in support of the claim of her sons William Huss and Jefferson Blaylock for 640 acres and improvements totaling $11297, noting that John Huss's name was "The Spirit". See RG75 E250 018. It is noteworthy that the Payne-Butrick papers frequently call him "Spirit" or "Captain Spirit".

148. He participated in several 1842 claims on his own behalf and in support of the children of his wife Nancy Gourd. Details of the claims are discussed in Chapter 17.

149. He was paid $65 that year for his work with the Light Horse. See James Mathew Martin, *The Cherokee Supreme Court: 1823-1835*, University of Nevada Reno (2018), p. 26.

150. Jeremiah Evarts wrote a letter on July 24, 1824 noting: "Captain Spirit has been baptized by the name of John Huss, his wife Nancy, his mother Mary and his sister by the name of Christianna." Michael Wren sent me a copy of the letter in 2021.

151. Nancy (No-Na) Gourd was born around 1794 to Sallie Lowrey. She had a son with John Huss in 1814 named William, who died in 1844. She was married for a time to Alexander McCoy, with whom she had one son, John Lowrey McCoy, born on December 12, 1812. She also had a son with John Blaylock around 1816 named Jefferson. All of these children filed claims in 1842 about her 640-acre reservation along Battle Creek. The claims state she died in Rossville in 1833. John Huss also was married to Nancy Dorcas Mush, probably known by that name because her brother was known as Laugh At Mush and her sister Nellie also used the Mush name. Nancy Dorcas was married earlier to Crawfish, with whom she had a daughter named Rachel, and to an unknown man with whom she had Jane Jennie about 1817 and Mary Sally around 1818. Jane Jennie

by all accounts was a beautiful woman and had liaisons with or married five men: Rider Fields, James Landrum, Jr., George Lowrey, Jr., Nelson Ore and Jefferson Pack. She had five children with them, several of whom were adopted by John Huss.

152. Cherokee Phoenix, July 2, 1828. Most likely the article was translated by Boudinot. See discussion in McLoughlin, Cherokees and Missionaries, 1789-1839, p. 234.

153. This statement written by Huss on behalf of a man just before being hung for murder at Crawfish Creek on April 18, 1828: "This day I address you, my Uncles, that you may abandon the practice of drunkenness. Forsake all evil, ye whom I leave behind. I desire you to believe that the practice of drunkenness which you follow is evil. Follow that which is good. Abandon drunkenness. If you believe, we shall meet again. I have relinquished my sins to God, who only, I believe, is able to save me." Speaking about this on May 3rd, Huss noted: "it is manifest that the great prevalence of drunkenness amongst us is the source of multiplied evils." Elias Boudinot translated this in the Cherokee *Phoenix* on May 28, 1828. See https://www.wcu.edu/library/DigitalCollections/CherokeePhoenix/Vol1/no14/communications-page-2-column-3b-5b.html.

154. *Cherokee Phoenix and Indians' Advocate*, Wednesday, May 27, 1829, Vol. II, no. 8, Page 2, col. 5a-Page 3, col. 2a.

155. See https://en.wikipedia.org/wiki/Jan_Hus.

156. The Missionary Herald, Volume XXX, No., 3 (March 1834), pp. 98-101. See Robert Sparks Walker, Torchlights to the Cherokees: The Brainerd Mission (The Overmountain Press, Johnson City, Tennessee 1933), pp. 126-127 for a detailed description of that day. See also McLoughlin, Cherokees and Missionaries, 1789-1839, p. 133. The full text of that edition of The Missionary Herald is contained in Appendix 6, courtesy of the Log College Press: https://static1.squarespace.

com/static/590be125ff7c502a07752a5b/t/5cdd57b1e4966b42acec1 4a8/1558009778787/Huss,+John,+Ordination+Sermon.pdf.

157. Annual Report of the Select Committee of the Society for Propagating the Gospel Among the Indians and Others in North America (Samuel N. Dickinson, Boston, 1843), p. 6. See https://books.google.fr/books?id=j0gwzOiYYVoC&pg=PA6&lpg=PA6&dq=reverend+john+huss+cherokee+preacher&source=bl&ots=ZJc9uHjwYP&sig=ACfU3U3TRGBinwTmadZMEwsrjLWEHUt-pg&hl=fr&sa=X&ved=2ahUKEwini8Hzgun4AhUU1IUKHRxgCFEQ6AF6BAgdEAM - v=onepage&q=reverend john huss cherokee preacher&f=false.

158. See RG75 E250 012 - John Huss for Nancy Gourd heirs William Huss/Jefferson Blaylock for reservation under 1817-19 treaties on Battle Creek.

159. See Butrick, *Journal* 31 Dec 1844.

160. This letter was written from Park Hill and is included in the American Board Archives (ABCFM 18-3-1 v13 Item 215 R747 mfr 661-665 K4193). It was provided to me by Michael Wren in 2021.

161. A chart showing Sam's ancestors is in Appendix 27.

162. Shadburn and Strange, p. 14.

163. He served in the 2nd Spartan Regiment as a Lieutenant under Captain Robert Faris and Colonel Thomas Brandon from December 1780 to May 1781, and under Captain James Crawford and Colonel Brandon until October 1781. See https://www.carolana.com/SC/Revolution/patriot_military_sc_lieutenants.htm.

164. A chart showing George's ancestors is in Appendix 27.

165. A chart showing Nannie's ancestors is in Appendix 27.

166. In those days Georgia prisons were grim, although Middedgeville was built in 1816 as part of a prison reform effort. Food rations were decent

and the rooms for prisoners ventilated.

167. Walker, *Torchlights to the Cherokees*, p.269.

168. Perdue and Green, pp, 34-43. At this time Ross estimated the Cherokee Nation comprised more than ten million acres, and provides many details about his people, their government, education and social relations. For the precise paragraph quoted see *Barbara R. Duncan and Brett H. Riggs, Cherokee Heritage Trails Guidebook* (The Museum of the Cherokee Indian, The University of North Carolina Press, Chapel Hill and London 2003), p. 263.

169. Eaton, pp. 4-5.

170. Print made in 1948 of a daguerreotype in the 1830s. Courtesy of the Tennessee Virtual Archive, see https://teva.contentdm.oclc.org/digital/collection/p15138coll18/id/2121/.

171. Courtesy of www.sharing.com. William created a New Echota website called "A Touch of William" with scores of drawings, photos, paintings and maps. See https://wsharing.com/WSphotosNewEchota2.htm.

172. I took these photos of the reconstructed New Echota in 2017.

173. I took this photo in New Echota in 2017.

174. Charles C. Royce, 1884. Courtesy of the Smithsonian Institution Bureau of Ethnology.

175. The Missionary Herald published an excellent summary of the new Constitution in 1828, which is quoted verbatim in Cheever, pp. 60-61.

176. See Cherokee Phoenix, May 18, 1828, pp. 1-2. https://www.wcu.edu/library/DigitalCollections/CherokeePhoenix/Vol1/no14/correspondence-page-1-column-4a-and-page-2-column-3a.html.

177. Leland R. Johnson, *Engineers on the Twin Rivers: A History of the U.S. Army Engineers Nashville District 1769-1978 (U.S.Army Core of Engineers 1978)*, p. 52. https://www.google.fr/books/edition/Engineers_on_the_

Twin_Rivers/kE0sAAAAYAAJ?hl=fr&gbpv=1&dq=Was+the+Hiwassee-Conasauga+Canal+built%3F&pg=PA51&printsec=frontcover.

178. Hoig, *The Cherokees and their Chiefs*, p. 139.

179. McKenney. The original painting was copied by Charles Inman and lithographed.

180. Moore and Takatoka, *History of the Kituwah People*.

181. See William Joseph Thomas, *Creating Cherokee Print: Samuel Austin Worcester's Impact on the Syllabary* (Cornell University 2008), p.8, who cites a War Department letter referring to an original copy of the syllabary prepared by "Captain Spirit (a Methodist convert and exhorter later renamed John Huss, who worked for the ABCFM to teach Cherokees reading and writing in their own language)."

182. This description of their work is from a Presbyterian mission pamphlet.

183. This extract is from the *The Missionary Herald*, an occasional publication of the American Board of Commissioners for Foreign Missions. A web page maintained by the Presbyterian Church is dedicated to John Huss, see https://www.logcollegepress.com/john-huss-1858/.

184. Grant Foreman, *Sequoyah* (University of Oklahoma Press, Norman 1939) pp. 75-77. Although there are other theories, I agree with Foreman that he is the most likely father, as acknowledged in the family records. George Washington was a friend of Gist, who served as a Colonel in the Revolutionary Army. He was a noted explorer in the Cherokee Nation, and they gave him Long Island in the Tennessee River

185. Grant Foreman, *Sequoyah* (University of Oklahoma Press, Norman 1939) p. 3.

186. See Cherokee Emigration Rolls, 1817-38, transcribed by Jack Baker. Sequoyah is number 187, in the emigration party that departed on May 21, 1818. He is listed as moving from Willstown, Alabama. These records

are held in the National Archives, with a copy at Cherokee Heritage Center in Tahlequah, Oklahoma, which provided me a photocopy of this page.

187. Foreman, *Sequoyah*, p. 7. Foreman concluded that Sequoyah's father was Nathaniel Gist, who had lived in the Cherokee Nation supporting himself as a hunter and explorer. Not everyone agrees with that conclusion, but of all the theories published, it makes the most sense to me.

188. Courtesy of Sequoyah Birthplace Museum, Vonore, Tennessee.

189. Ibid. pp. 45-46.

190. John Ehle, *Trail of Tears: The Rise and Fall of the Cherokee Nation* (Doubleday, New York 1988), p. 161.

191. John Alexander visited Sequoyah in 1840 and wrote this diary entry: "He has had five wives and 20 children; his present wife had 5 children, the youngest 2 years old; 10 dead and 10 alive; his son Jos 8 years old." Quoted in Grant Foreman, *Sequoyah*, p. 40. My research indicates that he had the following wives: Rebecca Bowles (with whom he had a daughter Sallie); Seven Fields (with whom he had a daughter Susan); Utiyu Langley (with whom he had two daughters, A-yo-ka and Polly) and two sons George and Richard); Sally Waters (with whom he a son Tessey and a daughter E-ya-gu); and Betsy Spirit (with whom he had one son, Big Dollar George). It is very difficult to pin down all the details of these relationships.

192. A chart showing the family from his perspective in in Appendix 27. See Shadburn and Strange, p. 482.

193. Foreman, *Sequoyah*, p. 8.

194. I took these photos in the reconstructed print house in New Echota in 2017.

195. Foreman, *Sequoyah*, p. 17.

196. Cheever, p. 62.

197. The cabin is open to the public, see https://visitcherokeenation.com/attractions/sequoyahs-cabin-museum.

198. Foreman, *Sequoyah*, p. 27. Much of Knapp's interview was also published in the *Phoenix* and also an article by Elias Boudinot published in the Annals of Education in 1832.

199. Moore and Takatoka, *History of the Kituwah People,* https://manataka.org/page838.html.

200. Foreman, *Sequoyah*, pp. 36-37.

201. Ibid. p. 40.

202. William Addison Phillips, *Sequoyah. (*Harpers Magazine, September 1870).

203. John B. Davis, *The Life and Work of Sequoyah*, Chronicles of Oklahoma, Volume 8, No. 2, June, 1930. See also Hughe, *The First Sequoyah*, Sunset, Vol. 59, Sept. 1927, p. 27.

204. *Statue of Sequoyah, Proceedings in Statuary Hall of the United States Capitol upon the Unveiling and Presentation of the Statue of Sequoyah by the State of Oklahoma*, Sixty-Fifth Congress, June 6, 1917 (Government Printing Office, Washington 1924, p. 25.

205. *The Cherokee Advocate*, June 26, 1845. Grant Foreman provides a longer version of the story in *Sequoyah*, pp. 44-67, based on The Worm's account.

206. Grant Foreman, *Sequoyah*, pp. 70-71. See also https://cherokeeimages.com/wp/%E1%8F%8D%E1%8F%8F%E1%8F%89%E1%8F%AF-%E1%8F%A3%E1%8E%B3%E1%8E%A9-%E1%8E%A0%E1%8F%8F%E1%8E%BE%E1%8F%8D%E1%8F%9B-the-genius-cherokee-7-things-surprising-about-sequoyah/ and https://en.wikipedia.org/wiki/Sequoyah.

207. *Statue of Sequoyah*, p. 9.

208. McKenney, p. 36. The original was painted by Charles Bird King

around 1830 and published in History of the American Indians in 1837. But the original was lost in the Smithsonian fire on January 24, 1865. An exact copy was painted by Henry Inman the 1830s and is the version hanging in the National Portrait Gallery. See also https://commons.wikimedia.org/wiki/File:Sequoyah,_Cherokee_inventor,_by_C.B._King,_1836.jpg.

209. Jahoda, p. 214.

210. McKenney, p. 412.

211. Ibid. p. 424.

212. Ibid. p. 423. Portrait by Charles Bird King, Courtesy of Wikimedia Commons. The original is in the Library of Congress.

213. Ehle, p. 303.

214. Elias Boudinot, "From The Cherokee Nation," letter to the editors of the Boston Recorder and Telegraph, July 29, 1825 in Perdue, Cherokee Editor, 46. Cited in Johathan Filler, *Arguing in an Age of Unreason: Elias Boudinot, Cherokee Factionalism, and the Treaty of New Echota* (Master of Arts Thesis, Graduate College of Bowling Green State University 2010), p. 26.

215. <?>   Filler, pp. 129-130 citing Wilkins, P. 146. The letter was published on December 20, 1823.

216. Elias Boudinot, An Address to the Whites (William F. Geddes, Philadelphia May 26, 1826). See https://acdc.amherst.edu/view/asc:427890/asc:427892.

217. Boudinot, Cherokee Phoenix, March 13, 1828 in Perdue, Cherokee Editor, 95-96. Cited in Filler, p. 52.

218. Boudinot, Cherokee Phoenix, July 17, 1829 in Perdue, Cherokee Editor, 108-109. Cited in Filler, pp. 59-60.

219. McKenney. The original is in the Smithsonian American Art Museum in Washington, D.C. and is in the public domain.

220. See https://avalon.law.yale.edu/19th_century/jackson1.asp.
221. Stephens, p. 188. See John Henry Eaton to the Cherokee Chiefs, April 18, 1829, Niles' Weekly Register, June 13, 1829.
222. Their letter was prepared at a large public meeting on February 9, 1829 and published in Vol. 1, No. 51 of the Phoenix. It is a moving document, reproduced in Appendix 3.
223. Perdue and Green, p. 18 and pp. 94-105.
224. William Penn, *On the Present Crisis in the Condition of the American Indians* (Boston: Perkins & Martin 1829), p. 8. These essays were first published in the *National Intelligencer*. William Penn was the pseudonym for Jeremiah Evarts. See also Stephens, pp. 197-198.
225. McLoughlin, Cherokees and Missionaries, p. 247.
226. Francis Paul Prucha, *Protest by Petition: Jeremiah Evarts and the Cherokee Indians* (Proceedings of the Massachusetts Historical Society, Third Series, Vol 97 1985), p. 48)
227. Included in E.C. Tracy, *Memoir of the Life of Jeremiah Evarts, Esq.* (Crocker and Brewster, Boston 1845).
228. See http://historymuse.net/readings/cherokee.htm.
229. See Perdue and Green, pp. 116-117 for the text of the Removal Act.
230. Cherokee Phoenix and Indians Advocate, Vol 4, Issue 1, June, 25, 1831.
231. Ibid.
232. Cherokee Phoenix and Indians Advocate, Vol 4, Issue 2, July, 2, 1831.
233. Memorial of the Cherokee Nation, December 1829, published in the Cherokee Phoenix on January 20, 1830, Vol. II, no. 40, Page 1, col. 3a-5b. It was reprinted in the March 13, 1830 issue of Niles Weekly Register published in Baltimore, Maryland.
234. Francis Paul Prucha, *American Indian Treaties: The History of an*

Anomaly, "The William Penn Essays" (University of California Press 1997), p. 165. See also 11. Register of Debates in Congress, 6:1049, cited in Filler, p. 63 and See https://www.revolvy.com/page/Frederick-Theodore-Frelinghuysen.

235. Wikiwand. Photograph by Mathew Brady. Courtesy of the Library of Congress Prints and Photographs Division.

236. Stephens, p. 220. See Register of Debates, Senate, 21st Cong., 1st Sess., April 9, 1830, 309-10.

237. Ibid. p. 227.

238. Courtesy of the Texas State Library and Archives Commission. See https://www.tshaonline.org/handbook/entries/houston-sam.

239. John S. Abbott, *David Crockett: His Life and Adventures* (Bottom of the Hill Publishing, Memphis, Tennessee 2012), p. 125.

240. Ibid. p. 127.

241. Remarks on the floor of Congress May 19, 1830. See https://citaty.net/citaty/1930438-davy-crockett-it-was-expected-of-me-that-i-was-to-bow-to-the-nam/.

242. Abbott, p, 136.

243. Courtesy of the University of Tennessee, Knoxville, Library Development Review/1993-94

244. Perdue and Green, pp. 63-68.

245. Cherokee Nation v. Georgia, 30 U.S. 5 Pet. 1 (1831). See also Carter, p. 113. For a detailed analysis of the various Cherokee cases see Brian W. Wildenthal, *Native American Sovereignty on Trial: A Handbook With Cases, Laws and Documents* (ABC CLIO, Santa Barbara, California 2003).

246. Ibid.

247. See Appendix 3 for the complete text.

248. Carte, pp. 119-120.

249. Ibid. p. 269. See also Vicki Rozema, Voices from the Trail of Tears,

p. 60 and Walker, p. 269.

250. Ibid.

251. Walker, pp. 273-275.

252. A copy of his handwritten letter is available at https://www.ancestry.com/mediaui-viewer/tree/105271716/person/422114082966/media/e42e5cb4-ea7f-4efb-aa82-.f5c5d481f3f3?_phsrc=fDs1&usePUBJs=true.

253. Ibid. pp. 285-286.

254. Ibid. pp. 239-240.

255. Smith, *An American Betrayal*, p. 129.

256. Ibid. pp. 130-131.

257. 31 U.S. (6 Pet.) 515 (1832). See also Perdue and Green, pp. 70-75; Wildenthal, pp. 42-47, which discusses the legal bases for the opinion. Although the reasoning in *Worcester* guided courts at various levels during the ensuing decades as they considered Indian treaty cases, the fact that it didn't recognize full Cherokee sovereignty led avalanche of actions undercutting it, culminating in laws such as *Dawes* and *Curtis*. As Paul Prucha wrote, "The Treaties themselves, to a remarkable degree, were instruments intended to transform the culture of the tribes." Prucha, *The Indian Treaties*, p. 9.

258. Edward Everett Dale and Gaston Litton, *Cherokee Cavaliers: Forty Years of Cherokee History as told in the Correspondence of the Ridge-Watie-Boudinot Family* (The Civilization of the American Indian Series, Book 19, University of Oklahoma Press 1995) pp. 5-6, Elias Boudinot to Stand Watie, March 7, 1832. Cited in Filler, p. 77.

259. Grant Foreman, *Indian Removal: The Emigration of the Five Civilized Tribes of Indians* (Norman, University of Oklahoma, 1932), p. 245. Cited in Carter, p. 131.

260. Ehle, p. 255.

261. Letter from John Coffee to Governor Wilson Lumpkin March 17,

1832 from Headquarters, Etowah. Courtesy of the Georgia Historical Society. See https://dlg.usg.edu/record/dlg_zlna_tcc709 - item.

262. Ibid.

263. Foreman, *Indian Removal: The Emigration of the Five Civilized Tribes of Indians*, pp. 242-243.

264. See https://wsharing.com/WSphotosRedClay1.htm.

265. https://wsharing.com/D770 0095 CR R44.jpg

266. Foreman, *Indian Removal*, p. 246.

267. Ibid. pp. 237-246.

268. Carter, p. 88.

269. William G. McLouglin, After the Trail of Tears - the Cherokees' Struggle for Sovereignty, Introduction p. xi.

270. Courtesy of https://commons.wikimedia.org/wiki/File:Andrew_jackson_head.jpg *and the White House Historical Association. See* https://www.whitehousehistory.org/photos/andrew-jackson.

271. See https://www.wikitree.com/wiki/Cherokee-129.

272. Foreman, *Indian Removal: The Emigration of the Five Civilized Tribes of Indians*, p. 254.

273. Ibid. p. 257.

274. Ibid. pp. 261-262.

275. Sconti's name was spelled "Scou-e-tah-hee". It was printed in the Congressional Register for the 23rd Congress, 2d Session as Doc. No. 91.

276. Mary Bondurant Warren, Whites Among the Cherokees: 1828-1838 (Heritage Papers 1987), p. 188

277. Hill, All Roads Led From Rome, Southern Spaces, p.10, recording Wesley Shropshire's description of Quatie's ouster.

278. Ibid. Courtesy of the Thomas Gilcrease Institute of American History and Art, Tulsa, Oklahoma.

279. Courtesy of the National Park Service.

280. Ehle, pp. 275-278. Courtesy of the Hargrett Library and part of the Digital Library of Georgia: https://dp.la/primary-source-sets/cherokee-removal-and-the-trail-of-tears/sources/1506.

281. Gary Evan Moulton, John Ross, Cherokee Chief (PhD Thesis, Oklahoma State University 1974), p. 118.

282. Ibid. p. 120.

283. Smith, *An American Betrayal*, p. 165.

284. Jahoda, p. 221.

285. Ibid. p. 124.

286. Smith, *An American Betrayal*, p. 170.

287. Jahoda, p. 225; Ehle, p. 294.

288. Ibid. P. 209.

289. Royce, *The Cherokee Nation of Indians: A Narrative of their Official Relations with the Colonial and Federal Governments*, p. 378.

290. Jahoda, p. 128.

291. Ibid. p. 130.

292. John Sedgwick, Blood Moon: An American Epic of War and Splendor in the Cherokee Nation, p. 246.

293. Moulton, John Ross, Cherokee Chief, p. 135.

294. Carolyn Thomas Foreman, An Early Account of the Cherokees, in Chronicles of Oklahoma, p. 143.

295. William G. McLoughlin, After the Trail of Tears, The Cherokees Struggle for Sovereignty, p. 76.

296. Hoig, The Cherokees and Their Chiefs, p. 155.

297. Perdue and Green, p. 77. They note that the "Memorial of Protest" was printed in the United States Congressional Serial Set as House Document 286, 24th Congress, 1st Session. They also note that an index to material dealing with Indians in the serial set was written by Stephen L. Johnson, Guide to American Indian Documents in the Congressional

Serials Set, 1817-1899 (Clearwater Publishing Company, New York, 1977).

298. Sedgewick, p. 253. See also Ehle, pp. 297-298.

299. For an excellent overview of General Wool's role, see Laurence M. Hauptman, *General John E. Wool in Cherokee Country, 1836-1837: A Reinterpretation* (The Georgia Historical Quarterly, Vol. 85, No. 1, Spring 2001).

300. http://www.electricscotland.com/history/johnross/letter.htm.

301. Hauptman, p. 14.

302. William G. McLoughlin, *Champions of the Cherokees: Evan and John B. Jones* (Princeton University Press, Princeton, New Jersey 1990).

303. Ibid., p. 15.

304. http://www.electricscotland.com/history/johnross/letter.htm.

305. John Ross speech at Red Clay Council Ground, September 28, 1836. See John Ross, The Papers of Chief John Ross, vol 1, 1807–1839, Norman OK, Gary E. Moulton, ed. University of Oklahoma Press, 1985, p. 458–461. See also http://historymatters.gmu.edu/d/6598/, and http://www.cherokeecommunityie.org/history-culture/trail-of-tears/.

306. Charles O. Walker, 1949. See https://gpbweb.smugmug.com/Destinations/Inside-Georgia/New-Echota-Historic-Site/Boudinot-House-Site/.

307. http://www.electricscotland.com/history/johnross/letter.htm.

308. *Cherokee Ration Books 1836-1838, New Echota*, Mountain Press, Signal Mountain Tennessee, 1999. The man in charge of keeping these books was Elbert S. Lenoir, whose family lived on the border of Cherokee territory and knew many Cherokees personally. He was trained in record keeping by his father, and these records were left to his granddaughters Mrs. Zeboim Cartter Patten and Mrs. Z. Cartter Patten. They became part of the library's permanent collection in 1939. The Murray County Library

in Chattsworth, Georgia has copies of many of the individual pages.

309. Grant Foreman, Cherokee Census 1835, Superintendent for the Five Civilized Tribes, which includes typed summaries of every Cherokee household, p. 198. This is a marvelous resource and has been digitized so it is searchable.

310. Ibid. p. 197.

311. Ibid. p. 13.

312. Shadburn, Cherokee Planters in Georgia 1832-1838, p. 99). See also Cherokee Valuations, Book 1, Office of Indian Affairs, 25th Congress, 3rd Session Senate: Report from the Secretary of War, July 25, 1835, p. 8.

313. Michael Wren provided copies of Hemphill's and Watters' detailed evaluations of Buffalofish's extended family farms along the south side of the Etowah in Floyd County. See Appendix 8.

314. Cherokee Valuations, Book 1, Office of Indian Affairs, 25th Congress, 3rd Session Senate: Report From the Secretary of War, July 25, 1835, p. 31.

315. Carter, p. 256. He notes that Sawnee (Sawney) Vann, one of Buffalofish's sons-in-law, received a total of just $1250 for his extensive holdings.

316. Ibid. p. 168.

317. Ibid. p. 76.

318. Ibid. p. 147.

319. Ibid. p. 79.

320. Ibid. pp. 38-39.

321. Ibid. See also Ehle, p. 298.

322. Personal communication from Michael Wren, based on the muster roll for the group.

323. See https://www.electricscotland.com/history/johnross/letter.htm, which contains the full version of Ross's letter to a Gentleman of

Philadelphia on May 6, 1837.

324. General Wool presented this address at Army Headquarters in New Echota. See https://babel.hathitrust.org/cgi/imgsrv/download/pdf?id=emu.010001341369;orient=0;size=100;seq=2;attachment=0.

325. Courtesy of the Library of Congress.

326. Sedgwick, p. 254.

327. Sarah H. Hill, Cherokee Removal: Forts Along the Georgia Trail of Tears, National Parks Service and the Georgia Department of Natural Resources/ Historic Preservation Division, 2005, p. 35.

328. Carolyn Thomas Foreman, George Featherstonhaugh's A Canoe Voyage up The Minay Sotor, An Early Account of the Cherokees (1847), Chronicles of Oklahoma, p. 146.

329. Ibid. p. 150.

330. Lamar Marshall, et al, p. 24, detail of John LaTourette map ca. 1837.

331. See Office of Indian Affairs, July 25, 1835, Report from the Secretary of War to the 25th Congress, 3rd Session Senate, listing all the evaluations prior to removal. This report includes the instructions given by C. A. Harris, Commissioner to Major B. F. Currey in Calhoun, Tennessee regarding methodology for carrying out the individual evaluations. See also NA RG75 E224, Rawlings and Massey Valuations (October 3, 1836).

332. The map was drawn by Evan Jones and published in The Baptist Arrow.

333. Jahoda, p. 229.

334. The full letter is in Appendix 9. See https://cherokee.org/About-The-Nation/History/Trail-of-Tears/Ralph-Waldo-Emersons-Letter. See also Ehle, p. 168.

335. Steve Inskeep, *Jacksonland: President Andrew Jackson, Cherokee Chief John Ross, and a Great American Land Grab*, p. 321.

336. Ibid. p. 326.

337. Hill, Cherokee Removal Forts, p. 23.

338. This map of removal forts, routes and distances in the Cherokee Nation was drawn in 1838 by Lt. Erasmus Darwin Keys. The original is in the Museum of Cherokee Indian in Cherokee, North Carolina.

339. Inskeep, p. 329.

340. Courtesy of the American Bureau of Ethnology and Britannica. See https://www.britannica.com/biography/John-Ross-chief-of-Cherokee-Nation.

341. Jonathan Siler, Arguing in an Age of Unreason: Elias Boudinot, Cherokee Factionalism, and the Treaty of New Echota, University of Bowling Green (Thesis, 2010, published in *History of the Cherokee Indians*). p. 159, quoting a valuation agent writing that the Spirit family living on the Southside Etowah River, want to "move this fall."

342. It is difficult to read this fragment. It seems that the children weren't recorded correctly since Annie Spirit was eleven or twelve in April 1838. It also is strange that her grandmother Chi-wa-yu-ga, who was around seventy, isn't listed in the family group.

343. This roll is available via Ancestry: *https://www.ancestry.com/imageviewer/collections/26356/images/dvm_LocHist011134-00057-0?ssrc=&backlabel=Return&backurl=https%3A%2F%2Fwww.ancestry.com%2F.*

344. See https://ualrexhibits.org/trailoftears/eyewitness-accounts/journal-of-edward-deas-cherokee-removal-april-may-1838/.

345. RG217, General Accounting Office, Treasury Department, Second Auditor, Indian Accounts, 1817-1922, Edward Deas File. See *https://ualrexhibits.org/trailoftears/places/mcleans-bottom-arkansas/.*

346. Courtesy of the Smithsonian American Art Museum, Washington, D.C.

347. See https://www.loc.gov/resource/rbpe.1740400a/?st=text.

348. The original document is in the Library of Congress. For the full text,

see https://www.loc.gov/resource/rbpe.1740400a/?st=text.

349. Letter to David Greene. See King, The Cherokee Trail of Tears, p. 44.

350. Foreman, *Indian Removal: The Emigration of the Five Civilized Tribes of Indians*, p. 288. Cited in Carter, p. 234.

351. Find a Grave. See https://www.findagrave.com/memorial/61781109/evan-jones.

352. Hill, Cherokee Removal Forts, pp. 58-59.

353. Rachel Caroline Eaton, John Ross and the Cherokee Indians (George Banta Publishing Company, Menasha, Wisconsin, 1914), pp. 117-118.

354. The Journal of Reverend Daniel S. Butrick, May 19, 1838 - April 1, 1839 (The Trail of Tears Association, Oklahoma Chapter, 1998). The case of Sweet Water and his wife Ooloocha was typical: In her claim filed on March 5, 1842 she stated: "The soldiers came and took us from home, they first surrounded our house and they took the mare while we were at work in the fields and they drove us out of doors and did not permit us to take anything with us, not even a second change of clothes, only the clothes we had on, and they shut the doors after they turned us out. They would not permit any of us to enter the house to get any clothing but drove us off to a fort that was built at New Echota. They kept us in the fort about three days and then marched us to Ross's Landing. And still on foot, even our little children, and they kept us about three days at Ross's Landing and sent us off on a boat to this country." Hill, Cherokee Removal Forts, pp. 27-28.

355. Hill, Cherokee Removal Forts, p. 23.

356. Courtesy of the Georgia Historical Society.

357. Hill, All Roads Led from Rome, especially the section titled "The Cleansing of Floyd County", https://southernspaces.org/2017/all-roads-led-rome-facing-history-cherokee-expulsion. Inventory and Sale of

Property Belonging to the Indians in Floyd County, 1838, (Recorded by Harvey Dan Abrams, Courtesy of the Digital Library of Georgia, Georgia Historical Society).

358. Inskeep, p. 327.

359. Sharon P. Flannagan, The Georgia Cherokees Who Remained: Race, Status, and Property in the Chattahoochee Community, Georgia Historical Society Quarterly Vol, 73, No. 3, Fall 1989, p. 585.

360. Ibid. pp. 598-600.

361. Eaton, p. 116.

362. Ibid.

363. Ronald T. Takaki, *Iron Cages: Race and Culture in Nineteenth Century America*, (Knopf-Random House, New York 1979), p. 103.

364. Lamar Marshall, et al, pp. 83-126. The phrase was first used by Professor Tom Hatley in 2003.

365. See https://cherokeeregistry.com/trail-of-tears-deas-detachment/.

366. See https://ualrexhibits.org/trailoftears/eyewitness-accounts/journal-of-edward-deas-cherokee-removal-june-1838/.

367. Foreman, *Indian Removal*, p. 293.

368. This transcription of that roll is incomplete as it doesn't include Weely Vann and his wife, while another document that mirrors the muster roll format, with numbers of people in various age groups, does list them.

369. See Rozema, Voices from the Trail of Tears, pp. 111-113 for the full report.

370. National Archives Record Group 75, Records of the Bureau of Indian Affairs, Letters Received, Cherokee Emigration, Roll 115, S1555 No. 3.

371. See https://www.facebook.com/removal.ride/posts/one-of-several-disbandment-sites-more-than-3500-cherokees-passed-through-akie-we/2254880974581242/.

372. Sedgwick, p. 279.

373. See *http://www.senaa.org/TrailOfTears/contingents1.html*.

374. This Resolution was signed by Richard Taylor, Going Snake and nine others on behalf of the Nation. See https://cherokeeregistry.com/index.php?option=com_content&view=article&id=240&Itemid=318. See also Sue Vänder Hook, Trail of Tears, ABDO Publishing Company, Edina, Minnesota (1949), p. 69.

375. Woodcut by an unknown artist. Courtesy of the *Penelope Johnson Allen Brainerd Mission Correspondence and Photographs collection*, University of Tennessee at Chattanooga.

376. National Park Service, Rivers, Rails and Roads, Transportation During the Cherokee Removal 1837-1839 (Middle Tennessee State University 2020). See https://www.mtsuhistpres.org/wp-content/uploads/2021/01/TRTE-Transportation-Booklet-spread-compressed-and-reduced.pdf.

377. Shadburn and Strange, p.482.

378. Thanks to the Thomas Gilcrease Institute of American History and Art in Tulsa, Oklahoma for sharing this part of the Deas June 6, 1838 muster roll.

379. Reverend Charles O. Walker was pastor at the First Baptist Church of Jasper, Georgia from 1960-1997, and spent decades researching Cherokee history in Pickens and Gilmer County, Georgia. He published several books of photographs and illustrations, including Cherokee Images and Cherokee Footprints Vols. 1-3, whose copyrights were bequeathed to the Georgia Trail of Tears Association.

380. King, The Cherokee Trail of Tears, p.88; Carter, p. 256.

381. Foreman, Cherokee Removal, p. 290. See also Jahoda, p. 233.

382. Rozema, Voices from the Trail of Tears, p. 32: Probably went from McMinnville to Nashville, crossed the river and on to Hopkinsville, Kentucky, crossing the Ohio River at Golconda, then through southern

Illinois to Green's Ferry on the Mississippi River. After crossing the Mississippi River the route wound through southern Missouri to Springfield and then into the new territory. In recent years there has been investigations about the routes actually taken, which varied in some important respects. The best overview I've located was done in 2013 in connection with designation by the National Register of Historic Places in Missouri, submitted by the Missouri Division of State Parks. Differing significantly from other reviews such as that done by Duane King, the Benge route map in particular was updated significantly. The report provides many previously undocumented details about the routes taken by all detachments that took one of the Northern Routes, with maps indicating key places where they stopped in Missouri and Arkansas. See https://mostateparks.com/sites/mostateparks/files/Cherokee ToT MO.pdf.

383. See https://commons.wikimedia.org/wiki/File:Trail_of_tears_map_NPS.jpg.

384. Duncan and Riggs, p. 282.

385. Robert Lindeux, Trail of Tears (courtesy of the Woolaroc Museum's Granger Collection, Bartlesville, Oklahoma).

386. Carter, p. 262.

387. Ibid. p. 262. That was the edition published on December 8, 1832.

388. Jahoda, p. 235, quoting Foreman, Indian Removal, pp. 304ff.

389. Carter, p. 257.

390. The Memories of Samuel Cloud, see http://www.angelfire.com/ny4/HOMEPAGE/writings/tearsmemory.html. He enlisted with John Drew's regiment in November 1861 at the age of twenty-nine, and left the Confederate side to fight on the Union side the remainder of the Civil War

391. A photo of the Inn is in King, The Cherokee Trail of Tears, p. 116.

392. Foreman, Cherokee Removal, p. 303.

393. The Original Keetoowah Society, http://keetoowahsociety.org/

whitepath.htm.

394. Foreman, pp. 306-307. The letter was published in the New York Observer on January 29, 1839. See also Hoig, p. 106, King, The Cherokee Trail of Tears, p. 104 and Jahoda, p. 237.

395. The Journal of Rev. Daniel S. Butrick, May 19, 1838 - April 1, 1839, Cherokee Removal, Monograph One, p. 58 (The Trail of Tears Association, Oklahoma Chapter).

396. Ibid.

397. Robert Lindeux, Trail of Tears (courtesy of the Woolaroc Museum's Granger Collection, Bartlesville, Oklahoma).

398. King, The Cherokee Trail of Tears, p. 135 and p. 162. The cost of this detachment's move was $112,504 (King, p. 175). See also Report Number 271, House of Representatives 27th Congress Third Session, February 25, 1843, which contains details about all the detachments.

399. A chart of Martha's family is in Appendix 27.

400. See Daniel F. Littlefield, Jr. and Lonnie Underhill, Fort Wayne and the Arkansas Frontier, 1838- 1840, The Arkansas Historical Quarterly 35:334-359, 1976; National Register of Historic Places Registration Form for Beattie's Prairie, January 23, 2014; and Will Chavez, Cherokee Phoenix, April 27, 2014, "Groups dedicate site as part of Trail of Tears", https://www.cherokeephoenix.org/Article/Index/8146.

401. Sedgwick, p. 295.

402. Foreman, *Sequoyah*, p. 33.

403. Gerard Reed, Postremoval Factionalism in the Cherokee Nation, in King, The Cherokee Indian Nation, p. 151.

404. Jahoda, p. 240.

405. Filler, p. 114.

406. Ibid. p. 238.

407. Foreman, *Sequoyah*, p. 34. See also Carter, p. 272.

408. Foreman, *Sequoyah*, p. 35.

409. Vänder Hook, p. 81.

410. Shadburn and Strange, p. 483; Shadburn, *Unhallowed Intrusion: A History of Cherokee Families in Forsyth County Georgia*, McNaughton & Gunn, Saline, Michigan 1993, p. 645.

411. Shadburn, *Unhallowed Intrusion*, pp. 645-646.

412. I received copies of these handwritten and signed 1842 claims from Michael Wren in 2019, and Kevin Cason, Archivist at the Tennessee State Library and Archives was kind enough to send higher-quality scans in June 2020.

413. Ibid. Mayes lived in Cass County and owned five farms and had five slaves. A separate evaluation for the ferry and its lost use totaled $2866.66. The ferry was first claimed by Mr. Quinton in 1836, and then by Mr. Parlier the following year.

414. Shadburn, Unhallowed Intrusion, 1993, p. 658.

415. Michael Wren provided a scan of the original, RG75 E250 012, in which he described himself as "John Huss or Spirit".

416. Michael Wren provided a scan of the original, RG75 E250 022.

417. His affidavit was sworn before Justice Jesse Bushyhead on February 15, 1842. Michael Wren provided scans of the original, RG75 E250 020 and 021.

418. Michael Wren provided scans of the originals, RG75 E250 018 and 019.

419. See Letter from the Secretary of War to the Committee on Indian Affairs on May 16, 1848, which contains a detailed abstract compiled by the Fourth Board of Commissioners. Sawney Vann's claim is #1096; Rachel Buffalo's is #1098; John Buffalofish's is #1110; Crying Snake Buffalofish's is #1138; Nelly Buffalofish's #1145; Rider Fields's is #1238. Altogether $1,520,982 was claimed and only $31,578 was

awarded. See https://digitalcommons.law.ou.edu/cgi/viewcontent.cgi?article=1756&context=indianserialset.

420. Her ECA 5585 is filled with Adair and Vann family information, including her mother Chi-yu-ka. A copy is in Appendix 26.

421. A chart showing Ti-es-kee's ancestors is in Appendix 27.

422. Daniel Davis's and Rachel Martin's family is most likely where Buffalo Fish and his wife stayed with in Georgia, but it's been impossible to confirm this.

423. A chart of the family from Rachel's perspective is in Appendix 27.

424. Shadburn and Strange, pp. 46-49.

425. Ibid. p. 46.

426. He helped dispense funds under the Silar Roll of 1851, with seven of his children paid under roll number 84. In 1852 he lodged claims pursuant to the Chapman Roll on behalf of his children and grandchildren. Daniel died in Lumpkin County, Georgia on June 9, 1868.

427. See Charley Buffalofish's April 1, 1842 Flint Book 3 Claim 53 on behalf of his deceased father, for three horses stolen by a white man named William Baker.

428. Rozema, Voices from the Trail of Tears, pp. 172-173.

429. This 1825 portrait was painted by Charles Byrd King. It was published by McKenney and Hall, see https://en.wikipedia.org/wiki/Fingerweaving. Courtesy of the Library of Congress.

430. McLoughlin, Cherokees and Missionaries, p. 162.

431. American Baptist Magazine, v. 24, no. 10 (Oct. 1844). See https://en.geneanet.org/fonds/bibliotheque/?collection_id=bibliotheque_premium_5460178&go=1&nom=BUSHYHEAD&nom_collection=The+American+Baptist+magazine+-+v.+24%2C+no.+10+%28Oct.+1844%29&size=50.

432. E. C. Routh, The Story of Oklahoma Baptists. Oklahoma City: Baptist General Convention, 1932, p. 51. See http://baptisthistoryhomepage.com/ok.bapt.routh.ch4.buckner.html.
433. Courtesy of the Cherok.ee Registry. See https://cherokeeregistry.com/jesse-bushyhead/.
434. Starr, p. 142.
435. Messages and Papers of the Presidents, IV [1846-1849], 429-431, cited in Dale and Litton, p. 43.
436. Starr, p. 137.
437. Ibid. p. 141.
438. Sedgwick, p. 350.
439. Theda Perdue, Stand Watie's War: The Last Confederate General (Historynet, December 15, 2016), https://www.historynet.com/stand-waties-war-the-last-confederate-general/.
440. Courtesy of the Smithsonian American Art Museum, Washington, DC.
441. J. M. Stanley, p. 18. See https://repository.si.edu/bitstream/handle/10088/23061/SMC_2_Stanley_1852_3_1-76.pdf?sequence=1&isAllowed=y.
442. Reverend William H. Good provided a personal account of the event, as well as a transcription of the letter inviting the various tribes to come to Tulsa. The Cherokee TV station Osiyo has prepared a short video for the Cherokee Almanac about the International Indian Council, focused on Stanley's painting. See https://www.facebook.com/watch/?v=1018098342091132.
443. Ibid.
444. Lowrey was made a Major by Andrew Jackson for meritorious service at the battle of Tohopeka and was an officer during the 1814 Creek War. His son George, Jr. married Jane Jennie Huss, who bore him a son,

Charles..

445. Carolyn S. Conway and Kelly E. Houston, eds., *Shorey W. Ross's Memories of the Cherokee Nation* (Little Rock, Arkansas 2005), based on interviews by Elizabeth Ross in 1937-38, p. 42. See https://ualrexhibits.org/tribalwriters/artifacts/Ross-Memories-of-the-Cherokee-Nation.html

446. J. M. Stanley, pp. 18-22.

447. Courtesy of the Thomas Gilcrease Institute of American History and Art, Tulsa, Oklahoma. The painter may not have been Stanley, according to the museum.

448. J. M. Stanley, pp. 22-23.

449. Ibid, pp. 23-25. See https://repository.si.edu/bitstream/handle/10088/23061/SMC_2_Stanley_1852_3_1-76.pdf?sequence=1&isAllowed=y

450. Courtesy of the Smithsonian American Art Museum, Washington, DC.

451. Augustus W. Loomis, *Scenes in the Indian Country*, p. 269, in Grant Foreman, *Advancing the Frontier, 1830-1860* (Norman: University of Oklahoma Press, 1933), p. 317. See https://library.nsuok.edu/digital/nsucentennialhistory/01.pdf.

452. Devon A. Mihesuah, *Cultivating the Rosebuds: The Education of Women at the Cherokee Female Seminary, 1851-1909* (University of Illinois Press 1993), p. 31.

453. Mihesuah, *Cultivating the Rosebuds*, pp. 31-32.

454. Brad Agnew, Northeastern: Centennial History (JVL Digital Library, John Vaughan Library Northeastern State University Tahlequah, Oklahoma 2009), Chapter 1. See https://library.nsuok.edu/digital/nsucentennialhistory/01.pdf

455. Volume 1, Number 2, p. 1: https://gateway.okhistory.org/ark:/67531/metadc99289/m1/1/?q=cherokee indians.

456. Starr, pp. 233-234.

457. Ibid. p. 19.

458. Mihesuah, *Cultivating the Rosebuds*, p. 2.

459. Ibid. p. 49.

460. Ibid. p. 73.

461. Ibid. pp. 73-74.

462. Ibid. p. 74.

463. *An Illustrated Souvenir Catalogue of the Cherokee National Female Seminary, Tahlequah, Indian Territory 1850 to 1906* (Arranged and Printed at the Indian Print Shop, Chilocco, Oklahoma 1906). This pamphlet wasn't sold and its pages are unnumbered; this photo is on page 38. It provides an excellent overview of the Seminary, its history and the key people involved in its operation, as well as numerous photos of students carrying out various activities, a list of all the graduating classes, and the courses for each grade. It begins with an historical overview by Mrs. R. L. Fyte. I have a copy in my library, a present from my grandmother Maude Mayes Barnes. To read an on-line version, see https://archive.org/details/Ayer_389_T128_C522_1906/page/n67/mode/2up.

464. Ibid. p. 46. Except for the photo of the 1902 graduation class by Jennie Ross Cobb, and Janana Ballard's group photo, the other photos in this section are from the Illustrated Souvenir Catalogue.

465. Jennie Ross Cobb was born Jennie Fields Ross in Tahlequah, Indian Territory on December 26, 1881. Her great-grandfather was Chief John Ross. She took many photographs of Cherokee life between 1896 and 1905 before becoming a teacher at the Cherokee Nation Owen School near Christie. She was the first-known female Native American photographer in Indian Territory, graduating from the Cherokee Female Seminary in 1900. Some of her earliest subjects were her fellow seminarians. Courtesy of the Oklahoma Historical Society, Jennie Ross

Cobb Collection, Collection number 20661.14. See https://anadisgoi.com/index.php/culture-stories/434-cherokee-nation-celebrates-the-life-and-photography-of-jennie-ross-cobb; https://www.hcn.org/issues/54.4/indigenous-affairs-photos-images-from-the-first-known-native-american-female-photographer. See also Jennifer E. Till, Thesis: Seven Female Photographers of the Oklahoma and Indian Territories, 1889 to 1907 (Oklahoma State University 1994). https://shareok.org/bitstream/handle/11244/12398/Thesis-1997-T574s.pdf?sequence=1.

466. Courtesy of the Cherokee National Archives.

467. *An Illustrated Souvenir Catalogue of the Cherokee National Female Seminary*, p. 20.

468. Ibid. p. 45.

469. Grant Foreman, *Students of Cherokee Male Seminary 1876-1909* and *Students of Cherokee Female Seminary 1876-1904*. These are Volumes 15 and 16 of Foreman's transcripts. The Male Seminary book is available at: https://www.okhistory.org/research/digital/foremantrans/foreman.sup15.pdf. The Female Seminary book is available at https://www.okhistory.org/research/digital/foremantrans/foreman.sup16.pdf.

470. See https://search.ancestry.com/cgi-bin/sse.dll?_phsrc=voB1&_phstart=successSource&usePUBJs=true&indiv=1&dbid=8054&gsfn=Samuel Houston&gsln=MAYES&_83004003-n_xcl=f&msbdy=1803&msbpn__ftp=georgia, usa&msbpn=13&ssrc=pt_t105271716_p422114082966&new=1&rank=1&uidh=iwf&redir=false&msT=1&gss=angs-d&pcat=35&fh=0&h=18021677&recoff=&ml_rpos=1&queryId=249a3c6f338fc1bb17561393f8ffff98.

471. R. Halliburton, Jr., *Red Over Black: Black Slavery Among the Cherokee Indians*, (Praeger Publishers 1977), pp. 110-111.

472. A chart showing Samuel's ancestors is in Appendix 27. Samuel Adair's ECA #411 is in Appendix 26, showing family relationships going back

several generations.

473. A chart showing her illustrious family is in Appendix 27.

474. See McLoughlin, *After the Trail of Tears*, pp. 117-119.

475. Ibid., p. 119.

476. Hoig, The Cherokees and Their Chiefs, p. 216.

477. Abel, Annie Heloise. *The American Indian as Slaveholder and Secessionist: An Omitted Chapter in the Diplomatic History of the Southern Confederacy* (The Arthur H. Clark Company, Cleveland, Ohio 1915), Vol. 1, pp. 46-50. I found these extremely well-researched and detailed books to be the best overall guide to understanding the Civil War in Indian Territory. She spent years reviewing documents that no one before her had taken a deep look at, and quotes extensively from them, weaving a rich tapestry.

478. Ibid. pp. 58-59.

479. See generally Megan Kate Nelson, *The Three-Cornered War: The Union, the Confederacy, and Native Peoples in the Fight for the West*, Scribner, New York, 2019. Navahos and Apaches were the most immediate victims but all Indian tribes in the Southwest and West would suffer grievously.

480. Ibid. p. 61.

481. Perdue, Cherokee Planters, in King, The Cherokee Indian Nation, p. 118.

482. Jeffrey Robert King, New Georgia Encyclopedia, *Slavery in Antebellum Georgia*. See https://www.georgiaencyclopedia.org/articles/history-archaeology/slavery-in-antebellum-georgia/.

483. I took these photos in 2017.

484. N. Michelle Williamson, New Georgia Encyclopedia, July 20, 2021. https://www.georgiaencyclopedia.org/articles/history-archaeology/joseph-vann-1798-1844/.

485. McLoughlin, p. 127.
486. McLoughlin, p. 127. Laws of the Cherokee Nation, p. 37.
487. Ibid. p. 120. Laws of the Cherokee Nation, pp. 118-129.
488. For general information on slave-holding practices among southeastern Indians see Barbara Krauthamer, *Black Slaves, Indian Masters: Slavery, Emancipation, and Citizenship in the Native American South* (University of North Carolina Press, Chapel Hill 2013).
489. Theda Purdue, Cherokee Women, 1998, p. 126.
490. Herman McDaniel, *Vann Slaves Remember* (Murray County Museum 2003). This site contains the recollections of several Vann slave families. See https://www.georgiaencyclopedia.org/articles/history-archaeology/joseph-vann-1798-1844/.
491. McLoughlin, *After the Trail of Tears*, p. 128. Laws of the Cherokee Nation, p. 19.
492. Ibid. p. 39.
493. McLoughlin, *After the Trail of Tears* p. 128.
494. McLoughlin, *After the Trail of Tears* p. 128, citing Halliburton, p. 87.
495. 267 F. Supp. 3rd 86 (2017). Tiya Miles wrote an important chapter in the *1619 Project* titled "Dispossession", covering in detail the history of African Americans enslaved by Indians. See Chapter 5, pp. 135-155.
496. All of the men born to Samuel Mayes and Nannie Adair were Masons, as was Annie Spirit's son William Penn Mayes and many other male relatives.
497. Patrick Minges, The Keetoowah Society and the Avocation of Religious Nationalism in the Cherokee Nation, 1855-1867, Chapter 2, The Birth and Growth of the Keetoowah Society.
498. Tahlequah Daily Press.
499. Ibid.
500. Patrick Minges, "Are you Kituwah's son?" Cherokee Nationalism and

the Civil War, p. 9 (Union Theological Seminary in the City of New York 1994). See also McLoughlin, *After the Trail of Tears*, pp. 153-157.

501. Frederick E. Hoxie, *What Was Taney Thinking? American Citizenship in the Era of Dred Scott*. Chicago-Kent Law Review, Vol. 82, Issue 1 (2006). See https://scholarship.kentlaw.iit.edu/cgi/viewcontent.cgi?article=3580&context=cklawreview.

502. Dred Scott v. Sandford, 60 U.S. (19 How.) 393, 403 (1857).

503. See McLoughlin, *After the Trail of Tears*, pp. 158-159.

504. Minges, "Are you Kituwah's son?" Cherokee Nationalism and the Civil War, p. 9 (Union Theological Seminary in the City of New York 1994). See also William G. McLoughlin, After the Trail of Tears: The Cherokees' Struggle for Sovereignty, p. 156.

505. Courtesy of my cousin Robert Lee Fleming, whose family has had the pipe since Annie died. His great-great grandmother was Charlotte Mayes, Annie's and Samuel Houston Mayes' daughter. Lee received the pipe as a graduation gift from his Aunt Frances Cecelia Fleming Poplin (1914-2005) when he graduated from Northeastern State University in 1983. Frances was a sister of Lee's father, Joe Lindsay Fleming (1921-1971).

506. Minges, "Are you Kituwah's son?" Cherokee Nationalism and the Civil War, p. 9 (Union Theological Seminary in the City of New York 1994), p. 11.

507. Minges, The Keetoowah Society and the Avocation of Religious Nationalism in the Cherokee Nation, 1855-1867, Chapter 2, The Birth and Growth of the Keetoowah Society.

508. Ibid.

509. Robert C. Wright, Indian Masonry, Tyler Publishing Company, Ann Arbor Michigan 1907, p. 104. See https://ia800500.us.archive.org/20/items/indianmasonry00wrig/indianmasonry00wrig.pdf.

510. Ibid. p. 107.

511. Minges, The Keetoowah Society and the Avocation of Religious Nationalism in the Cherokee Nation, 1855-1867, Chapter 2, The Birth and Growth of the Keetoowah Society.

512. Ibid.

513. The Choctaws had formally resolved to that effect on February 7th, but also assured Washington of their neutrality. See Abel, *The American Indian as Slaveholder and Secessionist*, p. 73.

514. Ethel Crisp Taylor, *Dust in the Wind: The Civil War in Indian Territory* (2005), pp. 6-7.

515. Abel, *The American Indian as Slaveholder and Secessionist*, p. 71. Abel, *The Slaveholding Indians: Native Americans as Slaveholders as Participants in the Civil War & Under Reconstruction*, Kindle Edition, p. 233.

516. Ibid. p. 186.

517. Zachary C. Cowsert, *The Civil War in Indian Territory, 1861-1865* (PhD Dissertation, Eberly College of Arts and Sciences, West Virginia University, Morgantown, West Virginia 2020), pp. 16-20. He describes the desperate escape of Colonel William Emory and his 750 troops from Indian Territory during the summer of 1861, which arguably laid the foundation for Confederate success in convincing various Indian nations to sign treaties.

518. Abel, *The American Indian as Slaveholder and Secessionist*, pp. 153-154. Abel, *The Slaveholding Indians: Native Americans as Slaveholders as Participants in the Civil War & Under Reconstruction*, Kindle Edition, p. 71.

519. Ibid. p. 150. Sell also Ehistory, *War of the Rebellion*, https://ehistory.osu.edu/books/official-records/003/0597.

520. Ibid. illustration, unnumbered page.

521. Taylor, *Dust in the Wind: The Civil War in Indian Territory*, p. 18, quoting Daniel O'Flaherty in *General Jo Shelby – Undefeated Rebel*.

522. Wikipedia.

523. Abel, *The American Indian as Slaveholder and Secessionist*, 222-223.

524. Clint Crowe, *Caught in the Maelstrom – The Indian Nations in the Civil War, 1861-1865* (Savas Beatie, Eldorado Hills, California 2019), p. 39.

525. Taylor, *Dust in the Wind: The Civil War in Indian Territory*, p. 23.

526. Crowe, p. 40.

527. Ibid. pp. 224-225.

528. Taylor, *Dust in the Wind: The Civil War in Indian Territory*, p. 22. See also Cowsert, p. 49.

529. Ibid. p. 59.

530. Ibid. p. 72.

531. See generally Ethel Crisp Taylor, The Forgotten Indian Soldiers: Indian Territory 1861-1865, and W. Craig Gaines, *The Confederate Cherokees: John Drew's Regiment of Mounted Rifles* (Louisiana State University Press, Baton Rouge and London 1989). Both books contain detailed commentary on the battles and skirmishes. Taylor's book includes several key letters written by General Pike and John Ross about a treaty. Appendix 1 of Gaines' book lists the officers in Drew's regiment and Appendix 2 lists the individual Cherokees who were serving at the beginning of the War. Most of them defected to the Union within months of joining.

532. Taylor, *Dust in the Wind: The Civil War in Indian Territory*, pp. 32-33.

533. Cowsert, p. 56.

534. Ibid. pp. 87-90.

535. Ibid. pp. 53-54, 94-104. This is by far the most complete account of this battle that I have found, drawing on numerous original resources including official reports and diaries.

536. Abel, *The American Indian as Slaveholder and Secessionist*, pp. 203-204.

537. Cowsert, pp. 107-110. This also the most comprehensive account of this battle that I have found.

538. McKenney, O-Poth-Le-Yo-Ho-Lo, Speaker of the Councils (Lithographed, colored and published 1836-44 by J.T. Bowen, Philadelphia).

539. Ibid. pp. 111-125.

540. Abel, *The American Indian as Slaveholder and Secessionist*, p. 262.

541. In her Miller Roll application dated November 7, 1907 she gave her original name as "Ah-na-wa-ki Spirit". She claimed on behalf of herself, her mother (Chow-e-you-cah), her Uncle Poorbear, Cousin Charles Poorbear and Tee-saw-yah. She stated that her mother died about 1861.

542. Cowsert, pp. 140-141.

543. Courtesy of the Oklahoma Historical Society.

544. Courtesy of American Battlefield Trust. See https://www.battlefields.org/learn/maps/battle-pea-ridge-elkhorn-tavern-march-7-1862.

545. The Battle of Elkhorn Tavern, Confederate Military History, Vol. 10, Chapter IV, pp. 7-8. See http://civilwarhome.com/pearidge.html.

546. This print is included in Frank Leslie's *Illustrated History of the Civil War*, p. 197 (1895), which can be found in the Internet Archive: *https://archive.org/stream/importantevents00franrich?ref=ol - page/n6/mode/2up/search/cherokees*. Also courtesy of the Oklahoma Historical Society: https://gateway.okhistory.org/ark:/67531/metadc1620118/m1/1/?q=civil war.

547. Frank Leslie's *Illustrated History of the Civil War*, p. 86.

548. Taylor, *Dust in the Wind: The Civil War in Indian Territory*, pp. 86-87.

549. Courtesy of the Oklahoma Historical Society: https://gateway.okhistory.org/ark:/67531/metadc1620118/m1/1/?q=civil war.

550. The Battle of Elkhorn Tavern, Confederate Military History, Vol. 10, Chapter IV, p. 88. See http://civilwarhome.com/pearidge.html.

551. Ibid. p. 91.

552. Ibid. pp. 98-99.

553. Ibid. pp. 108-109.

554. JSiler, pp. 158-159.

555. American Battlefield Trust, see https://www.battlefields.org/learn/maps/battle-honey-springs-july-17-1863.

556. History Net, see https://www.historynet.com/battle-honey-springs-1863.htm.

557. See Cowsert, pp. 232-250 for a detailed account of the battle, based on an analysis of original documents.

558. It was published in Frank Leslie's Illustrated Newsletter on August 29, 1863. Courtesy of the Oklahoma Historical Society: https://gateway.okhistory.org/ark:/67531/metadc1595245/?q=civil war.

559. Dale and Litton, p. 157.

560. Annie Heloise Abel, *The American Indian in the Civil War, 1862-1865, Volume 3, The Slaveholding Indians*, pp. 33-34. This volume of her trilogy was republished in 1993 as *The American Indian and the End of the Confederacy*, 1863-1866 (University of Nebraska Press, Lincoln and London 1993), with an Introduction by Theda Perdue and Michael D. Green. The cover was drawn by Frankie Dreadfulwater, husband of my cousin LeeAnn Thompson Dreadfulwater.

561. The photographer was John Whipple. The original is in the Harvard Art Museum, Cambridge, Massachusetts and the image is in the public domain.

562. Arthur C. Parker, *The Life of General Ely S. Parker: Last Grand Sachem of the Iroquois and General Grant's Military Secretary* (Buffalo Historical Society 1919), p. 133.

563. The original is in the Library of Congress and the image is in the public domain.

564. Frank Leslie's *Illustrated History of the Civil War*, p. 11.

565. Abrams, p. 16.

566. Ibid., p. 22.

567. Cowsert, p. 5.

568. Report of D.N. Cooley, *Annual Report of Commissioner of Indian Affairs for the Year 1865* (October 30, 1865), pp. 297-298 See also Cowsert, pp. 315-317, who described the scene in detail.

569. Abel, *The Slaveholding Indians, Volume 3*, p. 185. Abel, *The Slaveholding Indians: Native Americans as Slaveholders as Participants in the Civil War & Under Reconstruction*, Kindle Edition, p. 739. See also Cowsert, p. 316.

570. Abel, *The Slaveholding Indians, Volume* 3, p. 200.

571. Ibid. pp. 213-214. Abel, *The Slaveholding Indians: Native Americans as Slaveholders as Participants in the Civil War & Under Reconstruction*, Kindle Edition, p. 748.

572. Ibid. p. 255.

573. Ibid. p. 256.

574. Heritage of the Hills: A History of Delaware County, p. 188 (1979), from a project of the Oklahoma Historical Society in 1936-37.

575. A chart showing the family from Sarah's perspective is in Appendix 27.

576. The delegation included Smith Christie, James McDaniel, Thomas Pegg, White Catcher, Daniel Ross, John B. Jones and Samuel Benge. See https://dburgin.tripod.com/indians.html.

577. Abel, *The American Indian in the Civil War, 1862-1865, Volume 3, The Slaveholding Indians*, p. 355.

578. See http://www.southerncherokeenation.com/historyofscn3.htm.

579. One of the most illuminating documents showing US ill will towards Chief Ross and President Johnson's negotiating position is D. N. Cooley, The Cherokee Question: Report of the Commissioner of Indian Affairs to the President of the United States, June 15, 1866. See https://babel.hathitrust.org/cgi/pt?id=loc.ark:/13960/t3nv9kn60;view=1up;seq=7.
580. Photo by A. Zeno Shindler, Courtesy of the Amon Carter Museum of American Art, Fort Worth, Texas.
581. Moulton, p. 358.
582. McLoughlin, *After the Trail of Tears*, p. 229.
583. Wikiwand, see https://www.wikiwand.com/en/Timeline_of_Cherokee_history. The original is in the Thomas Gilcrease Institute of American History and Art, Tulsa, Oklahoma.
584. Ibid., p. 232.
585. Ibid. p. 234.
586. In Delaware District the locations chosen were Delaware Town, Sequoyah's New Place and the Snell family farm; in Saline they were in Requa, Cul-car-law-skees and Little Spring Creek; in Going Snake there were school houses at Tyners, Rabbit Trap, Barren Fork and Baptist Mission; a large school was built in Tahlequah along with others at Caney and Killermore's in that District; in Illinois District there were schools in Fort Gibson, Seabolt's and White Oak Spring; in Canadian three were established in Webber's Falls, Brier Town and Jimmy Vann's; in Sequoyah there were three, at Joseph Coody's, Lee's Creek and the Court House; in Flint they were in Clear Spring, at John Glass's place and near Alexander Scott's home; and in Cooweescoowee District they were established at Dog Creek, Lacey Hawkins on Grand River, and John Hatchett's place.
587. A chart showing William's family is in Appendix 27.
588. Don Shadburn thought she died in 1860 while other sources say1869; I've used the latter date.

589. A chart showing the family from Rosella's perspective is in Appendix 27.

590. A chart showing Martha's ancestors is in Appendix 27.

591. McLoughlin, *After the Trail of Tears*, p. 250.

592. McLoughlin, *After the Trail of Tears*, p. 245.

593. In 1842 the government of North Carolina acknowledged their presence and agreed to allow those Cherokees to remain. The 1849 census lists nineteen hundred and eighty-one Cherokees living in the mountains.

594. See https://digitalcommons.law.ou.edu/cgi/viewcontent.cgi?article=9039&context=indianserialset.

595. The full text of Downing's appeal and those who signed it is in Appendix 24.

596. 78 U.S. (11 Wall.) 616. This and other important related cases are discussed at length in Wildenthal, pp. 51-54.

597. http://www.sparksfamilyhistory.com/pix/ok1890.gif.

598. Courtesy of the Library of Congress Geography and Map Division.

599. A chart showing the family from Hunter's perspective is in Appendix 27.

600. Hunter Poorbear's 1906 ECA contains information about the family going back several generations and is reproduced in Appendix 26.

601. Given their genesis, neither marker noted that Watie was a slave owner who signed the New Echota Treaty. See https://www.kgou.org/native-american/2017-08-31/as-cities-remove-confederate-monuments-cherokees-grapple-with-civil-war-past. The statues are in storage in Tahlequah.

602. Journal of the General Council of the Indian Territory (Excelsior Book and Job Printing Office, Lawrence 1870), p.24. See https://books.google.co.ls/books?id=whqgvwEACAAJ&pg=PA24&focus=viewport&output=html.

603. See https://coloradoencyclopedia.org/article/indian-appropriations-act-1871-0.

604. A chart showing Dinah Otterlifter's ancestors is in Appendix 27.

605. A chart showing William's ancestors is in Appendix 27.

606. https://www.pinterest.fr/jamesbarnes1840/cherokee/.

607. Courtesy of the Thomas Gilcrease Institute of American History and Art, Tulsa, Oklahoma. See https://collections.gilcrease.org/object/43263680a-b.

608. Sarah Burrow's ECA #5885 is in Appendix 26. Her sisters also filed ECAs, which are available on line.

609. Annie Vann Adair's ECA #5585 is in Appendix 26. It contains a lot of information about family relationships and names.

610. Annie Harper Gladney Mayes ECA #5645 is in Appendix 26.

611. Betty Lou Dealy gave me my grandfather's letters before she died.

612. The bible and wedding certificate are in the possession of my cousin Daryl Crotts, whose mother was Mary Lycan, a daughter of Mary Hazel Mayes. A chart showing Annie Harper Gladney's family is in Appendix 27.

613. I have copies of many of those letters, which are posted on the website set up for this book.

614. A chart showing Elizabeth Alabama Scrimher's ancestors is in Appendix 27.

615. Hoig, The Cherokees and Their Chiefs, pp.248-49.

616. Ibid. p. 249.

617. https://gw.geneanet.org/tdowling?lang=en&n=bushyhead&oc=0&p=dennis+wolf.

618. John Bickers, *The Dawes Act*, in Origins, Current Events in Historical Perspective (Ohio State University, February 2022). https://origins.osu.edu/read/dawes-act?language_content_entity=en.

619. Carolyn Ross Johnston, Cherokee Women in Crisis: Trail of Tears,

Civil War, and Allotment, 1838-1907, p. 131. This collection of first-person accounts by Cherokee women from letters, diaries, newspaper articles and oral histories is unique, a valuable resource.

620. Ibid.

621. Wikipedia.

622. For the text of the law see: https://www.archives.gov/milestone-documents/dawes-act.

623. See Bickers.

624. Minority Report by Russell Errett, Charles Hooker and T.M. Gunter, House of Representatives, Report No. 1576, 46th Congress, 2nd Session, p.10. See also D.S. Otis, *The Dawes Act and the Allotment of Indian Land*, edited by Francis Paul Prucha (University of Oklahoma Press, Norman, Oklahoma 1973), Chapter 2. In my view, this is the most illuminating history of the Dawes Act available.

625. Bernard A. Weisberger, *American Heritage History of the American People* (1971). https://books.google.fr/books?id=KwJkCgAAQBAJ&pg=PT163&lpg=PT163&dq=Hunger+and+thirst+of+the+white+man+for+Indians'+land+is+almost+equal+to+his+hunger+and+thirst+after+righteousness."&source=bl&ots=_NQt6T4sbZ&sig=ACfU3U027awm15olBzmKTZ1AruK7r45EYA&hl=en&sa=X&ved=2ahUKEwjfl72okOz4AhUX8RoKHRq1Ah0Q6AF6BAgGEAM - v=onepage&q=Hunger and thirst of the white man for Indians' land is almost equal to his hunger and thirst after righteousness."&f=false.

626. Heritage of the Hills, p. 397.

627. For a short biography of William P. Mayes, see *History of Oklahoma*, http://genealogytrails.com/oka/hisofokbios17.html.

628. Heritage of the Hills, p. 188.

629. James E. Parins, *Elias Cornelius Boudinot: A Life on the Cherokee*

Border (University of Nebraska Press 2008). See *https://books.google.fr/books?id=YuaSjyiVc1YC&pg=PA214&lpg=PA214&dq=hunter+poorbear+ +cherokee&source=bl&ots=xuOQvD1WmF&sig=ACfU3U0UBKyhkUPLm 4SVPifTNQsCP6z4uQ&hl=en&sa=X&ved=2ahUKEwiglOTzt-7rAhUBx YUKHVmrACkQ6AEwBXoECAgQAQ - v=onepage&q=hunter poorbear + cherokee&f=false*

630. Mihesuah, *Cultivating the Rosebuds*, pp. 79-80. The photo is the frontspiece in *An Illustrated Souvenir Catalogue of the Cherokee National Female Seminary.*

631. https://gateway.okhistory.org/ark:/67531/metadc94737/.

632. https://en.wikipedia.org/wiki/Joel_B._Mayes.

633. See http://sites.rootsweb.com/~itchertp/history/chapter21.htm.

634. Hoig, The Cherokees and Th,eir Chiefs p. 251.

635. Heritage of the Hills, p. 379. See also Indian Pioneer Project for Oklahoma, http://okgenweb.net/pioneer/ohs/buffingtont.html. This is where the Ketcher community is located today.

636. Claude Hanna Retraces Memory's Road (compiled and edited by Jean E. Bohannan, Memory Road, Inc., Publisher, Grove, Oklahoma, 1969, p. 100, painted by Hazel Barnett).

637. Jess Fields recorded his memories on April 10, 1964 at age sixty-nine. See https://digital.libraries.ou.edu/utils/getfile/collection/dorisduke/id/10090/filename/10088.pdfpage/page/18.

638. Grant Foreman, Cherokee Census 1835, p. 37 and p. 167.

639. Penelope Johnson Allen Cherokee Collection, https://tsla.tnsosfiles.com/history/manuscripts/findingaids/.

640. See https://digital.libraries.ou.edu/utils/getfile/collection/dorisduke/id/10090/filename/10088.pdfpage/page/18.

641. Jack Grasshopper's Miller role file is 3054, filed in Southwest City, Missouri on November 10, 1906. See http://www.okgenweb.net/~apps/

grasshopper-jack.htm.

642. I am indebted to Devon A. Mihesuah's *Ned Christie: The Creation of an Outlaw and Cherokee Hero*, University of Oklahoma Press, Norman 2018, who undertook a detailed effort to counter the misinformation about Christie and his family. In particular, he criticizes Phillip W. Steele, *The Last Cherokee Warriors* and Bonnie Speer, *The Killing of Ned Christie: Cherokee Outlaw*. Mihesuah notes that Steele falsified many of his alleged interviews and took as fact newspaper stories across the decades, and states that Speer's book "contains misquoted, untraceable, fabricated, and incomplete sources, incorrect sequences of events, interviews with unidentified persons, data manipulation, as well as other faulty sources…." p. 17.

643. Ibid. p. 23.
644. Ibid., pp. 24-25.
645. Ibid. pp. 27-28.
646. Ibid. p. 32.
647. Ibid. pp. 34-35.
648. Ibid. p. 38.
649. Ibid. p. 20.
650. Ibid. p. 49.
651. Ibid. p. 53.
652. Ibid. p. 43. The image is in the Roy Hamilton Collection.
653. Ibid. p. 69.
654. Ibid. pp. 72-73.
655. Ibid. pp. 85-88.
656. Ibid. pp. 77-78.
657. Ibid. p. 99.
658. Ibid. pp. 105-107.
659. Ibid. p. 115.

660. Ibid. pp. 123-133.

661. Ibid. p.135.

662. Ibid. p. 146.

663. This is in my library and the original is in the Oklahoma Historical Archives.

664. See Find a Grave, https://www.findagrave.com/memorial/5178119/joel-bryan-mayes.

665. A chart of the family from Lucy Ann's perspective is in Appendix 27.

666. Joe Fox Raven's ECA# is 355 and John's is #373. Their mother likely was Sallie Tarpin (sometimes written Terrapin). Their grandmother Annie Vann Adair's grandmother was Polly Terrapin (1768-1833) based on the boys' ECAs. Sallie's father was Joseph Tso-Se and her mother was Jennie Ya-Kin-Nee (1820-1879). They had four other children, Claw-Ya-Kah, Ave (Ka-Ha-Goh), Ollie and James (Takee). James, born in 1861, married a woman named Betsy with whom he had three children. He died in 1932. John Leroy Raven married Nancy Welch and had two children, Pete Edwin (1908-1996) and Edna May (1909-1995). He also married Lucinda White, with whom he had Mary Louise (1919-2008).

667. Cherokee Advocate, unknown date. See https://www.cherokeephoenix.org/culture/cherokee_syllabary/sequoyah-schools-celebrates-150-years-of-its-establishment/article_63605c70-17d3-11ec-b589-abeec8371784.html.

668. Hoig, The Cherokees and Their Chiefs, p. 253.

669. Courtesy of the Library of Congress. See https://www.loc.gov/item/98687110/.

670. Hanna, p. 100.

671. Find a Grave, https://www.findagrave.com/memorial/11237574/samuel-houston-mayes.

672. https://en.wikipedia.org/wiki/Samuel_Houston_Mayes.

673. Tabatha Toney, *Until We Fall to the Ground United: Cherokee Resilience and Interfactional Cooperation in the Early Twentieth Century*, Phd. Thesis Oklahoma State University, Midwest City (1907), p. 78.
674. Ibid, p. 79.
675. Ballard family archives. A copy is in my library.
676. See https://www.findagrave.com/memorial/5382582/charlotte-ballard.
677. https://www.loc.gov/item/08010502/.
678. Talton v. Mayes, 163 U.S. 376, May 16, 1896, p. 986. Justice White delivered the Court's opinion.
679. Ibid. p. 988. Justice White cited Article 5 of the 1835 Treaty: "The United States herby covenant and agree that the lands ceded to the Cherokee Nation…shall, in no future time without their consent, be included within the territorial limits or jurisdiction of any state or territory. But they shall secure to the Cherokee Nation the right by their national councils to make and carry into effect all such laws as they may deem necessary for the government and protection of the persons and property within their own country belonging to their people or such persons as have connected themselves with them….This guaranty of self-government was reaffirmed in the treaty of 1866 (14 Stat. 803)…."
680. Ibid. p. 988. In 2020 the US Supreme Court ruled 5-4 in *McGirt v. Oklahoma* that eastern Oklahoma is still comprised of Indian reservations of the Creek, Choctaw, Chickasaw, Seminole and Cherokee Nations, one of the most important Indian sovereignty cases in many decades. Speaking for the Court Justice Gorsuch ruled: "Today we are asked whether the land these treaties promised remains an Indian reservation for purposes of federal criminal law," Justice Gorsuch wrote in the majority opinion. "If Congress wishes to withdraw its promises, it must say so. Unlawful acts, performed long enough and with sufficient vigor, are never enough

to amend the law. To hold otherwise would be to elevate the most brazen and longstanding injustices over the law," Gorsuch said, "both rewarding wrong and failing those in the right. Because Congress has not said otherwise, we hold the Government to its word." 591 U.S. (2020). The court partially overruled McGirt, ruling 5-4 in *Oklahoma v. Castro-Huerta*, 597 U.S. ___ (2022) that there is concurrent jurisdiction to prosecute non-Indians for state-law crimes committed against Indians in Indian territory. But the Court refused to overturn *McGirt* as Oklahoma had requested. Justice Gorsuch dissented, citing the continuing relevance of *Worcester v. Georgia*: "Where this Court once stood firm, today it wilts."

681. *The Cherokee Advocate*, Volume 20, Number 44, August 15, 1896, p. 1.

682. David C. Gideon, *Indian Territory: Descriptive Biographical and Genealogical Including the Landed Estates and County Seats, With a General History of the Territory* (Lewis Publishing Company, New York and Chicago 1901), p. 854.

683. The U of M Daily, March 27, 1895, P. 4.

684. University of Michigan, *Res Gestae* (1895), pp. 234 and 238. He is on the list of the Junior Class, p. 252.

685. Johnston, p. 133.

686. See Dave Roos, *How the Dawes Act Stole 90 Million Acres of Native American Land* (January 21, 2021). https://history.howstuffworks.com/american-history/dawes-act.htm.

687. US Congress. The Curtis Act, June 28, 1898. 55th Congress, 2nd sess., 1898.

688. Johnston, pp. 128-129.

689. https://visitcherokeenation.com/culture-and-history/fighting-and-healing.

690. Shadburn, Upon Our Ruins, p. 484. A chart showing his ancestors is

in Appendix 27.

691. https://en.wikipedia.org/wiki/Thomas_Buffington.

692. Moore and Takatoka, History of the Kituwah People.

693. This document was printed in the Knox City *Globe Democrat* newspaper and is in the collection compiled by Grant Foreman, Volume 13, Superintendent for Five Civilized Tribes. See https://www.okhistory.org/research/digital/foremantrans/foreman.sup13.pdf.

694. See article by Rose Stauber in the Grove Observer, April 13, 2007.

695. History of Indian Territory, p. 363.

696. Grove Sun, November 22, 1907.

697. Photo courtesy of John E. Pace, Heritage of the Hills: A History of Delaware County, p. 61 and the Colcord Museum.

698. Grove Sun, October 26, 1933, p.1. The hotel was estimated to be worth $7000 but only $3600 of insurance was carried. William Mayes was visiting his daughter Maude in Tahlequah that week.

699. Mihesuah, *Cultivating the Rosebuds*, pp. 66-67.

700. Mihesuah, *Ned Christie*, p. 129.

701. *An Illustrated Souvenir Catalogue of the Cherokee National Female Seminary*, p. 11.

702. Shadburn, Upon Our Ruins, p. 484.

703. Hoig, The Cherokees and Their Chiefs, pp. 257-58.

704. This document is in the collection compiled by Grant Foreman, Volume 13, Superintendent for Five Civilized Tribes. See https://www.okhistory.org/research/digital/foremantrans/foreman.sup13.pdf.

705. This is owned by my daughter Sociana Clark.

706. This is owned by my cousin Daryl Crotts, Hazel's grandson.

707. This is owned by my daughter Deborah Barnes.

708. See https://quizlet.com/20608803/cherokee-test-flash-cards/.

709. On September 17, 1907 the people of the Indian and Oklahoma

Territories voted favorably on statehood. The vote was certified and delivered to the President of the United States, Theodore Roosevelt, and on November 16, 1907, Roosevelt issued Presidential Proclamation 780 admitting Oklahoma as the forty-sixth state.

710. https://en.wikipedia.org/wiki/William_Charles_Rogers.

711. Johnston, p. 136.

712. Starr, pp. 481-482.

713. Courtesy of the Oklahoma Historical Society: https://gateway.okhistory.org/ark:/67531/metadc1622794/?q=cherokee indians.

714. Toney, p. 88.

715. https://en.wikipedia.org/wiki/State_of_Sequoyah.

716. See Frank J. Boudinot interview April 9, 1937, https://digital.libraries.ou.edu/cdm/singleitem/collection/indianpp/id/4721/rec/4, p.3.

717. United States v. Cherokee Nation, 26 S. Ct. 588, 202 U.S. 101; Id. 40 Ct. Cl. 252.

718. Chronicles of Oklahoma, Volume 4, No. 3, September 1926: James W. Duncan, The Keetoowah Society. Additional information about Boudinot's work can be found in Claim of Frank J. Boudinot: Hearings Before A Subcommittee of the Committee on Indian Affairs, House of Representatives,71st Cong. 2nd Session on H.R. 5847, April 12, 1930. I am indebted to my Michigan Law School classmate Greg Curtner, Dean Mark West and Professor Seth Quidachay-Swan for tracking down the details of Boudinot's time at the Law School. The Law School has an archive of material about him, including newspaper clippings and Law School publications.

719. Moore and Takatoka, History of the Kituwah People. This was originally published on the website of Manataka.org but has been removed.

720. The main family farm was in Township 24 North, Range 24 East.

I have a copy of that plat, which lists the parcels of all the children of William and Annie Mayes in contiguous plots, along with their Dawes Roll numbers. That farm (228 acres) was sold for $60/acre to a man named McCracken following William's death in 1944 and is maintained as one large farm owned by the Caudill family. Road E300 runs through the middle, east to west, and the other boundary roads are NS465 and NS466. It is lovely rolling land with forests, streams and several springs.

721. Bickers. https://origins.osu.edu/read/dawes-act?language_content_entity=en.

722. See the transcript of a Hearing in the US House of Representatives Committee on Indian Affairs, which took place during the second and third sessions of the Committee in 1930-31. Boudinot's claim for attorney fees to be awarded for his successful cases was introduced as HR 5487. The transcript contains a full record of legal work the Boudinot carried out starting in 1916 to recover compensation for the Cherokees. Ultimately, the Committee refused to approve his request, on the ground that he had already been paid part of the amount by the Cherokee Nation. In previous situations Boudinot convinced other Committees to provide additional compensation.

723. U.S. Statutes 253.

724. See Alexandra Witkin, *To Silence a Drum: The Imposition of Citizenship on Native Peoples* (Historical Reflections, Volume 21, No. 2, Spring 1995), pp. 353–83, https://www.jstor.org/stable/41299031?read-now=1&refreqid=excelsior%3A43831d741d9b266c0d07c8d794a5f145&seq=1.

725. See Paul Ridenour's home page about the Watie family. https://www.google.com/imgres?imgurl=https%3A%2F%2Fwww.paulridenour.com%2FFrankj.jpg&tbnid=zfoemWRkwqJ0pM&vet=12ahUKEwjLtbKu_dmBAxU7rycCHf40AUEQMygMegQIARBd..i&imgrefurl=https%3A

%2F%2Fwww.paulridenour.com%2Fpenn.htm&docid=TakLSaWQ79U NpM&w=189&h=229&q=Phot.

726. The letters among various family members from the early 1870s to the late 1930s were in the possession of Betty Lou Dealy in Muskogee and were given to me by her family after her death in early 2003.

727. *The* Grove Sun, November 27, 1908.

728. Mihesuah, *Cultivating the Rosebuds*, p. 76.

729. New State Tribune, Muskogee, March 11, 1909.

730. Commonly known as Shriners, membership requires one to be a Mason.

731. https://www.facebook.com/NNAIOP/photos/a.10150107218355578/10150253610065578/?type=3.

732. Mihesuah, *Cultivating the Rosebuds*, p. 69. A fire swept the Male Seminary in the spring of 1910, burning it to the ground. It was never rebuilt.

733. *The Grove Sun*, February 25, 1910, p. 5.

734. A list of Annie's grandchildren and great-grandchildren is in Appendix 29.

735. Hanna, p. 88.

736. Kenla Henson, Ceremony Honors 3 Trail of Tears Survivors, Cherokee Phoenix, November 20, 2017, p. 1. https://www.cherokeephoenix.org/culture/ceremony-honors-3-trail-of-tears-survivors/article_71c2e05a-d883-5c8c-9d14-588bc42c2511.html.

737. See for example https://edition.cnn.com/2022/09/27/us/cherokee-nation-push-for-congress-delegate-cec/index.html.

Bibliography

An Illustrated Souvenir Catalogue of the Cherokee National Female Seminary, Tahlequah, Indian Territory 1850 to 1906 (Arranged and Printed at the Indian Print Shop, Chilocco, Oklahoma 1906)

Abbott, Belle Kendrick. *The Cherokee Indians in Georgia* (published as a series in the Atlanta Constitution Oct. 27, Nov. 3, Nov. 10, Nov. 17, Nov. 24, and Dec. 3, 1889)

Abbott, John S. *David Crockett: His Life and Adventures* (Bottom of the Hill Publishing, December 21, 2012)

Abel, Annie Heloise. The Slaveholding Indians (Vol. 1-3): Native American as Slaveholder as Participants in the Civil War & Under Reconstruction (Madison & Adams Press 2021)

Abel, Annie Heloise. The American Indian as Slaveholder and Secessionist: An Omitted Chapter in the Diplomatic History of the Southern Confederacy (The Arthur H. Clark Company, Cleveland, Ohio 1915)

Abel, Annie Heloise. The American Indian as Participant in the Civil War, 1862-1865 (Torch Press, Cedar Rapids, Iowa; The Arthur H. Clark Company, Cleveland, Ohio 1925)

Abel, Annie Heloise. The American Indian Under Reconstruction (Torch

Press, Cedar Rapids, Iowa; The Arthur H. Clark Company, Cleveland, Ohio 1925)

Abel, Annie Heloise. The American Indian and the End of the Confederacy, 1863-1866 (University of Nebraska Press, Lincoln and London 1993), with an Introduction by Theda Perdue and Michael D. Green

Abram, Susan Marie. *"Souls In The Treetops:" Cherokee War, Masculinity, And Community, 1760-1820*, PhD Dissertation Auburn University 2009)

Agnew, Brad. *Northeastern: Centennial History* (JVL Digital Library, John Vaughan Library Northeastern State University Tahlequah, Oklahoma 2009)

Alderman, Pat. Nancy Ward: Cherokee Chieftainess: Her Cry was All for Peace; Dragging Canoe: Cherokee-Chickamauga War Chief: We Are Not Yet Conquered (Overmountain Press, Johnson City, Tennessee, 1978)

American Baptist Magazine (Volume 24, Number 10, Oct. 1844)

American Board of Commissioners of Foreign Missions, The Missionary Herald (Selected issues)

Boudinot, Elias. *An Address to the Whites* (Printed by William Geddes, Philadelphia, 1826)

Brown, John P. *Old Frontiers: The Story of the Cherokee Indians from Earliest Times to the Date of Their Removal to the West, 1838* (Southern Publishers Inc., Kingsport Tennessee 1938)

Bruchak, Joseph. On This Long Journey, The Journal of Jesse Smoke, A Cherokee Boy, The Trail of Tears, 1838 (Scholastic Press 2001)

Butrick, Daniel. *The Journal of Reverend Daniel S. Butrick, May 19, 1838 - April 1, 1839* (The Trail of Tears Association, Oklahoma Chapter 1998)

Calloway, Colin G. *The Indian World of George Washington: The First President, the First Americans, and the Birth of the Nation* (Oxford University Press 2018)

Carter, Samuel III. *Cherokee Sunset: A Nation Betrayed: A Narrative of Travail and Triumph, Persecution and Exile* (Doubleday & Company, Garden City NY 1976)

Catlin, George. *Illustrations of the Manners, Customs, and Condition of the North American Indians* (London, Henry G. Bohn, Ninth Edition 1857)

Catlin, George. *Shut Your Mouth and Save Your Life* (N. Truebner & Co., London 1870)

Charles River Editors. *The Trail of Tears: The Forced Removal of the Five Civilized Tribes* (Create Space Independent Publishing 2017)

Cheever, George Barrel. *The Removal of the Indians: An Article from the American Monthly Magazine: An Examination of an Article in the North American Review: And an Exhibition of the Advancement of the Southern Tribes, in Civilization and Christianity* (Pierce and Williams, Boston 1830)

Cherokee Phoenix (Selected issues)

Cherokee Phoenix and Indians' Advocate (Selected issues)

Civil War Society. *Encyclopedia of the Civil War* (Random House Value Publishing 1997)

Cooley, D. N. *The Cherokee Question: Report of the Commissioner of Indian Affairs to the President of the United States* (Government Printing Office, Washington, D.C. 1866)

Conway, Carolyn S. and Houston, Kelly E. editors, *Shorey W. Ross's Memories of the Cherokee Nation* (Little Rock, Arkansas 2005)

Cowsert, Zachary C. *The Civil War in Indian Territory, 1861-1865* (PhD Dissertation, Eberly College of Arts and Sciences, West Virginia University, Morgantown, West Virginia 2020)

Crowe, Clint. *Caught in the Maelstrom – The Indian Nations in the Civil War, 1861-1865* (Savas Beatie, Eldorado Hills, California 2019)

Dale, Edward Everett and Litton, Gaston. *Cherokee Cavaliers: Forty Years of Cherokee History as told in the Correspondence of the Ridge-Watie-Boudinot Family* (The Civilization of the American Indian Series, Book 19, University of Oklahoma Press 1995)

Davis, John B. The Life and Work of Sequoyah, Chronicles of Oklahoma, Volume 8, No. 2 (June 1930)

Duncan, Barbara R. ed. *Living Stories of the Cherokee* (University of North Carolina Press, Chapel Hill: 1998)

Duncan, Barbara R. And Riggs, Brett H. *Cherokee Heritage Trails Guidebook* (The Museum of the Cherokee Indian, The University of North Carolina Press, Chapel Hill and London 2003)

Eaton, Rachel Caroline. *John Ross and the Cherokee Indians* (George Banta Publishing Company, Menasha, Wisconsin 1914)

Ehle, John. *Trail of Tears: The Rise and Fall of the Cherokee Nation* (Doubleday, New York 1988)

Evans, Gen. Clement A. *Confederate Military History: A Library of Confederate States History, In Twelve Volumes, Written by Distinguished Men of the South* (Confederate Publishing Company, Atlanta, Georgia 1899)

Featherstonhaugh, George W. *A Canoe Voyage up The Minnay Sotor* (1847 - Republished by the Minnesota Historical Society Press 1970)

Filler, Johathan. Arguing in an Age of Unreason: Elias Boudinot, Cherokee Factionalism, and the Treaty of New Echota (Master of Arts Thesis, Graduate College of Bowling Green State University 2010)

Flannagan, Sharon P. *The Georgia Cherokees Who Remained: Race, Status, and Property in the Chattahoochee Community* (Georgia Historical Society Quarterly Vol, 73, No. 3, Fall 1989)

Forbes, Kathi. *Indian Reservations: Where History, Genealogy and Myth Collide*, https://www.indianreservations.net/2017/10/nanyehi-nancy-ward-beloved-woman-of.html (2017)

Foreman, Carolyn Thomas. *An Early Account of the* Cherokees (Chronicles of Oklahoma, Volume 34, No. 2, pp. 141-158, 1956)

Foreman, Grant. *Cherokee Census 1835, Superintendent for the Five Civilized Tribes*

Foreman, Grant. *Indians and Pioneers* (Norman: University of Oklahoma 1936)

Foreman, Grant. *Indian Removal: The Emigration of the Five Civilized Tribes of Indians* (Norman: University of Oklahoma 1932)

Foreman, Grant. *Notes of a Missionary Among the Cherokees* (Chronicles of Oklahoma, Volume 16, No. 2, pp. 171-189, 1938)

Foreman, Grant. *Sequoyah* (Norman: University of Oklahoma 1938)

Foreman, Grant. Students of Cherokee Male Seminary 1876-1909 (Volume 15, Superintendent for Five Civilized Tribes 1935)

Foreman, Grant. Students of Cherokee Female Seminary 1876-1904 (Volume 16, Superintendent for Five Civilized Tribes 1935)

Gaines, W. Craig. The Confederate Cherokees: John Drew's Regiment of Mounted Rifles (Louisiana State University Press, Baton Rouge 1989)

Gideon, David C. Indian Territory: Descriptive Biographical and Genealogical Including the Landed Estates and County Seats, With a General History of the Territory (Lewis Publishing Company, New York and Chicago 1901)

Grove Sun (Selected issues)

Hail, Raven. *The Cherokee Sacred Calendar: A Handbook of the Ancient Native American Tradition* (Denny Books, Rochester, Vermont 2000)

Halliburton, R, Jr. *Red Over Black: Black Slavery Among the Cherokee Indians*, (Praeger Publishers 1977)

Hampton, David. *Biography of Nancy Ward* (The Association of the Descendants of Nancy Ward)

Hanna, Claude. *Claude Hanna Retraces Memory's Road*, compiled and edited by Jean E. Bohannan (Memory Road, Inc., Grove, Oklahoma 1969)

Hauptman, Laurence M. *General John E. Wool in Cherokee Country, 1836-1837: A Reinterpretation* (The Georgia Historical Quarterly, Vol. 85, No. 1 Spring 2001, pp. 1-26)

Heape, Toye E. Trail of Tears National Historic Trail In Tennessee: Indian Removal In The Cherokee Nation (Native History Association, Nashville, Tennessee 2017)

Heritage of the Hills: A History of Delaware County, (a project of the Oklahoma Historical Society in 1936-37, published in 1979)

Hicks, Brian. *Toward the Setting Sun: John Ross, the Cherokees, and the Trail of Tears* (Atlantic Monthly Press, New York 2011)

Hill, Sarah H. *Cherokee Removal: Forts Along the Georgia Trail of Tears* (National Parks Service and the Georgia Department of Natural Resources/ Historic Preservation Division 2005)

Hill, Sarah H. Cherokee Removal Scenes: Ellijay, Georgia 1838 (Southern Spaces. August 23, 2012)

Hill, Sarah H. All Roads Led to Rome, Facing the History of Cherokee Expulsion (Southern Spaces, February 20, 2017)

Hoig, Stanley W. Night of the Cruel Moon: Cherokee Removal and the Trail of Tears (Facts on File, New York, NY 1996)

Hoig, Stanley W. The Cherokees and Their Chiefs: In the Wake of Empire (University of Arkansas Press, Fayetteville 1998)

Hoxie, Frederick E. *What Was Taney Thinking? American Citizenship in the Era of Dred Scott.* (Chicago-Kent Law Review, Vol. 82, Issue 1 2006)

Inskeep, Steve. Jacksonland: President Andrew Jackson, Cherokee Chief John Ross, and a Great American Land Grab (Penguin Press 2015)

Jahoda, Gloria. *The Trail of Tears: The Story of the American Indian Removals 1813-1855* (Wings Books, New York 1975)

Johnston, Carolyn Ross. *Cherokee Women in Crisis: Trail of Tears, Civil*

War, and Allotment, 1838-1907 (The University of Alabama Press, Tuscaloosa, Alabama 2003)

Journal of the General Council of the Indian Territory (Excelsior Book and Job Printing Office, Lawrence 1870)

Keys, Lucy Lowrey. *The Wahnenauhi Manuscript: Historical Sketches of the Cherokees* (The Smithsonian Institution, Bureau of American Ethnology, Bulletin 196, edited by Jack Frederick Kilpatrick)

King, Duane H. The Cherokee Trail of Tears (Graphic Arts Books, Portland, Oregon 2008)

King, Duane H., ed. The Cherokee Indian Nation: A Troubled History (The University of Tennessee Press, Knoxville 1979)

Krakow, Kenneth K. *Georgia Place-Names: Their History and Origins* (Winship Press, Macon, Georgia 1975)

Krauthamer, Barbara. *Black Slaves, Indian Masters: Slavery, Emancipation, and Citizenship in the Native American South* (University of North Carolina Press, Chapel Hill 2013)

Lenoir, Elbert S. *Cherokee Ration Books 1836-1838, New Echota* (Mountain Press, Signal Mountain Tennessee 1999)

Leslie, Frank. Moat, Louis Shepheard, ed. *Illustrated History of the Civil War* (Mrs. Frank Leslie, New York 1895)

Littlefield, Daniel F. and Underhill, Lonnie. *Fort Wayne and the Arkansas Frontier, 1838- 1840 (*The Arkansas Historical Quarterly 35:334-359, 1976)

Loomis, Augustus W. *Scenes in the Indian Country*, in Grant Foreman, *Advancing the Frontier, 1830-1860* (Norman: University of Oklahoma Press 1933)

Maddox, Jerry A. *The Legacy of Ludovic Grant* (Author House, Bloomington, Indiana and Milton Keynes, United Kingdom 2007)

Malone, Henry T. *The Cherokee Phoenix: Supreme Expression of Cherokee*

Nationalism (The Georgia Historical Quarterly, Vol. 34, No. 3, September 1950, pp. 163-188)

Marchione, William P. *A Brief History of Smyrna* (The History Press, Inc. 2013)

Marshall, Lamar et al, Gail King Project Director. *Alabama Collection Camps, Forts, Emigrating Depots and Travel Routes Used During the Cherokee Removal of 1838-1839* (Southeastern Anthropological Institute Northwest Shoals Community College, Muscle Shoals, Alabama and National Park Service 2009).

Martin, James Mathew. *The Cherokee Supreme Court: 1823-1835* (PhD Dissertation, University of Nevada Reno 2018)

McKenney, Thomas L. *History of the Indian Tribes of North America, With Biographical Sketches and Anecdotes*, 3 volumes (D. Rice and Co. Philadelphia 1837-44)

McLoughlin, William G. *After the Trail of Tears: The Cherokees' Struggle for Sovereignty* (The University of North Carolina Press, Chapel Hill and London 1993)

McLoughlin, William G. *Cherokees and Missionaries, 1789-1839* (University of Oklahoma Press, Norman, Oklahoma 1995)

McLoughlin, William G. *Cherokee Renascence in the New Republic* (Princeton University Press, 1986)

McLoughlin, William G. *Champions of the Cherokees: Evan and John B. Jones* (Princeton University Press, Princeton, New Jersey 1990).

Minges, Patrick N. *Slavery in the Cherokee Nation: The Keetoowah Society and the Defining of a People, 1855-1867* (Routledge 2003)

Minges, Patrick N. *Black Indian Slave Narratives* (John F. Blair, Winston-Salem, North Carolina 2004)

Minges, Patrick N. *The Keetoowah Society and the Avocation of Religious Nationalism in the Cherokee Nation 1855-1867* (PhD Thesis, Union

Theological Seminary, New York 1994 and 1998)

Moulton, Gary Evan. *John Ross, Cherokee Chief* (PhD Thesis, Oklahoma State University 1974)

Moulton, Gary E., ed. *The Papers of Chief John Ross, vol 1, 1807–1839* (Norman Oklahoma, University of Oklahoma Press 1985)

Mihesuah, Devon A. *Cultivating the Rosebuds: The Education of Women at the Cherokee Female Seminary, 1851-1909* (University of Illinois Press 1993)

Mihesuah, Devon A. *Ned Christie: The Creation of an Outlaw and Cherokee Hero* (University of Oklahoma Press, Norman 2018)

Miles, Tiya. *Dispossession,* Chapter 5, *The 1619 Project: A New Origin Story*, edited by Nikole Hannah-Jones, Caitlin Roper, Ilena Silverman and Jake Silverstein (The New York Times Company 2021)

Nance, Benjamin C. *The Trail of Tears in Tennessee: A Study of the Routes Used During the Cherokee Removal of 1838*, Tennessee Department of Environment and Conservation (2001)

Nelson, Megan Kate. *The Three-Cornered War: The Union, the Confederacy, and Native Peoples in the Fight for the West* (Scribner, New York 2019)

New State Tribune, Muskogee (March 11, 1909)

Norgren, Jill. *The Cherokee Cases: Two Landmark Federal Decisions in the Fight for Sovereignty* (University of Oklahoma Press, Norman 2004)

Office of Indian Affairs. *Report from the Secretary of War to the 25th Congress, 3rd Session Senate* (July 25, 1835)

Oklahoma Historical Society. *Heritage of the Hills: A History of Delaware County* (1979)

Otis, D.S. *The Dawes Act and the Allotment of Indian Land*, edited by Francis Paul Prucha (University of Oklahoma Press, Norman, Oklahoma 1973)

Parins, James E. *Elias Cornelius Boudinot: A Life on the Cherokee Border* (University of Nebraska Press 2008)

Parker, Arthur C. *The Life of General Ely S. Parker: Last Grand Sachem of the Iroquois and General Grant's Military Secretary* (Buffalo Historical Society 1919)

Penn, William. *On the Present Crisis in the Condition of the American Indians* (Boston: Perkins & Martin 1829).

Perdue, Theda. *Cherokee Women: Gender and Culture Change 1700-1835* (University of Nebraska Press 1998)

Perdue, Theda and Green, Michael D. *The Cherokee Removal, A Brief History With Documents* (Bedford Books of St. Martin's Press, Boston & New York 1995)

Perdue, Theda. *Slavery and the Evolution of Cherokee Society, 1540-1866* (The University of Tennessee Press, Knoxville 1979)

Perdue, Theda. *Cherokee Planters: The Development of Plantation Slavery Before Removal*, in King (ed.), The Cherokee Indian Nation: A Troubled History (The University of Tennessee Press, Knoxville 1979)

Perdue, Theda. Cherokee Editor: The Writings of Elias Boudinot (The University of Georgia Press 1983)

Phillips, William Addison. *Sequoyah* (Harper's Magazine, September 1870)

Presbyterian Mission Herald (American Board of Commissioners for Foreign Missions, Boston, Massachusetts 1849)

Prucha, Francis Paul. *American Indian Treaties: The History of an Anomaly* (University of California Press 1997)

Prucha, Francis Paul ed. *Jeremiah Evarts, Cherokee Removal: The "William Penn" Essays and Other Writings* (Knoxville 1981)

Prucha, Francis Paul. *Protest by Petition: Jeremiah Evarts and the Cherokee Indians* (Proceedings of the Massachusetts Historical Society, Third Series, Vol 97, pp. 42-58 1985)

Reed, Gerard. *Postremoval Factionalism in the Cherokee Nation*, in King, *The Cherokee Indian Nation*: A Troubled History (1979)

Richardson, James D., ed. *A Compilation of the Messages and Papers of the Presidents* (1902-1904)

Rouse, Karen. *The People v. Andrew Jackson* (West Sylvan Middle School, Portland Public Schools 2007)

Routh, E. C. *The Story of Oklahoma Baptists* (Oklahoma City: Baptist General Convention 1932)

Royce, Charles C. *The Cherokee Nation of Indians: A Narrative of their Official Relations with the Colonial and Federal Governments* (Fifth Annual Report of the Bureau of Ethnology to the Secretary of the Smithsonian Institution 1883-1884, Government Printing Office, Washington, D.C., pp. 121-378, 1887)

Rozema, Vicki. *Cherokee Voices: Early Accounts of Cherokee Life in the East* (John F. Blair, Winston-Salem, North Carolina 2002)

Rozema, Vicki. *Voices from the Trail of Tears* (John F. Blair, Winston-Salem, North Carolina 2003)

Sedgwick, John. *Blood Moon: An American Epic of War and Splendor in the Cherokee Nation* (Simon Schuster, New York 2018)

Shadburn, Don L. *Cherokee Planters in Georgia 1832-1838* (The Cottonpatch Press, Cumming, Georgia 1989)

Shadburn, Don L. and John D. Strange, III. *Upon Our Ruins: A Study in Cherokee History and Genealogy* (The Cottonpatch Press, Cumming, Georgia 2011)

Shadburn, Don L. *Unhallowed Intrusion: A History of Cherokee Families in Forsyth County, Georgia* (McNaughton & Gunn, Saline, Michigan 1993)

Siler, Jonathan. *Arguing in an Age of Unreason: Elias Boudinot, Cherokee Factionalism, and the Treaty of New Echota* (PhD thesis, University of Bowling Green 2010)

Smith, Benny. The Keetoowah Society of Cherokee Indians (Masters

Dissertation, Northwestern State College, Alva, Oklahoma 1967)

Smith, Daniel Blake. *An American Betrayal – Cherokee Patriots and the Trail of Tears* (Henry Holt and Company, New York 2011)

Stanley, John Mix. *Portraits of North American Indians With Sketches of Scenery, Etc.* (Smithsonian Institution, Washington D.C. 1852)

Statue of Sequoyah, Proceedings in Statuary Hall of the United States Capitol upon the Unveiling and Presentation of the Statue of Sequoyah by the State of Oklahoma, Sixty-Fifth Congress, June 6, 1917 (Government Printing Office, Washington 1924)

Stephens, Kyle Massey. *To the Indian Removal Act, 1814-1830* (PhD Thesis, University of Tennessee, Knoxville 2013)

Takaki, Ronald T. *Iron Cages: Race and Culture in Nineteenth Century America*, (Knopf-Random House, New York 1979)

Taylor, Ethel Crisp. *Dust in the Wind: The Civil War in Indian Territory* (2005)

Taylor, Ethel Crisp. *The Forgotten Indian Soldiers: Indian Territory 1861-1865 (Create Space Independent Publishing Platform 2014)*

The Cherokee Advocate (Selected issues)

The Payne-Butrick Papers: Volumes One to Six (William L. Anderson, Jane L. Brown & Anne F. Rodgers, eds., University of Nebraska Press 2010)

Thomas, William Joseph. *Creating Cherokee Print: Samuel Austin Worcester's Impact on the Syllabary* (Media History Monographs 10:2 (2007-2008, Cornell University)

Till, Jennifer E. *Seven Female Photographers of the Oklahoma and Indian Territories, 1889 to 1907* (Master's Thesis, Oklahoma State University 1994)

Timberlake, Henry. Memoirs (Londo 1765)

Toney, Tabatha. *Until We Fall to the Ground United: Cherokee Resilience and Interfactional Cooperation in the Early Twentieth Century* (PhD. Thesis

Oklahoma State University, Midwest City 2007)

Tracy, E.C. *Memoir of the Life of Jeremiah Evarts, Esq.* (Crocker and Brewster, Boston 1845)

Twohig, Dorothy ed. The Journal of the Proceedings of the President, 1793-1797 (Charlottesville, University of Virginia Press 1981)

Tyner, James W., ed. *1835 Cherokee Census*

Vänder Hook, Sue. *Trail of Tears* (ABDO Publishing Company, Edina, Minnesota 1949)

Walker, Reverend Charles O. *Cherokee Images* (1988)

Walker, Reverend Charles O. *Cherokee Footprints Vols. 1-3* (Industrial Print Service 1988)

Walker, Robert Sparks. *Torchlights to the Cherokees: The Brainerd Mission* (The Overmountain Press, Johnson City, Tennessee 1933)

Wallace, Anthony F. C. *Jefferson and the Indians: The Tragic Fate of the First Americans* (Cambridge: Harvard University Press 1999)

Wallace, Anthony F. C. *The Long Bitter Trail – Andrew Jackson and the Indians* (Hill and Wang, New York 1993)

Warren, Mary Bondurant. Whites Among the Cherokees: 1828-1838 (Heritage Papers 1987)

Wildenthal, Brian W. *Native American Sovereignty on Trial: A Handbook With Cases, Laws and Documents* (ABC CLIO, Santa Barbara, California 2003)

Wilkins, Thurman. *Cherokee Tragedy: The Ridge Family and the Decimation of a People* (The Civilization of the American Indian Series, Volume 169, University of Oklahoma Press 1989)

Witkin, Alexandra. *To Silence a Drum: The Imposition of Citizenship on Native Peoples* (Historical Reflections, Volume 21, No. 2, Spring 1995)

Wright, Robert C. Indian Masonry (Tyler Publishing Company, Ann Arbor, Michigan 1907)

INDEX

Note: References in *italic* refer to figures. References followed by "n" refer to endnotes.

Abel, Annie Heloise, 413n477, 416n513, 416n515, 416n518, 417n523, 418n536, 418n540, 419n560, 420n569–71, 420n577

abolitionism, 233

Act of Union, 178–79, 180

Act to Prevent Amalgamation with Colored Persons, 224–25

Adair, Andrew "Raven," 185–86, 215, 315, 354, 370n10

Adair, Annie Vann, 185, 214, 215, 276, 284, 315, 354, *355,* 370n10, 427n666

Adair, Black Watt, 62–63, 136

Adair, Edward Sylvester, 186, 214, 369n5, 370n10

Adair, George W., 182, 215

Adair, John Thompson, 213

Adair, John W., 136

Adair, Nannie. *See* Mayes, Nancy/Nannie Adair

Adair, Rosella, 186, 214, 276, 354

Adair, Walter Scott "Red Watt," 58
Adair, William Penn, 271
Adams, John Quincy, 77, 98, 126–27
"Address to the Cherokee Nation" (Wool), 139
Address to the Whites, An (Boudinot), 95
Alberty, Eliza Missouri Bushyhead, 356, *357*
Alexander, John, 87
Allotment Act of 1887, 306
Ama-Kanasta (Sweetwater), 48, 55
"Amazing Grace," 175
American Battlefield Trust, 418n544, 419n555
American Board of Commissioners for Foreign Missions, 29, 81, 92, 94
Amerindians, 56
Appalachian Mountains, 8, 11, 12, 157, 160
appraisals of Cherokee farms, 53–54, 135–36, 150, 156, 221, 339, 399n13
Arbuckle, Mathew, 40, 172, 179, 180
Archi Magus, xxxii
Arkansas Gazette, 87
Armstrong, William, 172, 179
Arrigoni, Giacomo Balardi, 59
Articles of Friendship and Commerce, 3
asylum, 283
Atlantic and Pacific Railroad, 274
Attacullaculla, 3–4, 10, 13, 90
Ayoka, 82, 83

Badger, 18
Baker, Teeartoonskie, 54
Ballard, Anna May, 281, 293

Ballard, Annie Fields, 281
Ballard, Archibald, 281
Ballard, Charlotte Mayes, 207, 214, 281
Ballard, Diana Otterlifter, 281
Ballard, Ethyl Savilla, 281
Ballard, Jane Anna (Janana), 209, 281, 293, 357
Ballard, Lucinda, 281, 293
Ballard, Ruth, 209
Ballard, Ruth May, 281
Ballard, Samuel, 281
Ballard, Sarah, 207
Ballard, Sarah Eleanore, 281, 293
Ballard, William Houston, 207, 209, 281
Ballard, Zoe Wyly, 281
Barnes, Nellie Maude Mayes, 285, 293, 323, 340–42, 352, *353, 354*
Barnes, Robert, 376n55
Battle of Bird Creek (Chusto-Talasah), 241–45
Battle of Elkhorn Tavern, 418n545, 419n55
Battle of Flint Creek in Alabama, 19
Battle of Honey Springs, 255–56
Battle of Horse Shoe Bend, 42, 43–47
Battle of Locust Grove, 250
Battle of Pea Ridge, 246–48, 275
Battle of Prairie Grove, 252
Battle of Preston, England, 2
Battle of Taliwa, 35
Battle of the Thames, 23
Battle of Tippecanoe, 22
beads, xxviii

Beamer, James, 5
Bean, Lydia, 36–37
Bell, James, 271
Bell, John, 180, 181
Benge, George, 313
Benge, John, 189
Benge, Sam, 268
Bird Clan, 304
Bishop, William, 121
Black Fox (Enolee), 78, 91, 118, 119
Blaylock, Jefferson, 184, 384–85n147, 385n151
Blaylock, John, 48, 58, 184
Blaylock, Mary, xvii, 48
blood law, xxxii
Bloody Fellow, 21
Blount, William, 20, 21
Bobcat, Charley, 308
Bohemia, 59–60
Boone, Daniel, 13–14
Boudinot, Elias, 60, 73, 84, 111, 112, 115, 118, 126, 134, 138, 178, 229, 235, 244, 257, 265, 268, 269, 294–95, 321, 325–26, 386n153
   Address to the Whites, An, 95
   editorial writing, 95–96
   education, 94
   execution, 176–77
   marriage, 94
   on prejudice, 95
   public lectures, 94–95
Boudinot, Frank Josiah, 325–26, 343, 348, 350–51, *351*

Boudinot, William Penn, 325
Bowl, The, 26
Boyle, John, 56
Brainerd Mission, 162
Brown, Alex, 184
Brown, David, 84
Buffington, Mary, 142, 187
Buffington, Thomas M., 299, 315, 329, *329,* 330, 337–38
Bureau of Indian Affairs, 31, 102, 274, 327
Burrows, Sarah A., 372n21
Burns, Samuel, 135
Bushyhead, Charlotte, 317, 318
Bushyhead, Dennis Wolfe, 7, 191, 213, 286–88, *287,* 296, 306
Bushyhead, Eliza, 169–70
Bushyhead, Eliza Missouri, 170
Bushyhead, Jesse, 7, 116, 123, 140–41, 144, 162, 165, 168, 169–70, 171, 176, 181, *192,* 216, 231, 272, 317, 356
   as judge, 191
   as a peacemaker, 190
Butler, Elizur, 109, 202
Butler, George, 219
Butler, Pierce, 88–89, 192–93
Butrick, Daniel, 140, 155–56, 169, 387n159, 402n354, 406n395
Buzzard Roost, 48–49, 51

Calhoun, John C., 28, 29, 31–32
Callis, 214
Calloway, Colin, 16, 26
Campbell, Duncan G., 33

Camp Gilmer, 63
Camp Homes Treaty, 41
Campo, 214
Canton Asylum, 311
Cass, Lewis, 28, 110, 111, 129, 130
Catherine, Susannah, 3
Catlin, George, 41, 373n31, 380n99
census, 218, 292
    of 1830, 51, 383n137
    of 1835, 120–21, 301, 399n309
    of 1849, 422n593
    of 1850, 213
    of 1872, 278
    of 2010, 362
    Guion Miller Roll, 1906, 302
Chambers, Henry, 313, 314
Charlotte, Sarah, 62
The Cherokee Advocate, 223, 291
Cherokee(s)/Cherokee Nation
    Articles of Friendship and Commerce, 3
    belief system, xxxii
    census (*See* census)
    clans, xv
    diplomatic and battle skills, 9–10, 13
    geographical area/spread in 1760, 8
    history, 8–34
    life, culture, and traditions, xx–xxxiii
    population, 10 (*See also* census)
    religious belief, 69

as sovereign political entity, 99
topographical map, *6*
written language, 68, 74
Cherokee Lodge #21, 229
Cherokee National Council, 38–39
Cherokee Nation v. Georgia, 108, 394n245
Cherokee Outlet, 217, 274, 279, 292, 297, 313, 318
Cherokee Phoenix, xxxiv, 52, 53, 58–59, 73, 77, 79, 84–85, 95, 100, 101, 108, 111, 115–16, 119, 124, 181, 273, 305, 350
Cherokee Phoenix and Indians' Advocate, 73, 100
Cherokee Rose Buds, 203, *204*
Cherokee Tobacco case, 278
Chester, Elisha, 115
chestnuts, xxi–xxii
Chickamauga Cherokees, 16
Chitwood, Thomas, 315
Chitwood, Walter Newton, 315
Chi-Wa-Yu-Ga, xvi
cholera, 118–19
Chouteau, August, 41
Chowyoucah, xv
Christian, William, 37
Christie, John, 304
Christie, Nede Wade, 303, 304–12
Christie, Smith, 232, 268
Christie, Watt, 304–5, 306
Chuleoa, 49
civilization policy, 90
Civil War, 219, 234–63

>   Battle of Bird Creek (Chusto-Talasah), 241–45
>   Battle of Honey Springs, 255–56
>   Battle of Locust Grove, 250
>   Battle of Pea Ridge, 246–48, 275
>   Battle of Prairie Grove, 252
>   casualties, 262–63
>   documents explaining Cherokees view, 268
>
> clan, xv
>   council, xxxii
>   wood, xxi
>   *See also specific clan*
>
> Clark, George Rogers, 17
> clay, xxvii
> Clay, Henry, 116, 126–27, 130
> Clayton, Judge, 63, 110, 112
> Cleveland, Grover, 291, 292, 293, 295, 315, 332
> Cloud, Samuel, 168
> Cocke, James, 77
> Coffee, John, xvi–xvii, 28, 43, 51, 52, 94, 113–14, 371n16
> "Coffee Line," xvi–xvii, 51
> Compact of 1802, 33–34
> Conrad, Hair, 165
> Constitution of Cherokee Nation, 69, 76
> Constitution of United States, 76
> Coodey, William, 99, 115, 165, 178
> Cooley, Dennis, 264–66, 268–70
> Coon, Wolfe, 329–30, 338
> Cooper, Douglas, 235, 241, 242–43, 252, 253, 255, 256, 269
> corn, xxxi, xxxiii

Cornsilk, A-toh-hee, 49

Corn Tassel, 15, 19, 32, 37, 38

Cornwallis, General, 18

Council of Constance, 59

Cowart, Robert J., 219

Crask, Phillip J., 56

Craven, Charles, 2

Crawford, George, 13, 46, 47, 179

Crawford, H.R., 302

Creekmore, Milo, 309–10

Creek Wars, 43

Crockett, Davy, 105–7, 394n239, 394n241

Cumming, Alexander, 3

Cunne Shote, 10, 12, *12*

Curry, Benjamin, 113, 115, 120–21

Curtis, Samuel, 246, 247–48

Curtis Act, 327

Daggett, Herman, 92

Dalasini, Tsatsi, 304

Dalasini, Wakigu, 304

Daugherty, Susan, 232

Davis, Daniel, 140, 188

Davis, Jefferson, 259, 261

Davis, John Barber, 68

Dawes, Henry, 289, *290,* 290–91, 306

Dawes Act, 296, 298, 327

Dawes Commission, 318, 321, 323, 324, 325, 328, 330, 349, 362

de las Casas, Bartholomé, iv–v

Deas, Edward, 150–52, 160
death penalty, 94
debt, 280, 287
Decatur Railroad, 160
Declaration of Independence, 100
Deer Clan, xv
Delaware Courthouse, 299–300, *300*
Dick, Nannie, 305
Dinwiddie, Robert, 8–10
divorce, 66–67
Doak, Samuel, 138
Downing, George Brewer, 276, 354
Downing, Lewis, 231–32, 258–59, 264, 265, 266, 267, 270–71, *271*, 272, 273, 276–77, 278, 279, 282, 296
Downing, Mary Eyre, 282
Downing, Samuel, 232
Dragging Canoe (Tsi'yu-gunsini), 13–16, *22*
    attacking/raiding white settlements, 18, 19
    death, 21
    Tecumseh supporting, 22
    Treaty of Holston and, 21
Drane, G. S., 161
Dred Scott v. Sandford, 230, 415n502
Drennen Roll, 302
Drew, John, 224
Drowning Bear, 51
Duncan, W.A., 317
Dutch, William. *See* Tah-Chee
DuVal, Edward, 40

Dwight Mission on Sallisaw Creek, 29, 119
Dykes Bend, x, 54, 135

Eaton, John, 96, 99
educational system, 68, 201–11
    schools/schooling, 34, 181–82, 275
    See also Female Seminary; Male Seminary
Edward, James Francis, 1
Emerson, Ralph Waldo, 146–47
emigration, 28, 40, 82
    forced (*See* Trail of Tears)
    Jackson pushing for, 101, 113–14
    White Path opposing, 114
Emory, Elizabeth, 7
Emory, Mary, 7
Emory, Robert, 7
Emory, Susannah, 171, 188
Emory, William, 7, 369n8, 374–75n41
Emory, William, Jr., 7
England, 1–4
    anti-Catholic riots, 1–2
    Cherokee delegation to, 3–4, 10–12
    Quebec Act, 13, 15
    religious issues, 1–2
    Royal Proclamation, 10–12
England, George, 276, 285, 293, 319
England, Joseph, 276, 285, 293, 319
England, Lucy Ann, 276, 285, 293, 315, 319
England, Sarah Mayes, 213, 275–76, 285–86, 293, 315

England, William, 275–76, 285
English colonial leaders, 8–10
Etowah River, xvi, xix–xx, xxii, xxiii, 54, 63, 75, 98, 99, 136, 140, 174, 182–84, 187, 188, 401n341
Euchela, 157
Eughioote, 3
Evarts, Jeremiah, 84, 100–101
exodus. *See* Trail of Tears

Featherstonhaugh, George, 19, 130, 141
Female Seminary, 201, *202,* 321–22
    Cherokee Rose Buds, 203, *204*
    daily schedule, 203
    enrollment, 205
    events, 205–6
    language classes, 202
    library, 206
    public examinations, 203
    subjects taught at, 202
Fields, Archibald, 58
Fields, Jess, 300, 301–2, 425n637
Fields, Richard, 7, 213, 239, *269*
Fields, Rider, 185, 281
Fields, Ti-es-kee, 187
Finn, Cynthia Ellen, 282
Finn, Daniel, 281–82
Finn, Elmira Mayes, 215, 275, 281–82, 322
fishing, xxiii–xxiv
Five Killer (Skayagustuegwo), 35, 36

Floyd, Charles, 148, 156

forced emigration. *See* Trail of Tears

Foreman, Grant, 211, 379n95, 389n184–85, 390n187, 390n191, 390n193, 390n195, 391n198, 391n200, 391n205–6, 395n259, 396n263, 396n266, 396n272, 399n309, 402n350, 403n367, 404n381, 405n388, 405n392, 406n394, 406n402, 406n407, 407n408, 410n451, 412n469, 425n638, 430n693, 430n704

Foreman, James, 120, 186

Foreman, Joseph, 181–82

Foreman, Nancy Gourd, 191

Foreman, Stephen, 60, 153–54

Forster, Thomas, 2

Fort Coffee, 160

Fort Loudon, 10

Fort Prince George land-cession treaty, 5

Foster, Lafayette, 266–67

Four Mothers Society, 326–27, 338–39, 344

Fox (warship), 3

free education, 68

Freemason "Blue Lodges," 229–30

Frelinghuysen, Theodore, 103–5

French and Indian War, 8–10, 36

Frisley, Sallie Tail, 50

Ga-ho-ga, 136

games. *See* sports and games

Gammell, William, 191

Gano, Richard, 257

Garfield, James Abram, 290

Garrett, John, 137
George, Big Dollar, 84
George Guess, 160
George II, King, 3–4
George III, King, 10–13
Georgia, 31–32, 47, 157
    Gold Lottery, 116
    gold rush, 116
    law denying Cherokee sovereignty, 99, 107, 113
    selling gold rights, 56
    Worcester v. Georgia, 63–64, 111, 113, 324, 428–29n680
    See also New Echota; Treaty of New Echota
Georgia Guard, 63, 109, 124–25, 221
Ghighau (Beloved Woman). *See* Nanye-hi
girls
    cooking and baking, xxxiiii
    weaving baskets and mats, xxvi
    See also Female Seminary; women
Gist, Nathaniel, 15, 81
Givens, Dora, 319
Gladney, Jackson, 282
Gladney, Joseph Foreman, 321–22
Gladney, William, 282
Glen, James, 5
Going Snake, 52, 125 141, 165, 404n374
going to water, xxx, xxxi
gold, 140, 214
Gold, Harriet Ruggles, 94
Golden Circle. *See* Knights of the Golden Circle

Gold Lottery, 116
gold rush, 116, 213, 286
Gourd, Nancy, xvii, 48, 58, 184–85
Grant, Ludovic, xv, 1, 2–5, 7, 90, 369n8
    as an indentured servant, 2
    death, 5
    marriage, 3
Grant, Mary, 3, 7, 369–70n8, 374–75n41
Grant, Susannah, 7
Grant, Ulysses S., 259, 260
Grasshopper, Daniel, 301
Grasshopper, Jack, 300–302
Grease, Nusi Goie "Nancy," 306
Great Tellico, 3
Green Corn Dance/Festival, xxxi–xxxiii, 3, 29
Gritts, Bud, 232
Gritts, Levi, 232, 349
Grove Sun newspaper, 333, 368n4, 430n696, 430n698, 433n727, 433n733
Guess, George. *See* Sequoyah
"Guide Me O, Thou Great Jehovah," 175
Guion Miller Roll, 302
Gunter, Edward, 99

Hair, Charles, 310–11
Hall, James, 41
Hanna, Claude, 360–61
hardwoods, xx
Harlan Bill, 264–67
Harney, William, 264

Harris, Bird, 321

Harris, Johnson, 315, 318

Harris, Joseph, 118–19

Harrison, Benjamin, 297, 314

Harrison, William Henry, 22, 23, 25–26, 181

Hasanoanda. *See* Parker, Ely Samuel

Haskell, Charles, 206

Hawkins, Benjamin, 37, 90

Hemphill, James, 156

Henderson, Richard, 13–14

Henry, Patrick, 16

Hesse, Hermann (Demian), iv

Hicks, Charles, 74–75

Hicks, Elijah, 73, 112, 120, 124, 132, 147, 165, 169, 189

Hicks, George, 159, 163–65, 168–69, 171

Hicks, Victoria, 205

Hicks, William, 77, 79, 115

Hiketiyah, 304

History of the North American Indians (McKenney), 102

Hiwassee Canal Company, 77

Hiwassee-Conasaga Canal, 77

Holocaust, 159

Hopewell Treaty. *See* Treaty of Hopewell

Hopper, Sookie, 36

Hoskin, Chuck, Jr., 363

Hotel Hazel, 330, 332–35, 339
    boarders, 333–34
    features, 332–33
    Grove Sun notice, 333

Houston, Samuel, 29, 105
Hoxie, Vinnie Ream, 89
Hoyt, Lucy Lowrey (The Wahnenauhi Manuscript), 369n6
Hubbard, James, 19
Humphrey, Richard A., 311
Hus, Jan, 59–60
Huss, Jane Jennie, 281
Huss, William, 184
Huttite movement, 59

immersion and bathing, xxx–xxxi
immigration, 13
Immortal Fourteen, 297
Indian Appropriations Act, 280
    Springer Amendment to, 298
Indian Removal Act, 98–117
    Crockett on, 105–6
    Frelinghuysen on, 103–5
    implications, 100
    public opinion, 102
    resolution opposing, 102–3
Indian rights to self-determination, 362
Indian trust funds, 220
Intercourse Act of 1834, 133
International Indian Council, 195–200
interracial marriage, 223
Intertribal Council at Creek Agency (1861), 234
Iroquois, 16–17
Isbell, L. P., 308

Jack, John, 36
Jackson, Andrew, 28, 29, 30, 33, 51, 53, 119, 170
    Battle of Horse Shoe Bend, 43–47
    Crockett on, 106–7
    Going Snake on, 141
    Inaugural Address, 99
    Indian Removal Act, 97, 98–117
    Junaluska on, 47
    land cession treaties, 28
    letter to Coffee, 28
    march of civilization, 99
    New Echota Treaty (*See* Treaty of New Echota)
    presidential election of 1828, 98, 99
    Takaki on, 159
    white nationalist rhetoric, 98
    White Path on, 141
Jacobites, 2. *See also* Treaty of Limerick
Ja-lu-na-hy, 301
James II, 1–2
James III, 2
Jefferson, Thomas, 8, 10, 16, 25–26, 91
Johnson, Andrew, 261, 264, 269, 270
Johnson, Robert M., 217
Johnson v. McIntosh, 30–31
Jolly, John, 29–30, *30,* 78, 82
Jones, Evan, 132, 140, 144, 154, *154,* 162, 179, 229, 267
Jones, John B., 233, 267, 268
Jones, Roger, 192–93

Jones, W. A., 339
Josephine, Mamie, 315
J.R. Williams (ship), 257
Junaluska (Chief), 47, 167, 188–89

Kahn-Yah-Tah-Hee, 82
Kansas-Nebraska Act and, 217
Keetoowah/Keetoowah Society, 34, 268, 380n108, 405n393, 414n497, 415n507, 416n511, 431n718
    anti-slavery, 218, 225, 227, 228, 230, 232–33
    Boudinot and, 326, 343, 348, 350–51, *351*
    Buffington and, 337, 338
    ceremonial ground, 305
    churches and, 228
    Constitution, 232
    Dawes Commission and, 349
    defiance to the Treaty Party, 172
    Downing and, 272
    First Cherokee Mounted Rifles, 239
    Harris and, 318
    Home Guards and, 253
    Masonic ideals and, 228
    McGloughlin and, 273
    militant group of "Pin" members, 232–33
    modernization, 232
    Ned and, 305, 306, 308
    Nighthawk, 318, 328–29, 344, *346*, 349
    O-Pothle-Yoholo and, 242
    Redbird, 328–29, 338, 344, *345*, 349

    sacred fire, 230–31
    Snell and, 245
    as United Keetoowah Band of Cherokees, 351
    Watie and, 253
    Wolfe Coon, 329, 330, 338
    women, 326
Ketagustah, 3
King, Charles Bird, 42
King, Gail, 159
Kingsley, Canon, 89
Kitchin, Thomas, 10
Kituhwa, 34, 228. *See also* Keetoowah/Keetoowah Society
Knapp, Samuel Lorenzo, 86
Knightkiller, Caty, 136, 142, 186, 187, 213, 276
Knightkiller, David, 61, 151
Knightkiller (Caty Spirit's husband), xviii, 142, 186, 187, 276
Knights of the Golden Circle, 218, 227, 229–30, 233, 235, 268
Knox, Henry, 16, 20, 21, 25, 26
Knoxville (ship), 138

Lawlo, 167
Lee, Robert E., 259, 260
Lenoir, Albert, 134
Lide, J. W., 156
Lightfoot, John, 136
Lightfoot, Nancy, 136
Lillybridge, Clark, 138
Lincoln, Abraham, 219
    assassination of, 261

Downing's letter with proposal to, 258–59, 264
portrait, *261*
Lipe, De Witt, 301
Lithia Springs, xvi, xvii, 48, 49, 54, 55–57, 126
Little Owl, 18
Little Turkey, 118
livestock, xxii
Livestock Association, 297–98
Long Hair Clan, xv, 3
Looney, John, 178
Louis XIV, 2
Lovely's Purchase, 33
Lowrey, George, 26, 48, 61, 79, 82, 130, 178, 187, 197–98, *198*, 369–70n8, 374–75n41
Lowrey, Jennie, 26
Lowrey, John, 43, 46, 288, 371n17, 382n124, 384–85n147
Lucy Walker (ship), 224
Lumpkin, John, 121
Lumpkin, Wilson, 113–14, 135–36, 137
Lynch, Mary Patsy, 171
Lyttelton, William, 10

MacDonald, Charles, 56–57
Madison, James, 46, 47, 92, 96, 371n16
Male Seminary, 201, *203,* 211
    literary magazine, 204–5
    subjects taught at, 202
    See also Female Seminary
Maples, Dan, 306–8, 311–12

marbles, xxv–xxvi
march of civilization, 99
marriage, 66–67
Marshall, John, 30–31, 108, 111–12
Martin, John, 7, 79, 124, 171, 188
Martin, Joseph, 37
Martin, Nannie, 171
Martin, Rachel, 140, 188, 408n422
Martin V, 60
Mary II, 1
Mason, John, 130
Mason, R. B., 192–93
Masonic Lodges, 228–29
masons, 227, 414n496, 433n730
maternal uncles, xxxii
Matthews, Asa, 261–62
Mayes, Andrew Jackson, 62
Mayes, Annie Harper Gladney, 316–17, 332–33, 334, 339
Mayes, Frank, 214
Mayes, George Wash, 317–18
Mayes, Joel Bryan, 63, 189–90, 205, 212, 276, 295–99, 313–15
Mayes, John, 62
Mayes, Maggie May, 285, 293, 323, *339*
Mayes, Mary Hazel, 319, 332, 334, 335
Mayes, Nancy/Nannie Adair, xxiii, 62, 63, 136, 202, 205, 212, 213, 218, 236, 319, 414n496
Mayes, Samuel Houston, xix, xxiii, 62–64, 109, 202, 296, 318
 Annie and, 212–16
 arrest and confinement, 63, 109

    released, 63–64

    slaves, 221

Mayes, Samuel Houston, Jr., 63, 189, 190, 276, 319–21, 330

Mayes, Sarah. *See* England, Sarah Mayes

Mayes, William Lucullus, 276

Mayes, William Penn, 215–16, 267, 284–85, 293–94, 302, 313–15, 319, 321, 330, 332, 333, 334, *339,* 339–40

McCloud, Dickerson, 102

McCoy, Alexander, 58

McCulloch, Ben, 235–38, 246, 247

McDaniel, Catherine, 36, 63

McDaniel, Charley, 119

McDaniel, James, 239, 268

McDaniel, William David, 36

McDaniels, James, 187, 268

McDonald, Collins, 165

McDonald, John, 16

McDonald, Mollie, 68

McGinnis, Charles F., 286

McGirt v. Oklahoma, 428–29n680

McGloughlin, William, 273

McIntosh, Daniel, 234, 242–43

McIntosh, Lachlan, 37

McKenney, Thomas, 102, 192, 379n96

McKinley, William, 336

McLeod, Dickson, 109

McMinn, Joseph, xvi–xvii

McNair, Martha, 189, 276, 297, 320

measles, 118–19

Medill, William, 193
Meigs, Return J., 45–46, 49, 91
Menawa, 44
Mihesuah, Devon, 306, 311–12, 426n642
Miller, Sarah Annie, 268
Miller, Susan Sconti, 268, 283–84
Miller, William Wirt, 268, 284
Miro, Don Estevon, 26
Missionary Herald, The, 60
missionary societies, 219
Mitchell, William D., 297
Moccasin flower, xxiii
Monroe, James, 31, 33–34, 92, 96
Montgomery, Hugh, 74, 103
Montgomery, James, 51
Moravian Christian Indians, massacre of, 17
Moytoy, Amatoy, 35
Moytoy, Nancy, 35
Moytoy of Tellico, 3, 4
Murrell, John, 214
Mush, Nancy Dorcas, xvii, 48, 58, 385n151
mushrooms, xxiii

Nanye-hi, 35–39
    as Agi-ga-u-e (War Woman), 36
    Battle of Taliwa, 35–36
    as chief negotiator, 37
    as Ghighau (Beloved Woman), 36
    as a healer and peacemaker, 36

See also Ward, Nancy
National Intelligencer, 100, 168
National Party, 178, 286, 295–96, 308
Nelson, C. H., 109
Neutral Lands, 274, 277, 279
New Echota
    buildings constructed in, 69
    first Council House, 69
    fortification, 145
    as modern town, 79
    as a new capitol, 34, 47
    treaty signed in (*See* Treaty of New Echota)
Newsam, Albert, 41–42
Nighthawk Keetwoowahs, 318, 328–29, 344, *346,* 349
Nine Years War, 2
Nitts (O-Ne-Hut-Tee), xviii, 50, 135, 138, 152, 187
Nixon, Richard, 362
North Carolina, 157–58
Northeastern State Normal School in Tahlequah, 357
Northrup, Sarah, 92, 94
Nowata Advertiser (newspaper), 344
Nuttall, Thomas, 80

Oconostota, 14, 90
Oklahoma Legislature, 357
Oklahoma v. Castro-Huerta, 428–29n680
Old Settlers, 29, 41, 80, 160, 173, 176–80, 187, 189, 193, 194
Olympus (Indian Territory), 332
O-Pothle-Yohola, 93, 234, 239–43

Ore, James, 21
origin of the universe, xxix–xxx
Osages, 27, 29, 39–40
Ostenaco, 9–12, 376n50
Outacite. *See* Ostenaco

Paint Clan, xv
Palmour, Silas, 140
Paloch, Thomas, 184
Parker, Ely Samuel, *259,* 259–60, *260,* 264, 419n562
Parker, Isaac C., 287, 307–8, 311, 325
Parris, John, 307–8, 311–12
Parsons, Francis, 12
Pathkiller, xxx, 43, 74–75
Payne, John Howard, 125, 165, 180
Peace of Paris, 18
peach, xxiii
Peavine Baptist Church, 230–32
Pegg, Thomas, 268
Perdue, Theda, iv, 368n1, 382n117, 388n168, 393n223, 393n229, 394n244, 395n257, 397n297, 409n439, 413n481, 419n560
Pettit, Elizabeth, 282
Phillips, William, 88, 252, 257
Pickens, Andrew, 37
Pickering, Timothy, 25
Pike, Albert, 235, 240, 242, 246, 269, 417n531
Pin members of Keetoowah Society, 232–33
Poinsett, Joel Roberts, 139, 147–48, 180–81
Polk, James, 193–94

Poorbear, Hunter, 50, 215, 279, 294–95, 369n5, 371n13, 422n600

poplars, xxi

Post, Mary Arminda, 282

Post, William, 282

Powder Springs, 55. *See also* Lithia Springs

Proctor, Henry, 23

Proctor, Isaac, 215

Prophetstown, 22

Protestant Church of England, 1

Protestants *vs.* Catholics, 1

Pulliam, R.H., 228, 229

Quahlate, Nan, 300

Quatse (or Betsy), 304

Quatsy, 35

Quebec Act, 13, 15

railroad construction, 160, 274

Randolph, P.G., 102

rations, 134

Ratt, Ailsey, 185

Raven, Eaw-Luh-Nuh, 315

Raven, Joe Fox, 315

Raven, John Fox, 315

Raven Warrior, 14

rebuilding, 172, 174–94

    Act of Union, 178–79

    court system, 179

    execution of traitors, 176–77

    families filed claims against the US government, 182–85

    schooling, 181–82

reciprocal hospitality, xxxii

Red Stick War, 47. *See also* Battle of Horse Shoe Bend

Reed, William, 110

Reese, Charles, 45

religious belief, 69

removal of Cherokees from their land. *See* Indian Removal Act; Trail of Tears; Treaty of New Echota

Resolution of defiance, 161–62

Revolutionary War, 15, 16, 37, 96

Reynolds, Joshua, 12

Ridge, John, 92, *93,* 115

    education, 92

    execution, 176–77

    Green Corn Dance, 124

    on Jackson, 112–13

    letter to Jackson, 138

    marriage, 92, 94

Ridge, The (Ka-Nun-Da-Cla-Geh), 75, 90–97, 118

    Battle of Horse Shoe Bend and, 43, 45, 46, 47

    constitution for Cherokee, 76

    execution, 176–77

    Hicks and, 74

    on Jackson, 93

    Jackson meeting, 129–30

    negotiations with the US, 93

    promoting Ross as the next Chief, 77, 79

    Treaty of New Echota, 125–26

war-like skills, 94
Rogers, William C., 115, 276, 343–44, *344*
Roman Nose, 132
Ross, Andrew, 58
Ross, Daniel, 68, 268
Ross, John, 41, 94, 114–15
    on annuities stopped by Jackson, 102–3
    as Assistant Principal Chief, 77
    attack on, 111
    Battle of Horse Shoe Bend and, 43, 45, 46
    on Cherokee relations with US, 31–32
    constitution for Cherokee, 76
    death of, 272
    drawing of, *68*
    early life and education, 68
    Eaton's response to, 99
    elected as Principal Chief in 1828, 79
    elections of 1865, 264
    ferry service, 75
    Georgia's law denying Cherokee sovereignty, 99, 107, 113
    grand tour of countryside, 218
    Hicks as mentor to, 74
    Hiwassee-Conasaga Canal construction and, 77
    Jackson's letter to, 113, 123
    Johnson's bill and, 217
    on *Johnson v. McIntosh* case decision, 31
    Kansas-Nebraska Act and, 217
    letter to Calhoun, 31–32
    letter to Gallatin on land and state of development, 67

    letter to Sequoyah on silver medal, 84
    meeting Jackson, 129
    "Memorial of Protest of the Cherokee Nation," 131
    National Committee leadership, 75
    National Party, 178, 286, 295–96, 308
    New Echota Treaty and, 124–25, 126, 127, 129–49, 150
    as persona non grata, 179, 269
    portrait of, *79*
    propaganda against, 179
    property (seizure and claim), 121–22, *122*
    Van Buren and, 138–39, 179
    See also Civil War; Trail of Tears
Ross, Lewis, 68, 108–9, 166
Ross, Louis, 282
Ross, Quatie, 121, 171
Ross, William P., 234, 280
    elected as Principal Chief, 272–73
    McGloughlin on, 273
Royal Proclamation of 1763, 10–12
Royce, Charles, 14, 127, 279
Rutherford, Mary, 62

sacred fire, 230–31
Samuels, Charlotte, 62
Saw-ka-ne, 301
Schaick, Goose Van, 16
Schermerhorn, John F., 123, 124, 125, 130
schools/schooling, 34, 181–82, 275
Schrimsher, Elizabeth Alabama, 286

Scott, Winfield, 148, 152–53, 156, 157, 159, 161
Scraper, Jennie, 305–6
Second Battle of Cabin Creek, 258
Sells, Elijah, 264
Selu, xxxiiii, 3
Se-ne-ka-naw-he-na, 301
Sequoyah, xvii, xviii, xxxiii–xxxiv, 80–89, 176, 177–78, 369–70n8, 374–75n41
    death, 88–89
    literary pension, 88
    painting, 86–87
    Phillips on, 88
    as polymath, 82
    Ross's letter to, 84
    silver medal, 84
    statue, 89
    Syllabary, xxxiii, 79, 82, 360
    teaching, 83
    Treaty of May 1828, 85–86
    wives and children, 84
Sequoyah Memorial, The, 204–5, 296
Sevier, John, 18, 19, 20, 377–78n75
Seward, William H., 219
sexual freedom, 66
Shawnees, 17
Shelby, Evan, 16
Shorey, William, Jr., 7, 369n8, 374–75n41
Sigel, Franz, 237
Situwakee, 147

Skyugo (chief), 39
slaves/slavery, 218–19, 220, 221–27
    education, 223
    Golden Circle (*See* Knights of the Golden Circle)
    interracial marriage, 223
    Keetoowahs and (*See* Keetoowah/Keetoowah Society)
    Masonic Lodges, 228–29
    plantation owners, 221, 224
    property rights in, 224
    revolt of 1842, 224
Smelter (ship), 151, 160, 161
Smith, Redbird, 328–29, 338, 344, *345*, 349
Smith, William, 121
Snell, Annie Spirit. *See* Spirit, Annie (Ah-ni-wa-ke)
Snell, Charles Ewing, 275, 299
Snell, Simon, xix, 245, 250, *251*, 252–53, 257, 258, 259, 261, 267, 275, 282, 284, 301, 305, 360, 369n5
Snowdale Farm, 320, 330
Society for Propagating the Gospel Among the Indians, 61
Sons of Temperance, 229
Sooners, 298
Southern Treaty Commission, 264
Spirit, Alexander Buffalofish, xviii, 49, 135, 171, 174, 187
Spirit, Annie (Ah-ni-wa-ke), 212–16
    boarding house, 299, 318–19
    cemetery, 360
    grave-marking ceremony for, 361
    Grove Press obituary, 359
    Hanna on, 360–61

Samuel Houston Mayes (husband) (*See* Mayes, Samuel Houston)
Simon Snell (husband) (*See* Snell, Simon)
Spirit, Ben Buffalofish, 49
Spirit, Betsy, xxxiii–xxxiv, 84
Spirit, Buffalofish, xvi–xvii, 48–54, 91
    appraisals of farms, 53–54
    children, 49–50
    family tree, *50*
    Lithia Springs and, 55, 57
    periodic references to, 49
    slaves, 221
    US document reference to, 49
Spirit, Caty. *See* Knightkiller, Caty
Spirit, Charles, xvi, 174, 214
Spirit, Charles Poorbear, 279, 294
Spirit, Charlie Buffalofish, xviii, 50, 187, 215
Spirit, Chowyoucah, xv
Spirit, Crying Snake Buffalofish, xviii, 49, 51, 100, 108, 135, 171, 174, 182–83, 187, 407n419
Spirit, David Sconti, 120, 142, 187, 212
Spirit, Eagle-on-the-Roost Buffalofish, xviii, 50, 135, 171, 174, 183
Spirit, John Buffalofish, 185
Spirit, John Huss, xvii, xxxiv, 41, 58–61, 117, 142–44, 186, 212–13, 215, 267
    adopted children, 58
    baptized, 58
    as a Cherokee evangelist, 58, 59–61
    death of, 200
    International Indian Council and, 195–200

philosophy, 58–59
Sequoyah and, 81
slaves, 221
Spirit, Lydia, 7, 369–70n8, 374–75n41
Spirit, Nakey/Naky, xviii, 50, 135, 138, 152, 187
Spirit, Nelly Buffalofish, 161, 185
Spirit, Old Sconti, xv, xvii, 7, 369–70n8
Spirit, Peggy, 7, 369n8, 374–75n41
Spirit, Poorbear Buffalofish, 134, 161, 279
Spirit, So-Wa-Chee, xviii, 50, 135, 156, 183–84
Spirit, Susannah, xvii, 26, 30, 48, 58, 80, 81, 98, 116, 135, 182–83, 215, 276, 371–72n17
Spirit, The, xv, xxxiv, 7, 8, 26, 48, 80, 150, 369–70n8, 374–75n41
Spirit, Watt, xvi
sports and games, xxiv–xxv. *See also* stickball
Springston, Anderson, 120
Stanley, John Mix, 195, 197, 199, 409n441–42, 410n446–49
Stapler, Mary Bryan, 192, 203
Starr, Emmet, 373–74n33, 381n111
Starr, James, 115
Steele, Frederick, 255
Steele, Phillip W., 426n642
Steele, William, 253
stickball, xxiv–xxv
stockades, 154–56
Stokes, Montfort, 172
Stuart, John, 87
Sullivan, John, 16–17
Supreme Court of Cherokee Nation, 68–69

Supreme Court of United States
    Cherokee Nation v. Georgia, 108
    Cherokee Tobacco case, 278
    Dred Scott decision, 230, 415n502
    Johnson v. McIntosh, 30–31
    Worcester v. Georgia, 63–64, 111, 113, 324, 428–29n680
Susannah (ship), 2
Sweetwater Creek, 48
Sweetwater Creek State Park, 49
Sweetwater Park Hotel, 57
Swimmer, Chowyouka, 49, 185, 212–13
Swimmer, Jess, xvi
Swimmer, Jim, xvi
Syllabary, xxxiii, 79, 82, 360

Tah-Chee, 35, 39–42
    Camp Homes Treaty negotiation, 41
    Catlin on, 41
    Chouteau on, 41
    as diplomat, 41
    Hall on, 41
    as warrior, 39–41
    Washington treaty, 41
Tahlequah Capital, 350
Tahlonteskee, 26–29, 78, 91, 133, 193
Tahnoovayah, 68
Takaki, Ronald, 159
Takatoka, 32–33, 83
Talton v. Mayes, 318 {plus page# in FN}

Taluntuskee, 82

Taney, Roger B., 230

Tarpin, Sallie, 315

Tatsi. *See* Tah-Chee

Taylor, Richard, 99

Taylor, Zachery, 199

Tecorhurtuski, Skyaheta, 304, 305

Tecumseh, 22–23, *24*

Teehee, Kimberly, 363

Teehee, Stephen, 313, 315

Tennessee Militia, 46

Tennessee Yazoo Company, 20

Tenskwatawa, 22

Terrell, Lige, 214

Thanksgiving Proclamation, 314

Thomas, W. H., 157–58

Thomas Yeatman (ship), 114, 119

Thompson, Rachel, 62–63, 136

Thompsons, Franklin, 171, 174

Thompsons, James, 171, 174

Thrower, Lydia. *See* Tecorhurtuski, Skyaheta

Timberlake, Henry, 9–10, 12

Tocqua "The Whale," 45, 46

Tohopeka. *See* Battle of Horse Shoe Bend

"To the Cherokee People," 100

Trail of Tears, xv, xxxiv, 24, 26, 60, 64
    Deas' water detachment, 150–52, 160
    hardhip and death, 159–73
    rounding up and, 150–58

stockades, 154–56
See also Treaty of New Echota
Trainor, Bub, 307–8, 311–12
Transylvania Company, 13
Treaty of August 7, 1846, 193–94
Treaty of Dover, 4
Treaty of Holston, 15–16, 20–21, 41
Treaty of Hopewell, 19–20, 37–38, 108
Treaty of Indian Springs, 51
Treaty of July 19, 1866, 269–70, 277, 278, 287
Treaty of Limerick, 2
Treaty of May 1828, 85–86
Treaty of New Echota, 61, 118–27, 172–73, 176, 292, 325
    Adams on, 126–27
    Article 5 of, 324
    Article 6 of, 363
    Article 9 of, 159
    Clay on, 126
    Foreman and, 181
    Mayes on, 299
    money and annuities under, 181, 193
    Ross opposing, 123–25, 126, 127, 129–49, 150
    Senate debate on, 130
    setting deadline for removal of Cherokee, 131
    US Supreme Court on, 363
    Watie and, 262, 422n601
    See also Trail of Tears
Treaty of Peace, 265
Treaty of Philadelphia, 41

Treaty of Sycamore Shoals, 13–14
Treaty of Tellico, 21–22, 100
Treaty of the Cherokee Agency, 28
Treaty of the Chickasaw Council House, 27–28
Treaty of the Holston, 41
Treaty of Washington, 41
Treaty Party, 61, 117, 118–27
    "Cherokee" (political body), 178
    Confederacy and, 235, 239
    Constitution of 1839, 193
    Lighthorse Brigades and, 194
    plantation owners from, 224
    Treaty of August 7, 1846, 193–94
    US government and, 179–80
    Wilkins proposal, 189
    See also Treaty of New Echota
Trott, James, 102, 109
Tsali, 157–58
Tsu-la Red Fox Kingfisher, 35
Tucker, Peggy, 305, 310
Turtle-at-Home, 18
Tyler, John, 181, 189, 193

Unassigned Cherokee Lands, 298
Union, 88, 225, 228. *See also* Civil War
Union Pacific, 274
universe, origin of the, xxix–xxx

valuation of Cherokee property, 135–37

Van Buren, Martin, 137, 138–39, 147, 167–68
Vandeventer, Christopher, 28
Vann, Alcie, xviii, 49, 187
Vann, Annie. *See* Adair, Annie Vann
Vann, David, 179, 189, 276, 296–97, 320
Vann, David Rowe, 356
Vann, George, xvi, 134, 185, 212, 216, 370n10
Vann, James, xvi, 221
Vann, Joseph, 221–22, 224
Vann, Lydia, 185
Vann, Martha Elizabeth, 191, 276, 320
Vann, Mary Delilah, 190–91, 276, 296–97
Vann, Sawney, xviii, 50, 135, 156, 183–84, 185, 187, 407n419
Vann, Weely, 161, 215, 258
Victoria (ship), 171
Virginia, 14–15

Wadaya, 304–5
Wagoner Record (newspaper), 337
Wa-ja-lun-ty, 301
Walker, Charles, 163
Walker, John, Jr., 119–20
Walkingstick, 45, 48
Ward, Bryant, 36
Ward, George, 215, 275
Ward, George Monroe, 215, 275
Ward, Lucy Mayes, 215, 275
Ward, Nancy, 372n21, 380n109, 381n110, 381n111
War of 1812, 23

war/warfare as beloved occupation, 262
Washington, George, 8–10, 12, 14–15, 37
    Bloody Fellow on, 21
    Calloway on, 16, 26
    Cherokee chiefs letter to, 19–20
    civilization policy, 90
    English treaties and, 15
    as the first US President, 24
    as General of American forces, 15
    investments in Indian lands, 24
    land patents, 13
    letter to state governments, 25
    Mississippi Company, 13
    war against Iroquois, 16–17
Wasituna, 158
water
    going to, xxxi
    immersion and bathing, xxx–xxxi
    postpartum and post-menstrual cleansing, xxxi
water drum, xxxii
Waters, Sally, 84
Watie, Stand, 180, 191, 194, 268, *269*, 271, 275, 320, 325
    anger against, 176
    Civil War (supporting Confederacy), 235–63
    death of, 280
    escape, 177
    Freemason "Blue Lodges" and, 229–30
    John Ridge's letter to, 112–13
    killing Foreman, 186

Knights of the Golden Circle, 218, 227, 229–30, 233, 235, 268
lobbying against Ross, 193
New Echota Treaty and, 130
printing press seizure and, 124
promotion to Brigadier General, 257
railroad companies and, 270
slavery and, 218, 262
surrender, 261–62
Treaty of July 19, 1866, 269, 270, 271
Treaty Party and, 124
as warrior, 262
Watters, Joseph, 135, 156
Watts, John, 21
Wat-ty, 301
Wauhillau, 305
Weatherford, William, 44, 45
weaving baskets and mats, xxvi
Webber, Akie, 161
Webster, Daniel, 31, *31,* 130
Western Cherokee, 77–78
White, Gideon S., 310, 311
White, Hugh, 130
White Catcher, 268
White Owl Raven, 35
White Path, 76, 114, 132, 141, 147, 165, 168–69
Wickett, Sehoyah, 90
Wild Potato Clan, xv
Wilkerson, Eliza, 317
Wilkins, William, 189, 192–93

William III, 1–2
Wilson, Ann Florence, 336
Wilson, Florence, 357
Wiper, Assetetu, 54
Wirt, William, 107–8
Wise, Henry, 126
Wistar, Thomas, 264
Wo-de-yo-he, xvi, xviii, xxii, xxxi, 48, 49–50, 56, 99, 123, 135, 163, 174, 183, 187, 371n13
Wolf Clan, xv, 35, 36
Wolfe, Arch, 308, 310–11
women
    stick ball song, xxv
    equality, 66
    matrilineal culture, 66, 67
    menstruating, taboo against, xxxi
    postpartum and post-menstrual cleansing, xxxi
    of Wolf Clan, 36
    See also Female Seminary
Women's Council, 36, 38
woods, xx–xxi
Wool, John, 131–32, 137–38, 139–40, 148, 400n324
Worcester, Samuel, 61, 84, 109, 175, 177, 286
Worcester v. Georgia, 63–64, 111, 113, 324, 428–29n680
Woyi, 10
Wren, Michael, 150
Wright, George, 356
Wu-te-he, 81

Young, John, 138

Zolnay, George Julian, 89

www.ingramcontent.com/pod-product-compliance
Lightning Source LLC
Chambersburg PA
CBHW030514230426
43665CB00010B/607